MW00762865

Iron Rails in the Garden State

Railroads Past and Present | George M. Smerk, Editor

# Iron Rails in the Garden State

## Tales of New Jersey Railroading

Anthony J. Bianculli

INDIANA UNIVERSITY PRESS

BLOOMINGTON AND INDIANAPOLIS

This book is a publication of

*Indiana University Press*

601 North Morton Street
Bloomington, IN 47404-3797 USA

http://iupress.indiana.edu

*Telephone orders* 800-842-6796
*Fax orders* 812-855-7931
*Orders by e-mail* iuporder@indiana.edu

MANUFACTURED IN THE UNITED STATES OF AMERICA

Library of Congress Cataloging-in-Publication Data

Bianculli, Anthony J., date-
  Iron rails in the garden state : tales of New Jersey railroading /
Anthony J. Bianculli.
       p.     cm. — (Railroads past and present)
  Includes bibliographical references and index.
  ISBN 978-0-253-35174-6 (cloth)
  1. Railroads—New Jersey—History. I. Title.
  TF24.N5B53 2008
  385.09749—dc22

                                                            2008001942

1  2  3  4  5  13  12  11  10  09  08

*For my family . . .*
  *the special people in my life.*

# CONTENTS

# Acknowledgments

I am indebted to many individuals and organizations who helped me in my quest for accurate information about railroading in New Jersey. Many of them provided background and obscure facts that are not available in the previously written accounts of the tales that I have included in this book.

First and foremost, a special word of thanks is due to Bob Yuell, executive director of the Plainsboro Museum, for his generous contribution of the fruits of his research about the Fast Line that he had painstakingly gathered over a long time. His sharing of this information made my job much easier in preparation of the chapter on the Fast Line and greatly improved its accuracy. Without the voluminous data that he contributed and his critical edit of my written words, the chapter would have been less authoritative and considerably abbreviated, if written at all. Although he has spoken to several groups about the Fast Line, I can only hope that Bob will consider preparing a more comprehensive and permanent record of this unique railroad of central New Jersey.

The chapter about the bicycle railroad was a challenge because a purist would say that the subject really has nothing to do with railroading. However, in the broadest sense, the bicycle railroad shares many features with a true railroad . . . rails, vehicles, passengers, and others. Margaret Frame at the Burlington County Historical Society and the reference staff at the Burlington County Library helped me immeasurably through access to their extensive files about the enterprise. Those files defined the character and usefulness of the bicycle railroad and showed how it fulfilled a railroad's mission to transport people from home to work.

Paul Schopp, coauthor of a definitive book about the Jersey Central Railroad, clarified several areas of (my) puzzlement about the bicycle railroad in a telephone conversation. Paul, like Tom Taber, willingly and accurately helps seekers of railroad material.

I took advantage of Tom Taber's long-standing offer to provide railroad information by asking for specifics about the Palisades tunnels and also a cartoon published long ago about ferryboat racing on the Hudson River. As usual, he responded with helpful data and constructive suggestions. Equally important was the rich source of railroad information in an unpublished manuscript that was meticulously researched and written by T. T. Taber, Tom's father. I mined that manuscript thoroughly, gleaning information about little-known or little-remembered incidents and people.

Many thanks are also due to Bill McKelvey, who shared with me a chronology of significant railroad events, spanning hundreds of years, that he had assembled over a long period. I found this listing to be a valuable source of incidents that deserved further investigation. Bill also deserves kudos for his unceasing devotion to the goal of establishing a Transportation Heritage Center in the state of New Jersey, a venue where transportation history will live and be accessible to all.

Beverly Weidl, the curator of the Hopewell Museum, uncovered some documents relative to the Frog War, which occurred on the outskirts of Hopewell. Those papers, which included an old program of a locally produced play and a long, if not memorable, poem about the incident, added much color to my account and sets it apart from other published versions. I also thank the Board of Trustees of the Hopewell Museum for their permission to use excerpts from these papers.

Regina W. Murray, the author of the delightful

book *Profiles in the Wind,* wrote about a young Billy Moore who "hijacked" a trolley car. Ms. Murray graciously gave me permission to recount that story in my own words.

Bill Hittinger, a friend and a trustee of Lehigh University, was instrumental in obtaining information about Henry Drinker, the supervisor of construction for the Musconetcong Tunnel. Biographical knowledge about Drinker's engineering career was hard to come by because the man was also an attorney, a vocation in which he spent the greater part of his career. Fortunately, in later life he became president of Lehigh University, and information became available through that source.

Michael Rosenthal is a photographer for New Jersey Transit and he . . . and the organization for which he works . . . graciously granted permission to use a photograph that he took to illustrate the chapter that talks of a railroad renaissance in the Garden State and NJ Transit's part in it. Rick Klittich, who is a customer service correspondence coordinator for NJ Transit, also provided valuable information about the organization.

When I had difficulty finding a copy of an old periodical with a story about the dirigible railroad, the author of the article, John J. Hilton, and several other readers responded to my query and donated copies of the publication. Rick Zitarosa, vice president of the Navy Lakehurst Historical Society, in a lengthy e-mail correspondence, also supplied much background information and answered questions that I posed about the dirigible railroad.

Geoff Greene, a member of the Pacific Southern model railroad club, helped with constructive suggestions about some technical distinctions in model railroading. He also contributed a photograph, taken by Cliff Moore, a local newspaper publisher, for the chapter about Lionel trains and model railroading in general.

Many, many others assisted me as I struggled to find obscure references, photographs, statistics, and anecdotes in New Jersey railroad history. A few of those good and helpful folks are:

Jeannette Cafaro at the Princeton Historical Society who helped me review files concerning the Princeton Branch of the Pennsylvania Railroad, the "Dinky."

In a telephone conversation, Jack DeStefano, director of the Paterson Museum, provided information and statistics about the 100-year-old locomotive that is displayed outside of the museum.

Frank Miklos, a railroad enthusiast and member of two railroad historical societies from which I obtained photographs that were used to illustrate the text, granted permission for their use in the appropriate chapters.

Robert Long furnished photographs from his large collection and willingly permitted me to use them to illustrate the text.

Frank LaPenta, an eyewitness to the Pennsylvania Railroad accident at Woodbridge, offered interesting observations about the scene when he arrived almost immediately after the accident occurred.

Scott E. Randolph, the collection curator of the Erie-Lackawanna Historical Society, submitted comments about the tunnels through the Palisades in response to my questions.

Substantial research was conducted among the New Jersey collections at numerous libraries. The staff at all of these organizations, in several counties . . . Burlington, Mercer, Morris, and Somerset . . . and at public libraries in Hopewell, Princeton and Somerville, were unfailingly helpful and unsparing of their time. Particular note must be made of the assistance provided by the staff at the Mary Jacobs Library, a member of the Somerset County System. There, Helen Morris and Bobbie Woloshin secured for me old, out-of-print books and researched many remote and hidden facts.

I must express a debt of gratitude to John Cunningham, whose book *Railroads in New Jersey: The Formative Years* is a classic. Its lively style reads like newspaper reports of incidents that may have happened yesterday. Indeed, this should be no surprise because Cunningham was a journalist as well as a prolific book writer. His book was a road map to important nineteenth-century mileposts in the history of railroads in the state. Also, I had the good fortune to meet Cunningham in person, and at that meeting he provided encouragement and guidance in my search for a publisher for my first book.

In addition to Mr. Cunningham's book, I consulted many publications, some recently published and some out of print. These are too many to acknowledge individually. I hope that the reader will consult the bibliography to identify these most valuable resources.

Special thanks are due to my copy editor, Elaine

Durham Otto, who provided an exceptionally detailed edit of the manuscript. She uncovered several errors and improved my less-than-perfect grammar and sentence construction. She trimmed superfluous verbiage to make the narrative read more crisply. But, amazingly, she also conducted meticulous research on the Internet and elsewhere to augment many of my findings. The depth and scope of her effort are truly impressive. She is hereby offered, and richly deserves, my sincere gratitude.

I also wish to thank the many others at Indiana University Press who helped me along the way: George M. Smerk, editor of the Railroads Past and Present series; Linda P. Oblack, Railroad Books editor; Miki Bird, managing editor; Ben Garceau, assistant editor; Peter Froehlich, assistant sponsoring editor; Brian Herrmann, project editor; Chandra Nanette Mevis, editorial assistant; and the many others who worked (anonymously to me) in the production of this book.

Finally, I thank my wife, who tolerated, without complaint, the many hours I spent at my computer.

# Introduction

New Jersey, the fourth smallest state in land area, is a gateway to New York City in the north and to Philadelphia in the south. Furthermore, it was an essential land link between those two great eighteenth-century cities. In 1750, stagecoaches, advertised as "flying machines," raced from the western shore of the Hudson River to the banks of the Delaware River opposite Philadelphia in less than three days. But in the nineteenth century, New Jersey became a "railroad state." By 1900, it had the highest track density of any state in the union. The first state charter ever granted to a railroad was written in New Jersey in 1815; the first locomotive and the fifth railroad built in the United States were located here. Being a small state in area, railroad mileage in the state of New Jersey was never as large as in its neighboring states. By 1860, only 560 miles of track were laid. One might argue that the monopoly enjoyed by the Camden and Amboy Railroad contributed greatly to the paucity of rail mileage, yet the legislature had authorized over 100 charters by that time but only 20 were exploited. Since the state government provided no direct aid to railroads, the few lines that were built served existing needs. Speculation was discouraged in favor of solid, revenue-producing investment. Still, entering the twentieth century, no town in the state, with very few exceptions in the northern mountains and the southern "pine barrens," was more than eight miles from a railroad![1]

By 1964, New Jersey's eleven major railroads, although in decline, still operated nearly 2,000 miles of lines in the state, making New Jersey the rail density leader in the country. The Pennsylvania Railroad's main line crossed the state from Trenton on its way to New York City and, measured at Rahway, was the busiest railroad in the world; a train passed that town every three minutes. The Central Railroad of New Jersey, with more miles of track in the state than any other, was built originally to bring coal from Pennsylvania, but by 1964 it was primarily a commuter railroad. These two roads and the many others--the Delaware, Lackawanna & Western, the Reading road, the Lehigh Valley, the Erie, the Pennsylvania-Reading Seashore Lines--were still prominent railroads in 1964, but that was soon to change. Within a few years their "flags had fallen" and they had disappeared, their rights-of-way abandoned or subsumed into government-owned or subsidized rail systems.[2]

This book chronicles stories of New Jersey railroads, beginning with its first, the Camden and Amboy, and proceeding to the most recent revivals, New Jersey Transit and Conrail Shared Assets, the creations of government intervention in the railroad scene. It is an eclectic collection of tales: it tells of railroad pioneers, builders, financiers, and technicians; of consequential railroad companies and their grand achievements and, in counterpoint, of shortlines and a most unusual industrial railroad whose raison d'être was to jockey dirigibles into various locations. The book digresses into the arena of electric traction with a number of short narratives about trolley cars and interurban cars, including a recounting of the time a 10-year-old boy stepped into the breach and assumed the controls. It reports on two horrific accidents and the heroic actions of passengers and onlookers, and it describes a few of the "frog wars," when railroad companies resorted to violence to protect their turf. There are other intriguing stories involving the Lionel Company and other model train makers and the "bicycle railroad" at Smithville and a little remembered, but significant, railroad strike that followed

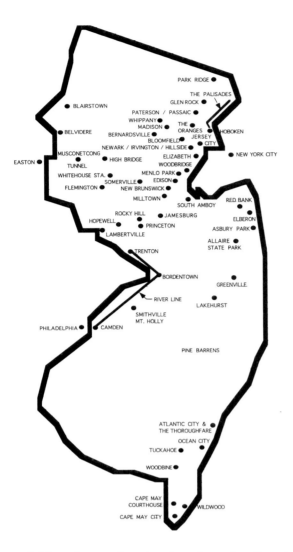

Map of New Jersey showing location of railroad sites mentioned in this book.

World War I. All in all, it discusses people, places, and incidents that are informative and interesting, and it serves as a travel guide to some sites of New Jersey railroad history. However, even though the railroad associations no longer exist at several of the locations, the book serves another important purpose: it provides a record of events that should be remembered as part of New Jersey heritage. One caveat is that the reader is cautioned that the current locations of historical actions or artifacts that are pinpointed are a "moving target" and may, in this time of rapid change, no longer be there or accessible. Real estate sales and new construction, the depredations of vandals, and the ravages of time or sudden fire may have obliterated some of the sites. The map on this page will serve to orient the reader to the railroad sites mentioned in the book.

Finally, readers are invited to lean back, get comfortable, and reflect on a New Jersey railroad scene of yesterday. Perhaps you can recall a favorite trackside location where, through three senses remembered-- sight, sound, and smell--it is possible to conjure up an image of a steam locomotive speeding by, a great iron horse whose labored breathing, the staccato chuff-chuff-chuff of its exhaust as it hauls a long train up a grade, assails the ears and then leaves the lingering aroma of coal smoke as it disappears into the distance. I hope that the following tales will bring similar images to life. Climb aboard and enjoy railroading in the Garden State!

Iron Rails in the Garden State

# 1 The Colonel Takes to the Rails (1825)

Railroading in the United States began in Hoboken, New Jersey. There, in February 1825, near his estate overlooking New York City, Col. John Stevens III operated the first locomotive to be built in this country. Twenty years earlier, Oliver Evans had built the *Orukter Amphibolos*. Evans was just as visionary as Stevens and predicted steam carriages on railways a generation before they appeared, but his creation was intended for water travel. The fact that it was self-propelled as it ran along city streets from his shop in Philadelphia to its launch point on the Schuylkill River in 1805 was incidental to its true function as a dredging scow. Stevens indisputably built the first American locomotive in 1825. Archibald Turnbull mentions that years after the colonel's death, his son, John Cox Stevens, contended that Stevens had constructed a steam carriage in 1795 but abandoned it because it was too "cumbersome."[1] Stevens was a technical innovator who had experimented with steam-driven boats. He built a steam ferry, the first in the world, to bring travelers across the Hudson River.[2] But his everlasting fame was based on his visionary proposals and actions regarding railroading.

Stevens attempted to influence legislators and prominent citizens regarding the benefits of this new means of transportation, but to no avail. For many years, Stevens hoped that the federal government would take an active role in the development of railroads. According to Seymour Dunbar, he believed that "under private auspices . . . [railroads] were usually brought into being without sufficient regard for their need, cooperation, or location; were built with more thought of cheapness than of efficiency and safety;

sometimes became political machines that ruled cities or dominated whole commonwealths; occasionally came into the hands of unscrupulous men who systematically used them to filch money from others." Stevens's fears were justified, and the negatives that Dunbar enumerated were real, not imagined.[3]

In 1811, Stevens approached the New Jersey legislature to request a charter to build a railroad, but he was dismissed as an impractical dreamer.[4] Yet, in all fairness to his detractors, the existing modes of transportation, roads and canals, were relatively safe and easily understood systems with entrenched supporters. It was about this time that the Erie Canal was proposed as an instrument to open up the West to trade with New York City. Determined to make his case, Stevens wrote a treatise explaining railroad technology. He used the facts and arguments that he developed in these writings to approach DeWitt Clinton, then mayor of New York City, and others to suggest that a railroad be built, instead of a canal, upon pilings three to six feet high along its route. These powerful individuals and other formidable interests aligned themselves in opposition to Stevens and rejected his arguments. Digging of the canal commenced in 1817.[5]

Rebuffed again, Stevens decided to publish his writings as a pamphlet. *Documents Tending to Prove the Superior Advantages of Railway and Steam Carriages over Canal Navigation* was published in the spring of 1812, and in it he delineated the overwhelming superiority of railroads over canals, their competitive costs, and operating details. Publication exposed Colonel Stevens to even further ridicule,

1

some based on statements that the author made, such as the possibility of traveling at 100 miles per hour, and in other instances based on the ignorance of his readers. One reporter in Philadelphia, upon perusing the tract, asked his editor, "What's a railroad, sir?" The editor replied that he did not know but that he was against it![6] Many years later, an official of the Pennsylvania Railroad, reading the tract for the first time, exclaimed that it was "the birth-certificate of all railroads in the United States."[7]

John Stevens would not accept defeat. He resolved to approach the New Jersey legislature again for a railroad charter but only after he had strengthened his theoretical arguments by walking the entire route that he intended to propose. That route was the key to the facilitation of trade between New York and Philadelphia. He chose the terminal points of his railroad to be Trenton and New Brunswick because both were river ports; passengers and freight transported along the Delaware from Philadelphia could be received at Trenton, then moved by rail to New Brunswick. One more transfer from rail to ship at New Brunswick on the Raritan River enabled direct access to New York Bay and New York City's great market.[8]

The 65-year-old Stevens left his estate at Hoboken and rode by carriage to New Brunswick where, "at George Road, at a corner of John Van Noice's fence," he began to walk toward Princeton and his ultimate destination, Trenton. Armed with firsthand information that confirmed the fact that there were no serious obstacles in the path of a railroad between New Brunswick and Trenton, he petitioned the lawmakers once more. Again he was turned down.[9]

Finally, after a third attempt, a charter, the first railroad charter awarded in America, was granted on 6 February 1815 "to erect a Rail-Road from the River Delaware, near Trenton, to the Raritan, at or near New Brunswick." Stevens's next hurdle was to finance the proposed New Jersey Railroad Company. This task was to prove as formidable as his original struggle to convince legislators of the desirability of a railroad. Potential investors just could not understand what Stevens was proposing, at least in a practical sense. There were no models to point to in the entire country, and he could not stir up any interest in the proposal. As a result, he was compelled to forfeit the franchise. Although he lacked support for his New Jersey railroad, Stevens continued to promote

his plans in other venues. He suggested lines in Pennsylvania, Virginia, and New York State, all without success.[10] Finally, several years later and in typical Stevens fashion, he devised a plan to convince the naysayers of the practicality of a railroad: he would build and demonstrate a locomotive!

In 1825, when Stevens was 75, he had a 630-foot-long circular track built so that one side was raised 30 inches above the other side. Stevens's intent was to demonstrate the engine's grade-climbing ability. Of course, the fact of its being a rack locomotive undoubtedly ensured its capability for climbing grades. Some writers placed Stevens's track at his "Castle" on his property at Castle Point,[11] but it was actually some distance south of the Stevens residence. The track was built on the lower lawn behind the Hoboken Hotel in an area bounded by Washington and First streets; it was located on the northwest corner of the intersection.[12] Today, the Hoboken City Hall sits directly across the street on the southwest corner of the intersection.

Next, he undertook construction of a 16-foot-long "Steam Waggon." This widely reproduced illustration shows that the locomotive carried a boiler with external tubes. Some historians were thus led to believe that this represented the actual machine, but for proper working the tubes had to be installed within the boiler. They were shown outside only to provide detail regarding their construction. Unlike steam engines built to that time, Stevens's boiler was capable of operating at extremely high pressures. A piston (through a connecting rod) drove a pinion gear mounted at the deck of the machine. The pinion meshed with a larger spur gear that engaged a rack mounted between the rails. In 1897, Stevens's grandson recalled that, although the wheels did not have flanges, the Steam Waggon ran on iron-capped wooden rails. Wooden fences extended from the outside of the stringers to keep the wheels "on track." However, the inventor noted excessive friction between the wheels and the side fences and "sent the carriage down to Van Velsen's shop and directed him to insert rollers into each end of two bars . . . so as to roll against the upright pieces placed on the outer sides of the ways." Carl Mitman, curator of mechanical technology at the Smithsonian Institution, described the improvement as follows: "Four vertical posts, extending downward from the floor of the truck near each corner and terminating in rollers in

**Figure 1.** John Stevens's locomotive, built in 1825, was the first railroad locomotive to be built in the United States. From Dredge, *A Record of the Transportation Exhibits at the World's Columbian Exposition of 1893.*

contact with the inner surface of the rails, guide the truck on the track."[13]

Now Stevens was prepared to demonstrate the practicality of a railroad once and for all. He wrote, "Rail Roads have nowhere yet been made, on this side of the Atlantic. Let the experiment be fairly tried."[14] Once built, Stevens invited members of the Society for Internal Improvement, which he had founded, to participate in trials of his machine.[15] In 1826, public demonstrations of the locomotive were scheduled. The *New York Evening Post* reported on May 12 that "Mr. Stevens has at length put his steam carriage in motion. It travelled around the circle at the Hoboken Hotel yesterday, at the rate of about six miles an hour. . . . It will be in motion again tomorrow, from 3 o'clock until sundown." It was a courageous pas-

senger who stepped aboard the Steam Waggon and rocketed along at the fearsome rate of 6 to 12 miles per hour! Yet this was not the "outrageous" velocity of 16 to 20 miles per hour that was originally planned. During the demonstrations, the little engine carried as many as half a dozen people while whirling around the 630-foot track.[16]

The boiler and steam valve of John Stevens's little Steam Waggon were later given to the Smithsonian Institution.[17] In November 1928, a replica of the tiny locomotive was built and operated around a circular track at Stevens Institute of Technology as part of the festivities surrounding the inauguration of a new college president.[18]

Finally, events caught up with the man who was years ahead of his time. Public railroads were established in England during the mid- and late 1820s, and local enthusiasm for railroads was kindled in Pennsylvania, South Carolina, Maryland, and New York. Despite that enthusiasm, there were still many skeptics, some of whom attributed darker motives to the idea of a steam-powered railroad. Anna Brakeley noted, "There were many who had not yet forgotten the tales that had come to them direct from the days of witchcraft, and this new undertaking was . . . but another scheme of the Prince of Darkness to entrap them, body and soul, or of the conjurer to untie their purse-strings."[19]

Casting all objections aside, Stevens's sons revived their father's hopes for a New Jersey railroad and secured a charter. The object of that charter, the Camden and Amboy Railroad, was the first railroad built in the state, and it was the fifth to be in operation in the country. This, then, was the culmination of a dream and vindication of a determined campaign by the man who wrote to John Gulick in February 1814, "I am anxious and ambitious that my native country should have the honor of being the first to introduce an improvement of such immense importance to society at large."[20] Had it not been for the shortsightedness of politicians and potential investors, who did not understand railroad operation or capabilities and whose money went into proven canal technology, Stevens might have built the first public railroad in the world a decade or more before any others.

# 2 From Camden to Amboy by Rail in Seven Hours: Fare, $3 (1833)

The history of the Camden and Amboy Railroad (C&A) has been recounted many times, and there is very little new information available. However, the planning, construction, and operation of New Jersey's first railroad are too important to ignore. We have seen how Col. John Stevens III was rebuffed in his attempt to secure a state charter for a railroad in 1811 and how in 1815 he was granted the first railroad charter awarded in the United States. Unfortunately, he failed to attract sufficient capital to undertake construction. It remained to his sons, Robert and Edwin, to build a railroad that, arguably, became the most important link in the mighty Pennsylvania Railroad (PRR) system.

By the end of the 1820s, railroads had been established in England, and the English locomotive *Stourbridge Lion* had rolled along tracks in Pennsylvania. The time was now ripe to build a railroad in New Jersey, but canals were the darlings of the legislators and the wealthy. Proponents of each, railroads and canals, lobbied for charters, but there was considerable concern in the New Jersey legislature (and elsewhere) that these were competitive enterprises, each with the potential to seriously affect the profitability of the other. A compromise was reached when Robert Stockton, a canal advocate, had a chance meeting with John Stevens's sons at the Park Theater in New York City. Their plan to seek charters for both a railroad *and* a canal was adopted by the legislature. As a result, the Camden and Amboy Railroad was chartered on 4 February 1830 to the Stevens brothers. On the same day, a charter was granted for constructing the Delaware and Raritan Canal (D&R).[1]

Unlike earlier railroad charters, important features were added to that obtained by the Stevenses on that winter day. In lieu of taxes, the charter specified that the State of New Jersey would share in the profits of the company, a flat fee for every passenger or ton of freight carried on the road. Even more important was the clause that these fees would no longer be paid if the legislature granted charters to any other railroad "from Philadelphia to New York to terminate within three miles of the commencement or termination of this road." These features made the railroad charter a much more desirable instrument than the canal charter. This was demonstrated by the fact that the entire subscription of railroad stock, in the amount of $1 million, was sold within 10 minutes, whereas it took nearly a year to sell an equal amount of the canal stock.[2] The canal charter specified that if all of its stock had not been sold within a year, the charter would be revoked. Robert Stockton, who was appointed president of the Delaware and Raritan Canal Company, saved the day when, at the last minute and with his father-in-law's assistance, he arranged for the purchase of the remaining unsold stock. Even after completion of the canal, it continued to be known as "Stockton's Folly."[3]

On 15 February 1831, to eliminate competition between the canal and the railroad, which might affect the profitability of both, the state legislature was persuaded to pass the so-called Marriage Act that joined the two together under a corporate umbrella known as the "Joint Companies." The Joint Companies worked out an agreement to pool all profits, thereby working in concert rather than as adversaries. But more threatening to the C&A from a competitive standpoint was the fear that another railroad, even though adhering to the restrictions placed in the original charter, might locate nearby in New Jersey and steal business from it. The second concern was addressed two weeks later, on March 2, when the act was strengthened in the Joint Companies' favor by an amendment that prohibited the construction of *any* railroad between Philadelphia and New York without the express consent of the Joint Companies. This monopoly was justified by the need to assure the investors in the railroad company that their profits would not be siphoned off by a rival if they were to invest in an as yet unproved transportation system. Of course, unremarked was the state's own interest, now fixed at an annual payment of $30,000 plus a percentage of profits.[4] Henceforth, throughout the nation, New Jersey was known as the "Camden and Amboy State." At least one historian justified the system by writing, "It was the duties paid by these companies that built our State Prison and Lunatic Asylums . . . also our beautiful State House . . . and . . . all our internal improvements, as well as a large amount toward the support of our magnificent system of public schools."[5]

The monopoly engendered continuing criticism and discontent that was notably expressed in a privately printed tract, *Beauties of the Monopoly System of New Jersey,* written anonymously in 1848 by Henry Charles Carey as "A Citizen of Burlington." In it he gathered numerous letters that he had produced denouncing the evils of the railroad monopoly. Robert Stockton felt obliged to answer this critic in a rebuttal volume that contained letters that he had written to the *New York Evening Post* in "Defence of the System." He argued that the so-called monopoly was really "a franchise, granted for a limited time, and for a fair equivalent or annual rent." He further pointed out that many railroad charters had been granted and that the C&A's franchise only restricted railroads operating between Philadelphia and New York, a perfectly normal situation in granting a charter. He then launched a moral argument that justified the private financing of railroads, a lesson learned well (he said) by New Jersey politicians when they viewed the enormous debt racked up by the State of Pennsylvania when it was the railroad builder. Finally, Stockton declaimed that "this franchise has cost more than it is worth. For the money paid for

this lease originally, and for its continued protection, the Companies could have bought all the roads ever proposed to be made between New York and Philadelphia, and taxed the public to pay for such an expenditure."[6] While the monopoly persisted, the C&A was a potent political force in the state. It had a strong influence in choosing candidates for election, from the governor down to local officials. The arrangement continued until 1 January 1869, when the monopoly expired under legislation that had been enacted in 1854.[7]

In 1830, Robert Stevens, the president and chief engineer of the pioneer railway, sailed to England, where momentous railroad activities were under way. England was the Mecca for all fledgling railroad officials. His principal reason for making the journey was to order rails and a locomotive for the C&A. There were no foundries in the United States with the capability for rolling any but ordinary strap rail with a rectangular cross section or simple shapes that required a "chair" to hold them in place. The use of a chair required very precise assembly with hard-to-manufacture bolts.[8] Pondering this situation and hoping to eliminate the chair, while en route Stevens designed a rail form that he fancied and whittled a model of it from a block of wood. This iron rail, with a broad base that could be fastened directly to a substructure, eventually became the universally accepted and employed T-rail that is still used worldwide. He also invented the hook-headed spike and "iron tongue," or splice plate that joined two rails, devices that survive to this day in nearly their original form. While in the British Isles, Stevens finally found Guest, Lewis and Company, an iron works in Wales that, after much difficulty, managed to produce his rail design in iron. Stevens was remiss in not patenting the design promptly, and when he belatedly sought patent protection, he found that the invention had passed into the public domain. Turnbull, however, acknowledged Stevens's contribution as "Robert's imperishable monument."[9]

Stevens's second quest, to purchase a locomotive, was fulfilled when he acquired the *John Bull* from George Stephenson's works at Newcastle-on-Tyne for about $4,000.[10] (The story of the *John Bull* and Isaac Dripps, the young mechanic who erected it upon its arrival in New Jersey, is told in chapter 3.)

The original path of the C&A, from Camden to Amboy, was established by the charter to lie between

"Cooper's and Newton's Creek" (on the New Jersey bank of the Delaware River) to "some point on the Raritan Bay."[11] (Although Perth Amboy had a fine harbor and was considered by some to have the potential to rival New York City as a future metropolis, the railroad would have been required to build a bridge over Raritan Bay to reach Perth Amboy. South Amboy was chosen as the terminus instead.)[12] The route was surveyed in 1830 by crews directed by Maj. John A. Wilson, a West Point graduate.[13] Typical of surveys at that time, the line was established using local references and landmarks. For example, a part of Wilson's survey put the right-of-way "south of Buccleugh's house. Thence to the dividing ridge between the waters of the Raritan and South rivers; thence north of Bloodgood's house, and after curving through a ravine which opens to the turnpike, is located to the south of Brown's Tavern."[14] Of interest is the fact that, although the charter specified that Bordentown should be on "a lateral road from the main line," which was not to be built until the main line was completed, the promoters ignored that restriction and began construction of the main line at Bordentown.[15]

A passenger traveling from Philadelphia to New York City could cross the Delaware River by ferry and entrain at Camden. At the northern terminus, South Amboy, that passenger could transfer to a steamship to complete his journey. The single-track section from Bordentown to the Amboys, a distance of 26.5 miles, was constructed first and was ready for service by December 1832. The first passengers, 40 or 50 strong, were carried over this portion of the line in horse-drawn cars on a rainy 17 December 1832.[16] Work continued on the Bordentown-Camden section, and when it was finished, the *John Bull* was put into service (between Bordentown and South Amboy) in September 1833.[17] Soon thereafter, regularly scheduled steam-powered service commenced over the 61-mile-long railroad; the seven-hour trip between the two terminals (Camden and Amboy) cost three dollars.[18]

It should not be presumed, however, that travel over the road was reliable and expeditious in the early days. A British actor, Tyrone Power, who visited the United States in the early 1830s, wrote of his several journeys on the Camden and Amboy. On one trip "everyone was delighted to find that the locomotives were now in operation." That delight soon changed to panic when "an alarm is given from the rear and loud cries of 'Stop the engine!' come from the windows of every carriage upon the train. One of the rear coaches had broken an axle, and several passengers were killed and injured." Although an inquest was hastily organized, it does not seem to have delayed the train for any substantial period of time, because the travelers arrived in Philadelphia later in the afternoon. Equally interesting is the matter-of-fact description of the accident, which resulted in the deaths of passengers.

On a subsequent trip, an axle on the tender failed and the engine was "speedily arrested." The problem was resolved by replacing the broken axle with one removed from a following car. That car was withdrawn from the train, its passengers transferred to other coaches, and the trip resumed. This incident occurred at a time when the railroad terminated at Bordentown and the trip to Philadelphia was to be concluded by steamboat. But on this occasion ice on the Delaware River precluded travel by boat, so the travelers continued by horse-drawn coach:

> The real terrors of the journey now began. The coaches first traveled through a narrow lane, with ruts over a foot deep. Mr. Power rode on top of the coach, and was kept busy dodging the branches of trees. . . . The frozen ruts were so bad that he fully expected the driver to give it up, but he coolly steered around all impediments. In one case he abandoned the road for a hundred yards, crashing through shrubs breast high on the right bank. . . . At Camden, with much trouble, the frozen river was crossed and Philadelphia was reached at four in the afternoon.[19]

The Camden and Amboy rails from Bordentown almost to South Amboy were laid on individual granite blocks, a practice then thought to provide the best construction. The blocks were obtained from quarries worked by inmates of Sing Sing prison in New York. Track work went well until South Amboy was neared; at that point the prison authorities failed to deliver the granite blocks as quickly as needed. As a temporary expedient, Stevens ordered hewn wooden ties to be laid instead of stone, and the rails were spiked directly to them. When the road began operations, it soon became evident that the wooden ties performed much better than the stone blocks, and the latter were replaced with wood as quickly as possible. Stevens noted that it was easy to see that, with very little attention, the exact line of direction and

**Figure 2.** This monument, erected in 1891 at the site of the first movement of the *John Bull* locomotive along the Camden and Amboy tracks, was relocated to downtown Bordentown in 1970. Photograph taken by the author, summer 2006.

perfect parallelism of the ways could be maintained by the wooden ties. With this innovation, Robert Stevens had single-handedly invented the forerunner of modern American railroad track: rails, crossties, spikes, and fishplates.[20]

In his book *Railroads in New Jersey*, John Cunningham noted the bonanza experienced by locals along the path of construction. Farmers in Dutch Neck (in West Windsor Township) discovered that stones required by the railroad for ballast would bring more than a dollar per perch (about 25 cubic feet) or an extra dollar if crushed to pebble size. Sawmill owners increased their incomes substantially by furnishing wood for all manner of railroad structures and for crossties.[21]

Originally, the tracks of the Camden and Amboy Railroad were laid in a more or less direct path from Camden to South Amboy. Then, in order to forestall the Philadelphia and Trenton Railroad (P&T) from extending their line to New Brunswick (their threat to do so just ignored the C&A's state-granted monopoly between Philadelphia and New York) to meet the tracks of the New Jersey Railroad and Transportation Company (NJRR), which went from that city to Jersey City across from New York, the C&A acquired control of the Philadelphia and Trenton Railroad and the Trenton Delaware Bridge Company. The C&A then (1838–39) built a connecting link from Bordentown to Trenton and continued with a branch north to New Brunswick. The tracks of the branch line followed the D&R canal closely from Trenton to Kingston and then continued northeast toward New Brunswick where they joined the NJRR on 1 January 1839. Through a lease arrangement with the NJRR, the C&A was then able to provide through service for passengers from Philadelphia to Jersey City (and thence by ferry to New York City). This avoided the longer ship passage from South Amboy to New York City.[22] Until 1840, all passengers had to leave their cars and walk across the bridge at Trenton to continue their trips because the gauges of the C&A and the P&T differed. Edwin Stevens took advantage of this situation to evade transit taxes; he took the position that the passengers were "way traffic" and not through passengers because they did not arrive at either New Jersey or Pennsylvania by rail.[23] At a later time (1867), the Joint Companies and the New Jersey Railroad were officially joined by an act of the legislature.[24]

After the Civil War ended, railroad officials executed a plan to eliminate the winding right-of-way along the canal, which hindered the passage of higher speed trains. Although the first suggestion was to relocate the track so that it passed through Princeton, perhaps along the main street, vociferous protests by the locals and more reasoned study by the officials resulted in establishing the main line about a mile and a half eastward. A new station, Princeton Junction, was built there (and recently rebuilt) along the two tracks, which were essentially straight from Trenton to New Brunswick. A consequence of this relocation was that the town of Princeton, a bustling community, would no longer be situated near the main line of the railroad. This situation was addressed by the provision of a shuttle train between Princeton and

**Figure 3.** A section of the original track of the Camden and Amboy Railroad showing the rail designed by Robert Stevens supported on granite blocks. This photograph was taken near Jamesburg, N.J., in 1932, a century after the track had been first laid. Author's collection.

Princeton Junction, about which more information is provided in chapter 10.[25]

The company's name passed into history in 1871 when the Camden and Amboy Railroad was leased to the Pennsylvania Railroad for a period of 999 years.[26] Henceforth its trackage was known as the Amboy Division of its parent. (A takeover of the C&A was also sought by the Philadelphia and Reading Railroad (P&R), which, along with the PRR, desired the C&A's strategically located rights-of-way.[27] A second option contemplated by the P&R, the one that was implemented, involved a new line from Philadelphia to meet the Central Railroad of New Jersey tracks at Bound Brook. The beginnings of the conflict between the two giants is told in chapter 14.) An audit conducted in conjunction with the leasing disclosed that the United Companies were more than a railroad and a canal company. As assets they also listed ownership in 13 railroads, two ferry enterprises, three horsecar lines, two bridges, four turnpikes, a steamboat company, and several telegraph services.[28]

In 1891, on the sixtieth anniversary of the first operation on the road, the Pennsylvania Railroad erected a monument that now stands in Bordentown on Farnsworth and Railroad avenues. This granite obelisk, five feet square and seven feet high, bears a bronze tablet with a bas-relief of the *John Bull,* its tender, and two coaches. Beneath is written:

> First movement by steam on a railroad in the State of New Jersey, November 12, 1831, by the original locomotive 'John Bull,' now deposited in the United States National Museum at Washington. The first piece of railroad track in New Jersey was laid by the Camden and Amboy Railroad Company between this point and the stone, thirty-five hundred feet eastward, in 1831.

The monument was encircled by a section of the original T-rail designed by Robert Stevens, resting on stone sleepers that were used during early construction. Isaac Dripps, then 82, contributed to the construction of the monument by driving stakes marking the ends of a short section of track at the site where the first movement of the *John Bull* was made in November 1831. A second bronze tablet at the base on which the monument now stands declares, "This monument moved from its original site on Amboy Road to its present location" on 1 October 1970.[29]

In 1893, the Pennsylvania Railroad converted its entire main line through New Jersey to four tracks, with the two inside tracks reserved for freight trains.[30] This route remains essentially unchanged to this day, and its directness facilitates the high speeds achieved by Metroliner and Acela express trains along the Northeast Corridor.

# 3 Isaac Dripps and the *John Bull* (1831)

On 4 September 1831, Engine Number One (the name *John Bull* was conferred at a later time), the Camden and Amboy Railroad's (C&A) first locomotive, arrived at Bordentown from George Stephenson's works at Newcastle-on-Tyne in England. This machine was delivered unassembled at Philadelphia and brought to Bordentown by sloop. A boiler, wheels, and other parts were scattered among several boxes and described as "a picture puzzle in iron." The engine was assembled by a 21-year-old Scottish-born mechanic, Isaac Dripps, who was employed by the Stevens family at their steamboat maintenance shops. Dripps, who had never seen a locomotive and was provided with no instructions by the builder, had expected guidance from Robert Stevens, but Stevens was unavailable at the time. Employing only his prior experience with marine engines, Dripps eventually sorted out the parts and put them together properly. Summoning Stevens from Hoboken, Dripps conducted a test of the machine, driving the locomotive with Stevens at his side. The *John Bull* operated with a boiler pressure (gauge) of only 30 pounds per square inch. Dripps made further adjustments to improve the *John Bull*'s performance, including the creation of a tender to carry water and wood. A leather hose, made by a local shoemaker, served to carry water, pumped by hand, from the whiskey barrel mounted on the tender to the six-foot-long boiler of the tiny engine.[1]

To celebrate the arrival of Engine Number One, Col. John Stevens arranged a midsummer lawn party at Hoboken. Two hundred guests were brought by special ferry from New York City, and their number was augmented by members of the New York and New Jersey boat clubs in "white jackets and trousers, round chip hats, and checked shirts." The food was superb, a highlight being turtle soup, and the "groves echoed with merriment and good humor, toasts, songs, and laughter."[2]

A demonstration of the *John Bull* was arranged for 12 November 1831. The festive occasion was described by an anonymous participant: "The members of the New Jersey Legislature were present, as well as all the dignitaries of the State and distinguished citizens of other States were included in the vast assemblage that gathered at the 'Mile Hollow' to witness the great event. Flags were numerous and refreshment tables, at which hot oyster soup predominated, were plentiful. Everybody came in carriages, and the vicinity was crowded with four- and two-wheeled vehicles."

Although many of the onlookers were reluctant to ride behind the fearsome, flame-belching locomotive, Madame Murat, wife of an exiled French nobleman who was residing in Bordentown, accepted Stevens's invitation and sat in one of the coaches. Spurred on (or shamed) by her example, others climbed into the coaches and the train moved off. The trial of the machine was successful, and the passengers, with ash-strewn clothes and smoke-filled eyes, retired to Arnell's Hotel to enjoy the sumptuous luncheon.[3]

An account appearing the following week in the *New Jersey State Gazette* observed that about 1.25 miles of track had been laid for the demonstration,

Figure 4. Isaac Dripps, the first master mechanic of the Camden and Amboy Railroad, and the locomotive *John Bull*. From Watkins, *The Camden and Amboy Railroad, Origins and Early History.*

and the Hoboken-built coaches that were attached to the locomotive were drawn with "great velocity." (In truth, the length of the demonstration track was 1,067.5 feet, less than a quarter of a mile.) Based on the *John Bull's* performance that day, it was estimated that the entire distance between Bordentown and Amboy could be traversed in less than one hour.[4]

After the celebrations were concluded, the locomotive was stored until the track was ready for it. During that hiatus and in anticipation of the need for additional locomotives, the construction of three engines based on the *John Bull* pattern began at Stevens's shops at Hoboken. The boilers were made at Hoboken, but valves, cylinders, and pistons were imported from England. These machines were completed by the spring of 1833. Dripps continued on with the Camden and Amboy Railroad as master mechanic and, in collaboration with Robert Stevens, outshopped several unique engines. In the late 1830s, they designed the *Monster*—and a monster it was, weighing 27 tons and sporting eight drivers, driven by a combination of side-rods and gears.

In the late 1840s, Stevens returned from another trip to England where he had seen a high-speed engine invented by Thomas Crampton. Back in America he immediately set about to design a copy of the Crampton machine, which he turned over to the Norris Brothers for construction. Photographs of the resulting locomotive, made in 1850, show an unusual engine whose forward weight was carried by three small wheels under the boiler. A single driving wheel, eight feet in diameter, placed behind the boiler, was driven by a piston sliding in a cylinder mounted alongside the boiler. The first of the Cramptons exploded near Bordentown after a short time in service, and its engineer was thrown 50 feet. The three remaining Cramptons were reworked, and although they remained in service for many years, they lacked tractive power and were never considered successful.

After the *John Bull* began regular operation, Robert Stevens came to the conclusion that it would benefit from the addition of a pilot truck. A pilot truck is essentially one or more sets of wheels that can swivel, or move from a straight line, independently of, and mounted before, the fixed (nonswiveling) driving wheels. The principle of its operation and usefulness in guiding a locomotive into a curve was already understood in England when Robert made his pilgrimage, and its first American application had been made to a Mohawk and Hudson Railroad locomotive in 1832. Ordered to design such an appurtenance, Dripps produced a two-wheel pilot truck. Although it did not swivel in the usual sense, it had sufficient play that its wheels could move from a straight line to lead the machine into and through a curve.[5] It served a second purpose of sweeping track obstacles aside, a function whose usefulness was demonstrated when the locomotive struck a hog. The hog was decapitated, but the engine "plunged with its head into the gutter," causing one male passenger to fall out of a window.[6] David Stevenson, an English engineer, recalled riding on a C&A train: "The train in which I travelled, while moving with considerable rapidity, came in contact with a large waggon loaded with firewood, which was literally shivered to atoms by the concussion. The fragments of the broken waggon, and the wood with which it was loaded, were distributed on each side of the railway, but the guard [pilot] prevented any part of them from falling before the engine wheels, and thus obviated what might in that case have proved a very serious accident."[7]

Shortly after the demonstration run of the *John Bull,* another young man, Matthias Baldwin, traveled from Philadelphia and obtained permission from Isaac Dripps to examine the small engine. He had been commissioned to build a working model of a locomotive for the Peale Museum in his city. The Baldwin Locomotive Works, which he founded, grew to be the most important and extensive locomotive factory in the United States.[8]

In 1850, Dripps designed a wide-tread locomotive to operate on tracks of different gauges. The variation between track gauges at that time was a serious problem because they could vary by as little as an inch or as much as a foot or more. A few years later (early 1850s), four additional locomotives based on the *Monster* design were built at the Trenton Locomotive and Machine Manufacturing Company for the Camden and Amboy. Isaac Dripps, in the employ of the C&A when the order was placed, left to become a partner at the Trenton concern. He retired

from that position in 1858 and later was appointed superintendent of motive power for the Pennsylvania Railroad (PRR). He passed away at the age of 82.[9]

The *John Bull* worked as a road locomotive until the late 1840s and then continued to be used in various services to haul work trains, as a switching engine, for hydrostatic testing of new boilers, and as a stationary engine to power a saw. Beginning in the 1850s, the engine was displayed at various fairs and expositions, including the 1876 Centennial Exposition at Philadelphia. In 1884, the engine was given to the Smithsonian Institution. The *John Bull* played a starring role at the Columbian Exposition in Chicago. Taken from the Smithsonian, the 60-year-old engine, in company with some of the restored early carriages, one of which had been serving as a chicken coop on a nearby farm, traveled from Bordentown to Chicago under its own power, making numerous stops along the way to be shown off. Although it proceeded at an average 30 mph pace, the trip took five days because of the many stops.

It was operated, under steam, at the 1927 Fair of the Iron Horse in Halethorpe, Maryland, and again at the Century of Progress in Chicago in 1933. When, in 1939, similar arrangements were sought to operate the locomotive at the 1939–40 World's Fair in New York City, the Smithsonian Institution demurred. The locomotive was simply too valuable to risk damage by operating it. At the Fair, its working was simulated by drawing the machine across a stage by cable in front of an audience. However, the managers of the Pennsylvania Railroad were disappointed by this performance, and they immediately authorized their Altoona Works to build an operable replica of the *John Bull,* identical in all respects to the original (although a small, inconspicuous steam injector was added for safety). This was done and for the 1940 fair, a *John Bull* clone worked under its own steam power for the entertainment of countless spectators.

The original engine was returned to the Smithsonian Institution in Washington, where it is exhibited as the oldest original locomotive in the country. However, in appearance, the museum piece is substantially different than the engine that arrived in this country. Notably, its smokestack and tender were altered, a cab has been added, and other features were changed. In 1981, the *John Bull* was reconditioned and made operable and then, in honor of its 150th birthday, brought out to run under its own power on Chessie System tracks near the nation's capital. Following this demonstration run, the engine was flown to Dallas to be exhibited there for a year.

The replica continued to be used, and finally, in the early 1960s, when the fortunes of the Pennsylvania Railroad had declined and its financial problems had become insurmountable, its management sold off assets. The *John Bull* replica, which by that time was part of a collection of historical PRR locomotives, was purchased by the Commonwealth of Pennsylvania and now is housed in an outstanding railroad museum at Strasburg, Pennsylvania, where it is the only operable steam locomotive in the collection.[10]

# 4 Ashbel Welch, Railroad Man (1836–74)

Ashbel Welch Jr. was an important, yet nearly forgotten, New Jersey railroad dignitary who was born in New York State in 1809. He resided in Lambertville for much of his adult life. He was noted as an engineer, a canal builder, a champion of an Atlantic–Pacific canal, a president of the Camden and Amboy Railroad, and the inventor of the first block signals to be installed on any railroad line in the country.

At 17, he was surveying the Lehigh and Delaware Canal in Pennsylvania. This experience led to an assignment as engineer in charge of building the feeder canal for the Delaware and Raritan Canal (D&R) in New Jersey. The feeder canal was to bring water from the Delaware River at Bull's Island (near Raven Rock) to Trenton, a high point between the main canal's termini at Bordentown and New Brunswick. Canvass White, chief engineer of the project, died before the D&R was completed, and Welch was promoted to his position. The D&R Canal was completed in 1834, and the following year, though only 24 years old, Ashbel Welch was appointed chief engineer of the "Joint Companies."

The Joint Companies were a venture that embraced the D&R Canal and the Camden and Amboy Railroad (C&A).[1] Shortly after charters were granted to the C&A and the D&R Canal, it became clear that competition between the canal and the railroad might destroy the profitability of both. To address this concern, the legislature now approved the so-called Marriage Act on 15 February 1831, and the two companies were joined. They agreed to pool all profits, effectively eliminating harmful effects of competition.

The Camden and Amboy Railroad (and later the Pennsylvania Railroad) spawned or acquired several connecting lines throughout its territory, and in 1836 Welch was appointed chief engineer of the Philadelphia and Trenton Railroad, a road that the C&A had acquired to preclude its becoming part of a through route between Philadelphia and New York. In 1850, Welch began construction of the Belvidere and Delaware Railroad (Bel-Del), which was to occupy the east bank of the Delaware River for much of the distance between its two end points. Although incorporated in 1836, the depression of 1837 adversely affected stock sales, and it wasn't until 1855 that the line was completed from Trenton to Belvidere.[2]

Concurrently, during the winter of 1852–53, his office was engaged in enlarging the locks along the D&R Canal in order to increase their capacity. This was done in time for the spring reopening of the canal. One of the reasons for completing the work on time and within budget was an imaginative method he developed for heating newly poured concrete to prevent it from freezing as it set.[3]

Meanwhile, work continued on the Bel-Del, which entered Phillipsburg on June 6, 1854, and was finally completed to Belvidere in 1855. The Bel-Del had been built primarily to serve the Trenton Iron Works, a company with facilities in Trenton and in Phillipsburg. Because of Ashbel Welch, Lambertville became a factor in railroad activities. Rather than locating major shop facilities in Trenton, Welch turned Lambertville into a busy railroad center that included the main offices of the Bel-Del and a shop for building and repairing locomotives and cars. An offshoot (later a branch of the Bel-Del), the Fleming-ton Railroad and Transportation Company, was also constructed from Lambertville to Flemington to tap that agricultural region. Welch also became president of the Bel-Del and the short Flemington railway.[4]

One of the commodities that made up a substantial portion of the C&A's traffic was coal. Mined in Pennsylvania, it was brought to South Amboy and thence shipped, by boat or barge, to New York City. A major problem was that the handling facilities at the South Amboy docks were inadequate for the volume of traffic. Welch applied his engineering talents to the problem which, as he related to J. Elfreth Watkins, "led me to invent and adopt barges so constructed that loaded wagons [railway cars] could be driven on board, the freight not being handled, but once until unloaded at destination . . . by this means the terminal expenses were reduced so that it equalled the expense of transportation for one hundred miles."[5]

During the Civil War, in 1862, Welch was made vice president and executive officer of the Joint Companies, a position he held until 1867. During this period he negotiated a lease arrangement with the New Jersey Railroad and Transportation Company that brought "the whole system of railroads and canals between New York and Philadelphia into one interest and under one management."[6]

The C&A was at this time a vital link in the movement of war materiel along the eastern seaboard and traffic increased tremendously along the line. Although it had experienced accidents since its inception, one incident became the catalyst for the application of a monumental invention. On 7 March 1865, two troop trains collided on the Philadelphia and Trenton Railroad at Bristol, Pennsylvania, killing 6 and injuring 40.[7] This accident disturbed Welch greatly, and he realized that a safer method of train operation was necessary to prevent similar disasters in the future.

Up to that time, American railroads operated under "time-interval" scheduling. Train movements were governed by scheduled departure and "meet" times. In other words, a train was obliged to be at certain points at specified times. They were not permitted to run ahead of schedule, but obviously there were times when they fell behind schedule. When a train stalled for any reason, flagmen were dispatched to the rear to prevent a following train from overtaking and crashing into it. Trains operating on a single track line had defined meet points where one train was to run onto a siding to allow another to pass. This system, with its confusing and sometimes conflicting rules, was fraught with danger, as evidenced by a high incidence of accidents.[8]

Welch had been looking into a better traffic control system, but wartime pressures had put the project on a back burner. The troop train accident brought it front and center and accelerated the introduction of Welch's "banner box signals." This first block signal to be installed on an American railroad involved "a white board, and a white light at night shown through an oraface [sic] two feet in diameter in a black signal box. . . . A partition in the box separates the signals for the opposite directions."[9] A red flannel banner, mounted in a rectangular frame within the box, could be raised or lowered to cover or uncover the white board.

The system worked as follows. A train was permitted to pass a banner box signal only if the white board (or a white light) was showing. As soon as the train passed the signal, a nearby signalman/telegrapher dropped the red banner in front of the white board. This red indicator stayed in place and halted any subsequent train until word was telegraphed that the first train had left the block (a length of track which, in this case, was "from one to two miles long") that was protected by the signal.[10] When such word was received, the red banner was raised and a white indicator was presented to the engineer of the second train, thus allowing him to proceed. Obviously, no more than one train could occupy a block at any time.

Ashbel Welch moved swiftly to implement his system of block signals, which he called "the American safety system," and he reported in a presentation that he made at a railroad conference in New York City in 1866 that his "plan has been in use for a year past between Philadelphia and New Brunswick on the main passenger route between Philadelphia and New York and experience confirms our confidence in its value." Welch's block signals were installed from New Brunswick to Jersey City by 1867, and they protected the entire main line, from Jersey City to Philadelphia by 1876, in time to handle the enormous traffic generated by the Centennial Exhibition in that year.[11]

The greatest shortcoming of this invention was the fact that it relied on human operators to function properly. Yet it truly was monumental and historical-

**Figure 5.** This photograph, taken about 1870, shows one of Ashbel Welch's banner box signals mounted on the station roof at Princeton Junction, N.J., a stop between Trenton and New Brunswick. In 1862, in order to accommodate heavy wartime traffic, the main line of the Camden and Amboy Railroad between those two cities was double-tracked and relocated in the Princeton area about three miles farther east of its original right-of-way near the Delaware and Raritan Canal. Author's collection.

ly significant because, despite its mechanical crudity, it was effective and provided the first instance where a railroad in the United States adopted block signaling. It blazed the way for other inventors to improve upon it and for other railroad executives to adopt block signaling for their operations.

Ashbel Welch was also instrumental in the construction of the Mercer and Somerset Railroad (M&S), a line that was built primarily to thwart the establishment of a competing line. He was appointed its president (see chapter 14).

In 1867, the Joint Companies, under lease arrangements, combined with the New Jersey Railroad and Transportation Company and the Philadelphia and Trenton Railroad, and Ashbel Welch became president as well as chief engineer of the new corporation, which eventually became known as the United Companies of New Jersey. As president, Welch embarked on a program of improvements which, although beneficial, drew down invested capital, a contributor to high dividends. By 1871, when dividends fell below the 10 percent return that the stockholders had long enjoyed and continued to expect, Welch's critics, especially John Read, a major stockholder, attacked Welch's policies. He strongly recommended that the Companies should accept the Pennsylvania Railroad's offer of a 999-year lease. (The PRR assured the stockholders that it would resume paying 10 percent dividends if their offer was accepted.) Further, believing that Welch's actions were influenced by his technical background, Read rebuked him by stating, "One thing is certain, our official head, the general president, must not be an engineer." Ironically, it was Welch's acquisitions and improvements, especially the port facilities on the west bank of the Hudson River, that influenced the PRR to seek to lease the Joint Companies. The directors accepted the Pennsylvania's offer on 30 June 1871 and removed Welch from the post of president. The offices of president and chief engineer were separated, and Welch was appointed a vice president of the Pennsylvania Railroad. One of the negative effects of the consolidation, insofar as Lambertville was concerned, was the withdrawal of locomotive and car building from the town.[12]

In January 1882, Ashbel Welch was elected president of the American Society of Civil Engineers, an honor well earned and richly deserved. He died on September 25, 1882, in Lambertville and, according to J. Roscoe Howell, "was buried in Mount Hope Cemetery, on a hill overlooking the Delaware River and the feeder canal he had built so long ago. Below the hill, also, lies the roadbed of the Belvidere and Delaware, the railroad he promoted, built, and managed, Sabbatarian during his lifetime, and Sabbatarian out of respect for him, for eight years after his death."[13]

Ashbel Welch's home was located at the southeast corner of York and North Union streets in Lambertville, a few blocks away from the Bel-Del shop and office complex that lay between the river and the feeder canal. The substantial brick residence re-mains and has not changed appreciably in appearance. The D&R feeder and main canals still exist and form the Delaware and Raritan State Park, one of the longest and narrowest state parks in the country. The Belvidere and Delaware Railroad ceased passenger operations on 16 October 1960, but freight service survived for a time. In February 1976, New Jersey representative Helen Meyner reported that freight service would be continued when the Consolidated Railroad Corporation (ConRail) assumed control of the line (from the then-merged Penn-Central). This assessment proved to be wrong because Con-Rail abandoned the Bel-Del tracks between Trenton and Milford on 1 April 1976. The abandoned right-of-way lies within the boundaries of the D&R feeder canal and is used by hikers, bicyclists, and horseback riders. At this writing, trains still operate at the Bel-Del's northern and eastern reaches but as a much diminished version of the original railroad. The Black River and Western Railroad (BR&W), which is a passenger and freight carrier, purchased the Flemington Branch in 1965 and operates excursions between Ringoes and Flemington, using steam and diesel motive power. It also services chemical and lumber enterprises along the route, and it interchanges freight with the Norfolk Southern at Three Bridges, N.J. (over Jersey Central rails acquired in 1976). More recently, the BR&W incorporated the Belvidere and Delaware River Railroad. This short railroad serves industrial customers in the area between Milford and Phillipsburg and connects with the Norfolk Southern, whose tracks use the old Bel-Del right-of-way north of Phillipsburg.[14]

# 5 Locomotives: From New Jersey to the World (1837–1926)

Of necessity, there being few firms dedicated solely to locomotive building, many early locomotives were built in the shops of the railroads upon which they were to be used. However, as outside sources became available, many railroad managers realized the advantages that might be secured by purchasing, rather than building, their locomotives. This approach conserved scarce capital for operations, utilized the specialized experience built up at the outside shops, and accelerated the movement to standardized forms of engine and accessories. Early on, New Jersey, a highly industrialized state, was at the forefront of locomotive building and became an important supplier of engines to the railroads of the United States and the world.

The first outside (non-railroad) builder in the state was Seth Boyden, who was a skilled mechanic with a shop at Newark, New Jersey. Boyden had a wide range of interests: he repaired watches, made improvements to patent leather manufacturing, and invented machines for making nails, cutting files, and heading tacks. He assisted Samuel Morse in perfecting the telegraph. Although he had never seen a steam locomotive, Boyden produced one, the *Orange,* for the Morris and Essex Railroad (M&E), which he delivered in 1837. In July of that year, with Boyden at the throttle, the six-ton engine ascended the mountain to Orange, a feat that had been accomplished previously only by teams of horses. Newspaper accounts of the first day of operation, when the little engine hauled about 100 passengers over the mountain, exaggerated its speed in excess of a mile a minute. It became a usual practice to "get a running start" at

full throttle on the level before the hill and, with a man dropping sand on the rails ahead of the machine to reduce slippage, attack the grade at full speed, but not likely at 60 miles per hour. Boyden produced only two more engines: the *Essex,* which was also sold to the M&E, and a second one, which was exported to Cuba. In later life, Boyden turned to horticulture and developed the Seth Boyden strawberry, a large and succulent fruit. A statue of Boyden, standing beside an anvil and a large hammer, was sculpted by Karl Gerhardt, a famous contemporary of Saint-Gaudens, and erected in Washington Park in Newark.[1]

Breese, Kneeland and Company, based in Jersey City, was also known as the New York Locomotive Works. Organized in 1853, it delivered its first machine to the Hudson River Railroad in 1854. It customers were countrywide, and one of its engines, made for the Milwaukee and Mississippi Railroad, is preserved at El Paso, Texas. Forced into bankruptcy, it was reorganized as the Jersey City Locomotive Works and continued to build locomotives for a few years. After the Civil War, the factory began to function again, but it stopped making engines in 1873. All told, about 300 locomotives were produced by Breese, Kneeland and its successor.[2]

The Trenton Locomotive and Machine Manufacturing Company was launched in 1854 by three principals. Messrs. Van Cleve and McKean, machinery builders, had no experience in locomotive building, so they brought Isaac Dripps, the talented Camden and Amboy master mechanic, into the firm as their partner.[3] Their intent was to build the company on Dripps's reputation and contributions to design and production. They did produce several engines for the Camden and Amboy, the Lehigh Valley, and others, but the Panic of 1857 left the firm without orders, and no further engines were erected by the company thereafter. Isaac Dripps resigned in 1858. The firm continued to make other products, and in 1863 it was reorganized as the Trenton Car Works. Grice and Long (G&L), a firm organized in 1858 to build railroad cars at Trenton, also built small locomotives. The company outshopped gear-driven passenger cars, dummy engines (steam locomotives generally used on street railways and shrouded to convey the appearance of an ordinary horsecar in order to avoid frightening nearby horses), and mining locomotives. Generally unsuccessful in breaching the streetcar market, the firm restricted its products to small locomotives. In the 1860s, Grice and Long acquired the Trenton Car Works. An advertisement in the *American Railroad Journal* in 1869 listed G&L's offices and works at Philadelphia. The company failed in 1871.[4]

The aforementioned, and short-lived, locomotive builders operated in three large cities of the state, but eventually locomotive construction centered at Paterson. Paterson had great natural advantages for manufacturing of any type and it was strenuously promoted by the state to become a manufacturing center. The Great Falls at Paterson is a stunning natural feature that attracts visitors to this day. However, it is only the most dramatic manifestation of the area's abundant water resources; five notable rivers flow through Passaic County, one of which, the Passaic River, is the most important insofar as the commercial development of Paterson was concerned.

Alexander Hamilton was appointed secretary of the treasury in 1789, and one of the responsibilities of that position was the development of manufacturing capabilities. In 1791, Hamilton presented his findings to Congress in a report that envisioned a centralized manufacturing location that would produce basic products essential to the nation's prosperity, if not survival. Using this report, he persuaded the New Jersey legislature to charter a committee to choose a site and establish a "Society for Establishing Useful Manufactures." Bids were received from many regional towns, but the area near the Great Falls was selected and named Paterson in honor of the sitting governor. The overwhelming reason for that decision was the plentiful power that could be harnessed by waterwheels placed in the fast-running Passaic River.

Unfortunately, the Society suffered setbacks and losses and flirted with bankruptcy. In 1814, its directors asserted their intention to revive the enterprise, and they were modestly successful. It was later, though, with the introduction of two industries, silk making and locomotive building, that Paterson's renaissance flowered. As an aside, John Sullivan was a civil engineer employed by the Society. In 1828, before there was a single railroad in the United States, it was Sullivan who proposed a railroad be built across the state from the coal fields of Pennsylvania to the Hudson River. Although Paterson's great natural resources were essential to the establishment of locomotive and other manufactories, the true catalyst for locomotive building in that town was a young man's ambition and industry and a little bit of luck.[5]

Thomas Rogers arrived in Paterson in 1812 when he was 20. Employed as a carpenter in John Clarke's machinery shop, he became a partner of the firm. Later, he sold his interest in the firm and established his own factory, the Jefferson Works. By the time he was 39, he was wealthy enough to retire, but he was persuaded to join with two new partners, Morris Ketchum and Joseph Grosvenor, to start a concern making axles and wheels and some bridge parts. He located his new shop in a sparsely settled area of Paterson, one of his few neighbors being the Paul and Beggs machine shop. His interest in locomotives was stirred by a mobile steam engine that was under construction at Paul and Beggs' yard and then reignited in 1835, when he was commissioned to reassemble an engine, the *MacNeil*, that had been shipped from England in pieces. (Actually, the machine that Rogers saw at Paul and Beggs's yard was the first locomotive built in Paterson. It was nearly completed in 1835 when fire swept through the establishment and destroyed the engine. Rogers later took over the ruined shops.)

The *MacNeil* had been ordered by the Paterson and Hudson River Railroad (P&HR). Looking at the finished work, Rogers saw an opportunity for his firm and undertook to build a locomotive based on the English design. (Trumbull, based on William Swinburne's recollections, states that Rogers's first locomotive was designed by a Mr. Hodge, with Swinburne making patterns. According to Swinburne, he realized that Hodge's design was inadequate and brought the errors to Rogers's attention. Rogers discharged Hodge and then expressed concern that he had no one available to complete the engine. He considered pulling out from locomotive building, but Swinburne stepped forward, confident that he, Swinburne, could complete the task. Trumbull continued, naming Swinburne as the mechanic who examined the *MacNeil* at work on the nearby P&HR and copied its design. This entire version is contradicted in the 1876 *Rogers Locomotive Catalog,* which included a history of the Rogers Works. There it is related that the first locomotive had been worked on by Thomas Hogg (or Hodge) since its commencement.)

In any event, the machine came out of Rogers's shop and was delivered to the New Jersey Railroad and Transportation Company (NJRR) in 1837 and, while undergoing trials, was observed by the president of the Mad River and Lake Erie Railroad, then building in Ohio. That individual prevailed upon Rogers to sell the machine to him, and it was named *Sandusky* and delivered to Ohio. Because the *Sandusky* had been intended for use on the NJRR, its gauge was 4 feet 10 inches. As the first locomotive in Ohio, its gauge established the standard track gauge for the state. The NJRR insisted that another locomotive, named the *Arresseoh* and sister to the *Sandusky,* be built for them. From this modest beginning, locomotive production accelerated at Rogers's works; seven were built in 1838, and by 1854 it was outshopping more than 100 engines per year.[6]

Thomas Rogers was an innovator, and his machines received high praise from the *American Railroad Journal* in 1839. They were powerful, durable, and delivered outstanding performance. He was an early user of hollow iron, counterbalanced, spoked driving wheels. (A patent application in which he disclosed counterbalancing techniques was filed in 1837.) His engines were ornamented with brass and brightly painted surfaces. The Erie Railroad became an important customer. Thomas Rogers died in 1856, and the firm was renamed the Rogers Locomotive and Machine Works. The Rogers factory was swept by fire in 1879 and rebuilt almost immediately, allowing 240 locomotives to be built in 1881.[7]

William Swinburne left Rogers's employ in 1845, and in 1848 he joined with Samuel Smith to form Swinburne, Smith and Company, the second locomotive builder at Paterson (if the ill-fated Paul and Beggs is not considered). They received their first order from the Erie Railway and fulfilled it in 1848. Speaking of the Erie Railway, it is told that on the first through

trip on the newly built railroad, a Rogers locomotive, hauling the inaugural train, developed a problem and had to be replaced by a Swinburne, Smith engine. In 1851, the company was reorganized as the New Jersey Locomotive and Machine Company (NJL&MC), and Swinburne left the partnership and opened a third Paterson locomotive factory. He was modestly successful, building 104 engines before the 1857 recession precipitated the failure of the company. Meanwhile, the NJL&MC went on to build engines for the Erie and other roads. It weathered the 1857 recession and had completed 225 machines in 1859. Its most famous engine, the *William Crooks,* built for the Minnesota and Pacific Railway and named for the chief engineer of that road, was built in 1861 and was the first locomotive to operate in the state of Minnesota. It was rebuilt after being in a disastrous fire in 1867, and today it is on display at the Lake Superior Railroad Museum in Duluth, Minnesota, the last NJL&MC engine extant. All told, the New Jersey Locomotive and Machine Company built about 330 locomotives. It became the Grant Locomotive Works in 1863.[8]

Indicative of the aggressiveness of the Rogers's Works is an anecdote included in John Cunningham's book, *Railroads in New Jersey.* When one of their local customers, the Jersey City and Albany Railroad, failed in 1877, it also failed to pay for a new Rogers engine that it had received. Rather than joining the line of creditors making claims on the receivers, the Rogers management took matters into their own hands. They dispatched a "messenger" to retrieve the locomotive. He tracked the engine down and found it where it had stopped for lack of fuel. He scavenged wood from nearby fences, built a fire in the engine, and drove it back to the Rogers Works. Unquestionably, the relative nearness of the engine to Paterson was instrumental to the success of his mission, but in retrospect, one must question his initiative: he did retrieve the engine, but probably illegally and at the expense of some farmer's fence.[9]

Sandwiched in time between the two giants of the industry described here, Rogers above and Grant below, was a small, obscure shop in Paterson that produced a locomotive in 1860. The Todd and Rafferty company was selected by Robert Rennie to build a 2-4-0 engine for the Lodi Railroad. Rennie, a director of the Hackensack and New York Railroad, had the Lodi Railroad built and arranged for the construction of the engine to replace an eight-mule team that hauled its cars. This unusual locomotive had two cylinders, mounted in a vertical plane, 90 degrees apart. The pistons drove a crankshaft that was connected via gears to the wheels. The last two pairs of the six, uniform size wheels were coupled by side rods. Locomotive number 2 of the road was of a more conventional design.[10]

The Grant Locomotive Works became one of America's important producers of locomotives. Successor to the New Jersey Locomotive and Machine Company and well financed, the firm had ratcheted up production to 110 locomotives in 1870. By 1872, including the machines made by its predecessor, it outshopped its 1,000th engine. Eight years later, despite some reversals during a general economic slowdown and its inability to fulfill a contract to deliver engines to Russia, it produced its 1,500th locomotive. Before closing in 1893, Grant built 1,888 locomotives. One of these, the *America*, was known as the "Silver Engine." This machine, completed in 1867, was displayed at the Universal Exposition in Paris and was described as "a poem in iron and silver." All of her fittings and trim and the jacket on the boiler were fashioned of German silver. Zerah Colburn, who had been superintendent of the New Jersey Locomotive and Machine Company but was now editor of the British journal *Engineering,* enthused over the engine and wrote, "The cab, made of curled maple and walnut wood, is more than usually smart, but the cabs of American engines are generally showy, sometimes very much so, and we have seen them decorated with prints and photographs, as if they were the offices of professional gentlemen rather than the posts of duty of hard-handed engine drivers."

The engine garnered a gold medal, first in show, and then was delivered to the Chicago, Rock Island and Pacific Railroad and placed in fast mail service between Omaha and Chicago. She continued in this service until 1886 and then was successively degraded to hauling a pay train. Around 1900, she was dismantled, and her boiler was used in a stationary installation. In this role, it exploded and was purchased to provide low-pressure steam to a greenhouse. It saw its last service in 1910.

Three other Grant engines were noteworthy for their bizarre design. The first was a machine designed by Eugene Fontaine and, like the Holman locomotive described in chapter 22, was intended to run at high speed through a friction drive arrangement between upper and lower driven wheels of different diameters. Raub's "Central Power" locomotive was built so that, through its longitudinal and transverse centerlines, each side was a mirror image of the other. This design was expected to produce a perfectly balanced locomotive. Then there was, in Carter's words, "the wonderful 'hydrocarbon' locomotive . . . heralded throughout the world with extravagant assurances that it would revolutionize railway motive-power." It was intended to burn hydrogen gas generated from water by a recently invented process. After months of testing, a trial of the locomotive was held on the Erie Railway. When the passengers on that test ride were nearly suffocated by the engine's fumes, its designers admitted defeat, and no more was heard of the machine.[11]

The last of the Paterson locomotive builders was the Cooke Locomotive and Machine Works. This business was begun in 1852 under the aegis of Clarke's machinery firm. One of the principals, John Cooke, had been superintendent at the Rogers works since replacing William Swinburne in 1845. (When Cooke left Rogers, he was replaced by William S. Hudson, a brilliant locomotive designer who introduced many new features to Rogers engines.) Organized as Danforth, Cooke and Company, it completed its first locomotive in 1853 and over the next six years turned out more than 160 engines. The company produced one of the first anthracite coal–burning engines made in the region, ordered by the Delaware, Lackawanna and Western Railroad in 1853. (Allegedly, an earlier coal burner had been produced in Trenton.) In 1883, by which time 1,236 engines were produced, the company name was changed to the Cooke Locomotive and Machine Company. In 1889 the company relocated to new facilities in suburban Paterson and continued to grow. Cooke became one of the locomotive builders that were consolidated as the American Locomotive Company (ALCO) in 1901. Between its beginning in 1853 and 1901, Cooke outshopped about 2,750 locomotives. Unlike some of the other firms that were part of this consolidation, Cooke's plant was modern and the best equipped. This fact influenced the new management to maintain locomotive production there, albeit small locomotives, not road engines. ALCO-Cooke received a large order to produce locomotives for the building of the Panama Canal and delivered 100; 44 others were supplied by other Paterson builders. The Cooke Works closed its doors in 1926.[12]

In terms of output, the Rogers Locomotive Works was second only to the Baldwin Works in Philadelphia. In fact, at the time of the Civil War, the Paterson builders and the Baldwin Works supplied 75 percent of America's locomotives, in addition to enjoying a substantial export trade. One of Rogers's famous locomotives was Union Pacific's (UP) number 119. This was one of the two locomotives depicted in the well-known tableau depicting the driving of the golden spike that joined the UP with the Central Pacific at Promontory, Utah, in 1869. But probably the most celebrated Rogers locomotive was the *General*. This engine, built in 1855 for the Western and Atlantic Railroad, was captured by a daring band of Union spies at Big Shanty, Georgia, during the Civil War. The captors then drove the engine northward intending to tear up the track and burn bridges in order to cripple the railroad and prevent its carrying Confederate reinforcements to an impending battle at Chattanooga. They were thwarted in this effort by a valiant pursuit directed by W. A. Fuller, the conductor of the captured train. Fuller used the locomotive *Texas* (among others) to pursue the raiders and finally, eight hours later, caught up with the *General* after it ran out of fuel. The *Texas* was another Paterson product, made by the Cooke Works. The two locomotives have been lovingly restored and are exhibited in Georgia.[13]

The following statistics are to be found in Trumbull's 1882 book: between 1837 and 1881, 5,871 locomotives had been produced in Paterson by the various builders. There were 17,720 locomotives in the country at that time. Of course, there is no direct correlation between the two numbers, but it is obvious that the Paterson builders had made a significant contribution to the country's inventory of steam locomotives. It was estimated that, up to 1881, Paterson had contributed engines with an aggregate value of over $86 million. All told, by the time that the last Paterson builder closed its doors in 1926, almost 10,000 engines had been produced there. The Grant Locomotive Works relocated to Chicago in 1885. As mentioned earlier, Cooke was absorbed into the American Locomotive Company consolidation in 1901; Rogers followed into that fold in 1905, and locomotive production was ended in 1913. The demise of locomotive building at Paterson has been at-

tributed to the rise of the silk industry at that city and the consequent competition for workers at the various plants. Another reason was the distance that a newly built locomotive had to be carried through the city's streets to the railhead.

The builders had established their factories along the banks of the Passaic River raceway in order to utilize the hydropower, and the nearest railroad, the Paterson and Hudson River Railroad, passed through the town at some distance removed. Thus, for many years, locomotives built by the major makers had to be hauled through the streets of Paterson to the tracks by teams of horses. Only Swinburne, who had relocated his new plant next to the railroad tracks in 1851, could avoid this problem. On the other hand, he lost the benefit of the plentiful waterpower derived from the river. In 1863, the three Paterson builders pooled their interests and established the Paterson Horse Railway. The horsecars did carry passengers, but its raison d'être was to carry locomotives from the factories to the P&H tracks. The City of Paterson permitted only horses to pull the heavy loads, and in some instances as many as 40 horses were needed to move one engine. Finally, beginning in 1901, the engine transfers could be made by a small steam engine, but not over rails.[14]

In the railroad field, Paterson was also noted for the manufacture of rotary snow plows. Early on, railroads employed wedge or "bucker" snow plows. Attached to the front of a locomotive, they were expected to clear a track by "bucking" their way through snowdrifts. They were effective in light snow, but deep snow often overwhelmed them. In 1884, Orange Jull, a Canadian mill owner, patented a rotary snow plow, and he assigned the patent rights to the Leslie brothers, who built a working model. Once interest was established, the Leslies turned to the Cooke Works to produce the machines in quantity. The "Rotary," as it was known, soon gained a reputation as the best plow to deal with deep snow. During trials on the Union Pacific Railroad in 1887, it cleared drifts as deep as 15 feet without a problem. The Rotary was adopted extensively in the West but less so by eastern roads. Cooke (and Grant, a licensee) continued to build the Leslie plows even after Cooke's amalgamation with ALCO.[15]

Finally, although it does not concern locomotives, Paterson was the birthplace of the first iron railroad passenger car. Dr. Bernard J. LaMothe was aware of

**Figure 6.** The Paterson Museum is housed in the erecting shop of the former Rogers Locomotive Works in Paterson, N.J. A Cooke-built locomotive, Number 299, is on display outside the Museum. Photograph taken by the author, summer 2005.

the inherent hazard presented by wooden railroad cars in the event of an accident: not only were they easily damaged, but they were also susceptible to fires started in the wreckage by the wood stoves used for heating the cars. LaMothe invented an all-metal car. Touted as a "life-preserving car," it was made of "contiguous steel bands, bent to the proper shape of the car. Transversely—the bands extend from one side of the frame to the other in pairs, one precisely over the other. . . . The single bands run in a longitudinal direction . . . and pass between the transverse bands, forming . . . rectangular squares. The three are firmly riveted together in each intersection, thus making the whole frame a complete network . . . [of] great strength and elasticity." LaMothe cars were used on some of the street railways in New York City around 1855, but in 1859 the first so-called "long car" was built in Paterson at the shops of William Cundell, an

iron products manufacturer. This car was delivered to the Boston and Worcester Railroad and enjoyed a long life. The next two cars, passenger and freight combination cars, were built for Robert Rennie. The last "long car" to be made was ordered by the Hackensack and New York Railroad. Although LaMothe may have rightly been concerned about the shortcomings of wooden cars, he could not have anticipated the cause of this car's demise. About a month after its delivery, the train in which the car was a member dove into the Hackensack River through an open drawbridge at Secaucus. Remarkably, the car lived up to LaMothe's claims regarding crashworthiness and was not seriously damaged. Returned to Cundell's shop for repairs, it was lost in a fire that swept through Cundell's establishment. Thus, ironically, this "fireproof" car was destroyed by fire.[16]

The erecting shop (1873–1901) of the former

Rogers Locomotive Works currently houses the Paterson Museum. The museum exhibits artifacts and displays that are associated with Paterson's industrial past, and conspicuous among these are silk-making machinery and products dating from Paterson's prominence as the "Silk City." The collection also includes the hulls of two pioneer submarines built by John Holland, a native son. Alas, within the museum there is little to remember Paterson's glory days of locomotive building: a model railroad, a few railroad items, and some photographs. Outside though, there is a Cooke 2-6-0 Mogul type locomotive, number 299, on display. This engine, the last of 100 built for the Panama Canal Commission, was completed in January 1906 after Cooke had been acquired by the American Locomotive Company. It worked during the construction phase and thereafter at the canal until it was retired in 1953 and displayed in Panama. In 1978, the mayor of Paterson arranged for the locomotive to be returned to Paterson, where it now stands proudly, recalling the days when thousands of its sisters rolled along the nearby streets on their way to customers worldwide. The museum, located at 2 Market Street in Paterson's National Historical District, also maintains extensive photographic archives that are rich in images of the Paterson locomotive builders.[17]

Postscript: This account of New Jersey locomotive builders is concerned mainly with those located at Paterson. However, there were numerous other builders: railroad shops within the state and builders of lesser note, who erected special-purpose or amusement locomotives or who constructed few machines. Even Thomas Edison's Electric Railway Company of America is numbered among the latter. According to a listing prepared by Frank Reilly in 1982, six New Jersey railroads built locomotives within the state: the Belvidere-Delaware at Lambertville; the Camden and Amboy at Bordentown; the Central Railroad of New Jersey at Elizabethport; the Delaware, Lackawanna and Western at their Kingsland Shops; the New Jersey Railroad and Transportation Company at Jersey City; and the Pennsylvania Railroad at Jersey City and Lambertville. All told, Reilly listed 43 individuals or concerns that built locomotives in the state, including the Paul and Beggs Company of Paterson, which almost, but not quite, built the first locomotive made in that city.[18]

# 6 Piercing the Palisades (1838–1910)

For the entire nineteenth century, rail traffic to New York City from the south and west passed through New Jersey and terminated at the western shoreline of the Hudson River. From there, passengers were carried by ferry, and freight was lightered across the river. Unfortunately, nature had provided a formidable barrier that denied easy access to the Jersey waterfront. The Hudson Palisades are a line of steep cliffs along the west side of the lower Hudson River. This ridge extends for miles and seriously impacted railroad operations in the area.[1]

The first breach of this barrier was made jointly by the New Jersey Railroad and Transportation Company (NJRR) and the Paterson and Hudson River Railroad. Their early locomotives, coming from New Brunswick in the west or Paterson in the north, lacked the power to climb Bergen Hill in order to reach Jersey City and the Hudson shore. Prior to the completion of the Bergen Cut in 1838, travelers had to detrain on the west side of the hill and be carried over it by horsecar.[2]

The Bergen Hill Cut was begun in November 1832, but the rock was so hard that progress was slow. Blasting was the only recourse, but drills, necessary to make holes for the powder, dulled rapidly. Hundreds of workers labored for more than five years to create the 40-foot-deep (average), mile-long open passage through the hill. The cut was not straight but, rather, included many sharp curves. This was a consequence of the path that the engineers chose, following an ancient waterway that had partially carved itself across the ridge. Eighteen men and two women died during construction, and hundreds of others were injured.

The Cut was finally completed in January 1838, and the first train passed through it on January 22.[3]

Eventually, the Cut was opened to the trains of four railroads, the New York & Erie, the Morris & Essex, the Jersey Central, and the Northern Railroad of New Jersey, in addition to the two that built it. Upon opening, other roads were charged six cents per passenger and ten cents per ton of freight carried over its tracks. When the broad gauge (six foot) Erie Railway entered the equation, it had to lay down an extra rail to accommodate its cars, and this rail was the cause of accidents involving derailments and interferences due to close clearances. Furthermore, as reported by Thomas McConkey, "switch-tenders had trouble distinguishing one train from another, often sending broad-gauge Erie trains bumping along the ties on the line toward Newark. Subsequently, the NJRR&TCo. painted the smoke stacks on their engines red as an identifying symbol to alert switch-tenders as to what train was coming." Rockslides in the Cut were another common cause of accidents.[4]

After the Pennsylvania Railroad (PRR) had officially joined with the NJRR in the 1880s, it decided to eliminate some of the many curves and to widen the cut. Although the trap rock through which the new, four-track-wide cut was made was no less hard, better tools made the difficult task a little easier. The four tracks enabled the road to separate their freight and passenger traffic. After the failure of the Penn-Central Railroad in 1976, the Bergen Cut was used by the Consolidated Rail Corporation (Conrail). In 1998, Conrail was broken up. Assets were divided between CSX Corporation and Norfolk Southern,

**Figure 7.** It took more than five years to carve the one mile long Bergen Cut through the hard basaltic rock of the Hudson Palisades. It provided access to the New Jersey waterfront opposite New York City. The first train passed through it in January 1838. Author's collection.

but Conrail retained ownership of tracks in three major metropolitan regions, including the greater New York area. Here operations, including the use of the Bergen Cut, are managed by the Conrail Shared Assets Corporation (CSAC). Port Authority Trans-Hudson (PATH) trains also still use the Cut at the Journal Square station in Jersey City.[5]

The next piercing of the Palisades, a tunnel for New York and Erie Railroad (NY&E) trains to reach Jersey City, was begun on 1 June 1856. More than half of its length passed through 4,311 feet of the volcanic rock common to the area. Twenty-three feet high and almost 30 feet wide, it could accommodate a double-tracked, broad gauge Erie line. Eight perpendicular shafts provided ventilation and the opportunity to attack the rock from 18 faces. Thirty-five horsepower engines, placed at the opening of each shaft, pumped air into the tunnel and were also used to remove water and the dislodged rock. The rock that was removed was then carried to the waterfront as fill and to build a bulkhead for six piers. On average, about 700 workers labored daily to build the tunnel. Relative to pay scales today, daily wages paid were ridiculously low: miners received $1.38, foremen $2.00, and laborers $1.12.[6]

During construction, six weeks after the tunnel drifts met and were "holed through," the laborers struck the job because their pay was one month in arrears. The strike was acrimonious and turned into a riot when the strikers overturned dump cars and built huge rock piles to blockade the Erie tracks west of the tunnel. The workers numbered more than 500, and they manned the barricades to prevent their removal. Unable to operate over the blockaded line, the railroad was compelled to terminate their trains at Piermont, New York, and use chartered steamboats to bring their passengers to New York City. After three days, the railroad management called upon the Jersey City authorities to send policemen to quell the rioting. The police presence had no effect on the rioters, so on September 19, 1859, a force of New Jersey militia arrived with two field pieces. The strikers hooted with derision. A priest attempted to make peace, but he was shouted down. A violent engagement with the police ensued, and there were many casualties on both sides. At this point, the soldiers were ordered to charge the strikers with fixed bayonets, and this action dispersed the strikers. Order was restored after the arrest of the strike leaders and the tracks were cleared, but the mob reassembled that evening. The militia marched again against the disorderly crowd, and finally the situation was defused. The late wages were disbursed, and after a long period of inactivity construction was resumed under the supervision of the road's chief engineer and an Erie-affiliated contractor.[7]

The tunnel took almost five years to complete (6 February 1861), and casualties were much higher than the earlier toll at the Bergen Cut because the work was mostly underground. Fifty-seven men died, and scores were injured. The enormous cost of the project, about $1 million, was a major factor in the bankruptcy of the NY&E, which was then reorganized as the Erie Railroad.[8]

Upon its completion, the Erie Railroad agreed to share the tunnel "in perpetuity" with the Morris and Essex Railroad (M&E). This arrangement, made in consideration of a contribution made by the latter road during construction of the tunnel, was friendly until 1870, when the M&E's parent (the Delaware, Lackawanna and Western Railroad (DL&W) had leased the road in 1868) built a branch line from Denville to Paterson that competed with the Erie's Suffern to Paterson trackage. That provocation, combined with the fact that traffic had increased to the point where the capacity of the tunnel was pushed to its limit, ended the amicable collaborative relationship. A spark was ignited on 2 December 1870, when the Lackawanna began to modify rails near the tunnel entrance to handle larger coal cars. Jim Fisk, controller of the Erie, was determined to prevent the DL&W from modifying the tracks, and he blockaded the tunnel connection with a locomotive and 1,000 men. But Fisk had miscalculated, because his impetuous action, which closed the tunnel to trains of both railroads, inconvenienced and incensed thousands of commuters, many of whom were influential businessmen. New Jersey governor Theodore F. Randolph alerted the militia and hurried to the confrontation site. In an ultimatum to Fisk, Randolph threatened that, unless Fisk lifted the blockade, the state militia would be mobilized to deal with it. Fisk backed down, but spitefully orchestrated a general slowdown of all trains using the tunnel, a situation that was resolved after a few days. This incident may have been the catalyst that spurred the DL&W into building its own tunnel.[9]

The DL&W began to dig through the Palisades in September 1873, using hand drilling for powder charges. Although steam drilling machines were available and had been used for the construction of earlier tunnels, the contractor believed that manual methods were more economical than the use of power equipment. Since the Lackawanna's tracks met those of the Erie near the portal of the existing tunnel, it was necessary to plan the new bore so that it did not interfere with the old one. Accordingly, its elevation was raised so that the DL&W tracks passed over those of the Erie and entered Bergen Hill about 30 feet higher than the Erie tunnel. The new 4,600-foot tunnel continued straight through the hill and emerged some 2,700 feet north of the old tunnel on the eastern side. The project was completed on 17 May 1877, and its total cost, including new approaches, was approximately $2,750,000.[10] The Lackawanna tunnel is now used by New Jersey Transit trains and can accom-

**Figure 8.** The tunnels of the Erie and the Delaware, Lackawanna and Western Railroads were only a few feet apart at the point where they entered the western side of Bergen Hill. A violent confrontation in 1870 at the portal to the original Erie Railroad tunnel, which was shared by the two roads, resulted in the Lackawanna's construction of its own bore. *Scientific American,* 26 May 1877.

modate 23 trains per hour in either direction.[11] In 2005, in order to provide more frequent service, New Jersey Transit announced that it would undertake the construction of another pair of single track tunnels just south of the ones that they presently use. The new tunnels, with an estimated completion date in the year 2015, would proceed to a new station to be built at 34th Street in New York City.[12]

A third tunnel through Bergen Hill was begun in 1880 for the New Jersey Midland Railroad (NJM). Wide enough for a double track with generous clearances between tracks and away from the walls, the 3,985 foot long bore brought the NJM to piers it owned at the river's edge in Weehawken. On average, 650 men worked on the project: 450 in the tunnel with about 200 preparing the approaches. Before the tunnel was completed, the NJM was controlled by the New York, West Shore & Buffalo Railroad (NYWS&B). Ownership of the NYWS&B in turn passed to the New York Central and Hudson River

Railroad in 1885, but the east shore tracks of the Central, heralded later in advertisements as "the water level route," became the preferred route to upstate New York. Deprived of a leading role in the long-distance passenger traffic to Albany and points beyond, the West Shore Branch of the Central became an important commuter road and, in more recent times, a significant freight carrier for Conrail. The West Shore tunnel is now used by the Hudson-Bergen Light Rail Line.[13]

A fourth bore, dug by the New York, Susquehanna & Western Railroad in the 1890s, penetrated the rock at Weehawken Heights. The mile-long (5,072 feet) tunnel enabled the Susquehanna to control its own trains, which had been using other railroads' rights-of-way to reach the Hudson River. The new tracks led to newly acquired land at Edgewater, New Jersey (about two miles north of Weehawken and opposite 110th Street in New York City). Ground was broken on 1 August 1892, and more than 1,000 men

**Figure 9.** Rather than boring through the Palisades, the North Hudson County Railroad chose to leap out from the top of the hill by means of a trestle. Huge elevators carried passengers from the water level to the railroad tracks above. *Scientific American*, 31 October 1891.

were assigned to the task: 900 worked on the tunnel; 150 built the piers and necessary structures at the river's edge. Completed in 1894, the total cost, including land acquisition, piers, and approach trackage, was about $1.7 million.[14]

Many years after the Erie Railroad's Bergen tunnel was completed, traffic demands had again taxed its capacity. Rather than building another tunnel, the Erie chose to dig an open passage nearby. Actually, although mostly open cut, at strategic locations,

where streets above crossed the track, the rock was not removed completely; instead, tunnels were bored. The cut, completed in 1910 and known as the Bergen Arches because of the periodic tunnels, was large enough to accommodate four tracks, and it enabled the road to move all of its passenger traffic through the new cut. The old tunnel was relegated to serving freight trains only. The now abandoned cut is being considered for recycling as a vehicular expressway.[15]

By this time, the difficult barricade that was Bergen Hill had become honey-combed with passages. No longer an obstacle, its various tunnels and cuts permitted trains to reach the Jersey shoreline where they were blocked from direct access to New York City by another, even more formidable barrier, the Hudson River. That barrier was overcome by a tunnel, actually two, single-track tunnels, under the river built by the Pennsylvania Railroad and described in the next chapter. Part of this project involved yet another piercing of Bergen Hill, essential as an approach to the new tunnel.[16] But before the conquest of the Hudson is described, it is of interest to mention a different approach that was taken by another railroad to cross the Palisades.

In the early 1890s, the North Hudson County Railroad (NHC), rather than boring through Bergen Hill, elected to build a viaduct extending from the top of the hill on its eastern face. North Hudson trains, instead of stopping at the cliff's edge, ran out on this bridge and detrained their passengers onto an elevator landing. There, three independent elevators, the largest in the world at the time, each capable of carrying 135 people, brought the passengers 148 feet down to the pier below. From that point they could board a West Shore train at the station nearby or a ferry for the short trip to New York City. This impressive structure, while expensive, was a cheaper alternative to a tunnel. It, like the Hillside Line of the NHC, which was built later using loops and very steep grades to climb the Palisades, was abandoned long ago.[17]

# 7 The Final Barrier: Crossing the Hudson River (1838–Present)

Once the Palisades were conquered, the railroads that reached the Hudson River were frustrated by that broad and busy waterway. Their destination and major market was New York City, almost a mile away on the eastern shore, but throughout the nineteenth century, access was limited by the terminal facilities and the number and capabilities of the boats that could be used to ferry people and goods across. Yet, despite the obvious disadvantages associated with the surface crossing, there was no easy solution. Long, high bridges that would allow heavy marine traffic to pass below them were prohibitively expensive, and subaqueous tunneling could not be considered until techniques became available to prevent water entry during construction.[1]

Many individuals applied themselves to the problem of crossing the river. One of the earliest, and undoubtedly the most visionary, was Col. John Stevens III of Hoboken. Stevens was already associated with ferry service in the area. It was he who, in 1811, introduced the first regularly scheduled steam-powered ferry, the *Juliana (II),* which was a conventional steamboat, not a double-ended ferryboat. (The original *Juliana,* named for his daughter, was an experimental craft launched in 1804.) He also suggested spanning the Hudson with a pontoon bridge and then a bridge "of so great a height and so wide a span as to admit vessels of every description to pass through freely." In 1806 Stevens wrote about his idea for a tunnel under the waterway. He would have built it of wood, eight feet wide, to allow carriages to pass through. As with many of Stevens's conceptions,

the idea was commendable but far in advance of the technology needed to bring it to fruition.[2]

Toward the end of the century, a high-level, triple-deck bridge, twice the length of the Brooklyn Bridge, which would carry 14 tracks plus roadways, was proposed by the Pennsylvania Railroad (PRR) but was rejected by the War Department because its piers might present a hazard to navigation on the river.[3] The only way to cross the Hudson into Manhattan was by water, and to this day there is no railroad bridge between that borough and the opposite shore.

## FERRYBOATS

Before the railroads arrived, the vessels that were used to ferry people and goods across the Hudson River assumed many shapes and sizes; some were powered by hand, some by wind, and others by steam engine. A favored type was the "team boat," a trimaran driven by horses or mules walking on a treadmill that was connected to a paddlewheel. Scull reported that Stevens invented the team boat, but there are records of the employment of "horse boats" at least five years before Stevens became involved with ferry operations.[4] Many years after they disappeared from the Hudson scene, team boats were memorialized by a landscape painter and writer named John Banvard. His opening stanza was written about East River operations, but it is equally applicable to the Hudson:

> How well I can remember the
> horseboats that paddled
> 'Cross the East River
> ere the advent of steam;

Sometimes the old driver the
horse would straddle.
And sometimes rided round on
the circling beam.[5]

The railroads, however, brought with them a new and imposing problem. The amount of merchandise and the number of people that they brought to the west shore towns increased substantially, and most of the existing ferries were relatively small and inadequate for the task. To meet the demand, by the mid-1860s the Morris and Essex (M&E), the Erie, the New Jersey Railroad and Transportation Company (NJRR), and the Jersey Central (CNJ) railroads had initiated their own ferrying services. Five impressive passenger terminals were erected on the Jersey side, including those at Hoboken (Delaware, Lackawanna and Western Railroad) and Jersey City (CNJ), two that still stand today. Large passenger ferries were launched, and these eventually reached leviathan dimensions. Unpowered lighters, or car floats, meant to be towed by tugboats, were put into service to handle freight traffic. The invention of the car float, in 1866, was credited to John H. Starin, an entrepreneur who had established a business transporting goods across the Hudson River for various railroads. Entire trains of loaded freight cars were placed aboard such barges and carried to piers located along the New York City shoreline. This procedure was extended to include passenger cars so that travelers from the south and west could complete journeys to New England without changing cars. These cars were transported by float from New Jersey to a railhead on the far side of New York City.[6]

In the 1890s, railroads were using dozens of large ferryboats and hundreds of car floats across the waterway; by 1925, seven ferry routes crossed the river from Jersey City, Hoboken, and Weehawken to landings in midtown and downtown Manhattan. Other boats left New Jersey bound for Brooklyn and Staten Island. Railroad ferryboat service continued for over a century, and it has been only about 50 years since the last of the great railroad ferries was retired. Because of a relatively recent revival of limited ferryboat service, Harry Smith, author of the *Romance of the Hoboken Ferry*, may not have been overly optimistic when, writing in 1931 of ferryboats in the metropolitan district of New York, he predicted that "possibly another hundred years will elapse before this system of transportation is abandoned."[7]

Robert Louis Stevenson wrote about a ride he took in 1879 from New York on a Pennsylvania Railroad boat to reach his train:

I followed the porters into a long shed . . . [where there] was no fair way through the mingled mass of brute and living obstruction. . . . At length . . . the crowd began to move. . . . We were being filtered out into the river boat for Jersey City. . . . I found myself on deck under a flimsy awning and with a trifle of elbow room to stretch and breathe in. This was on the starboard; for the bulk of the emigrants stuck hopelessly on the port side, by which we had entered. In vain the seamen shouted [at] them to move on, and threatened them with shipwreck. These poor people were under a spell of stupor, and did not stir a foot. It rained as heavily as ever, . . . and we crept over the river in darkness, trailing one paddle in the water like a wounded duck. . . . The landing at Jersey City was done in a stampede. . . . People pushed, and elbowed, and ran, their families following how they could. . . . There was no waiting-room, no refreshment room; the cars were locked; and for at least another hour . . . we had to camp upon the draughty, gas-lit platform.[8]

This inauspicious start to Stevenson's journey was repeated many times by businessmen and families alike, but eventually the railroad operators provided adequate facilities. Stevenson mentioned that his boat was paddle-wheel driven, the usual method of propulsion at the time. The first successful screw-driven, double-ended ferryboat was the *Bergen*, which was owned by the Hoboken Ferry Company and launched in 1888. The last of the paddle-wheel ferryboats to ply the Hudson was the *Montclair*, a Delaware, Lackawanna and Western Railroad (DL&W) boat that made its last crossing in 1944.[9]

During the Civil War, several New York ferryboats were drafted for naval service, but it appears that only one railroad ferryboat was among these. The *John P. Jackson*, owned by the New Jersey Railroad and Transportation Company, had had the honor of carrying President-elect Lincoln across the Hudson when he was en route to Washington to be inaugurated. The trip across the water was festive. Dodsworth's Band provided stirring music, and other vessels sounded their whistles while cannons were fired to mark Lincoln's passage. Later, in 1860, the boat was sold to the Navy, where she served admirably as part of the West Gulf Blockading Squadron. A much more somber trip was made by the *Jersey City*, which

**Figure 10.** The ferryboats *Bergen* and *Hoboken* crossing the Hudson River. The *Bergen* was built in 1888 and was driven by two propellers, running off a single shaft, so that one screw pulled and one pushed the boat. The *Bergen* was scrapped in 1953. *Scientific American Supplement,* 1 November 1890.

worked for the Pennsylvania Railroad when, on 24 April 1865, she brought the slain president's body across the river on its journey back to Illinois.[10]

The Morris and Essex Railroad, a predecessor to the DL&W, used the Hoboken Ferry Company's boats to bring passengers to New York. (The Hoboken Ferry Company was owned by the Stevens family from 1821 until 1897.) The M&E came under DL&W control in 1868, and the latter road leased the ferry facilities in 1903. In 1905, a fire destroyed the ferry house and station in Hoboken, the fourth terminal on the site, but two years later a more imposing ferry complex rose from the ashes (see chapter 21).[11]

At first, the Erie Railway brought passengers across the river at Piermont, New York, about two miles north of the New Jersey state line. Then a Jersey City terminal was completed in 1869, and boats departed from the Pavonia Avenue docks. Erie Railway service ended in January 1957. The New York, West Shore and Buffalo Railroad absorbed the New Jersey Midland's ferry slip at Weehawken in 1884; the demise of its ferries occurred in 1959. The Central Railroad of New Jersey, the successor to the Elizabethtown and Somerville Railroad, was extended from Elizabeth to the Communipaw district in Jersey City in 1864, and its new ferry service originated in that area. The last CNJ boat crossed the river in

1967. The Pennsylvania Railroad (PRR) erected an extensive facility at Exchange Place in Jersey City; from there ferryboats ran to several destinations in Manhattan and Brooklyn. Service from Exchange Place was abandoned in 1949, and the last Pennsylvania boat, the *New Brunswick,* was retired. The last railroad ferry service to Manhattan was operated by the DL&W, and it was finally abandoned on 22 November 1967 when the *Elmira* made its last run.[12]

Before 1908, the ferryboat was "the only game in town," and despite some brave talk by Captain Emery, a DL&W captain and later manager of the road's marine department, who believed that the opening of the trans-Hudson tunnel of the Hudson and Manhattan Railroad (H&M) would have a negligible effect on ferry revenues, DL&W commuter ferryboat traffic tumbled almost immediately. A decade or so later, patronage across the Hudson (below 59th Street in Manhattan) was about equally divided between the ferries and the Hudson Tube trains, each with approximately 150,000 passengers per day. Another 18,000 travelers entered New York City each day via the new Pennsylvania Railroad tunnels. Then a new player entered the scene: the Holland Tunnel, completed in 1927. This vehicular passageway and its younger sisters, the George Washington Bridge and the Lincoln Tunnel, siphoned off many of the motor vehicles that formerly had been ferried across in the big boats. Even television was cited as a reason for the decline of ferry traffic; in 1954, the Interstate Commerce Commission noted "a decline in the number of persons attending Manhattan entertainment events because of the popularity of television broadcasts." Railroad river crossing is now made below the surface through tunnels whose origins extend back to the 1870s. One of the last of the railroad-operated boats, *Elizabeth,* was sold to the Public Service Electric and Gas Company when it was withdrawn from ferry service. It was established as a floating museum at the Salem, New Jersey, nuclear power plant and renamed *Second Sun.* Later, after a brief stint as a restaurant and despite private efforts to preserve and exhibit it at Liberty State Park, *Elizabeth* was purchased by the New Jersey Department of Environmental Protection and brought offshore near Brielle, where it was scuttled to serve as part of an artificial reef. Another ferryboat, the *Thomas N. McCarter,* was operated by the Public Service Corporation between Edgewater, New Jersey, and 125th Street in Manhattan. Built in 1926, it shuttled across the Hudson for years and then passed into other hands. Its last reincarnation was as a houseboat named *Sardinia.* This boat was abandoned along the Delaware River waterfront in northeast Philadelphia in 2004, where it remains.[13]

There is an exception to the demise of the ferryboats operated by railroads. By the late 1980s, the Port Authority Trans-Hudson (PATH) system was experiencing saturation during rush hours. The solution was to sponsor a ferryboat line that would drain off some of the peak traffic. In October 1989, New York Waterway, privately operated but under contract to PATH, instituted service between Hoboken and downtown Manhattan. A decade later, ridership had increased to 2.5 million trips per year, equal to 4 percent of the PATH patronage. Although a small quantity, it did relieve PATH to some extent and brought the Hudson River ferryboat saga full circle.[14]

It should be mentioned that marine freight service by car float continued after the big boats left the scene but almost had expired by the end of the twentieth century. In the words of Joe Greenstein, it underwent a "30-year near-death experience." Only one shortline railroad still operates car floats across the Hudson. Despite the fact that if it were not for cross-harbor marine operations, freight rail traffic

reaching the west shore of the Hudson at New York City would be compelled to be routed almost to Albany before crossing the river, a detour of almost 200 miles, there is no assurance that the car floats will survive. A potential competitor is a cross-harbor tunnel, a possibility that is being touted by local politicians and government agencies. Although its benefits have yet to be quantified in economic terms, tunnel proponents reach back almost two centuries and compare its building to the construction of the Erie Canal, a project that assured New York City a position as the preeminent port on the East Coast.[15]

A charming addendum to this tale of the railroad ferries involves a proposal made by the New York Chapter of the Railway and Locomotive Historical Society in 1935. At that time it was suggested that, in addition to generating nationwide publicity for railroads during the difficult years of the Great Depression, a "ferryboat race on the Hudson River, each railroad represented by one boat . . . [would arouse] the interest, enthusiasm, and support of its patrons." The chapter chairman, Tom Taber, offered "a suitably engraved silver cup to the winning boat." That race, which never took place due to resistance on the part of the railroads, would have been held over a long course from the George Washington Bridge to Bear Mountain, some distance upriver. Although the practicality of racing many huge ferryboats raises many issues, there is no question but that it would have been a grand spectacle to observe, akin to the Mississippi River steamboat races of yesteryear. Incidentally, the idea was not a new one. In 1909, rival DL&W ferryboat captains engaged in a famous race, presumably with the approval of their management. On 1 October, the *Ithaca* and the *Lackawanna* raced between Hoboken and Newburgh, New York, a course of about 60 miles. The honor of "carrying a broom at her masthead" went to the *Ithaca,* which traversed the distance in 3 hours and 35 minutes. Very likely there have been many other unsanctioned, unheralded races between rival captains.[16]

## THE HUDSON AND MANHATTAN RAILROAD (HUDSON TUBES)

Not until techniques had been developed for digging in a pressurized environment could a subaqueous tunnel under the Hudson River be contemplated. Aware of James Eads's success with the Mississippi River bridge at St. Louis when he constructed the

**Figure 11.** In 1935, in the depths of the Great Depression, Thomas T. Taber, who was chairman of the New York Chapter of the Railway and Locomotive Historical Society, proposed a railroad ferryboat race up the Hudson River as a way to reinvigorate railroad interest and travel. This contemporary cartoon poked mild fun at the idea. Kay in the *Hudson Dispatch*, Thomas T. Taber Collection.

deep piers within a pressurized caisson, a technique that Eads had observed at Vichy, France, a year earlier, Dewitt Clinton Haskin promoted the construction of a Hudson River tunnel to connect Jersey City and New York City. He and his financial partner, Trenor W. Park, launched the Hudson River Railroad Tunnel Company to undertake the project. Excavation began in 1874, but as soon as Haskin sank his first shaft at Jersey City, work was halted for five years! (The entrance to this first shaft can still be found near the present Newport Tower residences.) The DL&W served him with an injunction because it feared that its huge investment in railroad facilities on the two riverbanks would become obsolete if the tunnel were successful. (It took almost a century for that to happen.) The legal issue was finally resolved, and the laborers were called back in 1879 to resume work on the tunnel.[17]

Although tunneling shields had already been used to build other tunnels, Haskin believed that air pressure alone would be sufficient to prevent the incursion of water during construction. Instead of using a shield, he chose to sink a vertical shaft on land at a point from which he could intercept the river bed and then begin tunneling nearly horizontally. An air lock was erected in the heading beyond the bottom of the vertical shaft, and compressed air was introduced ahead of the lock into a chamber where laborers excavated the soft earth. Although a test of the pressure system was made and found wanting, Haskin pressed ahead until disaster struck. As the tunnel extended out beneath the river, the roof failed and allowed pressurized air to escape suddenly. Without internal pressure to support it, the roof collapsed and water engulfed the work chamber. The door to the air lock slammed shut, and 20 workers died.[18]

The accident did not deter Haskin. He had a caisson built, essentially a sealed dam that excluded water, and pushed a pilot tunnel out from it. Supporting

plates for the main tunnel were erected in the pilot tunnel. Despite numerous small leaks and one major rupture that took no lives, the technique worked reasonably well.[19] By late 1882, 1,550 feet of the north tube and 560 feet of the south tube had been built and a heading was begun from New York City. Unfortunately, Trenor Park, Haskin's major backer, died that year. Work slowed because of funding difficulties and then stopped. Five years later, having raised more capital, Haskin resumed construction, and work continued at a slower pace into the 1890s.[20]

A new project manager, funded with British capital, was appointed in the 1890s, and the project moved ahead on a more professional, technically sound basis. A tunneling shield was introduced, and the relatively thin supporting plates lining the tunnel were replaced by strong cast-iron segments.[21] When more than two-thirds of the tunnel was completed, funds ran short again, and the company was sold to the bondholders in 1899.

In 1902, William Gibbs McAdoo organized the New York and Jersey Railroad (NY&J) and added more ambitious objectives. The company was tasked to construct a tunnel from the Exchange Place (Jersey City) station of the Pennsylvania Railroad to a new station site (Hudson Terminal) at Cortlandt and Church Streets in New York City. The NY&J also undertook completion of Haskin's original tunnel from 15th Street in Jersey City to Morton Street in Manhattan. The twin tubes of this tunnel would eventually continue along the west side of Manhattan to midtown and approach the proposed location

Figure 12. This hydraulic shield, erected in the Hudson River tunnel, is in place to commence excavation in soft ground. The face of the heading is timbered in front of the cutting edge. *Illustrations of Incidents in Tunnel Construction,* Plate 4.

of Pennsylvania Station, then in a planning stage. This integrated approach joined the Pennsylvania, the Erie, and the Lackawanna terminals on the Jersey shore of the Hudson to New York and eventually brought railroad passengers from Newark and Manhattan Transfer. The Manhattan Transfer facility was established to change motive power from steam to electric to make the underwater run across the river. After the main line of the PRR was electrified to Philadelphia in 1933, it was no longer necessary to switch locomotives at Manhattan Transfer. In addition to tracks facilitating the motive power exchange, Manhattan Transfer consisted of a pair of 1,100-foot-long platforms serving both the Hudson and Manhattan Railroad (the NY&J was so renamed) and the PRR, which allowed the latter's commuters to reach H&M stations in New York. It was unique in that it was located in a marsh and was accessible only by rail. The Pennsylvania Railroad's position regarding the use of its tunnels only by long-distance passenger trains (announced in 1901, long before they were completed) probably aided McAdoo's efforts to raise capital for the NY&J, which he proposed as a "commuter only railroad." However, several engineering problems had to be solved. Ingenious solutions were applied, and the north (midtown) tubes were finally completed in 1908. According to Black, the outside diameter of the north tube is 19.5 feet and its inside diameter is 18 feet 2 inches; the other tunnels are almost 3 feet smaller in diameter. The first train rolled on these tracks of the now-named Hudson and Manhattan Railroad in response to a telegraphed signal sent by President Theodore Roosevelt in Washington. Thirty thousand tickets were sold to the general public in the first 12 hours following the official opening of the tubes at midnight on 25 February 1908. The first paying passenger was Mrs. Barbara Schlatter, who, although seventh in an early-forming queue, was accorded the privilege of being first by the gallant men ahead of her. The south (downtown) tubes to Hudson Terminal at Cortlandt Street were completed in 1909.[22]

Although trains were now running below the mighty Hudson, work continued (mostly in New Jersey) on the tubes. The tracks were completed from Exchange Place to Grove Street in 1910 and then extended beyond Journal Square (then called Summit Avenue station) to Manhattan Transfer, which they reached the following year. From there they ran through Harrison, crossed the Passaic River, and terminated at Park Place in Newark in 1911. Park Place was the "end of the line" until the Pennsylvania Railroad completed its new Art Deco station in Newark in 1937. At that time the H&M was brought into the new station so that passengers could conveniently transfer from one road to the other. Manhattan Transfer was closed during that year.[23]

To the detriment of their own ferry facilities, the DL&W touted the new H&M service available at their Hoboken terminal by releasing a new Phoebe Snow jingle:

> Now Phoebe Snow direct can go
> From 33rd to Buffalo
> From Broadway bright the "Tubes" run right
> Into the Road of Anthracite.

Phoebe Snow was the fictional maiden attired in white garments that were intended to emphasize the cleanliness of the DL&W's anthracite coal-burning locomotives.[24]

In retrospect, it was well that this tunnel, the tunnel that wouldn't die, took so long to complete. If done sooner, no adequate motive power would have been available to propel trains through it without generating enormous clouds of noxious black smoke.

It wasn't until 1895 that the first viable electric locomotive tunnel application was made in Baltimore.[25]

Shortly after the tubes began operating, the Women's Municipal League campaigned for a dedicated "ladies' car" during rush-hour service. That group complained about the crushing and crowding of women and children when the cars were overfilled. Management agreed to the request on a test basis. The experiment failed for two reasons: journalists jeered the trial, writing about the "Hen Car" in most uncomplimentary terms, and a complaint was received that the practice was illegal and discriminatory. The Interstate Commerce Commission found in favor of the road, but the damage to the continued use of "ladies' cars" had already been done by the press, and use of the special cars was ended.[26]

The peak traffic year for the Tubes was 1927, when over 113 million commuters were carried. Traffic declined sharply during the Great Depression; the vehicular crossings of the river also contributed to the decline. The Hudson and Manhattan Railroad filed for bankruptcy in 1954 when its annual ridership measured only 37 million. In 1962, the Port Authority Trans-Hudson Corporation was formed to run the failed road. With an infusion of money brought by the new owner, service recovered, and today PATH provides more than satisfactory service through the old McAdoo tunnels.[27] One remnant of the original H&M is an architecturally stunning building that housed the railroad's electrical plant. At this writing it still stands on the Jersey City waterfront. Although abandoned in 1929, the shell of the "Powerhouse" remains, described by Christopher Gray, a *New York Times* columnist and architectural historian, as a "masterpiece of brickwork" that is "like some ancient, partly ruined cathedral." Another, less imposing memento of the tubes is a manhole cover that remains functional on the north platform of the Exchange Place station.[28]

A final monumental railroad project to span the Hudson River is the tunnel built by the Pennsylvania Railroad during the first decade of the twentieth century.

## THE PENNSYLVANIA RAILROAD TUNNELS

All of the Class A railroads that terminated on the Jersey side of the Hudson River had an interest in reaching New York City by rail alone, but the various alternatives were expensive. Of the railroads stalled at the western shoreline, one, the Pennsylvania Railroad, unquestionably had the strongest incentive to reach New York City without the need for marine operations because its major competitor from the west, the New York Central Railroad (NYC), did not require passengers (or freight) to transfer. The NYC entered the city from the north along the east shore of the Hudson, having crossed the river on a bridge near Albany.

In 1892, George Roberts, then president of the PRR, assigned his assistant, Samuel Rea, to study the subaqueous tunneling that was under way for the London Underground. Upon his return from Britain, Rea presented three possibilities to his management. One involved a tunnel from Jersey City to Manhattan and then under the East River to the Long Island Railroad (LIRR) yards in the borough of Queens. (The LIRR came under the Pennsylvania's control in 1900.) The second plan contemplated a roundabout route: building a new right-of-way in New Jersey and across Staten Island, a tunnel under the Narrows between upper and lower New York Bay into Brooklyn, and a bridge crossing the East River to Manhattan, with the tracks proceeding to a terminal in midtown. The third and preferred plan visualized a big bridge carrying 14 tracks across the Hudson, but its cost was astronomical (about $100 million). The PRR sought support among a consortium of railroads to build this bridge but was unsuccessful. Although tunnels were mentioned in two of Rea's proposals that he advanced for a Hudson River crossing, railroad management was reluctant to plan in that direction. It is not difficult to understand that position because at the time (1892), electric motive power was a new and uncertain quantity and the only practical means of locomotion involved steam engines. The PRR did not want to build and operate a smoke-filled underwater railroad tunnel.[29]

An attempt to resuscitate the bridge project in 1900 also failed. However, by that time the possibility of using electric power for railroad trains had broadened considerably. Under Rea's supervision, a trans-Hudson tunnel was planned. The finalized design contemplated "a double-track railroad starting from the main line east of Newark, crossing the Hackensack Meadows on a high fill, passing through Bergen Hill by separate single track tunnels and under the Hudson River to Ninth Avenue, Manhattan, in two single-track tubes." The line was to be continued under Manhattan and below the East River to a connection with the LIRR at Long Island City. Obtaining the necessary franchises and approvals was time-consuming, and it was not until 1904 that the first construction contracts were awarded. On 27 November 1910, the first PRR trains rolled into the newly built Pennsylvania Station in New York City. (Long Island Railroad trains were using the terminal almost three months earlier.) This great and costly undertaking was worth every cent because it gave the PRR an edge over its rivals coming from the south and west, and it leveled the playing field with its northern rival, the New York Central Railroad.[30]

By the time the tunnels were ready for use, the railroad had also developed an electric locomotive that was up to the task of moving heavy steel passenger cars up tunnel grades that approached 2 percent, higher than PRR trains encountered through the Allegheny Mountains. That engine, featuring a 225-ton electric motor, powered its driving wheels via a crankshaft, connecting rod, and side rods, much like the steam locomotives that it displaced. Earlier tests of an engine with direct drive, axle-mounted motors, conducted in New Jersey in 1907, convinced engineers that the rod connections would provide a more stable machine. The locomotive, assigned the class designator DD-1, generated 2,000 horsepower. It was the most powerful locomotive built to that time and was key to the tunnel project's success.[31]

In the nearly 100 years since the Pennsylvania tunnels were opened, they have performed well, but they are now approaching saturation in rail traffic with attendant potential safety problems. On the drawing board is a plan, approved by NJ Transit's board of directors, to dig an entirely new tunnel (Trans-Hudson Express [THE] Tunnel) under the Palisades and Hudson River that will lead to a new terminal in Manhattan. The project, with an estimated completion date of 2016, would cost $6 billion overall; the tunnel portion is estimated to cost $2.3 billion and would allow rail traffic into the city to be doubled.[32]

To the deep regret of architectural historians and many ordinary citizens, the exceptional Pennsylvania Station is no more. Demolition began in 1963, and it was replaced by a pale shadow of its former magnificence, a building that is more noted for the entertainment hall that it houses than its continuing role as a railroad station. Vincent Scully, a noted architectural historian, wrote of a traveler's entry into the city since the original station's demise: "One entered the city like a god, one scuttles in now like a rat." Recently, a grander Pennsylvania Station has been designed and is intended to occupy space under the New York General Post Office building, which is a block west of the present station. Unfortunately, the design is still not firm, and the schedule for completion of construction is being pushed farther into the future.[33] The most recent proposal envisions THE Tunnel to be constructed much deeper than originally designed in order to avoid disruption to existing vehicular traffic above and rail traffic below street level. If approved, this change would bring the new station 175 feet below ground level, necessitating a four-minute escalator ride to the surface.[34]

Much of the rubble derived from the razing of Penn Station, including some of the carved statuary, now lies in a landfill in Secaucus, New Jersey. Happily, some of the priceless statuary was saved when it was donated to worthy beneficiaries. Particularly significant were four identical sculptures that were fashioned in pink marble by Adolph Weinman. These groupings of maidens representing Night and Day with accompanying eagles framed clocks above the principal entrances to the terminal. One of the works was donated to the State of New Jersey and ensconced at Ringwood State Park. Some consideration is now being given to moving this sculpture to Newark's Penn Station or to the railroad station at Trenton.[35]

The Lackawanna (or Erie-Lackawanna, if one prefers, since the two roads merged in 1960) Terminal still serves NJ Transit passengers on their way to New York. But now, instead of embarking on magnificent ferryboats, the commuters rush to the PATH trains below the terminal to conclude their journey.

# 8 The Railroad and the New Jersey Bedroom Communities (1840–2006)

New York and Philadelphia operated (and still do) like two great magnets, attracting thousands of commuters to their very heart each weekday morning and then releasing them to return to their homes in New Jersey every evening. Of the two cities, New York saw the greatest number of commuters by far, and, as explained in chapter 7, the problems attending their transportation were huge and almost defied solution, at least with the technologies available in the nineteenth century. This chapter explores the role that railroads played in the development of the New Jersey bedroom communities, those towns and villages whose citizens left each working day for their daily excursion to the "big city."

## FROM NEW JERSEY TO THE SIDEWALKS OF NEW YORK

Before the coming of the railroad, if a person lived in a small town, they usually walked to work; in the city, slow, crowded omnibuses extended the range of a commuter somewhat, but that range was still limited. Railroads, in general, were the facilitators of an ability to work at some distance from one's home. Nowhere was this fact more applicable than in northern New Jersey because of the great business and commercial magnet that was New York City. By 1840, only a few years after the first railroad had been established in the state, more than 700 workers were traveling to New York City from Newark and Jersey City via the New Jersey Railroad and Transportation Company's trains and ferryboats. Twenty years later, that number had swelled to over 4,300 commuters. The early railroads encouraged this daily

traffic by offering reduced commutation rates. There is a record of a Mr. Lathrop who purchased one of the first commutation tickets on the Morris and Essex Railroad in 1841. For his payment of $100, Lathrop enjoyed the privilege of traveling between Madison and Newark for six months. (Incidentally, the word *commuter* is derived from the commuted, or discounted, fares. It followed that the commuted riders became known as commuters.)[1]

In almost all instances, when a railroad was built in northern New Jersey (and most other places), it quickly brought an influx of settlers. For instance, when the Paterson and Ramapo Railroad entered Godwinville (now Ridgewood) in 1848, a small farming community within the town of Paramus, 20 families resided there. Three years later, 59 homes were occupied, and 25 years after that, the population had swelled and the town boasted about 1,200 houses. Whereas, before the railroad, the center of community life in most towns had been the local church, by 1876 business and social activity revolved around the railroad depot. More than just a catalyst for town expansion and development, railroads were also instrumental in building new communities. After the state legislature severed part of Bloomfield to create the new township of Montclair, the New York and Oswego Midland Railroad routed its tracks through the new municipality. Within 10 years, the community had expanded and property values had increased 250 percent in many instances.[2]

The peculiar nature of the commutation phenomenon, namely, that passengers had to be transported within a relatively short time window, say, two hours, morning and evening, presented a problem that has never been solved satisfactorily. Maximum operating staff and equipment were required for those two-hour periods, and then near minimum levels were needed for the interval between the peaks. "Rush hour" became "crush hour" as trains and ferryboats were jammed with people only to become nearly empty during the midday hours.[3]

Before 1900, the various New Jersey railroads had staked out claims to commuters in their territories. Fingers snaked out from the waterfront opposite New York City to Essex and Morris counties (Delaware, Lackawanna and Western, DL&W), Bergen and Passaic counties (Erie), Somerset County (Central Railroad of New Jersey, CNJ), and Middlesex and Mercer counties (Pennsylvania, PRR and the Philadelphia and Reading). The CNJ and the PRR shared patrons in Monmouth and Ocean counties.[4] These commuters performed a twice-daily routine that involved up to four changes of transport each way. Unless they lived within walking distance of the railroad, they had to be brought by carriage or hack, then by train, to the waterfront. Ferryboats brought them across the river, and again they had to employ a carriage or hack, unless they worked within walking distance of their place of business. Gustav Kobbé expressed the phenomenon thusly: "It may be said that thousands of the best citizens of New York are not citizens of that city at all; in the evening they ebb away . . . of New York's best citizens thousands are citizens of New Jersey."[5] Although the ride across the water could be a very pleasant experience on a summer day, not all passengers were enthused about the trip. One woman, in a letter to the New York Times in 1873, complained that the "Ladies' Cabins" of the Pennsylvania Railroad ferries "are not, as a rule, as clean as a well-regulated pig-pen."[6]

The various commuter railroads vigorously promoted the idea of living in New Jersey and working in New York. For example, a map of metropolitan New Jersey, undated, but circa 1900, was published by the Erie Railway. It showed the Erie network in the region and was titled "The Land of Suburban Homes on the Lines of the Erie Railroad System Adjacent to New York."[7]

After the Hudson and Manhattan Railroad (H&M) began operation, the development of northern New Jersey exploded. By 1909, the Hudson Tubes offered quick, dependable service to midtown and downtown Manhattan and acquired their own commuters from Newark, Harrison, and Jersey City, some stolen from the preexisting railroads. Realtors touted the new railroad, making much of the fact that it took less time now to reach New York City. A representative New Jersey real estate page from the New York Tribune of 25 February 1908, headlined "Opportunities for Home-Seekers in New Jersey Tunnel Zones," listed several advertisements of houses available in communities near railroad facilities: in East Orange "on D.L.&W.R.R." and at "Passaic, opposite Erie Depot." An accompanying article described the advantages of Passaic, the "Ideal City," since "Tunnels Bring It Much Nearer to New York." The gist of the article was that buyers should hasten to buy New Jersey real estate:

> It is the consensus of opinion among realty experts that the Hudson and Manhattan and the Pennsylvania Railroad tunnels between New Jersey and New York will result in large areas of vacant land in New Jersey being quickly transformed into ideal suburban towns, and also in making all New Jersey towns in the tunnel zones many times bigger and much more attractive places in which to live than they are today.

Incidentally, the newly built three-story houses in East Orange, with nine rooms and bath on a "Beautiful Parkway" two minutes from the Grove Street DL&W station and only "35 minutes from New York by Hudson Tunnel," were offered by the builder for $7,300. Although the Tribune story implied that the soon-to-be-built Pennsylvania Railroad tunnels would be a boon to commuters in nearby New Jersey towns, this was not so. The president of the Pennsylvania Railroad made it clear that the road's tunnels would be used for long-distance passenger travel exclusively; local train passengers would use the ferries, as usual. However, New York–bound commuters could connect with the H&M at Exchange Place, and the PRR later arranged to bring H&M trains into the new Penn Station at Newark, where an easy transfer was effected.[8]

Commutation from New Jersey to New York City continued into the twentieth century. The years before the Great Depression established many records in numbers of commuters carried by rail and by ferryboat. The Depression affected commutation adversely as workers lost their jobs, especially in the financial center in downtown New York. World War

**THESE BEAUTIFUL HOUSES ON BEAUTIFUL PARKWAY**
For sale by owner and builder; 9 rooms and bath; all latest improvements, tiled bath, steam heat, parquet floors; finished in hard wood; price, $7,300.00. Easy terms if necessary. Two minutes from East Orange, Grove St. Station, on D., L. & W. R. R. Apply DAVIS, 6 North 15th St., East Orange. Three sold last week. Thirty-five minutes from New York by Hudson Tunnel.

Figure 13. Anticipating the 1909 completion of the Hudson & Manhattan Tubes, real estate development in the New Jersey suburbs with access to the Tubes exploded. This advertisement, published in the *New York Tribune* on 23 February 1908, was typical of the many offerings.

II brought a resurgence of traffic, but after the war, rail commutation faced a new threat from automobiles and buses passing across the George Washington Bridge and through the new vehicular tunnels under the Hudson. Slowly the commuter railroad business declined, causing the retirement of the "big boats" and then substantial losses for the railroads. The Erie lost almost 20 million passengers, about 80 percent of its patronage, between 1930 and 1960. Ironically, the Port Authority of New York and New Jersey, the agency that built the vehicular trans-Hudson crossings that, in large part, caused the railroad commuter decline, became a railroad factor itself when it assumed control of the Hudson and Manhattan Railroad, the Hudson Tubes. By improving service on the now-named PATH [Port Authority Trans-Hudson], it checked that decline and steadily increased rail ridership. In 2001, it suffered a major setback with the destruction of the World Trade Center twin towers; its major terminal was beneath the buildings. Work began almost immediately to restore service to lower Manhattan, and the trains are now running into a new subterranean terminal at the site.

## NEW JERSEY COMMUTING, SOUTHERN STYLE

In much the same manner that New Jersey was isolated from New York City by a great river, so was the state separated from Philadelphia. In both cases and for a long time, rail travelers were carried across the two rivers, the Hudson and the Delaware, by ferryboats, most operated by the railroads.

Many business commuters to Philadelphia came from the west, the "main line" communities along the Pennsylvania Railroad. Consequently, although established early and considered essential to the operations of several roads, the Camden and Amboy (C&A) in particular, Camden–Philadelphia ferry service never attained the epic proportions of the Hudson River crossing. Neither was the trip as long; the distance between the two terminals (between Market Street in Philadelphia and Federal Street in Camden) was slightly over a half mile. However, later there were large weekend crowds traveling to Camden where they could board a train to the Jersey Shore for a day's outing. Still later, many Pennsylvanians came by auto and were carried to the eastern shore of the river by the *Bridgeton, Salem, Millville,* or other big boats.

The first C&A train from the north arrived at Camden on 29 December 1834. Passengers were shepherded onto the Reeves and Knissel ferryboat *William Wray* to be brought to Philadelphia. The railroad then instituted its own ferry service across the Delaware from Camden to its wharf at Chestnut Street with two newly built boats. Although ferry services had existed at Camden for more than 100 years, the first steam ferry was established in 1836. In that year, the Camden and Philadelphia Steam Boat Ferry Company (C&PSBF) was established by Joseph Kaighn. The railroad and Kaighn reached an agreement whereby the new ferry company would acquire the C&A's two boats and would transport the road's passengers for five cents each. Beginning in 1838, it served C&A passengers between the railroad's dock at Camden and Walnut (later Market) Street in Philadelphia. In 1840, the C&A purchased the Reeves company, and its boats sailed from Reeves's Federal Street slips in Camden. In 1851, the railroad went back into the ferry business at Philadelphia and established new routes between the two cities. During the Civil War, it inaugurated a car ferry that brought entire trains across so that their patrons were spared the inconvenience of making a physical transfer. Then, in 1867, the railroad decided once more to terminate its ferry operations, and the C&PSBF assumed that responsibility again until 1883, when it was acquired by the Pennsylvania Railroad, which then continued the service.[9]

In 1866, the Kensington and North Jersey Ferry Company (K&NJ) began 14 years of operation between Camden and Philadelphia. This ferry was purchased in 1880 by the Camden and Atlantic Railroad, which then relocated the trans-Delaware route to Vine Street in Camden. When the Pennsylvania Railroad bought the C&A in 1885, it had all rail passengers use the C&PSBF facilities that it now owned; the K&NJ continued to operate, however. Another entity, the West Jersey Ferry Company, was incorporated in 1849, and it was merged with the Camden and Philadelphia Steam Boat Ferry Company and renamed the Philadelphia and Camden Ferry Company (P&C) in 1899. In 1901, the PRR built a new ferry facility at Federal Street in Camden to serve its rail traffic.[10]

When it began operations, the Camden and Philadelphia Steam Boat Ferry's boats were compelled to detour around Windmill Island near the Pennsylvania shore. To shorten its route, the company dug a canal across the island, a task it completed in 1840. Fourteen years later, the West Jersey Ferry Company agreed to share in the cost of enlarging the cut; its quid pro quo was permission to use the canal. In 1894, ownership of the portion of the island owned by the ferry company was conveyed to the federal government, which then removed the entire island.[11]

In 1883, the Philadelphia and Reading Railroad assumed control of the Philadelphia and Atlantic City Railroad (P&AC). A few years later, the Atlantic City Railroad (ACRR) was organized from P&AC and some Reading assets. The Reading road then incorporated the Delaware River Ferry Company of New Jersey to serve the Atlantic City Railroad. This ferry, operating to Kaighn's Point in Camden, was abandoned in 1936 after the Pennsylvania-Reading Seashore Lines merger, and the Reading's boats were acquired by the Pennsylvania Railroad.[12]

Bill Day, a columnist for the *Haddon Gazette* in the 1970s, recalled the Philadelphia and Camden ferry service in the 1920s. One of his vivid memories was of an ice-choked river between Philadelphia and Camden, a common winter occurrence. At times, ice floes two feet thick smashed against the steel-hulled boats, and floes often wedged themselves between the boat and its slip as the boat approached its dock, causing substantial damage to the piling buffers. The seriousness of the problem was underscored when the *Bridgeton* became trapped in the ice in January 1918. The *Hammonton* came to the rescue and evacuated the passengers safely. The steam engine-driven boats were fueled with coal, and Day recalled that horse-drawn wagons would come aboard the big boats twice daily to cart the ashes away.[13]

Unlike the situation at New York City, where almost all railroads serving that metropolis terminated within a few miles of each other on New Jersey's shoreline, only a few major roads, notably the Pennsylvania and the Philadelphia and Reading, entered Philadelphia and crossed the river at that point. The PRR dominated the traffic at Philadelphia yet never considered the construction of a tunnel between that city and Camden. Thus the ferryboats remained the only means for railroad passengers to cross.

Although the railroads contributed substantially

to the development of suburban communities in the metropolitan Philadelphia area, New Jersey commuter traffic exploded after the Delaware River (Ben Franklin) Bridge was built in 1926. In addition to vehicular traffic, the railroads' fierce competition, the bridge carried tracks of the city subway across the river. Later (mid-1960s), Port Authority Transit Company (PATCO) trains began to use the facility. The bridge, ending in the middle of an affluent neighborhood of Camden, also precipitated a migration of the city's wealthier citizens to more distant suburbs. A corollary of the bridge's popularity was the decline of ferry service. By the early 1950s, the Philadelphia and Camden Ferry Company was losing almost a quarter million dollars a year. Ferry service on the Delaware River between Philadelphia and Camden ended in 1952 when the *Haddonfield* made a last run across the water. Two years later, the PRR railroad and ferryboat terminal at Camden was destroyed by fire.[14]

But what about latter-day rail connections on the New Jersey side of the river? New Jersey Transit's River LINE (which begins at Trenton) ends at Camden where one can transfer to Port Authority Transit Company "High Speed Line" trains bound for Philadelphia or Lindenwold, New Jersey. Connections with NJT's Atlantic City Line can be made at Lindenwold. The Atlantic City Line, abandoned during NJ Transit's early years, was rebuilt in 1989 and now extends from Philadelphia to Atlantic City.

# 9 The Jersey Central (1849–1976)

Of the scores of railroads, large and small, that have operated in the state of New Jersey, one, the Central Railroad of New Jersey (CNJ), stands out as a sort of "native son." Other great railroads that traversed the state (perhaps with the exception of the Camden and Amboy before it became part of the Pennsylvania Railroad system) were, for the most part, more closely associated with other regions; lesser railroads never attained the influence and importance within the state as the Central (again, with the exclusion of the C&A). Arguably, the Central of New Jersey represented the essence of railroad transportation in New Jersey. From its beginnings in the Elizabethtown and Somerville Railroad (E&S) until its demise in 1976 when it was absorbed into Conrail, the Central *was* New Jersey.

The CNJ was formed through the reorganization of the Elizabethtown and Somerville Railroad, which was chartered on 9 February 1831, making it one of the very first roads in the state. Unfortunately, the E&S was not a fast-developing railroad. It did not begin to plan the right-of-way until 1835, and it did not begin operations until 1836. That beginning, along Broadway in Elizabeth, was accomplished using horsepower over a 2.5-mile road. A little more than two years later, the fledgling railroad had received a steam locomotive, the *Eagle*, from Matthias Baldwin in Philadelphia, and on 1 January 1839, the *Eagle*, hauling a passenger car, rolled into Plainfield. In his book *Railroads in New Jersey: The Formative Years*, John Cunningham tells of a race between the *Eagle* and a horse-drawn coach in which the latter far outdistanced the locomotive. But, according to

Cunningham, it was not long before stage drivers were chanting a requiem:

> Oh, once I made money by driving a team
> But now all is hauled on the railroad by steam.
> May the Devil catch the man who invented the plan,
> For it's ruined us poor wagoners, and every other man.[1]

Building from Plainfield, the E&S did not reach Somerville until 1842, almost 11 years after its charter had been granted. Short on funds, the road celebrated their arrival at Somerville, not with the usual lavish affair hosted by railroads, but by providing lemonade and cake at the local inn. Despite a depleted treasury, the road struggled to operate, but in order to save money, the railroad's managers undertook to build a brick engine house and turntable themselves. They did award a contract in the amount of $500 to James Castner of Somerville for the construction of a wooden passenger depot. Castner built the station, but later presented a bill for additional work that he had done; the E&S refused to pay the extra amount. Castner then sued and won a judgment and, through the sheriff, attached one of the road's locomotives (by this time they had four engines). The machine was then auctioned off and sold to a Mr. Toms for $10. The E&S superintendent demanded that Mr. Toms remove the locomotive from the company's property within five hours, an impossibility. Later the company settled the bill and recovered its engine.[2]

The original station at Somerville was situated in approximately the same location as the surviving 1890 depot. The latter is now occupied by a law firm and has been faithfully restored to its original

**Figure 14.** This Central Railroad of New Jersey depot was built at Somerville in 1890. The structure, made of gray Jersey sandstone, still stands, recycled as a law office and faithfully restored close to its original appearance. This photograph was taken by the author in February 2006 from a position northeast of the station.

appearance. (More information about this station is presented in chapter 31.) However, before the 1890 structure was built, a second station was constructed between the tracks in 1856. Upon its completion, the original depot was demolished, and its bell, which had been used to announce the arrival and departure of trains, was removed to the county fairgrounds where it was used to start horse races. Ten years later, a fire destroyed the station and a temporary building was erected to serve the community. The "temporary" station stood for 22 years until 1890, when the present structure was built.[3]

The road was originally built with strap rail, a common method of construction employed by early builders. The pioneer railroads had two choices insofar as rails were concerned: they could import heavy, expensive shaped rail from England (because there were no local iron fabricators that could roll the required cross-section) or use bar iron, essentially the material used to make barrel hoops, which was produced domestically. The E&S chose the latter, less expensive path. This was an acceptable decision when the railroad's trains were drawn at low speed by animals that walked between the rails. Once locomotives began to be used, their substantial weight played havoc with the track. One of the shortcomings of strap rail was its tendency to deform under the weight of the engine and cars and curl up at the ends when the spikes fastening them to the wooden stringers supporting them would work loose. Once freed, the raised end provided an opportunity for a wheel to roll *under* the rail and peel it away from its stringer suddenly and forcefully. Occasionally, in this situation, the iron rail would penetrate the floor of a car passing over it and present a serious hazard to the passengers within. Such a penetration was termed a "snakehead" because the rail rising through the floor looked, in its "writhing and twisting," much like a snake. The spike hole, near the end of the rail, reminiscent of a serpent's eye, accentuated the snakelike appearance. Numerous incidents of snakeheads were reported, including one in 1841 on the Morris and Essex Railroad, when the rail "passed through the thigh of one of the passengers." The Jersey Central had its own unfortunate incident: "On August 19, 1843, Isaac Staats boarded the train at Bound Brook, and someone asked where he was going. He replied, 'To Jericho.' The train had gone but a few miles when a "snakehead" passed up through the car, striking Staats under the chin and killing him instantly."[4]

By 1846, the Elizabethtown and Somerville Railroad had fallen into bankruptcy. This situation presented an opportunity to John Stearns and Coffin Colket, principals in the firm that built part of the original E&S. Acting as agents for the creditors, they purchased the defunct company for only $125,000, a true bargain. After the sale, Stearns was appointed to be the road's superintendent. The new owners reorganized the E&S as the "Elizabethtown and Somerville Railroad of 1846," and the following year the Somerville and Easton Railroad Company (S&E) was incorporated to fulfill the earlier charter promise of reaching the Delaware River. This development gave the new proprietors the right to build toward the Pennsylvania coal fields and the rich income that coal haulage was expected to generate. In anticipation of that advance, the strap rail was torn up and replaced with heavy T-rail. In 1849, the two charters were merged to form the Central Railroad of New Jersey. The driving force behind the reorganizations and the push to Easton, Pennsylvania, was John T. Johnston. Made president of the S&E in 1848 at the age of 28, Johnston remained as president of the Central Railroad of New Jersey until 1876. He instituted the practice of wearing uniforms for railroad employees in this country, and he was one of the founders of the Metropolitan Museum of Art in New York City. Jersey Central passenger conductors were fitted for blue uniforms, coat, pants, vest, and a cap with a CRR badge, all peppered with gold-hued buttons.[5]

When the CNJ began its westward advance, it encountered a few formidable obstacles. For instance, at Union Forge, the surveyors found a deep valley carved by the south branch of the Raritan River. There the construction crews built a quarter-mile, 120-foot-high wooden trestle to span the valley. Begun in 1859, the bridge contributed its name, High Bridge, to the station that the Central erected nearby. Built upon eight stone piers, the bridge acted like a living thing when a train passed over it. It undulated like ocean waves, deflecting between piers and rising at each pier. Though not actually unsafe, it terrorized those travelers who rode across it. In 1865, the CNJ responded to the entreaties of its patrons and solved the problem by filling in the spaces between piers with an enormous amount of material. This project cost $250,000.[6]

The CNJ arrived at the Delaware River at Phillipsburg in 1852 where coal brought to that town via the Lehigh Canal would be loaded. But the first order of business was a celebration. Eight "splendid" passenger cars, drawn by the locomotive *Pennsylvania,* brought railroad officials, businessmen from New York City and various villages along the line, and Dodsworth's "celebrated band." These participants met with the elected officials of Easton, Pennsylvania, and some of its citizens who were accompanied by the Easton Brass Band. The conductor on that first train into Phillipsburg was Levi Shattuck. His ambition had been to become a locomotive driver, and to fulfill this goal, he began working as a fireman for the E&S in 1838. After 11 weeks at this job, he was promoted to engineer of the *Eagle,* the road's first locomotive. In 1840, Levi, a religious man, approached Superintendent Stearns and declared that his conscience would not permit him to engage in Sunday work. Although Stearns relieved him of his locomotive duty, he continued Shattuck's employment with station assignments at Bound Brook and then Somerville. Shattuck returned to train duty as a conductor between Elizabethport (site of the road's marine facilities in Elizabeth) and Somerville, except on Sundays, and later was chosen to head up the crew of the celebratory journey to Phillipsburg.[7]

Once at the Delaware River, Pennsylvania beckoned and Jersey Central management was anxious to extend its reach into the neighboring state, its ultimate goal being the rich coal fields. Asa Packer, owner of the Lehigh Valley Railroad (LV), also had an interest in crossing the river, from the other direction. Packer's road built from Mauch Chunk to Easton in Pennsylvania where it, after crossing the river, was expected to join with the Belvidere-Delaware Railroad (Bel-Del) on the Jersey shore. A major problem existed, however. The CNJ tracks ended at the river on a high ridge while the Bel-Del's right of way was at water level. High ridges also dominated the Pennsylvania side of the river. Packer solved the problem by constructing a two-level bridge that brought the CNJ directly across at the ridge level while carrying the Lehigh Valley over at a much lower level. The LV then had to climb the ridge on the Pennsylvania side to meet its existing tracks. The bridge took two years to build, with a substantial amount of that time spent dealing with disasters, natural and manmade. First a flood destroyed some of the early spans, and then a canal boat smashed into the bridge. Finally, double-heading LV locomotives were too much for the new span, and it collapsed under their weight. But after this rash of unfortunate incidents, traffic finally flowed steadily, and the bridge enabled the CNJ to fulfill its objective of sharing in the lucrative coal traffic. Later, when as many as 300 carloads of coal were dumped into barges daily at Jersey City, the CNJ also encouraged tourist "Excursions to the Coal Fields of Pennsylvania." Such was the title of a broadside that touted travel to "some of the WILDEST and MOST ROMANTIC SCENERY IN PENNSYLVANIA." A traveler could board a CNJ steamboat at 7:30 AM, then travel by rail from Elizabethport to and through the Delaware Water Gap and over Pocono Mountain to Scranton and Wilkes-Barre (via other roads). He or she would continue to Mauch Chunk and ride on the Gravity Road at Mt. Pisgah over the "wonderful switchback." The return trip would be through Easton to New York, entirely on CNJ facilities. The entire excursion cost $5.25, and arrangements could be made to extend the tour for two or three days, if desired.[8]

The Jersey Central and the Delaware, Lackawanna and Western (DL&W) Railroads agreed in 1856 to join their respective tracks at Hampton, New Jersey. From there DL&W trains were hauled

**Figure 15.** This view of Easton, Pennsylvania (from Phillipsburg Rock), shows the bi-level bridge crossing the Delaware River. The bridge carried the Jersey Central tracks across the river at the high, ridge level while accommodating the Lehigh Valley Railroad at the lower level. New Jersey Historical Society Photograph Collection.

over CNJ tracks to Elizabethport. Since the DL&W operated on broad gauge track (6'0") instead of the more common standard gauge, a third rail had to be laid to accommodate the Lackawanna trains. The CNJ bought nine broad gauge locomotives to move the newcomer's consists. During the second year of this cooperative effort, the DL&W brought 224,000 tons of coal to the Central's tracks. This arrangement continued until 1875 when the DL&W acquired the Morris and Essex Railroad and brought their coal traffic to Hoboken over their own right-of-way.[9]

It is important to note that the extension of its tracks to Jersey City in the 1860s had been sought by the Jersey Central for a number of years. The New Jersey legislature, still dominated by Camden and Amboy Railroad (C&A) interests, had rejected the CNJ's attempts to secure permission to build to tidewater. The CNJ finally took a page from the C&A's book and distributed free passes to legislators, judg-

es, and other persons of influence, and hired a special train to carry a Trenton contingent to a gala affair at Phillipsburg. This "lubrication" of the wheels of government obviously was successful because a charter amendment was approved at the next session of the legislature.[10]

Upon leasing the Lehigh and Susquehanna Railroad in 1871, the CNJ was no longer reliant upon shared trackage, and it brought coal directly from the mines to its docks at Jersey City. But it now faced a more formidable enemy, the depression of 1873. The road was bankrupted and had to be reorganized in 1877. A reinvigorated Jersey Central rose like a phoenix by 1880, but the railroad that had pioneered a New York–Chicago route through Allentown, Pennsylvania, with the cooperation of its rivals, the LV, Reading, and Pennsylvania Railroads was eventually to see its freight and passenger business decline, a victim of those same competitors.[11]

**Figure 16.** A happy day in 1896 along the Sandy Hook Route of the Jersey Central! A locomotive, hauling a pay car, has just arrived at the East Long Branch station. It took the pay train 15 days to accomplish its monthly rounds over the entire system. North Jersey Chapter, National Railway Historical Society / North Jersey Electric Railway Historical Society.

The Central Railroad of New Jersey was also a major player in the southern part of the state. During the early 1860s, the Raritan and Delaware Bay Railroad (R&DB) operated the *Brooklyn and Camden Express* train between New York and Philadelphia (both ends of the journey were made by ferryboat). Because the five-hour trip was not competitive with the Camden and Amboy route, a new line was established, known as the Bound Brook Route or, unofficially, the "New Line." This brought passengers from Jersey City to Bound Brook on CNJ tracks, then continued on Reading rails on their newly built Delaware and Bound Brook Railroad to Philadelphia. In 1869, the R&DB became CNJ's Southern Division.[12]

A number of railroads had sought to tap the relatively sparse traffic in southern New Jersey by concentrating on produce from the farms in the region and then by developing a vacation trade by serving a few promising towns, including Cape May and Atlantic City. The CNJ's Southern Division joined them. The Southern extended from Red Bank, where it met the New York and Long Branch Railroad, a CNJ affiliate, to Bayside opposite the state of Delaware, where connections could be made with the Bombay Hook ferry to Delaware. The Southern Division was also an important factor in the development of a sand trade. The southeastern part of New Jersey is exceptionally sandy, and the material is an essential component of glass and concrete. Millions of tons of sand for glass products and for construction uses were carried by the Southern Division. Travelers to the North Jersey shore could reach the numerous resort towns along the Sandy Hook Route, which served them from Atlantic Highlands to Point Pleasant.[13]

Around 1880, speed began to be considered as an important competitive factor, and nowhere was it more important than on the New York–Philadelphia runs. Over the next several years, a speed rivalry between the Pennsylvania and Reading Railroads resulted in new records being set almost constantly. Probably the most celebrated speed queen of the era was the New York Central's number 999, which in

1893 exceeded 100 miles per hour over a measured mile near Batavia, New York. But, in the same year, the Jersey Central's camelback locomotive number 385 was timed by chronograph at 105 miles per hour as it passed through Fanwood.[14]

By 1881, the CNJ covered a good part of the state with three main routes, two extending from Jersey City to Pennsylvania (at Easton and at Philadelphia) and the third being the Southern Division. These routes were composed of numerous branches and leased tracks: the Main Line, the Southern Division, the High Bridge Branch, the Bound Brook Line, the Trenton Branch, the Newark and Elizabeth Branch, the Dover and Rockaway Railroad, the Ogden Mine Railroad, and the New York and Long Branch Division, operated jointly with the Pennsylvania Railroad. The Dover and Rockaway and the Ogden were leased in 1881 and 1882, respectively, for 999 years. The South Branch Railroad joined the system in 1888.[15]

In 1883, the Philadelphia and Reading Railroad (P&R) leased the total assets of the CNJ as part of a plan to achieve a monopoly of the Pennsylvania coal trade. A secondary interest was the development of a through line from New York City to Norfolk, Virginia, in which the Southern Division's tracks would play an essential role. Unfortunately for the P&R, these goals were more easily formulated than accomplished; the plan disintegrated, and the P&R defaulted on its payments to the CNJ. By 1887, the Jersey Central reestablished its control and began to upgrade its facilities and acquire additional assets, and by 1882, it operated over 427 miles of railroad lines in New Jersey and Pennsylvania. It also managed about 282 miles of railroad in Pennsylvania, Delaware, and Maryland.[16]

Despite the lesson learned in the early 1880s, the Philadelphia and Railroad management still believed that they could monopolize the coal-carrying trade. In 1890 they again concluded a lease with the CNJ to manage the road, a situation they engineered by promising CNJ stockholders a better return. Their expectations did not materialize, and the Reading road was soon bankrupted.[17]

During the 1890s, the Jersey Central, following the practice of many other railroads and trolley lines, developed an excursion destination at Lake Hopatcong. Nolan's Point, situated on the east side of the lake, encompassed picnic areas, hiking trails, flying horses and swings, and a dance pavilion. A rowboat could be rented for two dollars a day, and for an additional dollar boaters could enjoy the services of a rower. Most folks enjoyed the park on a day trip from New York City or Jersey City or Newark, although hotels were also available for those who wished to stay longer. The excursions, which cost two dollars a person, attracted over 50,000 fun-seekers each season and continued into the early 1900s. Kobbé mentioned that the railroad sought "respectable people only" who, "although they have no end of fun during their day's outing, are notably quiet and orderly." These folks were "concentrating a whole year's holiday into their one day at the lake." Until 1930, the branch was also busy in the winter transporting ice cut from the lake to markets at Newark and New York City. Nolan's Point had earlier been a terminal of the Ogden Mine Railroad, which became a CNJ affiliate. Iron and zinc ores recovered from mines in Jefferson Township were brought by the railroad to Nolan's Point and transshipped from there to the Morris Canal on canal boats towed by an OM steamboat.[18]

American railroads were notoriously deficient in the application of traffic control signals. The Pennsylvania Railroad installed the first comprehensive signal systems along its Philadelphia–New York route in 1876 (see chapter 4), one that relied upon human intervention to set the signal indications. However, the CNJ was one of the first roads to install automatic block signals; it applied automatic block signals to its tracks between the Jersey City terminal and Bergen Point in 1889–90. An electro-pneumatic system, it operated through relays from track circuits; the installation controlled semaphore arms. In 1893, the CNJ continued its innovation in railroad signals when it installed the world's first automatic, electric motor–operated semaphore signal at Black Dan's Cut, near Phillipsburg. The Jersey Central's experiments with signals in the early 1890s are significant because it was not until 1894 that the next extensive signal system, using Hall signals, was installed in New Jersey (by the DL&W, after a disastrous accident in the Jersey Meadows in 1894). Railroads all over the country soon began to turn to electric semaphore signals, which allowed the signal to be self-contained and eliminated the lengthy runs of pipe required for pneumatic applications. By 1902, about 2,000 electric semaphore signals were in use or on order. The all-electric signal, controlled by a track circuit and installed at Black Dan's Cut, was invented by J. W. Lattig, superintendent of telegraph for the Lehigh Valley Railroad. It was held by a counterweight to present normally a "danger" signal; when its motor was energized, a mechanism moved the blade to a "clear" position. Lattig received a medal from the Franklin Institute for his invention.[19]

The Jersey Central manifested its innovative spirit again in 1925 when it placed into operation the world's first diesel-electric locomotive. Number 1000, a switching engine, was built by Ingersoll-Rand at Phillipsburg, with major components from the American Locomotive and the General Electric Companies. This locomotive worked at the Central's New York City terminal in the Bronx where it remained in service until 1952. Then, after being used at Elizabethport for a time, the pioneer engine was donated to the Baltimore and Ohio Railroad Museum in Baltimore.[20]

During World War I, when the U.S. Railroad Administration managed the railroad industry, 22 New Jersey shortlines were absorbed by the Central Railroad of New Jersey. Three others were added to the family in 1930, and the CNJ was granted permission to abandon the Ogden Mine Railroad in 1935.[21]

## THE BLUE COMET, COACH TRAVEL AT ITS BEST

One chapter in the history of the Jersey Central that deserves a few words involves the *Blue Comet*. This was an assigned seat, deluxe coach train designed to attract shore-bound passengers from the railroad's competitors—perhaps as a last-ditch effort. The CNJ had been involved since 1889 in the Atlantic City trade. Their trains brought vacationers and excursionists to shore resort towns like Ocean Grove, whose auditorium featured attractions such as Helen Keller, evangelist Billy Sunday, and Irish tenor John McCormack. In May 1900, the CNJ, in cooperation with the Reading road, began running the "Lakewood–Atlantic City Special," an offering that was later matched by what was, arguably, the Jersey Central's most serious competitor, the *Nellie Bly*, a flyer operated by the Pennsylvania Railroad. This train, unnamed at first, was christened after a small girl, fascinated by her journey on the train, remarked to

the conductor, "This is much like Nellie Bly and her trip around the world." The comment, referring to a famous and crusading reporter for the *New York World* whose real name was Elizabeth Jane Cochran, was passed along to management.[22]

Replacing mixed coach and Pullman parlor car service, the no extra fare *Blue Comet* began operating in February 1929 with two trains daily, and it consisted of all-steel, roller-bearing-equipped cars. The exteriors of the baggage car, combination smoking car, three coaches, and an observation car were painted Packard blue with cream trim and gold lettering. A dining car, which was a remodeled wooden car with steel sheathing, was attached to the trains that traveled during the lunch period and at dinnertime, and its specialty was the Blue Comet Special Plate Dinner, a bargain at 75 cents. Ruth May Etheridge, whose father was a CNJ station agent, recalled receiving "a special treat from my Dad, when I was a teenager in the mid-1930s. He arranged for his twin sister, my Aunt Maymie, and me to take a free ride on the *Blue Comet* from Hammonton to Jersey City. . . . We had dinner on the *Blue Comet* and I remember that all the table cloths and the napkins were the same beautiful combination of colors as the *Blue Comet* cars."

Instead of the usual "Central Railroad of New Jersey" letterboard, the cars were identified as "The Blue Comet," and each car bore the name of a comet. All in all, the train was first-class, from its well-upholstered, mohair-covered reclining seats in the coaches and reed-covered armchairs in the observation car to its blue carpeted aisles. The company went all-out to promote it. The locomotives were fitted with distinctive whistles, and its schedule was posted at highway crossings so that viewers could time their arrival to catch a glimpse of the train as it sped by. Timetables that carried the Comet's schedule had a representation of a comet sailing through the sky in the time spaces left empty on the card at the stations bypassed by the train from Lakehurst to Winslow Junction. To heighten interest and awareness even further, the railroad engaged Mrs. Keith Miller, a famous aviatrix, to race the *Blue Comet* in an airplane. Miller lost the race, but was rewarded for her effort with a ride in the cab. On the anniversary dates of the beginning of *Blue Comet* service, a special birthday celebration was held at Jersey City. Patrons partook of servings of a blue-and-white frosted birthday cake. "The Sea-

Figure 17. The *Blue Comet* at Atlantic City on 17 July 1938. Even in this black-and-white photo, the distinctive paint scheme, Packard blue and cream with gold lettering, can be visualized. The powerful Pacific type engine that was a trademark of the *Blue Comet* is not at the head end at this time. Number 594's sister, another Camelback locomotive numbered 592, also hauled the *Blue Comet*. Number 592 was given to the B&O Railroad Museum at Baltimore. Robert L. Long Collection.

shore's Finest Train," as it was billed, was also represented as a tinplate model train made by the Lionel Corporation in 1930.[23]

Jerseyans along the route adopted the train as their own. As it raced through the Pine Barrens, train crews would toss their newspapers to some of the locals who lived in remote areas far from a newsstand. In a reciprocal gesture, those same crews often found buckets of blueberries awaiting them at Lakewood, a gift from the natives. Unfortunately, the *Blue Comet* had the misfortune to have been born just a few months before the start of the Great Depression. That economic disaster treated the railroads harshly, and the Jersey Central was no exception. In fact, because it lacked an extensive long-distance passenger business and its short haul run customers, both commuters and seashore pleasure seekers, suffered precipitous declines, its situation was more serious than many other roads. The *Blue Comet* was especially hard hit by the drop in seashore visitors and by competition from buses. Ridership declined from

over 62,000 in 1929 to 17,351 in 1933 and then to a low of 13,668 in 1939. In 1934, service was reduced to a single round-trip daily; off-season loading was rarely more than a dozen travelers. Despite its problems with its money-making capability, the train was retained for its publicity value. Further reductions in service were made, including the replacement of the powerful Pacific-type locomotives that were used since inception; the Pacifics were needed elsewhere.

The year 1939 was notable for the opening of a world's fair in New York City (and for the beginning of World War II). CNJ management attempted to capitalize on the fair by offering excursions to fair tourists to the Jersey shore. In August, the *Comet* derailed at Chatsworth because the rails had been washed out by torrential rains. No longer luxurious or color-coordinated, the train was splayed along the right-of-way. Thirty-eight people were injured, some seriously. Most of the injured passengers had been riding in the observation car and were struck by the loose wicker chairs, which flew in all directions. The dining car was badly damaged and was withdrawn from service. Cafe cars from an equipment pool replaced the damaged car.

Finally, on 28 September 1941, the CNJ was allowed to retire the train, and the *Blue Comet* made its last trip. This occasion also marked the end of passenger service on the Southern Division. Over the 12 years of its existence, the *Blue Comet* carried over 1,680,000 passengers. Her old rival, the *Nellie Bly*, survived for another two decades as "a near deserted dowager." Waltzer mentions that, as of 2001, two *Blue Comet* cars, stripped of their seats and interior fixtures, remained at Winslow Junction. A restored *Blue Comet* observation car attached to a restaurant at Clinton serves as a dining area, and another *Blue Comet* observation car is now in the possession of the Cape May Seashore Lines. Although the train is long gone, its memory lives on in a poem by Margaret Smith whose opening stanza reads:

> Throaty and clear through the silent night
> Echoes her clarion call
> A flash of blue
> with a creamy hue
> The "Glorious Queen" of them all.[24]

The Jersey Central itself survived for three and a half decades after its crack train was retired. Its story during those remaining years was not much different from many other railroads: heavy traffic during the war years and then a painful decline. Its commuter traffic, however, continued both on the main line and along the coast. Arguably, the most significant incident during the declining years of the railroad was a disastrous accident that occurred along the bridge from Elizabethport. The original trestle had been rebuilt in 1927, and a modern lift bridge was installed to accommodate marine traffic. On 15 September 1958, a commuter train plunged through the open draw into the waters of Newark Bay. Early reports feared that as many as 40 people had died in the wreck; by the following day, 27 bodies had been recovered. After the CNJ was melded into Con-

rail in 1976, government-funded rail service over the bridge between Cranford and Bayonne continued for two more years. Then, because the lift spans posed an obstacle to navigation, they were blown up and removed in 1980; today there is little evidence of the bridge.[25]

The Central entered bankruptcy in March 1967 and remained there until September 1979, emerging as Central Jersey Industries, Inc. Its new mission was not railroading, because it had divested itself of almost all of the tracks it had owned. In 1986 it reorganized as CJI Industries, Inc., and then was subsumed into the Pechiney Corporation in January 1989. From that time, all evidence of the Central Railroad of New Jersey disappeared.[26]

Many artifacts of the Jersey Central remain. Rights-of-way are still being used by NJ Transit and by ConRail Shared Assets. There are several interlocking towers still standing, and many bridges and stations are still in use, although several of the latter serve dual railroad and commercial purposes or commercial uses only. The slogan that the Jersey Central adopted in 1947, "The BIG Little Railroad," was apt. It signified a railroad that was big enough to handle any job that came its way while small enough to offer personalized service. The poem praising the road's glories that was published in 1906 in the *Suburbanite*, the company magazine, says it all:

> J is for Jersey, through which the trains go,
> E is for Equipment, the finest we know;
> R is for Roadbed, firm rock ballast in it,
> S for the Schedule that's kept to the minute;
> E stands again for the traveler's Ease,
> Y for the uniformed Yeomen who please.
>
> C means Convenience and Comfort and Care,
> E the Electric co-partner with air;
> N is for National, the scope of its fame,
> T indicates Trust, 'mong all hands the same;
> R is for Rolling Stock, staunch, safe and sound,
> A is the Agent who books where you're bound,
> L Locomotive, for speed it is crowned.[27]

# 10 The PJ&B, a Really Short Shortline (1865–Present)

After the Camden and Amboy Railroad (C&A) relocated its main line from the town of Princeton to a more direct route that bypassed the town, it provided shuttle rail service from the new station at Princeton Junction. The relocation was planned during the Civil War, when it became obvious that the winding single-track main line, which followed the Delaware and Raritan Canal (D&R) from Trenton to Kingston, was inadequate to handle the wartime traffic demands and to utilize the faster, more powerful locomotives and trains that were coming into service. The shuttle service was a necessity because there was no other convenient way to bring passengers and freight into Princeton. In response to complaints from Princetonians, the C&A management built the Princeton Branch. The line was 3.2 miles long, but the Princeton depot was moved and rebuilt four times, each move bringing the station closer to the main line. It ended up as a branch 2.7 miles long. At this length, it was distinguished by providing the shortest scheduled rail service in the country. Its "Princeton-town" patrons sometimes refer to the road as the PJ&B (Princeton Junction and Back), and its self-propelled rail car is generally and affectionately known as the "Dinky." The shuttle service still operates (under New Jersey Transit auspices), but it is threatened with replacement by a bus shuttle. Also, as discussed in the last paragraph, it appears that the PJ&B will again face truncation.[1]

When the Princeton Branch opened in May 1865, its motive power was a 4-4-0 American type locomotive, attended by the distinctive C&A tender, which was an enclosed car with a lookout cabin, known as

a "gig," at its rear end. Wood for fuel was carried in the tender, and makeup water for the boiler was contained in barrels mounted on a flat car following the tender. A lone passenger car included both side and end doors for the convenience of passengers alighting at the high station platform at Princeton Junction. Since there were no steps below the side doors, they could not be used at the Princeton end of the run. Figure 18 shows the train at Bear Swamp (Princeton Junction); the gantry-type turntable was used to turn the engine around for its return trip, although if time was limited, the engineer often chose simply to run the engine in reverse on its next shuttle trip. A turntable was also installed at Princeton. The train took 20 minutes to run between the two depots, and it made 12 round trips daily. A rule was established that a brakeman on foot must precede the train across the canal bridge.[2]

The wooden station at Princeton on Railroad Avenue (now named University Place) was of the type known as a "railroad barn." This structure permitted an entire train to enter the building through doors at its end. A waiting room and a freight and baggage room were attached to the main building. Following a prevalent railroad practice, a bell to announce departures was mounted on the roof of the station. A more durable masonry station was built around 1873 with a separate freight station nearby. Carriages and wagons could enter a courtyard via an opening between the two buildings, and a road led from the yard to University Place. About 1890, the road moved the station a short distance; the present-day building was constructed in 1920. In 1976, to present Princeton's

**Figure 18.** The Princeton Branch Line train at Bear Swamp, near Princeton Junction, circa 1870. A hand-powered turntable may be seen in the left foreground. From the collection of the Historical Society of Princeton.

best face during the national bicentennial year, the station was rehabilitated. The latest station was designed with high-level platforms that are at the same level as the waiting room and the street.[3]

In 1888, a monster blizzard with 60 mph winds hit the northeast and played havoc with all New Jersey railroads. Temperatures were below zero; 21 inches of snow fell, with drifts as high as 16 feet, and not a train moved in the state except over the Princeton Branch tracks. Service was maintained throughout the ordeal, and many passengers who had been stranded on the main line were shuttled into Princeton to be accommodated at local hotels and rooming houses. The main line was not cleared for operations for several days. In this emergency, the "little engine that could" did![4]

Princeton University students have contributed their share of anecdotal stories about the PJ&B. One incident involved three junior students who had attended the theater in Trenton one evening in 1876. Returning to Princeton Junction, they found that they had missed the last Dinky train to Princeton. Like many other late travelers, they began to walk into town. A short way into their hike they encountered a handcar on a siding and immediately appropriated

it to continue their journey in relative comfort. They were soon speeding along the track "in high glee" until one of the students remembered that the drawbridge over the Delaware and Raritan Canal was usually left open at night after train service was shut down. Just in time, he shouted for the others to leap from the speeding handcar which, an instant later, tumbled into the dark waters of the canal. The boys then continued their journey into "Princeton town" by "shank's mare" and agreed not to mention the adventure to anyone. Surprisingly, they saw and heard no references to the missing handcar in the next few days or, indeed, over the next 30 years. However, it was a story too good to keep secret forever, and when one of the participants in the escapade returned to Princeton for a reunion in 1907, he disclosed the particulars of the episode to his sister, Louisa Potter Strong. He then commented that "a large derrick would be required to lift that hand car to the surface from the bottom of the canal, so no doubt that car rests on the bottom of the Raritan canal to this day!"[5]

A more sinister walk over part of the same route was taken by Solomon Krauskopf on 10 March 1874. Krauskopf, "a peddler of dry goods and notions," traveled to Trenton that morning to collect on some accounts that were due. Returning to Princeton Junction on the 8 PM train from Trenton, he fell asleep and missed the stop. He detrained at New Brunswick and was given a pass to return to Princeton. Krauskopf took the train, which had left New York at midnight, and arrived back at the Junction at about 2:30 AM. By this time, the last Dinky of the evening had departed, and the salesman began the three-mile walk into town. On Wednesday morning his body was discovered by the bridge-tender's son at Stony Brook, near the canal crossing. "[Justice] Mount immediately summoned a jury of twelve men, who proceeded to the spot, and viewed the body as it lay. It was then removed to the Mansion house, in town, and the inquest sat." Krauskopf obviously had been murdered, shot in the chest at close range. It was established that he had left Princeton with about $175, but, when found, his wallet was empty. A money clip, overlooked by the murderer, held $12 in cash. Although the coroner's jury held a thorough hearing, eliciting testimony from numerous individuals who had seen the victim earlier, there was no evidence pointing to a possible perpetrator of the crime. Krauskopf's murder was never solved.[6]

In a lighter vein, George "Buster" Dey, a veteran conductor on the Dinky, related the following tale to the author many years ago. On a run from the Junction in 1963, the Dinky was held up by the "Princeton Gang." This was before Princeton University had become coed. It was a common practice for girlfriends of the students to take the train into town to attend football games and other functions at the school; sometimes as many as 400 girls would arrive on a prom weekend. On the day of the holdup in 1963, the train was halted by a car positioned on the tracks. Immediately, four masked students rode up on horseback and "kidnapped" four girls. According to one of the participants, "We had hats and bandannas and rented horses. I had a .38 pistol loaded with blanks. When the train came along, we galloped down and the conductor screeched it to a stop. We all climbed on and I fired off a couple of shots . . . it was very loud . . . and everybody was yelling and had their hands up and all the businessmen were throwing their wallets at us. We didn't have dates on the train. We just picked the four girls we thought were most likely to play along and told them what was going on. We all took off through the woods."[7]

Dey often helped his passengers above and beyond the call of duty. He told of noticing a dejected young lady who had arrived via his train for a party weekend featuring a dance. When asked, she told him that her luggage had been misrouted by the airline into New York, and she had nothing suitable to wear to the dance. Dey was up to the challenge. He sat the girl down in the station and told her to wait until he returned from his next run, when he expected one of his regular Princeton passengers, another young lady who might be able to loan her a dress. Sure enough, the regular was on her usual train, introductions were made, and the two women left together. Some time later, Dey learned that not only had the young woman enjoyed the dance but she had also become engaged to marry the brother of the good Samaritan who had lent her a dress.[8]

The Pennsylvania Railroad became aware of the potential danger of moving many special trains into Princeton for football games. In 1900, the PRR added three tracks to facilitate the unloading, temporary storage, and reloading of football specials on game days. (The 1904 Princeton-Yale game brought 30,582 passengers on 42 special trains.) Plans were made to enlarge the university's stadium to hold as many as 28,000 fans, and the branch line simply was not able to handle the traffic. On 18 December 1902, F. L. Sheppard, general superintendent of the Pennsylvania Railroad, wrote to F. H. Earle, a principal in a civil engineering firm that worked for the road.

> We have some very influential friends at Princeton, N. J., about equally divided in interests between New York and Philadelphia.
>
> They are as much impressed as we are with the dangerous character of our train service whenever there is a football crowd, &c., which sometimes amounts to eighteen or twenty special trains.
>
> They have got to the point where they have some assurance from our people in Philadelphia that, if I present a reasonable scheme for improving the Branch, including a double track, it will be given favorable consideration.

Sheppard asked Mr. Earle to "put this under your pillow some night, and see if anything feasible occurs to you."

On 11 February 1903, Earle responded with a proposal that would require a "change of alignment" and regrading leading to 24 tracks at the Princeton end. He included a turntable and a switching track

Figure 19. The "Dinky" leaving Princeton on 2 October 2006 for its short run to Princeton Junction. Author's photograph.

as well as double-tracking. Earle estimated that this project could be accomplished for less than $300,000, if "five deck spans of the old bridge from the Raritan at New Brunswick" could be made available. The old bridge spans were to be used to build a high bridge over the D&R Canal (51 feet of clearance above the water level) to eliminate the need for a drawbridge. A revised estimate on 14 February considered the possibility of electrifying the line. According to Sheppard,

> The attendance at these Games has been largely made up of young people, to whom excessive crowding and delays were accepted as part of the frolic. . . . The Army and Navy Games are attended by an older and more dignified class of people, who require Pullman accommodations, Dining Cars, &c., in addition to the Special Trains for the President of the United States and other public officials.

Sheppard then forwarded this information on 16 February to W. W. Atterbury, general manager, for consideration. Upgrading the line by adding an additional track and mitigating some of the worst grades and curves and building the 24-track yard to accommodate special trains was completed in 1905, and Sheppard's Princeton Branch could now serve the more mature and distinguished group of football fans. As it developed, at such times the shuttle train between the main line and the coaching yard at Princeton consisted of several cars, perhaps as many as nine. Incidentally, the high bridge was not included in the execution of the project; instead, a new drawbridge was added with 12 feet of clearance at "full head" in the canal.[9]

Palmer Stadium was built in 1914 (and rebuilt a few years ago) with a stated capacity of 41,000 persons; 10 years later, it had been enlarged to hold 56,000. At first, football games were well attended, but by the 1970s attendance by enthusiasts arriving by rail had dropped drastically, a casualty of the automobile and a greater interest in professional football. The railroad facilities were correspondingly reduced, inevitable in those days of serious railroad financial problems, until there is now little, if any,

railroad presence involving the transportation of football fans.[10]

Woodrow Wilson, who had been president of Princeton University and governor of New Jersey, was elected president of the United States in 1912. On 3 March 1913, he walked from his home to the Dinky station to board a special train to Washington for his inauguration. Although he had made the walk alone many times before, on this jaunt he was accompanied by a brass band and many well-wishers. Thirty-five years later, T. S. Eliot set off from the Princeton shuttle depot to receive the Nobel Prize in Literature in Stockholm.[11]

The Princeton Branch employed steam locomotives from the time of its inception until gas/electric cars replaced them in 1933. A test of a rubber-tired gas/electric was conducted on the branch line in 1934. Riding qualities were superior, but it could not climb some of the grades on the line. In 1936, the PJ&B was electrified, and Pennsylvania Railroad multiple-unit (MU) cars were run in tandem. In 1976, Conrail introduced stainless steel "Jersey Arrow" cars, which

Figure 20. Mile marker erected in the nineteenth century still stands on the Princeton University campus. It indicates the distance to Princeton (0 miles) and to Princeton Junction (3 miles). Author's photograph, October 2006.

were run individually. Occasionally, a second car would be added to make up a train.[12]

A notice (undated, but probably 1969) of a public meeting to protest possible abandonment of the Dinky is contained in the files of the Princeton Historical Society. It mentions that the Penn Central (PC) proposed abandoning Princeton Branch rail service because freight usage had fallen to practically zero since the Princeton University's power plant no longer used coal. More significant, however, was the fact that commutation traffic was reduced to only 200 daily riders. There was probably sufficient merit to the PC's arguments, but unwritten was the fact that many influential individuals had ridden the Dinky on a regular basis, including Albert Einstein, John Maynard Keynes, Toni Morrison, Brooke Shields, Paul Robeson, John Nash, Mikhail Baryshnikov, James Stewart, Nicholas Katzenbach, Peter Benchley, John McPhee, and F. Scott Fitzgerald. Their interests have trumped the several attempts to eliminate the service. In the year 2000, the Dinky made 39 trips and carried 838 passengers per day on average.[13]

Still remaining on the campus of Princeton University (on the side of Little Hall that faces University Place) is a triangular, cast-iron mile marker that indicated an earlier terminus of the branch. The three-foot-high marker reads "0" on one side and "3" on the other. These markings represent the number of miles to Princeton and the number of miles to Princeton Junction, respectively. As of this writing, a proposal has been made by Princeton University to reroute University Place so that it would circle around behind the Dinky station. This would allow the university to consolidate some arts facilities into a planned "arts village" surrounding McCarter Theater. The plan envisions that the Dinky tracks would terminate at a new station situated 460 feet south of the current station. The latter would be renovated and converted for retail use. If it comes to pass, this latest plan would bring the Princeton depot still closer to the main line.[14]

# 11 The Rascals at Bay in "Fort Taylor" (1868)

Daniel Drew, Jim Fisk, and Jay Gould were three of the legendary names associated with railroad financing in the late nineteenth century. Although they were not New Jersey natives, they earned a place in this book because of their manipulation of the stock of the Erie Railway, their retreat from New York City to New Jersey to avoid arrest, and their later associations with the Garden State. Theirs was a marriage of convenience. In Drew's words, Gould was "quiet as a clam; and Fisk, the devil's own. But both of them were handy in a stock-market dicker; and that was what I needed just now. The Erie war was rapidly coming on. I had to have partners that could help."[1]

Daniel Drew, born in New York State and the "old man" of the group, had enlisted in the Army in the war of 1812. Demobilized and using his enlistment bonus, he purchased a herd of cattle and drove them to market in New York City. He progressed to ownership of a tavern, then became a steamboat operator on the Hudson River. Drew's objective was to get "bought out" by the largest steamboat company on the river. He was simply following in the footsteps of another shrewd, ruthless operator, Cornelius "Commodore" Vanderbilt, who began a price war that resulted in his being paid off in return for leaving the steamboat field for 10 years. His interest, like Vanderbilt's, turned to railroads, and Drew eventually became treasurer of the ailing Erie Railway.[2] Adams and Adams found Drew to be "shrewd, unscrupulous, and very illiterate,—a strange combination of superstition and faithlessness, of daring and timidity,—often good-natured and sometimes generous,—he ever regarded his fiduciary position of

director in a railroad as a means for manipulating its stock for his own advantage."[3]

Jim Fisk was a Vermonter who had a checkered career that included stints as a waiter and circus barker. He was a flamboyant character who wound up working for Daniel Drew as a steamboat salesman. Drew supported him in his establishment of a brokerage firm, and Fisk became a director of the Erie Railway. Jay Gould, born in Roxbury, New York, received a spotty education yet was adept at business. He began to speculate in railroad stocks and bonds, and in 1867, when he was 32, he was appointed to a seat on the Erie's board of directors.[4]

The three, later known as the "Erie Ring," were implicated in 1868 in one of the most shameful incidents in a long history of railroad financial manipulations involving control of the Erie Railway. It was expressed concisely in a few lines written about Daniel Drew by the Benéts:

> With sleek Jay Gould and blithe Jim Fisk,
> Made other people's money fly
> And sucked the Erie Railroad dry.
> They foiled the law, they bribed the courts,
> They watered stock, they squeezed the shorts.[5]

As a consequence of the construction of the transcontinental railroad, it appeared that most eastern railroad traffic would pass through Chicago on its journey to Omaha, Nebraska, the eastern terminus of the Union Pacific Railroad. The Erie had made arrangements with midwestern roads that reached the Mississippi River, but through Cincinnati, not Chicago. Vanderbilt controlled the New York Central and

**Figure 21.** This oil painting of Daniel Drew hangs in Mead Hall on the campus of Drew University in Madison, N.J. Author's photograph, winter 2006.

Hudson River Railroad, a rival to the Erie but one with connections to Chicago. Vanderbilt feared that the Erie management would challenge the Central's commanding position, and he decided to buy sufficient Erie stock on the open market to control the company and replace its directors with ones favorable to him and the Central. Furthermore, if the Erie could be added to his New York holdings, he would have a virtual monopoly of New York State railroads. According to the *New York Times,* "This effort, it is charged, was met by Mr. Drew and his friends by the creation of such new stock, poured upon the market as from a never-failing fountain, and was taken up in large quantities." Vanderbilt soon discovered that the amount of stock in circulation was beyond belief, and even as he purchased large blocks, more and more became available. The explanation was simple: Gould and Fisk, allied with Daniel Drew, opposed Vanderbilt's move. Essentially governing the issuance of Erie stock, they just kept printing new shares until finally Vanderbilt realized that he was being "hornswoggled." The effect of the distribution of the additional stock was to drive down the price of all Erie stock, in essence leaving a large stockholder like Vanderbilt with securities that became less and less valuable while making his goal of control more and more distant.

The scheme was vintage Drew. He had a reputation for "stock watering," a term that was derived from his days as a drover when he would water his cattle just before they were weighed to fix their value. Although the General Railroad Act of New York permitted railroads to "borrow such sums of money as may be necessary for completing or furnishing their Railroad, and to issue and dispose of their bonds for any amount so borrowed . . . and the directors . . . may confer on any [bondholder] . . . the right to convert the principal due into stock," it was obvious that the issuance of large blocks of additional stock at this time was not supported by a necessity for additional funds. Thus Vanderbilt (or perhaps in this instance, *Vanderbilked*) questioned the legality of the action.[6]

The Commodore was not about to allow this outrage to be perpetrated upon him. He sought redress in the law and had his "pet judge," according to the Drew faction, issue orders restraining Drew and company from issuing more stock and order Drew's removal as the Erie's treasurer. Drew ignored the injunction and dispatched attorneys to Cortland, New York, where they found a more sympathetic judge from another district who stayed the original judicial order. The skirmishing continued into March, until finally arrest warrants for contempt were drawn up against the infamous trio. News of the warrants reached the Erie offices.

> At ten o'clock the astonished police saw a throng of panic-stricken railway directors—looking more like a frightened gang of thieves disturbed in the division of their plunder, than like the wealthy representatives of a great corporation—rush headlong from the doors of the Erie office, and dash off in the direction of the Jersey ferry. One individual bore away with him in a hackney-coach bales containing six millions of dollars in greenbacks.[7]

At first the policemen believed that a crime was in progress, but they soon realized it was the Erie directorate, fleeing with the proceeds of the stock sales and many of the financial records.[8] According to one stanza of a contemporary poem:

> Fleeing from jars—perhaps the jug—
> Dan looked to foreign lands,
> And to his brethren said, "Arise!
> These Bonds put off our hands;
> We will unto New Jersey, where
> My Seminary stands.[9]

Meanwhile, upon hearing that they were being sought, Drew departed New York City by ferryboat, but Gould and Fisk decided to enjoy one last dinner at Delmonico's. These two were advised during dinner that arrest was imminent, and they fled the restaurant on foot. At the Hudson River, they arranged for a boat to take them to New Jersey, and they had several close calls, nearly colliding with other vessels. Finally, they caught the paddle-wheel housing of a Pavonia (Erie Railroad) ferryboat and were hauled aboard, wet and bedraggled. Arriving at Jersey City, they and Drew established a new base at the waterfront Taylor Hotel. All told, about 50 Erie officers and employees decamped to Jersey City. An affidavit presented to the judge in New York represented these men as "disorderly characters, commonly known as 'roughs.'"

At Taylor's Hotel, the fugitives settled in for a long siege because they could not return to New York until Vanderbilt's wrath was appeased. They lived as though they had not a care in the world, and Fisk went so far as to ensconce his mistress, Josie Mansfield, in a suite in the building. Their defense was organized along military lines, with Drew becoming responsible for the land contingent and Fisk the naval element. (At this point in time, Fisk did not yet control the Narragansett Steamship Company, more commonly known as the Fall River Line, but he had inclinations to be remembered as a military man. Once in control of the steamship line in 1869, Fisk often affected the role of "admiral," strutting around in a custom-made imitation of a U.S. Navy admiral's uniform.) At Taylor's Hotel, "a standing army was organized from the employees of the road, and a small navy equipped. The alarm spread through Jersey City; the militia was held in readiness; in the evening the stores were closed and the citizens began to arm; while a garrison of about one hundred and twenty-five men intrenched themselves around the directors, in their hotel ."

The hotel was dubbed "Fort Taylor" and, incredibly, Fisk arranged to have three cannons set up to guard the approaches to the structure. Fifteen Jersey City policemen were assigned by the friendly local politicos to patrol the immediate area, and Erie Railway policemen augmented that force. Fearing attack by men from New York determined to enforce the arrest warrants or by gangs of toughs who might be interested in liberating the large pile of greenbacks in their quarters, they arranged for small boats to patrol the waterfront and installed signaling systems to keep all the defenders informed. An article in the *New York Herald* rumored that "underneath the box containing the valuable deposits, including bonds, was placed a pan of nitro-glycerin, in order that if the brave directory should be stormed in the upper room of a Jersey hotel . . . the last survivor would devolve the fearful alternative of consigning his body and the treasure to a common perdition."[10]

President Andrew Johnson was battling impeachment proceedings in Washington. However, in the New York–New Jersey area, all attention was focused on the exploits of the Erie Ring. It was as though Johnson and his problems were a world apart. Crowds gathered at the Taylor Hotel, hoping to catch a glimpse of one of the scoundrels. It would appear that the incident had assumed ridiculous proportions when an organized force of 50 men arrived from New York to arrest Drew. The Erie Railway police inspector assured them that Drew was not at the depot where they landed and that any effort to take him by force at the hotel would result in a catastrophe. It was never determined who had sent this group. Was it Vanderbilt, who, it was rumored, had posted a $50,000 reward for Drew's capture? Or had they been acting on their own to collect the reward? More Machiavellian was the possibility that it was Fisk's doing in order to impress Drew with the seriousness of the situation and to prevent him from making a separate peace with Vanderbilt. This was a real possibility because Drew, chafing under the enforced exile, began to take advantage of the immunity from arrest provided on Sundays. He would spend the day in Manhattan, returning at nightfall to his refuge across the river. When he, the Erie's treasurer, began to move money back to New York banks, his companions denied him access to the treasury. The standoff at Fort Taylor continued throughout the month of March, but much transpired behind the scenes.[11]

**Figure 22.** The *Pavonia,* one of the Pavonia Ferry Company fleet. The fugitives, Fisk and Gould, almost drowned when the boat in which they were escaping arrest was nearly swamped by near-collisions with other craft in midriver. They were saved by grasping the paddlewheel housing of a Pavonia ferryboat (perhaps this one) and hauling themselves aboard. *New Jersey Transport Heritage,* February 2006.

One of the most shocking deeds was the action of the New Jersey legislature, which granted a state charter to the Erie Railroad after less than two hours of deliberation. The charter enabled the road to continue operations in New Jersey under a legal umbrella. Suits and countersuits were initiated. Vanderbilt charged that the stock watering constituted fraud and solely benefited Daniel Drew. Drew countercharged that Vanderbilt's stock purchases were "mere speculation" intended to obtain control of the road and that the judge who issued the arrest warrants "was acting in the interests of the speculation." Of course, both were right, but they begged the question. In the end, it was the Erie shareholders who were unrepresented and the big losers. The *New York Times* castigated Vanderbilt's actions:

> No complaint ought to be made of any litigation undertaken in the true interests of the Erie Railroad to protect its stockholders; but it is not supposed that any

of the suits now depending are of this character, or have any object whatever beyond the aid they afford in enabling the managers of a competing road to obtain control of the one which competes, and to make a speculation successful.

The newspaper was equally critical of Drew's position:

> It is thought also that the effort of those in possession of the Erie road to continue such possession has for its object to conduct speculations successfully, much more than to manage the Company with true regard to the interests of its stockholders and of the public.[12]

While they remained in Jersey City, the three rogues were safe from the arm of New York justice, but shortly, risking arrest, Gould made an end run back into New York at Albany. He carried with him a half million dollars in cash, which he intended to use to bribe New York legislators to enact a law that would legalize the questionable stock scheme and

**Figure 23.** Mead Hall is located on the campus of Drew University in Madison. A Greek Revival mansion, it was built by William Gibbons, the owner of The Forest, the estate that Daniel Drew purchased for the establishment of Drew Theological Seminary. Mead Hall is on the New Jersey Register of Historic Places. Author's photograph, winter 2006.

to press for legislation prohibiting the merger of the Erie and the Central. Although Gould was arrested at Albany and brought to New York City, he persuaded his guard, with the help of a couple of Tammany Hall thugs, to accompany him back to Albany, where he worked his "magic" with the money in his valise. He obviously greased the right palms, because one branch of the legislature did pass favorable laws, but to the bitter disappointment of many legislators, before the lower house acted, a settlement had been reached with the Commodore. Vanderbilt remarked that "he could easily enough buy up the Erie Railway, but he could not buy up the printing-press." The legislation that legitimized the Erie's actions and position was later compared "to a bill legalizing counterfeit money."[13]

Even before the settlement with Vanderbilt, Drew's associates came to distrust him. Afterwards, they realized, the settlement terms were Drew's, not theirs, and they believed that Drew acted only in his own interest. Still fearing arrest, they were not prepared to return to New York. Around 25 April, a "treaty" was effected that allowed them to cross the river in safety. By July, Fisk and Gould were in absolute control of the Erie Railway. Gould was appointed president, Fisk became vice president, and Drew was forced out. Also appointed to the Erie's board was William "Boss" Tweed, the infamous leader of Tammany Hall, a good ally to have when you are trying to promote an illicit scheme. Now, relieved of their immediate legal problem, the Erie Ring continued their financial depredations.

Later, Drew returned to the Erie Railway because "Erie was still a money-maker" and he wanted "another turn or two at the milking stool." Partnered with Fisk and Gould in another of their schemes, he then broke away and operated against them. He sold Erie short while the others were going long. Further market manipulations affected his fortune for better

and then for worse. When the Panic of 1873 struck, "Uncle Dan'l" was ruined, and he died, impoverished, in 1879. In the same year, Gould was driven from his officership at the Erie, having bankrupted it again.[14]

Daniel Drew was a devout Methodist, seemingly incompatible with his shady financial activities. However, it appears that he drew upon divine assistance to justify those schemes, a position which, in his mind, was fully acceptable. In any event, about the time that the Civil War ended, Drew was approached by two clerics who suggested the idea of establishing a great theological institute. According to Drew, "I was making money so fast I could afford to give some of it away," so "I answered right up: 'I am willing to donate two hundred and fifty thousand dollars for the endowment of a Theological Seminary." Told of a property for sale, "The Forest" at Madison, New Jersey, he purchased it as the site of the seminary. The Greek Revival mansion on the grounds was built in 1836 by the owner of the estate, William Gibbons, who, coincidentally, was also involved in the steamboat business on the Hudson River. The mansion remains in use by Drew University as Mead Hall. The theological institution was opened in November 1867. Although he had also intended to provide a monetary endowment, his stock market reverses left him penniless and unable to meet that commitment. However, Drew University prospered. The institution has been greatly enlarged with the addition of a liberal arts college, and Drew Theological Seminary continues to educate ministers.[15]

When Jay Gould died at 56, most of his $100 million fortune was inherited by his son, George. George discovered Lakewood, New Jersey, in the 1890s and built a mansion on 200 acres that he named Georgian Court. George Gould was more a playboy than a businessman. He indulged in short workdays, commuting to New York City via the Jersey Central, and enjoying golf and polo. He arranged "entertainments," one of which was a chess game where the pieces, children dressed in appropriate costumes, pawns, knights, king, and so forth, were assembled and moved on a huge board. Upon his death, Georgian Court and its extensive grounds were sold to the Sisters of Mercy, who relocated their College of Mount St. Mary to the site. One of the conditions of the sale was that the name of the school be changed to Georgian Court College. The institution still functions at this location.[16]

As for Fisk, he continued his profligate ways, often at the playground of the rich and famous: Long Branch, New Jersey. He established his headquarters at the Continental Hotel, which became notorious for the elaborate private parties that he sponsored. He was involved in helping the fledgling Monmouth Park racetrack become established by contributing to the stakes of races during the short initial season. Always a showman, he gloried in driving through the seaside resort in an enormous carriage pulled by six horses and attended by four coachmen. He arranged for a regiment of the New York State militia, in which he had purchased a leadership position as colonel, to conduct maneuvers at Long Branch, where they were reviewed by President Grant. In 1872, Fisk was murdered in New York City by a rival for the attentions of Miss Mansfield.[17]

# 12 Henry Drinker and the Musconetcong Tunnel (1872–75)

One of the remarkable achievements in the saga of early railroad construction in the western reaches of New Jersey was the tunneling of Musconetcong Mountain. The mountain, known locally as Jugtown Mountain, lies about 10 miles from Phillipsburg along the route that the Easton and Amboy Railroad (E&A), a subsidiary of the Lehigh Valley Railroad (LV), desired to press through the state. Ground was broken for the tunnel on 10 April 1872, at a time when new techniques were coming into use; dynamite had been invented in 1866, and pneumatic drills made their debut in the same year. Despite the introduction of new tools and methods, tunneling was still a laborious and dangerous task, highly dependent upon experience and skill. So, considering that the projected tunnel would be the longest in the eastern United States at the time and also that the Hoosac Tunnel in Massachusetts was already 18 years in the making (and would not be completed until 1876), it is surprising that the New Jersey venture would be entrusted to a young, recently graduated engineer.[1]

Henry Sturgis Drinker was awarded the degree of engineer of mines by Lehigh University in 1871, when he was 21. Upon graduating, he was employed by the Lehigh Valley Coal Company, and one year later, he was transferred to its parent company, the Lehigh Valley Railroad. Engaged by the road's engineering department, Drinker was assigned as resident engineer responsible for overseeing construction of the Musconetcong Tunnel.[2]

The Easton and Amboy Railroad was built for the express purpose of carrying Pennsylvania coal to tidewater at Perth Amboy. Most of the route was reasonably flat and posed few problems, but the Musconetcong Mountain ridge, a divide from which water falling on its west slope tumbles toward the Delaware River and east slope rainfall flows to Raritan Bay, is several miles long. Musconetcong Mountain, the highest point along the ridge at 955 feet above sea level, is located near Pattenburg, New Jersey, and was directly in the path of the right-of-way. It had to be bored for a length of 4,893 feet.[3]

The western approach to the tunnel was dug through soft earth, and 68 feet was left as open cut; the next 702 feet was arched to prevent collapse. This first 770 feet was the easy part. The project next encountered 460 feet of limestone and then 3,731 feet of granular, igneous rock. The latter, which continued to the eastern portal, required masonry arched supports for most of the distance where water infiltrated and affected the earth and rock in the tunnel. Timber supports had to be constructed first, then a masonry arch of bricks two feet thick, resting upon sandstone walls, was installed below the timber supports.

All in all, work proceeded favorably from the eastern heading for about a year. However, at 3 PM on 7 May 1873, a drill struck a pocket of water whose pressure was such that it unleashed a geyser that shot 50 feet into the heading! By 5 PM, the water was rising so fast in the tunnel that the two steam pumps in use were in danger of becoming submerged. Only one pump could be withdrawn in time. The second pump was covered by water. Without any pumping, the water, emanating from an underground lake, continued to rise in the downward-sloped heading and reached its maximum level on 9 May, 120 feet from the top of

**Figure 24.** Much of the Musconetcong Tunnel was required to be supported by timber and/or masonry arches because the rock through which it was bored was loose and frangible. A timber support structure (1) through (4) was built first, then sandstone walls were erected and a two-foot-thick brick arch was added above the walls. Drinker, *Tunneling, Explosive Compounds, and Rock Drills.*

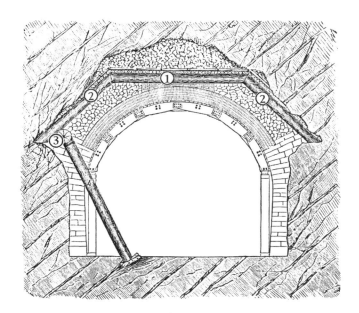

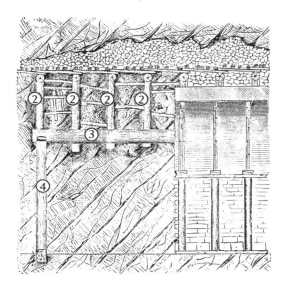

the slope. On 10 May, another pump was brought to the site, and the two available pumps began to work in tandem. The water had receded 40 feet by 15 May. Then, just when it appeared that the situation was under control, several sets of arches failed and, in a domino effect, caused others to break as well!

It was determined that all of the timber supports would have to be replaced, but the inflow of water prohibited working in the tunnel. Drinker's solution was to sink a shaft nearby. Once at the proper depth, headings were extended from the shaft to a low point in the tunnel from which point water could be channeled out to the open cut. While the shaft was being dug, work proceeded from the east, in a heading established from the east portal of the tunnel. At the time that the water entered the tunnel, the westward-driven heading was in limestone, some distance away from the flooded section. That heading, coming from the east, encountered no serious difficulties throughout the construction.

When work was resumed in the west heading, the rock was found to be so loose that drilling machines could not be applied due to the vibrations that they caused. New water springs were encountered as the digging advanced until hard rock was reached in May 1874. Some 1,725 feet of rock, which some experts said was the hardest rock "encountered in tunneling in our Eastern States," remained to be removed. Now Charles McFadden, the contractor for the tunnel, adopted Ingersoll drills driven by compressed air to drill powder holes. He also employed "giant powder," a name then applied to dynamite. First, the center of the face was blasted away to a depth of about 10 feet. Then three drills, mounted vertically on a carriage, were run over tracks to the face on each side of the center hole (in this manner six drills could work the face simultaneously). Holes in groups of three high were drilled approximately 10 foot deep at several positions along the sides of the face. Then the holes were filled with powder, and a blast was triggered by electricity. Since the center area was removed earlier,

a lesser blast than might otherwise be required was effective.

The tunnel was "holed through" in December 1874, after which the bore was enlarged. The tunnel was opened in June 1875, about a year late, by Drinker's own admission, due to the water problem. In truth, the entire Easton and Amboy Railroad was projected to be completed sometime in mid-1874. However, the cause of the road's delayed completion was not only the tunnel problem but also the effects of an economic downturn in 1873. The first E&A train left Phillipsburg on 28 May 1875 with 125 coal cars in tow. It negotiated the 11.5-mile upgrade to the tunnel and reached Perth Amboy 6.5 hours after leaving the Delaware River town. The official opening of the road to passenger and freight traffic came at the end of June.[4]

All materials for digging the tunnel were carried in over the tracks of the Central Railroad of New Jersey. At the west end it was necessary to move about 1,000 tons of coal alone by horse-drawn wagons from the Central's tracks to the tunnel workings keeping "some twenty-four four-horse teams in constant employment." About 85 tons of dynamite were expended to blast 82,000 cubic feet of rock; in addition, black powder was used before the dynamite was applied.[5]

Drinker had his hands full keeping his men and alcohol separated so that the job could continue smoothly.

> The experience at Musconetcong paralleled that on most public works in the obstacles encountered by every contractor—namely, the swarm of liquor-shanties, which, if not soon checked with a stern hand, will every month throw the work almost idle for a week following pay-day. New Jersey law, being proverbially infallible, might have been expected to be sufficient to stop peremptorily a large unlicensed sale of liquor; but though her laws may ordinarily do for the home-rule of the simple and peace-loving aborigines, it was found necessary, on the introduction of a more active community, to pass some special provisions for their benefit; among these laws was one rendering the sale of liquor, in quantities under five gallons at a time, within three miles of either extremity of the Musconetcong Tunnel, a crime punishable with a year's imprisonment. . . . Under this law, several convictions being at once secured, the nuisance was effectually abated for the time that the men were most needed.[6]

The tunnel workers came from different cultures, and racial overtones were injected into their efforts because many were newly landed European immigrants and others were native-born African Americans. The work was arduous, and the laborers were often exhausted, precipitating quarrels and disagreements among the crews. Violence erupted between the groups in November of the first year of construction, and in the ensuing conflict five workers died and many more were injured.[7]

One measure of Drinker's and McFadden's competence in tunnel building is the fact that, when it was "holed through," the headings and the grade mated within one-half inch. But probably Drinker's fame and reputation were enhanced more by his authoritative book, *Tunneling, Explosive Compounds, and*

*Rock Drills.* This 1,200-page volume was published in 1878 when its author was only 28 years old. It was the first comprehensive treatise on tunneling, and it remained the "bible" for many years. The work was all the more extraordinary for having been written while he was studying law; he was admitted to the bar before the book's publication.

Drinker's later professional life centered about the legal profession, but he took advantage of his earlier experience by practicing railroad and corporation law, first privately and then with the Lehigh Valley Railroad. He became the assistant to the president of the LV and then of the Philadelphia and Reading Railroad when it leased the Lehigh Valley. He had many other active interests and served as president of Lehigh University from 1905 to 1921, the only alumnus ever to assume that position. He died in 1937.[8]

The Lehigh Valley Railroad built Bellewood Park east of the Musconetcong Tunnel as an excursion destination and opened it for business on 4 July 1904. Day-trippers from nearby cities in Pennsylvania (Allentown, Bethlehem, and Easton) and from New York City, a two-hour train ride away, rode special excursion trains during the summer months to enjoy the attractions, including a roller coaster, a Ferris wheel, and a carousel. The park was closed at the end of the summer of 1916 and never reopened. According to one gentleman who had walked through the park many times as a boy, there are no longer any remains of the park. He recalled seeing the foundations of the many buildings, including "a round circle where the merry-go-round once was and the spring [was] still running . . . where once a footbridge crossed it.[9]

The old Musconetcong Tunnel was known by several names, including the Pattenburg Tunnel (for the nearby town) and the Bellewood Tunnel (for the amusement park). It was abandoned and replaced by another bore through the ridge that was built by the Lehigh Valley Railroad and opened in November 1928. Currently used by the Norfolk Southern Railroad, the *new* tunnel, originally accommodating two tracks, was reduced to one track in 1999 in order to allow large stack trains to use it. Abandoned though it is (although it may still be used to house track construction and maintenance vehicles), the old tunnel is still evident to a determined hiker, and travelers along Interstate Highway 78 might notice an exit sign reading "West Portal," an indication of the nearby tunnel.[10]

# 13 The Railroad King of Blairstown (1876)

John Insley Blair was born near Foul Rift north of Belvidere, New Jersey, in 1802 and became an entrepreneur at an early age: when he was 10 years old he earned money trapping muskrats and rabbits and selling their skins. Despite a minimum of formal education (he left school at the age of 11 and went to work for an uncle in a general store in Hope), Blair proved to be adept at business. By the time he was 19, he had established a general store at Gravel Hill (formerly named Butt's Bridge), and within two years he had bought out his partner. That store and others that he organized served to launch an impressive career. The enterprises in which he had an interest included mills and factories, a foundry, a bank, and railroads. When he was 37, Gravel Hill changed its name to Blairstown in his honor.[1]

Blair's railroad career began when, in partnership with a number of other prominent organizers, including the Scranton brothers from Pennsylvania, he built and consolidated the Legget's Gap Railroad and the Delaware and Cobb's Gap Railroad, both Pennsylvania railroads, to form the nucleus of the Delaware, Lackawanna and Western Railroad (DL&W). The DL&W was created to capture the lucrative Pennsylvania coal field traffic, a prize that was also coveted by the Morris and Essex Railroad (M&E). Blair and William E. Dodge undertook the construction of the Warren Railroad, which served as a connector between the DL&W on the Pennsylvania side of the Delaware Water Gap and the Central Railroad of New Jersey (CNJ) at Hampton, 19 miles away. This route encountered formidable mountains,

which necessitated digging two tunnels and erecting two major bridges. His partners in this undertaking, the DL&W and the CNJ, became concerned about the overruns in time and money and demanded that a temporary track be built so that revenue could begin to flow immediately. The first train was dispatched from Elizabeth on 27 May 1856 with great fanfare and reached the hurriedly built tracks of the Warren Railroad. The ladies from Washington, New Jersey, those "most select specimens of Jersey beauty," provided refreshments during a short stop before the train continued on to Scranton.[2]

A testament to Blair's managerial ability was provided by the fact that the entire business of founding the Warren Railroad—establishing subscription books, choosing directors and officers, adopting the survey route, and authorizing the president, Blair, to make a filing with the secretary of state—was accomplished in two hours! Of further note is Blair's single-minded follow-up. Two days later he was in Trenton, where he made the requisite filing about an hour before the agent of the M&E. The following day found him back in Warren County to stake a claim to the necessary mountain passes south of the Delaware Water Gap. The M&E interests meanwhile had arranged for rights to various passes north of the Gap and "paid exorbitant prices for farms, right of way, and two river crossings." Blair arranged to have the DL&W meet his Warren Railroad where it crossed the Delaware several miles south of the Gap, leaving his competitor with expensive real estate that became useless. An ensuing lawsuit over the Warren

Railroad's use of Van Ness Gap was settled in Blair's favor. By 1871, John Blair was the president of the 35-mile-long Sussex Railroad Company.[3]

Blair retired from his general store at the age of 57, and in 1860 he traveled by rail to the Republican National Convention at Chicago and then on to Iowa, where the rails ended. After the Civil War ended, convinced that a fortune awaited in the West, he participated in the surveying and building of the first railroad across the state of Iowa, a railroad that later was melded into the Union Pacific Railroad. His holdings in numerous western railroads led to his being known as the "Railroad King of the West." At one time or another, John I. Blair, the self-made man, had an interest in, or control of, more than 60 railroads and was president of 16. He was worth more than $60 million.[4]

In 1876, the Blairstown citizenry were interested in providing their town with a rail link to the nearby (11.3 miles away) Warren Railroad at Delaware, New Jersey, which by now was part of the DL&W. A committee was constituted with Blair as a prominent member. Reprising his efforts with the Warren Railroad, he immediately set about to acquire land. However, he found the local farmers to be recalcitrant, demanding excessive sums for their land. Blair managed to cobble together the needed property (even donating some of it himself), and ground was broken for the new railroad on 4 July. By May 1877, the railroad was finished and trial runs were made. The first regular trip was made on 4 July 1877 with a train was pulled by the locomotive *Blairstown,* a 16-ton woodburner built by the Danforth Locomotive Works. The riders on the inaugural day enjoyed free transportation and the stirring music of the Mount Herman Cornet Band. The occasion was to be memorialized by an address praising the town's major benefactor, J. I. Blair, but the speech was never delivered because its subject was a no-show that day. The great man did appear at the evening dinner held at the Methodist Church where he described the construction of the road and recognized two of its directors who were his grandchildren, 12-year-old Clarence Mitchell of New York and 10-year-old Clinton Blair.[5]

The second locomotive acquired by the fledgling railroad was the *John D. Vail,* a 15-ton, 4-4-0 Danforth-built woodburner that was named for Blair's secretary, who became a director and the superintendent of the road. In June 1880, the Blairstown Railway received its last piece of motive power, a steampowered inspection engine. This diminutive 0-4-0 locomotive carried eight people and was used as a passenger conveyance for the road; it shuttled riders between Blairstown and the DL&W mainline. Formally named the *Belle* (for Belle Scribner Fitzhugh, Blair's granddaughter), the machine was affectionately called the "Dinkey" by those who rode it. (According to Heilich and Schweiterman, the nickname "was used not only for the passenger train but for the entire railroad.") The locomotives *Blairstown* and *Vail* were scrapped in 1901.[6]

The Blairstown Dinkey was remembered in a poem printed in the *Blairstown Press* in 1892. Its last stanza shouted,

> Three cheers for the little Dinkey!
> She's rather slow, I know;
> And her coach is not so handsome,
> And she pulls out rather slow.
> But she has the sturdy spirit,
> Of which the poets sing,
> Three cheers for the little Dinkey!
> Loud may her praises ring.[7]

The short-lived, single-track Blairstown Railway was active and independent from July 1877 until October 1881, when it became part of the New York, Susquehanna & Western Railroad (NYS&W). For the six months, until April 1882 when it lost its identity and passed under the complete control of its new parent, the road operated as before. The NYS&W was, at that time, interested in competing for the lucrative coal traffic between Pennsylvania and New York City and immediately began to extend tentacles from the Blairstown tracks both eastward and northward. At a much later time (1925), passenger traffic between Blairstown and Delaware had fallen off appreciably, to the point that the Susquehanna decided to replace its steam trains with a Brill gasoline engine-powered car. Passenger service continued until 8 June 1928; shortly thereafter, the Delaware Branch was abandoned.[8]

From 1898 until 1940, the New York, Susquehanna & Western Railroad was under Erie Railway control. In 1940, the road became independent once again. In 1961 the Lehigh and New England Rail-

Figure 25. The *Belle*, a small steam-powered inspection engine, served as the sole passenger car for the Blairstown Railway. Seating eight riders, the locomotive shuttled between Blairstown and the main line of the Delaware, Lackawanna & Western Railroad 12 miles distant. North Jersey Chapter, National Railway Historical Society/North Jersey Electric Railway Historical Society.

road, which shared some of the NYS&W's tracks for 67 years, pulled out of that arrangement, and the diminishment of traffic resulted in abandonment of the Susquehanna line in the following year. The right-of-way was acquired by the City of Newark in 1963 to bring a pipeline from a proposed reservoir, and when that project was abandoned, the property was acquired by the State of New Jersey.[9]

John Insley Blair died at Blairstown in 1899, at age 97, but his name lives on at Blairstown (in New Jersey and in Iowa), at Blair Academy, and at Princeton University where Blair Hall is named for him. He built Blair Academy in his hometown and donated it to the Presbytery of Newton to be used to educate the children of ministers free of charge. He left other legacies at numerous other colleges and towns in the West.[10]

The Susquehanna depot no longer stands in Blairstown, but the Lackawanna station is being used by a local radio station. A trace of the Blairstown Railroad exists today as the Paulinskill Valley Rail-Trail, a 27-mile-long hiking and bicycle trail and linear state park that extends over part of the abandoned roadbed (nine miles between Blairstown and Columbia). Many landmarks and identifiable features (mostly of the successor road, the NYS&W) remain, and these are detailed in Craig Della-Penna's book, *24 Great Rail-Trails of New Jersey*. Della-Penna takes his readers on a step-by-step journey along the trail and identifies bridges and viaducts, station foundations, a turntable pit, whistle and mile markers, and other items and areas including "the site of the Kalarama Station. In 1891, the NYS&W wanted to move it to Vails, so they jacked it up onto timbers and put it on the rails. They slowly pulled it with a locomotive towards Vails until disaster struck. It slid off the rails and tumbled down an embankment where it became a source of fuel for wood-stoves in the area."[11]

# 14  The Great Frog War at Hopewell (1876)

At various times in the nineteenth century, railroads sought to forestall or prevent the entry of a competing road into or through their territory by denying permission to the competitor to cross their tracks. Legal or political remedies were often sought, but in some cases physical force was used to accomplish this goal. This vignette describes an instance where the latter course was proposed, an incident between crews of the Mercer and Somerset Railroad (M&S) and those of the Delaware and Bound Brook Railroad (D&BB) that occurred at Hopewell, New Jersey, and became known as the "Great Frog War."

A "frog," in railroad parlance, is that essential part of a railroad switch or crossover rails where two tracks converge or diverge. It is called a "frog" because of its resemblance to the triangular horny substance that is part of a horse's hoof and which bears the same name.[1] The term was applied to the Hopewell fracas because the bone of contention was a crossover that the D&BB workers attempted to install in M&S tracks in order to continue their rails across. A little background information is necessary in order to understand the issues that were in play.

From its beginnings in 1832 as the first railroad built in the state of New Jersey, the Camden and Amboy Railroad (C&A) enjoyed an exclusive monopoly in rail traffic, passenger and freight, between Philadelphia and the New York City gateway at Jersey City. This situation was legalized in the charter granted by the state where, in return for assurances that no other railroad would be chartered between the two cities, the railroad gave 1,000 shares of stock to the state. The monopoly persisted until the mid-1870s. Al-though other railroads were built in the state during those 40-odd years, none was permitted to operate a through route between the two important cities. The C&A went to great lengths to maintain the status quo and quickly responded to any such threats. So when Henry Hamilton, a New York City promoter, announced his National Railway Company in 1867, battle lines were drawn.[2]

The National Railway began life as the Attlebor-ough Railroad Company, a Pennsylvania corporation organized by Hamilton to build from Philadelphia to the Delaware River at Trenton. Hamilton then se-cured amendments to his charter that authorized an increase in capital and the purchase of controlling interests in a number of New Jersey railroads and the Yardleyville Bridge Company. The various Jersey companies were merged under the umbrella of the newly formed Stanhope Railroad Company, which was then leased to the National company. He also arranged that the voting stock in the Attleborough Railroad would be held by a trustee who was prohib-ited from voting it in the interest of the Camden and Amboy or other competitor.[3]

The Camden and Amboy management had re-alized that Hamilton's intent was to build a direct line from Philadelphia to New York, as indicated by the term "Air Line," meaning "as the crow flies" or "direct line," in the popular usage for the name of the road. As Brock Haussamen, a professor who has written extensively on railroads in Somerset County, states, referring again to that phrase, "'National' was grandiose, but . . . [any line connecting] New York with Philadelphia and tracks to the west was indeed, in a sense, national." The C&A's reaction was to seek an injunction against the National Railway and then to advance a counterproposal in the state legislature (which body it influenced greatly), a railroad that would parallel Hamilton's road in the state. The new road, the Mercer and Somerset, would join two existing C&A–controlled railroads and, for all intents and purposes, would make Hamilton's road unnecessary or, if built, redundant.[4]

In rebuttal and taking advantage of the public mood, Hamilton pushed for new legislation that would eliminate the legal roadblocks that prevented potential competitors from obtaining charters through C&A territory. This was accomplished in 1873, enabling the National Railway to commence construction. Financial problems ensued, and eventually the road was reorganized, and the link through New Jersey came to be known as the Delaware and Bound Brook Railroad.[5]

Although the *Somerset Unionist* newspaper opined that the M&S proposal was a sham and that the road would never be built, the first tracks were laid in 1870 and the road was opened in 1874.[6]

Because of its many curves for the first two miles out of Trenton, the M&S was known locally as "The Cork-Screw Railroad."[7] Meanwhile, control of the C&A passed to the Pennsylvania Railroad in 1871, via a long-term lease.[8] The Pennsylvania was just as protective of its position and as contentious as the C&A had been. But because the D&BB had a valid charter, nothing could be done to prevent it from building from the Neshaminy Falls Bridge over the Delaware River near Trenton Junction (where it connected with the North Pennsylvania Railroad running toward Philadelphia) through Pennington.[9] It was when the D&BB neared Hopewell, where it had to cross the M&S's tracks, that full-scale hostilities began.

In November 1875, anticipating trouble when the D&BB reached the Mercer and Somerset tracks, the M&S management had moved a heavy locomotive (Pennsylvania Railroad #679) onto their rails at the projected point of crossing.[10] This engine, running back and forth, maintained its patrol for several months, leaving its station only to move into a siding (some distance away in what is now Hopewell Borough) to allow regularly scheduled trains to pass.[11] When the D&BB finally reached the crossing point, their workers were instructed to insert a crossover in the M&S's tracks so that the line could be completed through Hopewell and Belle Mead and then on to a connection with the Jersey Central at Bound Brook. Stymied by the locomotive blocking the crossing point, about 200 D&BB employees congregated close by, awaiting an opportunity to install their crossover. Some were prepared to install the frogs, while protected by additional men armed with ax handles.[12]

On 5 January 1876, a bitterly cold night, at 7:30 PM, a regularly scheduled Pennsylvania train signaled its approach in order that the track-blocking engine used to forestall the D&BB efforts would be moved to allow passage of the main line train. (According to the *Somerset Messenger,* flagmen were stationed along the tracks to signal the standing locomotive when a scheduled train approached.)[13] As quickly as that occurred, a D&BB work gang chained the M&S engine to the siding and laid a barricade across the main line tracks. As the D&BB men labored to install the crossover, orders were transmitted to Millstone (the end of the line for the M&S) to send an engine to run the blockade. The telegraphed order instructed the engineer to "scatter it [the barricade] to the devil." Engine #336, driven by George Ellis, raced 11 miles in 15 minutes, charged through the eastern barrier, and was derailed in the process.[14] Perhaps the most vivid account of this incident was presented in a 1992 video production, *Frog War! The Mercer and Somerset Story.* In it, an actor portraying an eyewitness described the events leading up to the confrontation. When the relief engine thundered down from Millstone, he declared, "I never saw such a scene in my life. First there was a crash and then ties, timbers, tools, lanterns, and whatnot went flying in all directions like skyrockets on Fourth of July nights." Remarkably, Ellis and 500 spectators were not injured by the collision or the flying debris.

But by now, a D&BB engine was positioned atop the crossover to prevent the crossover from being removed.[15] As soon as this was done, a second M&S engine arrived from Lambertville to run the western obstruction. However, the engineer of this locomotive stopped just short of the barricade, unwilling to ram his way through.[16]

Violence was threatened when Pennsylvania Railroad officials arrived the next day bearing a court order requiring the D&BB to remove the frog. Although the crowd swelled with additional "observers," farmers armed with squirrel guns, muzzle load-

**Figure 26.** A newspaper artist's interpretation of the Great Frog War at Hopewell in 1876. *Daily Graphic* [New York], 10 January 1876.

ers, and even a few flintlock rifles, relics of the American Revolution, and "combatants" dispatched by the two railroads, a stalemate continued throughout the day. Reporters "swarmed over the scene like bees at a molasses keg." Fearing that the situation could turn ugly with very little additional provocation, local officials sought a state militia presence to keep the situation within bounds. Seventh Regiment troops dispatched from Trenton and a company of troops from Lambertville secured the scene on the morning of 7 January and maintained order. (Because there were only 24 houses in Hopewell at the time, feeding and resting the troops was a problem. However, according to Alice Blackwell Lewis, a local author, "everyone pitched in and did the best he could and the problem was handled in some manner.") The situation was defused when word was received that the state chancellor had determined that the Delaware and Bound Brook Railroad was legally entitled to cross the Mercer and Somerset tracks at grade.[17]

Hamilton's railroad built on to Bound Brook but was absorbed by the Philadelphia and Reading (P&R) Railroad in 1879. In the ensuing years, the P&R became the Pennsylvania Railroad's great competitor for the Philadelphia–New York traffic. As a postscript, the Mercer and Somerset, itself having become redundant, was abandoned in 1879, and by 1880 its tracks had been removed. This road, con-

ceived with one purpose in mind, to prevent a competitor from invading its parent's territory, and having no further raison d'être, cost more than $760,000 (about $34,500 per mile) to build, a sizable sum in those days. It turned a profit, a paltry one at that ($637.16), in only one of the eight years of its existence. The poor financial performance caused the directors of the road to deliberately default on payment of the interest on its bonds. On November 29, 1879, the M&S was sold at public auction for $50,000, becoming the first of the Joint Companies' roads to be abandoned. After the Frog War incident, the D&BB Railroad continued to operate (quite successfully) as the New York Branch of the Reading's Philadelphia and New York Division. It remained strong until the Great Depression when traffic began to decline. The Reading maintained its operations until it was subsumed into Conrail in 1976. Conrail, then New Jersey Transit, continued passenger operations until 1982. Freight operations survive today under the CSX flag.[18]

According to maps of Hopewell Township, one dated 1875 (but revised in 1971)[19] and the other a more recent representation, the crossing of the two tracks occurred a short distance from the current County Road 518, just outside of the western boundary of Hopewell Borough, along the line of the present CSX Corporation railroad tracks. In 1916, the *Trenton Sunday Times Advertiser* located the site near Marshall's Corner, a hamlet located equidistant from Pennington and Hopewell, but the action undoubtedly took place much closer to Hopewell Borough. On location, it is difficult to find the exact spot because in the twentieth century, when the line was under Reading management, the right-of-way was regraded and traces of the old M&S path were obliterated.[20] However, the exact location is marked on a contemporary (1876) map of the Delaware and Bound Brook Railroad tracks in Hopewell Township that is kept at the New Jersey State Archives in Trenton.[21] Richard W. Hunter discloses that "in Hopewell Borough, Model Avenue, part of Railroad Place, and Somerset Street follow the old Mercer and Somerset corridor." Hunter mentions other physical features and structures of both railroads that survived but are difficult to locate and identify.[22] Fortunately, a memorable remnant of the D&BB Railroad, its station in Hopewell Borough, a Second Empire architectural prize, not only remains but has been restored to near its former glory.

The Frog War incident is embedded in Hopewell history, and in addition to the countless references in various historical narratives, there are two other interesting accounts of the episode, both of which are excerpted here through the courtesy of the trustees of the Hopewell Museum and its curator, Beverly Weidl. One was a recounting of the action in a play about events in Hopewell's history. The play was presented as a fund-raiser to benefit the Hopewell Library and Museum in 1921; it was performed by local citizens, some of whom were present at the action in 1876. In one scene, the playwright expresses the prevalent opinion at the time: the local citizens were wholly sympathetic with the D&BB; they believed that the M&S provided "poor service and connections." The time is spring 1876, the place, the Hopewell Station

of the D&BB. A group of young ladies, on their way to the Centennial Exposition in Philadelphia, reminisce about the Frog War. They board the train and leave. One young lady, arriving late, admonishes the ticket agent, "Oh, why didn't you wait for us? You knew we were going." The ticket agent responds, "Madam, this is the Delaware and Bound Brook road. Like time and tide we wait for no man."[23]

The action at Hopewell was also memorialized in "The Battle of the Frog," a poem written at the time by William H. Johnson. This long (66 stanzas) poem was printed in the *Hopewell Herald,* and a copy is kept at the Hopewell Museum. The poem, in which Thomas Scott, the president of the Pennsylvania Railroad at the time, is cast as a villain, covers the incident in minute detail, beginning with the November blockade of the crossing point by the M&S locomotive. Then, in January, as an M&S train raced to the scene:

> The engine sped toward Hopewell vale,
> Like lightning it rushed o'er the iron rail,
> They reached the spot, but for fight don't care,
> For still three to one stood before them there.
>
> The news had spread from car to car,
> That Scott's reinforcements would soon be here,
> He has made his boasts, let them do their best,
> He'd have that frog ere the sun reached the west.
>
> Then from every shop and every farm,
> They rushed to save the frog from harm,
> Till nearly 800 by nerved men led,
> Did guard the frog in his little bed.

Fittingly, this chapter is concluded with the last stanza of the poem, a plaintive recitation by the frog itself:

> While Bound Brook trains will o'er me fly.
> While Tom Scott o'er my bed will cry,
> While M&S trains will o'er me creep,
> I'll lay me down in peace to sleep.

# 15  Frog Wars Redux (1879)

Several occasions of New Jersey "frog wars" are discussed in this book: chapter 6 recounts the confrontation between the Erie and the Lackawanna railroads on 2 December 1870, and chapter 14 tells of the meeting between the Delaware and Bound Brook and the Mercer and Somerset railroads on 5 January 1876. Other "frog wars" occurred. In March 1876, the Erie Railroad confronted the New Jersey Junction Railroad (a New York Central affiliate) near Weehawken. In September 1891, the Central Railroad of New Jersey met the Jersey City, Newark and Western Railway (JC, N&W, under the control of the Lehigh Valley Railroad) at Jersey City. Several years later, in 1897, the JC, N&W disputed a crossing by the Pennsylvania Railroad, again at Jersey City. Two other encounters are described below.[1]

About fifteen years after the well-known and well-documented "Frog War" at Hopewell, New Jersey, a similar incident occurred in South Jersey. Toward the end of the 1850s, the Cape (May) Island Council became concerned about the emergence (and competition) of Atlantic City as an ocean resort town. Atlantic City's prominence was due, in large part, to the Camden and Atlantic Railroad, which began regular service in 1854. Consequently, the Council appropriated $10,000 to encourage and aid the construction of a railroad in its area. A few years later (1863), the Cape May and Millville Railroad (CM&M) entered Cape May.[2] There the railroad built a hotel, and its trains ran directly to that building. With quick and comfortable transportation to the community and effective advertisement (e.g., "Every ocean breeze is an ethereal tonic, pure as the quintessence of the elixir of life"), Cape May flourished and grew as a beach resort destination.[3]

In 1879, the CM&M, the sole carrier into Cape May, became part of the West Jersey Railroad (WJ), controlled by the Pennsylvania Railroad. But in the 1890s, the Philadelphia and Reading Railroad (P&R) decided to extend their line, which ran from Camden to Atlantic City, south from Winslow Junction to Tuckahoe and ultimately to Cape May. The issue was that the Reading's branch, incorporated as the Cape May Railroad Company (CM), had to cross the West Jersey rails near Woodbine, New Jersey. Thus the stage was set for a reprise of the original Frog War with the same adversaries playing the leading roles.

Undoubtedly, the Hopewell incident was still fresh in the minds of railroad officials because, instead of blocking their tracks, the West Jersey management anticipated the problem and sought legal recourse. (Of more significance, perhaps, the WJ had recently made an unsuccessful attempt to thwart the CM's efforts to cross its tracks at Richland.) The lawyers for the two companies sparred in Chancery Court, which eventually prohibited the CM from crossing the West Jersey road at grade. The judgment specified that an overhead crossing be built instead, a victory of sorts for the WJ. The West Jersey was not truly triumphant, because it did not want the competition posed by a second railroad and would have preferred to keep the P&R out of Cape May completely.

Despite the court's opinion, the Cape May Railroad took direct action. One night in April 1894, a train carrying about 50 laborers came into view at the disputed crossing point. Half of the CM's crew dragged a crossover from their train and busied themselves unloading the frog in anticipation of installing it across the WJ track. The other half, armed with ax handles and other clubs, prepared to fend off anyone who might interfere. Interference came in the form of a crew of WJ employees, about 100 strong, who were stationed at nearby Belleplain in anticipation of trouble and were rushed to the scene. Reminiscent of the Hopewell situation, a WJ locomotive was positioned at the point of crossing to prevent laying the crossover. The CM contingent sent for curved rails to be sent from Tuckahoe to lay track around the WJ engine. Now, unlike the outcome at Hopewell, the "frog war" at Woodbine turned ugly, and a violent engagement ensued. Despite the violence and blood shed on both sides, the end result was that the frog was installed.

Again, the WJ sought a legal remedy and accused the Cape May crew of disorderly conduct and assault and battery. A local justice of the peace held court on the following day in a boxcar near the scene of the incident. A large crowd of local residents, who favored the CM's incursion, expressed their sentiments. The JP ruled that the accused men were not guilty of the charges and freed them.

The West Jersey Railroad continued to harass the Reading legally, and that legal skirmishing resulted in an opinion that the crossing at grade could remain only so long as it took to build a separated crossing at that point. That ruling was also extended to another crossing that was anticipated near Cape May Court House. Although the West Jersey could not prevent the latter road from completing to Cape May, it may have had the last laugh because the Reading extension never returned a profit to its owners.[4]

The two antagonists, the Pennsylvania and the Reading railroads, tangled again in 1898 at Ocean City, New Jersey, through their proxies, the West Jersey road (PRR-controlled) and the South Jersey Railroad (P&R-controlled). Ocean City was established on a barrier island south of Atlantic City, and its first railroad affiliation was with the narrow gauge Pleasantville and Ocean City Railroad (P&OC). This road was built into Somers Point, on the mainland, and it brought passengers across the Great Egg Harbor inlet by steam launch. The P&OC was later acquired by the West Jersey Railroad, which converted it to standard gauge. In 1896, the Ocean City Railroad (OC), extending their reach eastward from Tucka-

hoe, entered Ocean City along Haven Avenue. The Reading Railroad acquired this route in 1897 and assimilated it into the South Jersey Railroad.[5] Now the stage was set for another confrontation when, just as in their earlier encounter, the WJ sought to keep its competitor from building into its territory.

A more immediate reason for the WJ's concern was the fact that two years earlier, on 30 July 1896, one of their excursion trains was broadsided by a Camden and Atlantic (C&A, a Reading subsidiary) express train at a crossing near Atlantic City. Just west of the resort city, "the tracks of the West Jersey Road run parallel to those of the Camden and Atlantic until after they cross the drawbridge, when they switch off to the south, crossing the Reading Road at an obtuse angle." The engineer of the WJ train observed the C&A train nearing the crossing but proceeded without stopping because the signals were set in his favor. His locomotive cleared the crossing, but the center of his first car was struck by the engine of the Reading train. Following cars derailed or telescoped, and then, to compound the horror, the boiler of the Reading locomotive exploded; several people were scalded to death, and many were burned. By the time rescuers arrived, the scene was dark and bonfires were lit to facilitate the rescue effort. Forty-seven persons died, and more than 100 were injured. Because the injured overwhelmed the local medical facilities, 15 surgeons were dispatched from Philadelphia to aid the local physicians. As a postscript to this tragic incident, when the wife of the C&A's engineer was told of his death, her grief and shock caused her to "fall to the floor dead."[6]

Responsibility for the accident was hard to establish. One could argue that the WJ engineer, having seen the Reading train approaching the crossing point, should have stopped rather than pass the clear signal. On the other hand, the signal, which allowed the WJ train to proceed, also displayed a "stop" indicator to the C&A engineer. Although the coroner's inquest was inconclusive, blame was generally assigned to the C&A engineer for running the signal at high speed. Contributing to his performance may have been the fact that, two weeks earlier, he had been suspended for not maintaining schedule and was seeking to avoid a repetition. The two companies resolved the issue by agreeing to share the liability costs.[7]

Returning now to the action at Ocean City, the

WJ employees were ordered to keep their rivals from building into the city, without resorting to violence. The two lines met on Haven Avenue between 8th and 9th streets, and gangs from both railroads were dispatched to that locale. Wilson wrote, "From dawn to dusk the South Jersey workers fastened the rails into their section of the roadbed. From dusk to dawn the West Jersey workers pried up the rails and tossed them away." Actually, the WJ crew ripped up about 120 feet of South Jersey rail in June, and the SJ sought an injunction to prevent a reoccurrence. The conflict erupted again on 25 August when the SJ began to lay crossing frogs. Again, the WJ positioned a heavy engine to prevent the frog installation, and the SJ crew turned to a different section of track where they cut the rails preparatory to placing the frog. The WJ now pushed several freight cars across the cut rails and prevented further work. Newly laid SJ rail was removed by the WJ crew on the night of 30 August 1898. The *pas de deux* continued, and the farce ended only after a court determined that neither road could interfere with the others tracks.[8]

In 1896, the Pennsylvania Railroad consolidated its South Jersey railroads under a new umbrella named the West Jersey and Seashore Railroad Company.[9] A similar combination of Reading properties in the region was effected in 1901. In 1906, in a rare but not wholly altruistic spirit of cooperation, the Pennsylvania Railroad offered to build and maintain a second track on the Reading's right-of-way between Winslow Junction and Cape May, making it into a double-track line that would be used by both roads. This offer was precipitated by the PRR's electrification of their West Jersey line to Atlantic City, which left it in need of a new route into Cape May. Since traffic was seasonal, the PRR management suggested that the two roads could share upgraded rails rather than continue their money-draining competition.[10] Nearly three decades later, in 1933, in response to a precipitous decline in traffic and revenues as a result of the Great Depression, the two competitors merged their shore line holdings into a new corporate entity, the Pennsylvania-Reading Seashore Lines (PRSL).[11]

PRSL eventually was caught up in the Penn-Central merger, and then it passed under Conrail control. New Jersey Transit (NJT), through a contract with Conrail, assumed responsibility for some operations and maintained passenger (and some freight) service until a large gear failed on the Crook Horn bridge (in 1981) near the south end of Ocean City. That incident, combined with stringent speed limits on the branch to Cape May, compelled NJT to close down passenger service and substitute buses instead. One railroad landmark, the Pennsylvania-Reading Seashore Lines' 10th Street station, remains in Ocean City and was placed on the National Register of Historic Places in 1984. Alas, it now serves as a bus terminal.[12] A bicycle rail-trail exists today along Haven Avenue, from 10th to 35th Street in Ocean City. In addition to the 10th Street station, some interurban track was still embedded at 20th Street when *24 Great Rail-Trails of New Jersey* was published in 1999.[13]

In 1984, the Cape May Seashore Lines, Inc., was organized to operate rail service between Tuckahoe and Cape May. Operating over the old Pennsylvania-Reading Seashore Lines' right-of-way between the two cities, the 27-mile-long railroad carries freight and provides passenger service, mostly for tourists.[14]

# 16 Thomas Edison and Leo Daft: Electric Locomotive Pioneers (1880–83)

The first electric locomotive was reported to have been built in Vermont in 1837. Although that curiosity operated on a one and one-half foot gauge track it was little more than a miniature car, about four feet long. Through the following years, other inventors, in the United States and abroad, produced small electric locomotives, all operated from batteries, either on-board or external to the machine. A consultant engaged in 1848 by Peter Cooper of *Tom Thumb* fame found that electric motors "could never be substituted to any extent for other motors so long as the main dependence was upon chemical batteries." Locomotives powered by electric motors that did not rely on batteries became a possibility only after a number of crucial developments were unveiled over the next few decades. The first demonstration of a practical machine was made in Germany in 1879. Hard on the heels of that breakthrough was Thomas Edison's electric locomotive of 1880.[1]

Young Edison, born on 11 February 1847 at Milan, Ohio and home-schooled by his mother, exhibited a vivid imagination and an aptitude for numbers and science (although his spelling ability left much to be desired). His association with railroads went back to his teen years when he was a news butcher on the Grand Trunk Railway, but his most important railroad connection involved electric locomotives.[2]

In 1880, using a lighting dynamo as a motor, Edison built a full-size machine that collected electricity from the running rails. This 12 horsepower engine was operated on a 1,400 foot long track on the grounds of Edison's laboratory at Menlo Park, New Jersey. It debuted on 13 May 1880 before a crowd

of onlookers and about 20 of the assemblage availed themselves of the opportunity to ride on the locomotive and the car behind. A friction drive, like a clutch and controlled by the operator by means of a long lever, transmitted power from the motor to the driving wheels. The outbound trip on that May day was successful but, operated in reverse for the return trip, the friction drive failed and the riders had to push the train back to its starting point. Within a few weeks, the inventor had corrected the drive problem; he eliminated the friction drive and substituted a belt instead. In another test on 5 June before some of his investors, the machine worked flawlessly until it parted company with the rails while rounding a curve at 40 miles per hour.[3]

Accounts of rides on 13 May and 5 June were reminiscent of tales of locomotive trials conducted many years earlier, especially those of Colonel Stevens's machine of 1825 and the *John Bull*. Representatives from *Scientific American* magazine, who had been invited by the inventor to participate in the 13 May experiment, were aghast at the speed of the little train which raced "at a breakneck rate up and down the grades, around sharp curves, over humps and bumps, at the rate of twenty-five to thirty miles an hour." Later, one of the participants at the 5 June trial wrote,

I have ridden at forty miles an hour on Mr. Edison's electric railway—and we ran off the track. I protested at the rate of speed over the sharp curve (and although) said I did not like it, but would go along. The train jumped the track. . . . Kreusi [the driver, was thrown] with his face down in the dirt, and another man in a

The "GENERATOR."

**Figure 27.** The electric locomotive that Thomas Edison built in 1882 was intended to be used on the Northern Pacific Railroad. Here the engine is shown being operated on the grounds of Edison's laboratory at Menlo Park, N.J. The inset shows the generator that the inventor employed to operate the train. *Frank Leslie's Popular Monthly,* September 1889.

comical somersault through some underbrush. Edison was off in a minute, jumping and laughing, and declaring it was a "daisy." Kreusi (face bleeding and shaken) said "Oh! Yes, pairfeckly safe!"[4]

In 1881, Henry Villard, president of the Northern Pacific Railroad (NP) and one of Edison's investors, financed the development of an electric locomotive for his railroad. The NP ran through mountainous country with the potential to generate abundant hydroelectric power. Villard contracted for machines that could pull a 10-ton load at 60 miles per hour on the steep grades of his system. By the following year, Edison had built the two engines and was running them on his test track. Villard intended to electrify a 50-mile length of track to provide a proper and conclusive testing ground for the engines but the rail-

road encountered economic difficulties apart from the electrification plans and Villard was compelled to renege on the contract. Villard later was an organizer of the Edison General Electric Company, which evolved into the giant General Electric Company, an important factor in the fabrication of electric and diesel-electric locomotives.[5]

Meanwhile, Edison also encountered difficulties, but of a legal nature. Stephen Field, a competitor in the electric locomotive arena, sued Edison for patent infringement. In 1874, Field had disclosed an experimental electric railroad that used a third rail for energy collection, although he had deferred its construction until 1880, at about the same time as Edison built his tracks. Ultimately, the two inventors settled the suit and merged their separate interests in one new company, the Electric Railway Company of America. This company built an improved electric locomotive named *The Judge,* which was shipped to Chicago in 1883 for display at the Railway Exposition in that city. The machine engendered considerable interest because electric railway propulsion was beginning to be seen as a wave of the future, but Edison's interest in electric railways had waned. He stated, "I had too many other things to attend to." Another pioneer in the field, Frank Sprague, wrote of Edison that he "was perhaps nearer the verge of great electric railway possibilities than any other American."[6] Edison's response to the Field lawsuit was typical. He preferred to settle such differences by compromise and merger rather than direct confrontation. This attitude was evidenced in his later motion picture ventures. After Thomas Edison retired from the investigation and development of electric locomotives, he became interested in motion pictures. The association of that interest with railroading and with New Jersey was manifested in his production of one of the most famous movies ever made, *The Great Train Robbery.*

Edison's work with moving pictures began in the 1880s, and he pioneered the development of the Kinetoscope, a device in which a viewer could observe a series of images, presented rapidly and serially. The device had two flaws: viewing time was limited by the number of images that could be stored in the Kinetoscope box and only one person at a time could use it. Others were working on the development of projected images, but Edison stubbornly believed that his system was superior. Eventually he was persuaded to help advance the projected motion picture art.

During the 1890s, there were at least six stage plays with a railroad theme playing in various venues across the country. They usually involved a hero with a name like Fred Fearnot or Railroad Rob, who rescued a damsel from a terrible fate, thwarted a robbery, repulsed an attack on a train, or prevented a wreck. Spectacular effects were used onstage which simulated explosions or introduced a puffing locomotive. The year was 1896, and Edison was a member of the audience at a stage production of *The Great Train Robbery.* Extremely impressed by the story line and the special effects used in its staging, Edison retained the play in his memory for possible adaptation to a motion picture. Later, he moved from the making of short movies and produced *The Great Train Robbery.* Distributed in 1904, it was directed by Edwin S. Porter. Starring Justus Barnes, the film was shot at the Delaware, Lackawanna and Western Railroad's freight yards in Paterson, New Jersey.[7]

Now back to Edison's predilection toward settlement rather than confrontation. From the efforts of Edison and many others, the motion picture industry blossomed and grew quickly and tremendously. The great inventor had made an enormous blunder by not seeking patent protection in Europe for his contributions to the industry. Faced with lengthy legal battles, Edison generally settled by merging with his opponents.

Appropriately, the man who developed the first electric locomotive in New Jersey was chosen to inaugurate service on the newly electrified Delaware, Lackawanna and Western commuter lines. On the morning of 3 September 1930, "Thomas A. Edison started the first electric passenger train through the Oranges . . . when he pressed the controller of a 10-car train at 9:44 starting the train from South Orange." Edison was joined by his wife at the controls, and headlines in the local paper shouted, "'Phoebe Snow' among Big Happy Throng Riding Lackawanna's New Iron Horse from South Orange to Hoboken." Phoebe Snow's presence was a calculated marketing ploy that was meant to forecast "the eventual elimination of smoke and soot through the territory covered by the Lackawanna Railroad."[8]

As a postscript to this tale, Edison and his works are represented on several U.S. postage stamps. Scott numbers 654 and 655 (the Scott number is a unique identifier of postage stamps that is assigned by the Scott Publishing Company of Sidney, Ohio) are representations of Edison's first electric lamp. Scott 945 portrays the inventor, and 3182c commemorates *The Great Train Robbery.*[9]

Edison's laboratory at Main Street and Lakeside Avenue in West Orange is a National Historic Site. Edison's mansion, *Glenmont,* also a National Historic Site, where he lived between 1886 and 1931 is on Glen Avenue at Llewellyn park, an exclusive section of West Orange. Both are open to visitors. When the author visited the laboratory site a few years ago, an electric locomotive truck was displayed/stored outside the building. Inside, many of Edison's inventions are displayed and his original phonograph is exhibited. There are reproductions of early electric lights and the first motion picture studio, the "Black

Maria." Truly impressive is Edison's two-story office, where one can almost imagine the great man descending from a balcony to greet his visitors. Thomas Edison died in October 1931.

A monument (dedicated in 1925) memorializing the inventor and his invention of practical electric lighting is to be found in the Menlo Park neighborhood of Edison, New Jersey. Originally known as Raritan Township, the town was renamed Edison in honor of New Jersey's adopted son. The inventor had established his laboratory at Menlo Park, which was the site of an unsuccessful real estate development. A very impressive tower at 37 Christie Street marks the spot where the first successful incandescent light bulb was made and, appropriately, the tower is topped by what is billed as "the world's largest light bulb." A nearby museum houses many of his inventions and other memorabilia. The tower and museum, open to the public, were dedicated in 1938 on what would have been Thomas Edison's 91st birthday.[10]

Another New Jersey electric locomotive pioneer, Leo Daft, was a contemporary of Edison. Professor Daft was born in Great Britain and came to the United States in 1866. He formed the Daft Electric Company from the New York Electric Light Company, which he had joined in 1879. Located at Greenville, New Jersey (not far from Point Pleasant), Daft Electric constructed several small, narrow-gauge electric locomotives over a period of two years and ran them on a short length of track on their property. Finding these machines worked well, Daft went on to build a larger, 2-ton, 12-horsepower (some records say 25), electric locomotive that he named *Ampere*. The *Ampere* was the first standard gauge electric locomotive to be built in the country, and Daft conducted further testing at Newark, New Jersey. In November 1883, he brought the *Ampere* to the tracks of the Saratoga and Mount McGregor Railroad in New York State, where it underwent a rigorous trial. The locomotive, powered from a third rail situated between the two running rails, pulled a conventional passenger coach loaded with 75 passengers, a load estimated at 10 tons, up a one and one-eighth mile long, 1.5 percent grade in 11 minutes. The *Ampere* derailed on its return trip, the accident caused by the failure of a makeshift rope coupling or, by some accounts, excessive speed while rounding a curve. But the most notable incident during the trial was the stunning of four horses that inadvertently stepped on the third rail. The *Scientific American* account is interesting, if not electrifying: "although one could touch the rails without feeling any unpleasant shock, it was very evident that many were temporarily 'excited' in crossing the tracks . . . while no less than four horses fell on the track from the effect of the current, and had to be helped off." Although the two locomotives were built in the same year, in appearance the *Ampere* was unlike Edison's *Judge*. Whereas the latter was recognizable as a locomotive, in fact, it mimicked the outline of a small steam engine, the *Ampere* more nearly resembled a locomotive tender; it was low, little higher than the floor of the car it pulled, about 10 feet long, and the operator rode in an exposed position at the front.[11]

The *Tech*, a publication of the Massachusetts Institute of Technology, reported that, during the trial of *Ampere*, an alumnus, George W. Mansfield, one of Daft's assistants, attempted to coin a new word, "motorneer," referring to a driver of an electric locomotive as distinguished from an "engineer," who drove a steam locomotive. Though his motive was commendable, since the electric locomotive was a new quantity, he felt that its operator should be distinguished from an "engineer," he was roundly criticized by his alumni organization as well as the Boston *Transcript* newspaper. Fortunately, despite the early report in the MIT newspaper that the word was "simply unendurable" and its "employment by writers is spreading fast," it appears that the term died a quick and almost unnoticed death.[12]

Daft went on to install a number of electric railway systems, including the Sea Shore Electric Railway, a four-mile-long street railway built at Asbury Park in 1887. This system delivered electricity to the cars through overhead conductors and may have been the first electric railway installation in the state. An earlier one of Daft's installations, in Baltimore, was cited as being the first successful electric railway system in the United States. Arguably, his greatest recognition was for the Ninth Avenue Elevated Railway application in 1888 where his locomotive *Benjamin Franklin* pulled a 60-ton train despite wet and slippery tracks caused by a driving rainstorm. Leo Daft died in 1922 at the age of 79 during the heyday of the trolley, an industry in whose development he had played a major part.[13]

# 17  A Railroad Bicycle and a Bicycle Railroad (1880 and 1892)

In the early days of railroading, a number of "single" locomotives were built; these were machines with a single pair of driving wheels, usually of a sufficiently large diameter to ensure speed. They were also slippery, that is, they had low adhesion and consequently limited starting power that restricted the amount of weight that they could pull. According to W. Barnet LeVan, no more than 18 "single" locomotives had been manufactured in the United States before 1880.[1]

In the late 1870s, the Philadelphia and Reading Railroad (P&R) was flexing its muscles and meeting the Pennsylvania Railroad head-on in competition for the New York–Philadelphia passenger traffic (see chapter 14 for the beginnings of this rivalry). To provide a meaningful challenge, the P&R required a locomotive capable of maintaining a two-hour schedule between Philadelphia and Jersey City. Coincidentally, in 1880, the Baldwin Locomotive Works was to outshop its 5,000th locomotive, and its management decided to fill the P&R's needs by producing an engine that would be fast yet safe because, being a single, it would have no side rods that might break at the high speeds to which they would be subjected, a serious concern at the time. Baldwin overcame the adhesion deficiency common to single locomotives by incorporating a steam-actuated apparatus that acted on the equalizing levers to shift some of the locomotive's weight to the driving wheels when starting. This 4-2-2 engine, known as a "bicycle locomotive," became the P&R's number 507.[2]

On 14 May 1880, the P&R made a test run of its new speedster. Pulling a tender and four cars filled with dignitaries, a total weight of 148 tons, the train left Philadelphia, entered New Jersey near Trenton Junction, and sped on to Bound Brook, from whence it completed the trip to Jersey City over Central Railroad of New Jersey tracks. Total elapsed time for the 89.4-mile nonstop trip was 98 minutes, equal to a rate of 54.73 miles per hour. The fastest time, 81 miles per hour, was made on the 2.8-mile stretch, partially upgrade, between Willett and Langhorne in Pennsylvania. Number 507 made a few more trips over the Philadelphia and New York Division, but in light of financial difficulties that the company was experiencing, the engine was sold to Lovett Eames and exported to England to use for demonstrations of his patented vacuum brake system. The P&R then turned to 4-4-0 "American" locomotives built in its own shops (and some at Baldwin) for its passenger service via Bound Brook and also on the Atlantic City Railroad, which it controlled.[3]

Now, bicycle locomotives were designed to operate on true railroads having nothing to do with bicycles. But there was a true bicycle railroad built in New Jersey in 1892. Although not a railroad in the traditional sense, it nevertheless was a railroad where bicycles were used as the vehicles operating on rails. Our story begins when, in 1865, Hezekiah B. Smith, by many accounts an impulsive, eccentric genius, bought about 45 acres of land at Shreveville, New Jersey, about 2.5 miles from Mount Holly. The nearby railroad made Philadelphia or Trenton about a one-hour journey. His $20,000 purchase encompassed the existing village, including a Greek Revival mansion, and some of its surrounds. Here Smith es-

**Figure 28.** This "bicycle locomotive" was the 5,000th locomotive produced by the Baldwin Locomotive Works. It was delivered to the Philadelphia and Reading Railroad in 1880. *Journal of the Franklin Institute*, July 1880.

tablished a manufacturing business to make woodworking machinery and immediately changed the name of the town to Smithville. The energetic (and prosperous) Smith infused new life into the town; decaying buildings were restored, new workshops were built, and the antiquated water wheels that dipped into Rancocas Creek were upgraded to provide power to the factory. Parks and libraries were established, a theater suitable for a large congregation was added, a 110-foot-tall tower was erected, and a large boardinghouse, known as "Mechanics House," was built for unmarried mechanics who would work in the revived factory. The H. B. Smith Machine Company quickly became famous for producing excellent machinery based on Smith's own designs. At one time, the company produced one-quarter of the nation's woodworking machinery.[4]

At about the same time as Smith was organizing his business in New Jersey, bicycling became the rage countrywide. Although the bicycle had been invented early in the nineteenth century, it was still a dangerous contraption because of its design, which mounted a large wheel at the front and a small one behind. In 1880, a startling new design appeared. Invented

by George Washington Pressey of Hammonton, New Jersey, the Star bicycle reversed the large (about 39-inch diameter) and small (about 20-inch diameter) wheels, bringing the smaller wheel to the front. This made the bike more stable and easier to steer and less likely to pitch its rider over the handlebars if it struck something in its path. Pressey took his plans for the bicycle to Smith, who agreed to manufacture it at Smithville.[5]

Over the years, employment swelled at the plant to approximately 360 workers. Mount Holly was the principal source of labor. The workers were there and available, but their only means of commuting was by riding a bicycle or walking over bumpy and muddy roads. Commuting by train was a possibility but was inconvenient because of limited service and the fact that the Smith plant was half a mile from the stop at Smithville. At the time that Smithville was established, the community was served by the Burlington County Railroad, which later was absorbed by the Camden and Amboy Railroad. By 1878, when ownership had devolved to the Pennsylvania Railroad, local citizens told a newspaper article that they "could hardly point with pride to the TRAPS which the Pennsylvania Railroad Company runs, between Mount Holly and Burlington." Yet, accommodations aside, the train trip between Mount Holly and Smithville was accomplished in six minutes.[6]

Although Hezekiah Smith was credited by most authorities to have instituted the bicycle railroad at Smithville, it was not until after Smith's death in 1887 that the railway was contemplated, and then five years had passed before it was completed. Arthur Hotchkiss, seeking a manufacturer for the components of his newly conceived railway, came to Smithville because of the reputation of the Smith concern as a bicycle manufacturer and respected machine tool manufactory. (Some sources say that Hotchkiss was a New England friend of Hezekiah Smith, which, if true, may have influenced him to come to Smithville.) The company not only agreed to produce the required bicycles but also invested in Hotchkiss's project, and William Kelley, who was running the factory at this time, became a director of the railway company (along with seven other Smith employees). The H. B. Smith Machine Company built prototypes of the special cycles and constructed a test track at the factory for proving the system. In any event, Hotchkiss "brought the matter to the attention of the people of Mount Holly" and then built the Mount Holly and Smithville Bicycle Railroad Company, which was capitalized at $10,000. The 1.8-mile trip, which cost ten cents round-trip, took about six minutes when riders pedaled at maximum speed (about an 18 mile per hour rate, achievable over the smooth level rails). T-shaped metal rails were mounted atop wooden stringers that were, in turn, supported on four-foot-high posts firmly set into the ground. To maintain a level track, it was necessary to cut and fill high and low areas and to drive piles at other places. Although about half a mile of the railroad was double-tracked, most of the line was single, that is, traffic traveled in both directions along the same track. (Plans were made to complete the second track, but this never was done.) Because the route was laid out in an essentially straight line, it had to cross the meandering Rancocas Creek 10 times. Gates and removable sections were built into the fencelike supporting structure at intervals so that farmers could access their properties. (If the farmer was careless when closing a gate or replacing the fence section, a rider might be unceremoniously thrown to the ground or, worse, dumped into Rancocas Creek, when he passed over

that point.) At strategic locations, switching arrangements allowed the bikes to leave the "main line" for passing and turntables were provided at each end of the run for turning the bicycles around. If two travelers met at a point where there was no "passing siding," one rider had to physically lift his bicycle off the track to enable the other one to pass. Many tempers were frayed when "fast" riders overtook "slow" riders and were frustrated by their inability to pass. Since the railroad passed through various farms, another hazard involved the possibility of encountering an ill-tempered bull during the trip; at such times the rider would pedal furiously to reach safety in the next field.[7]

The system employed specially designed inverted bicycles made with large (20-inch diameter) and smaller (12-inch diameter) running wheels. Most of the cycles carried one passenger, but a number of two-passenger tandem machines were also provided. The running wheels were grooved, a feature that, with lower guide wheels on each side, kept the bike on the rail and made steering unnecessary; the rider's contribution was pedal power. "Mud guards" of a sort were provided "to prevent the throwing of water formed by dew settling on the track in the evening." Instead of the now familiar chain and sprocket drive, the rider, seated on a saddle between the two wheels, pumped a ratchet mechanism up and down to drive the cycles. At one time it was contemplated that electric-powered bicycles would be used on the line, but like so many of the grandiose plans that were suggested, this never came to pass. Running lights were provided for night riding, yet collisions occurred.

The bicycle railroad was opened (though still not completed) on the second day of the annual Mount Holly Fair. It was an immediate success as a fair attraction, and couples waited their turn for hours at the Pine Street terminal in Mount Holly. The railroad was unique, and parties traveled from as far away as Philadelphia to experience the ride. (To appreciate the attraction of the bicycle railroad, a present-day reader should understand that it was innovative and an advance over then existing means of self-powered personal transportation. Recalling that bicycles of the day were difficult to use and required substantial practice and skill, the railway provided a casual or occasional rider with a means to travel faster than any other wheeled system that was driven by the user.) Once the system was completed and as rider-

**Figure 29.** At an impasse on the "bicycle railroad." The bicycle railroad was built in 1892 by Arthur Hotchkiss to carry workers from Mount Holly to a manufacturing plant in Smithville, about 2.5 miles away. The structure supporting the monorail was about four feet high, and this illustration shows the track structure at one of its several crossings of Rancocas Creek. When riders met on the single track line, one of the riders had to remove his cycle from the rails in order to permit the other to pass. From the Collection of the Burlington County Historical Society, Burlington, N.J.

ship increased, Hotchkiss added more cycles and offered a two-dollar per month commutation fare to Smithville. The general public was permitted to use the facility during the workday, but the factory hands coming from Mount Holly enjoyed a priority during the morning and evening, going to and from work. (It is not clear how the dozens of bicycles that were used to bring the workers from Mount Holly were returned to their starting point so that others could utilize them during the day.) The managers permitted the use of the railway on Saturdays and after working hours, but in deference to Hotchkiss's wishes, they prohibited its use on Sunday.

Before the bicycle railroad was completed to Smithville and when it had been in operation only four days, it became the focus of a sensational murder. Most of the more recent accounts of the murder wrongly state that it took place when the victim, Lizzie Peak, was riding on the railroad, but the true facts are these. In 1891, Wesley Warner, who lived in Burlington City, deserted his family and took 23-year-

old Lizzie to Brooklyn to live with him. Some time later, they quarreled, and Lizzie returned home to Mount Holly. On the evening of 17 September 1892, Lizzie and her younger sisters went for a ride on the bicycle railroad with three local boys. Warner, her rejected lover, lay in hiding near her house, and when she returned home he leaped up and attacked her with a carving knife. Lizzie died from a stab wound in her throat, and Warner was arrested, convicted, and hanged at Mount Holly that same year.[8]

The railroad operated until 11 PM, and although it mostly ran through open fields and unsettled areas, there was only one authenticated account of attempted foul play along the line during its life. George Brannin, returning to Mount Holly late at night, was shot at by unknown assailants. Unharmed, he continued a short distance and was then attacked by a vicious dog, which apparently accompanied another attacker. In another noteworthy occurrence, during the spring of 1894, a five-day storm blanketed the Mount Holly area and caused widespread flooding.

The water level of Rancocas Creek rose substantially, and along most of the route of the bicycle railroad little more than the iron rail was visible above the flood waters. Despite the difficulty of pedaling his machine in the deep water, one of the road's managers did travel between the termini of the road.[9]

Arthur Hotchkiss entertained the belief that his invention would be adopted everywhere, but it never really caught on. He franchised others as "owners of the rights to make and operate the Hotchkiss Bicycle Railroad." In 1893, he left Mount Holly to go to Chicago to promote the bicycle railroad at the Columbian Exposition. According to a tale that was widely circulated at a later time, although it was never mentioned in contemporary newspapers, a few days after Hotchkiss left, his brother contacted the Mount Holly police to report that Arthur had never arrived at Chicago. This led to a story that Arthur Hotchkiss disappeared and was never seen again. That story was probably fabricated some time after the fact because local papers did report that Hotchkiss was in Chicago. However, Arthur never returned to the Mount Holly area except for brief visits. His brother, George, was also associated with the railroad at various times after 1893 and served as superintendent into 1898. Many reporters confused the names of the brothers at various times, and some stories relating to one or the other may have misidentified the brothers. That Hotchkiss did not disappear was proven by an article in the *Mount Holly News,* dated April 1898, which stated that "George L. Hotchkiss was taken to his home at Brooklyn . . . by his brother Arthur." In July 1898, the *Mount Holly News* reported that "Arthur Hotchkiss, of Brooklyn, was in town last week looking after the bicycle railway." In any event, Arthur Hotchkiss was definitely seen and heard from again.[10]

The fortunes of the Mount Holly–Smithville bicycle railroad eventually declined, and by 1898 it had fallen into disuse and was declared bankrupt. The default of the operation was blamed on the lack of an interested manager (by the proponents of the Hotchkiss "disappearance" hypothesis), but a more significant factor in its failure was the introduction of a new, modern street bicycle design that was safer and easier to ride than the old models. Although it still made sense for commuters from Mount Holly to ride the bicycle railroad to and from work, the enterprise required the support of the general public for its financial health. Once the pleasure riders turned to the new bicycles, Hotchkiss's project was doomed. General ridership declined in subsequent years (and concurrently, the Smith Company reduced its workforce), and by 1897 the *Mount Holly News* was reporting that the railway company might not be able to pay the interest due on its bonds.[11] Legend has it that the Lizzie Peak murder was also a contributing factor to the bicycle railroad's demise, but that notion, like so many other variations of the Smithville story, is untrue.[12]

A near-copy of Hotchkiss's bicycle railroad was built as a Midway ride on the grounds of the Columbian Exposition. There, the bicycles were propelled by an attendant who contributed the muscle power to carry a patron along without effort. The attraction was not financially successful, but it did command the attention of an Englishman who transplanted the idea to the British seaside resort at Blackpool. During the early 1890s, accounts of similar "elevated" bicycle railways were printed in the *Mount Holly News.* These systems, which were developed by the H. B. Smith Machine Company and reported to be installed at Atlantic City, Ocean City, and Gloucester, New Jersey, differed from the Smithville version in that the cycles hung from overhead, parallel steel rails that were mounted about 18 feet high. The rider sat astride the bicycle but close to the ground.[13]

The Great Depression dealt a punishing blow to the H. B. Smith Machine Company, yet it survived into the 1960s (although much reduced in size). The mill village of Smithville began a slow decline: most of its farmland was sold in the 1940s, Mechanics House was demolished in 1948, shortly thereafter, many of the residences were razed, and the observation tower, the gristmill, and the stables came down in 1952. Train service ended during the 1950s, and the Smith mansion was sold in 1962. The successor company, the Smith Machine Company, finally succumbed to the diminished demand for its last remaining product, a commercial size belt sander.[14]

Smithville Village is currently undergoing reconstruction to buildings, streetscapes, and other structures. Known as the Smithville Historic District, it is established in Smithville Park, one of the Burlington County parks. Located not far from the intersection of U.S. 206 and County Road 537, the Village is listed on the National and New Jersey Registers of Historic Places. The Smith Mansion is open to visitors during the summer months. Unfortunately, although Rancocas Creek, which was crisscrossed by the railway track, is widely traveled by canoeists today, there is absolutely no evidence of Hotchkiss's bicycle railroad remaining.[15]

\* \* \*

Author's Note: Although it had no connection with New Jersey or the bicycle railroad described above, for completeness it should be mentioned that the term *bicycle railway* was also applied to an ill-considered venture promoted by Eben Boynton. Boynton designed a monorail locomotive whose double-flanged wheels rode on a single track, but it was stabilized by rollers above the engine. The rollers pressed against an overhead wooden stringer mounted on a trestlelike structure. The inventor's 23-ton Cycle #1 was tested in 1889 on an abandoned stretch of railway track in Brooklyn, using only one of the two existing rails. Cycle #2, a 9-ton version, was only a small improvement over the earlier machine. Later, to achieve higher speeds, Boynton built a two-mile-long "bicycle electric railway" on Long Island. Although his electrically powered train sped along at 50 miles per hour, the system was no more successful at attracting investor support than his earlier efforts.[16]

# 18 Death of a President at Elberon (1881)

Elberon is a shore community in Monmouth County, part of the city of Long Branch, east of Tinton Falls, north of Asbury Park. The railroad had come to Long Branch in 1875 when, on 25 June, the Central Railroad of New Jersey (CNJ) inaugurated service from its terminal at Jersey City. On that day, the dignitaries participating in the trip included President Ulysses S. Grant, whose private car was attached to the train. In the 1880s, Elberon developed into an exclusive community, and many notables, including Grant, maintained summer homes here. It was here, in late summer 1881, that the ability of a railroad (in this instance, the CNJ) to respond to an emergency was demonstrated dramatically.[1]

James Garfield, a congressman and then a senator-elect, aspired to the presidency. But during the 1880 contest for the nomination, he withdrew from contention and became convention manager for John Sherman, a fellow Republican. Sherman was opposed by James Blaine and Ulysses Grant, who was running for a third term. Despite Garfield's strong efforts through 34 ballots, Sherman failed to receive a majority of votes on the convention floor. Recognizing that their candidate would not prevail, some of Sherman's supporters switched allegiance to Garfield and, on the thirty-fifth ballot, cast their votes for him. On the following ballot, Garfield was unanimously chosen as the Republican nominee. Although support from Grant's followers came late in the ensuing campaign, Garfield was elected twentieth president of the United States, a circumstance that determined his fate.[2]

Eight months later, on 2 July 1881, James Garfield proceeded to the Baltimore and Potomac Railroad station to travel to Long Branch and thence to Williamstown, Massachusetts, where he would attend the commencement exercises of his alma mater. As he entered the station and walked through the ladies' waiting room, he was approached by Charles Guiteau, a lawyer and supporter of the Grant faction. Guiteau, a mentally unstable man and disappointed office seeker, raised a .44 caliber "English Bulldog" revolver and fired two shots at the president. Garfield fell to the ground, bleeding.[3]

Removed from the station, Garfield was taken to the White House; the hectic trip back to the presidential residence in an army ambulance was described graphically in the *Philadelphia Times*:

> About twenty minutes after nine o'clock this morning the people on Pennsylvania avenue were startled by the sight of a team of powerful horses driven at full speed toward the White House. The first impression was that it was a runaway, but as the team swept by, the fact that it was a War Department covered wagon and the driver, of grim and soldierly bearing, sat urging his horses to a still higher speed, was a puzzle to everybody. The avenue was thronged with vehicles, and the soldier driver thundering along on the dead run waved them aside, while the people on the walks closed rapidly in behind with muttered comment and looks of astonishment. . . . [Following] was the President's empty carriage, with the driver on the box . . . bowling along at the same break-neck pace, the driver urging his animals with the whip.[4]

At the White House, the president was attended by a group of distinguished doctors. A telegram was sent to Mrs. Garfield, who was already at Long Branch awaiting her husband's arrival. Before one o'clock she was aboard a special train that took her to Washington, where she arrived before seven in the evening.[5]

For six weeks the physicians tried one procedure and remedy after another, including an attempt to locate the bullet using a metal detector devised by Alexander Graham Bell, all to no avail. Although most authorities indicated that Bell was unsuccessful in his attempt to find the bullet, McCabe provides a recounting of the exploration using Bell's modified "Induction Balance" in great detail. He asserts that the bullet was definitely located. Others disagree, and Bell's failure to find the projectile was later attributed to the fact that Garfield lay on a new type of mattress containing steel springs. The metal springs interfered with the metal detector and masked the location of the bullet in the president's back.[6]

Beginning around 15 August, Garfield's condition took a turn for the worse. Compounding the problem was the insufferable summer weather in the nation's capital. Because the president was known to favor the sea and had once claimed, "I have always felt that the ocean was my friend and the sight of it brings rest and peace," the suggestion was made that the president be moved to a cooler venue at the seashore. Although a few days earlier, his doctors contemplated the president's removal to a more beneficial climate only as a last resort, on 2 September, the Associated Press reported, "Dr. Bliss said to-night, in reference to the President's removal: 'He ought not to remain an hour longer than necessary, because September, in Washington, is a bad month. . . . I think it is probable that we shall take him to Long Branch by rail.'" In addition to the president's own wishes in the matter, another influence was the fact that earlier that year Mrs. Garfield had been gravely ill with malaria. As soon as she became able to travel, she was brought to Long Branch, New Jersey, where she recovered quickly. The deciding circumstance was Dr. Hamilton's opinion that to keep Garfield at Washington, where he would be subjected to the malodorous stench of the "Potomac Flats," "would be very serious upon him, if not fatal."[7]

The president had often vacationed at Elberon, his favorite seaside resort. Taking advantage of an offer of a 20-room summer "cottage" made by a wealthy New Yorker, Charles Francklyn, a decision was made to transport Garfield 228 miles to Elberon. The move was planned with military precision and thoroughness. The Pennsylvania Railroad assigned the task of fitting out a special car to Theodore N. Ely, its superintendent of motive power at the Altoona shops. The car had a spring-cushioned bed, and ice boxes were located under the bed to keep the car cool. A false ceiling was installed to allow air flow between it and the roof, the intent of which was to insulate the car from exterior temperatures while retaining the cooling benefits of the ice chests. The car was one of a three-car train that was assembled to transport the patient; the first car was Garfield's, the second for his wife, Lucretia, and the third carried a military detachment of 20 soldiers who were to carry the president's stretcher.[8]

On the morning of 5 September, Joseph Harris, the general manager of the CNJ,

received a dispatch from Attorney-General MacVeigh, asking him to lay a track from the depot to the Francklyn cottage and have it ready for use by 10 o'clock tomorrow. Word was at once sent to W. W. Stearns, the Assistant General Superintendent of the road, and surveying instruments were ordered from Jersey City so that the route could be laid out for the workmen. Track-master Murtagh was ordered to come from Newark by telegraph, and orders for ties and rails were hurried on to Jersey City and Elizabethport. About 2 o'clock ground was broken by Mr. Murtagh, with only 12 laborers, all who were here. An hour later laborers began to arrive from all parts of the road between Jersey City and Sea Girt, and by 9 o'clock tonight 300 skilled railroad-builders were hard at work. A full supply of ties and rails were on the spot long before that time. The length of the new track will be 3,200 feet. The route chosen is one containing very few obstructions. Beginning at a point about 800 feet north of the Elberon station, the route describes a wide curve to the eastward until it strikes the driveway leading from the station straight to the hotel. The rails are being laid along the southern side of this road, directly to the hotel grounds, where the track will describe another wide curve, and end in front of the entrance to the President's cottage. The material used in building the road is entirely new, and, when completed, the road will be as smooth as a parlor floor. 'They will have the last spike driven by daylight,' said Mr. Murtagh to-night, 'and a train can run over the road then, if necessary. We shall put in the time between daylight and the arrival of the Garfield train in leveling up the track, filling in between the ties, and doing other things which will serve to make the road more perfect and easy. By 9 o'clock in the morning we shall have over half a mile of railroad finished completely in every respect.' Crowds of ladies and gentlemen from the various hotels and cottages along the shore have visited the scene to-night, and watched the laborers at their work. Immense locomotive head-lights from the railroad shops and hundreds of smaller lamps and lanterns give light for the workmen. Hot coffee and sandwiches, furnished by Col. Jones, of the Elberon, are served to the industrious workers at frequent intervals and every man is working with a will to get the road in readiness.[9]

Although many accounts of this effort speak of "thousands of volunteers" working through the night to build the spur, it is probable that most of the work was undertaken and completed by the approximately 300 railroad workers. Some volunteers may have aided in the effort, but if there were 2,000 men at work on the spur, that would have equated to one laborer for every two feet of railroad track. Many of the volunteers most likely worked in ancillary roles, providing food or performing other chores. Also, the "thousand of volunteers" may have included the sightseers who attended the nocturnal construction.[10]

Of interest is the fact that the rail used for the construction of the spur was already installed as tracks west of Westfield. Before it could be sent to Elberon, it had to be removed by gangs of workers. After its installation to the Francklyn cottage, Superintendent Stearns read the following message of thanks from Harris to his employees on 6 September.

The receiver desires me to thank the officers and men whose patient and cheerful toil through so many hours has enabled the company to do the part allotted to it in making the President's long journey a comfortable one.

I doubt not that affection for the illustrious sufferer and the loyal wish to help the company make the work perfect, combined to animate the night labor and to relieve its weariness.

And now let us pray that God, who has shown the nation so many miracles, may raise up our President from his bed of suffering, and restore him to us and to his family, for many years of perfect health and grand usefulness.

It was reported in the *Long Branch News* on 17 September that the construction of the Francklyn spur cost the Jersey Central $3,000.[11]

Unremarked in most accounts is the fact that the Pennsylvania Railroad had also built an extension at the Washington depot across Pennsylvania Avenue near 6th Street. This extension had rails resting on crossties set in a fully ballasted right-of-way, and the special train waited for its distinguished passenger at that point. The seven-hour, nearly 230-mile journey from Washington, which began before 6 AM on 6 September 1881, was made at a reasonable rate so the president would not be disturbed unnecessarily. The trip was made over the rights-of-way of six railroads, leaving Washington on the Baltimore and Potomac Railroad. In New Jersey, most of the trip was made on the New York and the Amboy divisions of the Pennsylvania Railroad (from Mantua to Monmouth Junction to Sea Girt). From Sea Girt, the final 9.5 miles to the station at Elberon was completed on the Long Branch division of the Central Railroad of New Jersey.[12]

A pilot train, preceding Garfield's train, warned other trains along the route to stop and to refrain from blowing their whistles. Planning even extended to the selection and outfitting of houses at strategic points near the tracks in the event the patient required immediate medical attention that could not be provided on the train. A stop was made at Lamokin, Pennsylvania, for fuel and water; the tender took on water again at Tullytown. Ely directed the operation of the train, and a telegraph operator and lineman were on board in the event that additional emergency assistance had to be summoned. The special train, whose locomotive burned anthracite coal to reduce smoke, reached Elberon shortly after 1 PM. Since the load-carrying ability of the new stretch of track was questionable, the large road locomotive that had brought the president to this point was replaced by a smaller engine. As the train slowly proceeded along the newly laid track, it stalled on a small hill near the house, and 200 railroad workers, who were waiting nearby, approached and manually pushed the president's car up the grade.[13]

Despite the extraordinary arrangements made

**Figure 30.** Volunteers labored during the night of 5 September 1881 to build a spur from the main line to the Francklyn cottage. Calcium lights were used to illuminate the work area. Author's collection.

for his comfort and recuperation and the salubrious sea breezes, James Garfield died two weeks later, on the night of 19 September 1881. The same special train was dispatched to Elberon to return Garfield's remains to Washington to lie in state. The cars were then pressed into use a final time to bring the president to Cleveland for a public viewing before he was laid to rest at Lakeview Cemetery.[14]

Mrs. Garfield requested that the funeral train should stop only at those points that the railway officials deemed necessary. Thus it proceeded directly from Washington (leaving at 5:16 PM) through Baltimore and on to Marysville, Pennsylvania, where it left the Northern Central Railroad tracks and continued along the Pennsylvania Railroad. It passed through Pittsburgh and arrived at Cleveland at 1:30 PM the following day. Although most of the run was made at night, enormous crowds turned out at the towns and cities that it passed, and even in rural regions people lined the tracks. The funeral train was followed by another special train carrying dignitaries to the burial. One untoward incident was the combustion of a black drapery draped on the side of a car in the second train. A spark from the engine had caused the fire. Although fire consumed the drapery completely, it did not seriously damage the car.[15]

An editor for *Scribner's Monthly,* Josiah Gilbert Holland, wrote of Garfield that "his sympathy with the humble drew to him the hearts of the world."[16]

A postscript to this tale involves Garfield's predecessor, Ulysses S. Grant. He was also a regular vacationer at Long Branch, and in the year following Garfield's death, Grant was aboard a train heading down to the Jersey shore community. As the train passed over the Parker's Creek trestle, it derailed and fell into the shallow stream below. Five passengers were killed, but most of the others, including Grant, exited the cars, which lay on their sides, through the windows, "like bees out of a hive."[17]

Elberon, which takes its name from a phonetic play on the name of one of its founders, L. B. Brown, remains a popular beach resort, although it no longer enjoys the prestigious and fashionable reputation that it once did. Revitalization efforts have begun to revive the Long Beach waterfront, including Elberon. The New Jersey Transit North Jersey Coast Line serves Elberon today, but the railroad station that was built in 1899 and that residents considered "the most artistic and costly on the road" is no longer used. It has been replaced by a smaller, more utilitarian depot sited on Lincoln Avenue, about a quarter of a mile from Route 71.[18]

One remnant of the spur that was built to the Francklyn cottage remains in Long Branch. When the spur was no longer needed, it was torn up, and some of the ties were fashioned into canes and distributed as souvenirs. Others were sold to a local property owner who used them to build a small garden house that he called "Garfield's Hut." The cottager invited folks to tea parties in the hut, and over a century later the "Garfield Tea House" was relocated to the Long Branch Historical Museum, where it may be seen today. Incidentally, the museum itself is housed in St. James Chapel, where seven American presidents, including James Garfield, worshipped when they were in residence at the summer resort.[19]

# 19 William F. Allen and the "Day of the Two Suns" (1883)

Traditionally—one might say, tongue in cheek, "since the beginning of time"—the time at any point on the globe was measured by celestial observation and calculations proceeding from the observations. In other words, the time in your village might be established as 9 AM while, at the same instant, another observer in a town 60 miles away might conclude that it was 8:55 AM in her town. In fact, under the accepted "sun (or solar) time" measuring system, in the latitude of New York and Chicago, time varied about one minute for every 13 miles traveled east or west from a reference point. When there was slow and minimal travel between locations, time differences were inconsequential. After all, if you rarely left your village and you worked from dawn to dusk, it made little difference what the time was when your day started, 6 AM or 6:15 or even 7. Dawn to dusk in New York occupied about the same number of working hours as dawn to dusk in Chicago. However, the railroads brought increased traffic and faster travel speeds between towns. Now the standardization of time became an important consideration, and nowhere was it more important than on the railroad.[1]

Consider that when a train traveled on a single track railway from town A to town B some miles distant, it relied on "time-interval scheduling," a procedure that established certain "meet" times to avoid collisions with trains going in the opposite direction. One train was switched onto a siding before the meet time so that the other could pass safely. Under the existing time system, with conductors and engineers setting their watches to different standards, and saddled with ineffectual or nonexistent signals, the possibilities for errors and accidents were large. One instance of the problem, and probably the first manifestation of the problem affecting a railroad, was observed on the South Carolina Railroad, the first railroad in the country to operate with steam locomotives on a regular basis. There Horatio Allen, chief engineer of the road, declared that "the want of a uniform standard of time at the different points" made it difficult to maintain a schedule with faithful adherence to arrival and departure times. The South Carolina Railroad, 136 miles long, was the longest in the world at the time (1833), and each of its six stations functioned under solar time. The problem was solved by installing clocks at each station set to one standard.

In 1883, before the time zone system was established, *Scientific American* noted that 49 time standards existed in the United States. For example, in 1881, Connecticut set a uniform time for the entire state, the first instance of time legislation in the country. At Chicago, the Rock Island road advised passengers, "The clock in Sherwood and Waitley's store, at the corner of Lake and Dearborn Streets, is at present the adopted standard time, and the traveling public are reminded that the trains will arrive and depart promptly at the times stated, and as indicated by that clock." Private observatories, selling their services to businesses, offered "time services," where a standard time signal, based on local time, was routed to subscribers. The Western Union Company eventually reduced the number of local time standards by offering a uniform, less expensive time service based on U.S. Naval Observatory time measurements. Thus, a Western Union subscriber in Washington was able to synchronize his watch with another in New York. At the same time, the company excluded the competitive time signal providers from their lines, thereby reducing their effectiveness by limiting them to local distribution.[2]

Worse still, confusion reigned wherever railroads met. In Kansas City, where several railroads left from the same terminal, each used its official time, a time corresponding to the solar time at its home office. A traveler changing trains at Kansas City had to be cognizant of the variations between the two roads, an impractical requirement, if he or she wanted to make a close connection. One observer wrote: "The people of Kansas City never did have accurate information on the arrival and departure of trains, except such as was gained by going to the edge of the hill and looking down on the railway station." Again, a traveler going from Washington, D.C., to Boston, a journey of about 450 miles, and carried over the tracks of three railroads, would be required to reset his watch four times or else show a discrepancy of 24 minutes. Leaving Washington on the Baltimore and Ohio Railroad, he would be using Baltimore time. The next leg, on the Philadelphia, Wilmington and Baltimore Railroad, ran on Philadelphia time, seven minutes ahead of Baltimore. Then, catching a train on the New York, New Haven and Hartford Railroad, he would find that road using New York time, 12 minutes faster than Philadelphia. By the time he reached Boston, he would have made two other corrections, at New London and Providence.

It therefore made sense that railroads should be interested parties in attempts to develop a universal "standard" system of keeping time. They already had a mechanism in place that could address the problem. This was a group of general superintendents representing numerous railroads who met in St. Louis in 1872 to establish through timetables. However, they discounted the need for a uniform time standard, commenting that "the disadvantages the system seeks to avoid are not of such serious consequences as to call for any immediate action on the part of railroad companies." The system that they referred to was published by Charles Dowd in 1870 in which time zone boundaries coincided with meridians. Dowd was appalled by the fact that the "traveler's watch was to him but a delusion; clocks at stations staring each other in the face defiant of harmony either with one another or with surrounding local time and all

wildly at variance with the traveler's watch, baffled all intelligent interpretation." Even though the railroad officials did not believe that the establishment of a uniform time standard was a pressing problem, by the time they met in Chicago in 1875 the assembly was renamed the "General Time Convention of Railway Managers."

By 1881, the delegates were advised by the chairman of the Committee on Standard Time of the American Association for the Advancement of Science (AAAS) that "the importance of a uniformity in standards of time throughout the country is daily becoming more and more apparent. . . . I would beg you to please call the attention of your Convention [to this matter] . . . and sincerely hope a committee will be appointed to consider this important question." The AAAS position was reinforced by communications from the Army Signal Office and the American Metrological Society and other "distinguished gentlemen." Yet, although the delegates listened to various proposals politely, they "pigeon-holed" them at that meeting by referring them to the secretary of the group, William F. Allen. Rather than letting the matter drop, Allen solicited further opinions on the issue.[3]

Although it was apparent—it seems to all but the railroad men—that it was in the railroads' interests to establish a "standard" time in order to avoid the imposition of a patchwork quilt of local times, it took the perspicacity and tenaciousness of William Allen to move the issue of standard time along. Allen was the son of a railroad man from Bordentown who lost his life in the Civil War. At the age of 16, Allen began working for the Camden and Amboy Railroad as a rodman. He became a civil engineer, and in 1868 he was appointed to the position of resident engineer on the West Jersey Railroad. Based on his practical railroad experience and capacity for hard work, Allen was posted as the permanent secretary of the railway managers' group in 1875. At this time, Allen lived in South Orange and commuted daily to New York City. Fascinated by time and determined to be faithful in its keeping, he regularly advanced the minute hand of his watch one minute each morning as he traveled to work. Every evening, time demanded that the hand be moved back one minute when he reached South Orange. He made these changes at the direction of the "Comparative Time-Table" pocket chart that showed the instantaneous time at 102 cit-

**Figure 31.** William F. Allen, the architect of the plan to operate railroads in the United States to a uniform, standard time. *Frank Leslie's Popular Monthly,* April 1884.

ies, compared with a reference city. Based on the listings, he ascertained that the time difference between his home and work destination was one minute. The impracticality of such timekeeping was accentuated by the message printed across the top of the chart:

> There is no "Standard Railroad Time" in the United States or Canada; but each railroad company adopts independently the time of its own locality, or at that place which its principal office is situated. The inconvenience of such a system, if system it can be called, must be apparent to all, but is most annoying to persons strangers to the fact. From this cause many miscalculations and misconnections have arisen, which not infrequently have been of serious consequence to individuals, and have, as a matter of course, brought into disrepute all RailRoad-Guides, which of necessity give the local times. In order to relieve, in some degree, this anomaly in American railroading, we present the following table of local time, compared to that of Washington, D.C.

A conscientious traveler from New York who wished to notify his family of his train's arrival time at Chicago so that he would be met "on time" had better use the chart or risk a wait at the station if the family employed local time in their calculations![4]

In addition to being secretary of the Time Convention, Allen had two other advantages in influencing the strong-willed managers: he was editor of the *Travelers' Guide,* a publication that incorporated an editorial section where he could espouse his views, and he was also a member of the American Metrological Society. As part of the AMS, involved in the science of measures and weights, he became intimately aware of the efforts of those involved in time reform. Therefore, he was able to call attention to a variant of Canadian Sandford Fleming's 1875 concept, namely, to divide the earth into 24 time zones. He proposed that North America should be divided into five time zones, in each of which time (or its measurement) would be the same. Thus, 9 PM in New York City would correspond to 9 PM in Harrisburg and to 8 PM in Chicago, which was one time zone removed from the first time zone. This proposal was based on the

procedure employed by the AMS in the maintenance of a "public Standard Time Ball," namely, upon receipt of a telegraph signal, all time balls in the

> Atlantic Coast time zone will drop at noon on the 75th meridian; Gulf Coast time balls all drop at noon on the 90th meridian; Lake Coast time balls all drop at noon on the 90th meridian; Mississippi Valley time balls all drop at noon on the 90th meridian; Pacific Coast time balls all drop at noon on the 120th meridian.

(It is interesting to note that the current New Year's Eve practice of dropping a ball in Times Square in New York City at midnight in the Eastern Time Zone is a direct descendant of this procedure.)

Fortunately, Allen chose to ignore a suggestion that the "sun time" at Washington, D.C., the "Hub of the Universe," become the national time standard, a national "prime" meridian where noon at Washington would become noon at San Francisco. He displayed a sharp sense of humor when he scolded Washingtonians by asking "what right have you to claim that particular meridian as belonging to your city. The villages of Gum Tree and of Hard Scrabble are on the same meridian and have as much right to give it a name as your beautiful city has."[5]

Now, although the time was ripe for pressing forward with a uniform time standard, a rate war erupted among various trunk lines, and cooperation between them took a back seat. Allen, prepared to present his time plan to the convention in April 1882, decided to postpone its meeting indefinitely because he realized that it would not receive a fair hearing in the existing atmosphere. In October 1882, an abbreviated gathering of the delegates afforded him the opportunity to offer his plan for consideration. At that meeting some attendees suggested disbanding the group, but Allen emphasized the importance of the standard time question and pointed out the activity in the field that was being undertaken by government and private companies. He also secured agreement that a subsequent meeting should be held to consider his report.

Because Allen knew that the railroads were fearful that a government standard might be imposed upon them and that it was in their best interest to establish their own voluntary standard, he wrote an editorial in the *Travelers' Guide* in April 1883 urging immediate action: "We should settle this question among ourselves, and not entrust it to the infinite wisdom of the . . . State legislatures."

Later he declared, "Congressional action . . . is to be depreciated, as . . . there is little likelihood of any law being adopted in Washington, effecting [*sic*] railways, that would be as universally acceptable to the railway companies." Thus, through the force of his arguments and personality, Allen almost single-handedly brought the issue to a vote. Bartky, in the conclusion to his excellent treatise on the subject, wrote about Allen, "So the railroads began to care about uniform time because of the actions of one person, uniquely placed to appreciate the efforts that had been under way for years and able to effect change, who felt that the industry had to respond to prevent 'outsider' influence."

The "Allen Plan," adopted by the Time Convention in October 1883, defined the reference meridians in each time zone exactly 15 degrees of longitude, or one hour, apart. The zones were renamed as we know them today: eastern, central, mountain, and Pacific; the fifth zone, applying to the Canadian Maritime provinces, was centered on the 60th meridian and called intercolonial. There were some anomalies in

**Figure 32.** A map of the proposal for standard time made by William Allen. This plan, adopted by the General Time Convention of Railway Managers, was implemented by almost all American railroads in November 1883. From the appendix to the *Proceedings of the General Time Convention, 1893.*

the scheme because the boundaries of each zone were established at specified towns and cities, at the terminus of a railroad or one of its divisions. For instance, Pittsburgh was included in the central time zone because it was a terminus for many lines to the west. Thus the borders were not clean-cut; rather, they displayed considerable raggedness. As it developed, the central time zone was almost two hours wide, a consequence of using division points for boundaries. Rather than being a disadvantage, the consideration of railroad termini was an important selling point to the convention delegates. Although in the many iterations of his plan, Dowd had conceived of almost all of the standard time features that were ultimately adopted, he had lacked an understanding of the importance of attempting to maintain one time zone from beginning to end of a division. Allen, a railroad man, used this information to his advantage. (Not only was Dowd's proposal rejected by the railroads but the man himself experienced the misfortune of being killed by a railroad train at a crossing in 1904.)

To explain further, the 75th meridian, a line of longitude that passed through Philadelphia, was chosen as the reference meridian in Allen's eastern time zone, which stretched from Maine to a longitude near Pittsburgh. It was dictated that it was noon throughout the zone precisely as the sun passed over the 75th meridian. Saying it was so was the easy part. Implementing it was more difficult! A highly coordinated effort was necessary to change all the timepieces within each time zone at exactly the right instant. Allen issued orders from New Jersey detailing the exact steps that were to be followed. (He permitted individual railroad officials to decide, when the difference between sun time and standard time was less than 10 minutes, whether they would also modify and republish their timetables.) On 18 November 1883, railroad clocks were stopped throughout the time zone and set to noon. Upon receipt of a telegraphed signal from the Naval Observatory that

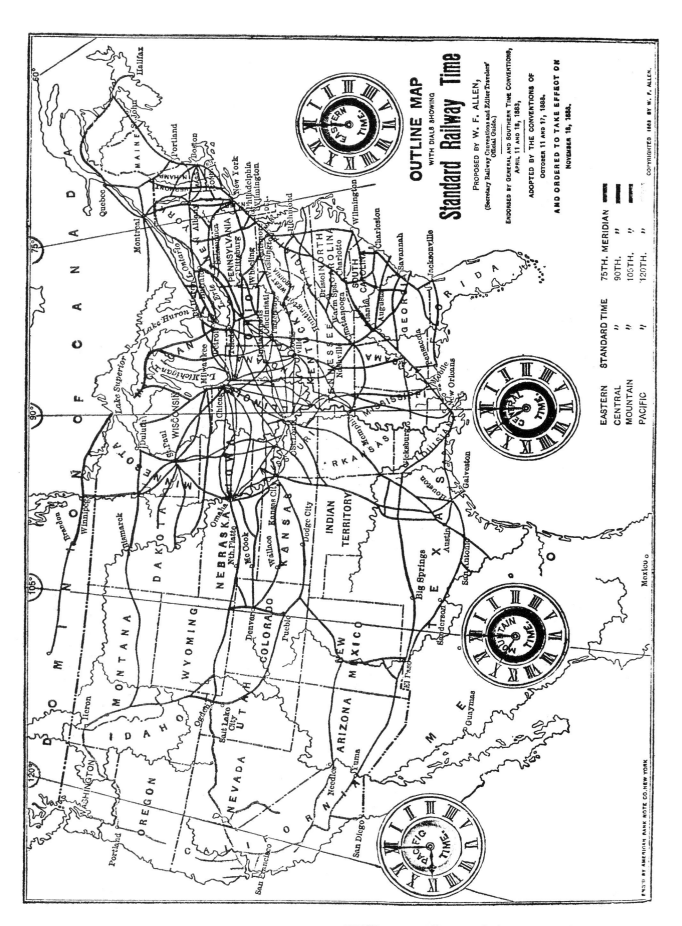

the sun was over the relevant reference meridian, the clocks were restarted. Now all clocks within the zone read the same time. It was a stupendous achievement to ensure that all clocks were in harmony. Fran Capo, an author who wrote about New Jersey, stated that Allen "made time stand still." When the event took place, Allen was in New York City at the headquarters of the Western Union Company. He described the moment as follows: "Standing on the roof of that building . . . I heard the bells of St. Paul's strike on the old time. Four minutes later, obedient to the electrical signal from the Naval Observatory . . . the time-ball made its rapid descent, the chimes of old Trinity rang twelve measured strokes, and local time was abandoned, probably forever."[6]

The Association of American Railroads published a pamphlet titled *The Day of Two Noons,* which described the changeover. Allen himself wrote a detailed explanation of his plan, along with historical information about the situation that preceded it, in *Popular Science Monthly;* it was reprinted in *Scientific American Supplement.* Though meant to apply to their operations, the railroads realized that public cooperation in terms of adopting the railroad standard as their local standard was important to its success. In fact, before the resolution was approved at the October 1883 meeting, the delegates insisted that the city of Boston adopt Allen's plan, which it did. Happily, most cities and villages followed suit, but there were some who disagreed with the concept or the subsequent reality. As might be expected, opposition was strongest at the time zone boundaries, where the variation from solar time was the greatest. However, the United States attorney general directed all federal agencies to reject the "Allen Plan." That individual stubbornly neglected to reset his watch to the new railroad time and consequently, when he departed work that evening, he missed his train. And there were others, like the mayor of Bangor, Maine, Frederick A. Cummings, who railed against the imposition of any standards and who vetoed his council's adoption of a standard time. He thundered that "neither railroad laws nor municipal regulation has power to change one of the immutable laws of God, that the hours of noon, sunrise, and sunset should occur at different periods of the day . . . this 'farce styled standard time' . . . [that] turns day into night . . . teaches wholesale falsehood and deception, and is in no way adapted to the wants of the general public."

Mayor Cummings's outburst was mild compared with that of the pastor of a church who felt that accepting the new time was "the worst case of total depravity on record . . . For a lie is a lie, be it big or little. [The Bible says] the sun was set to rule the day, and the moon to rule the night." The mayor's and pastor's opinions notwithstanding, all of the railroads in the United States and Canada (except parts of the Central Pacific and Southern Pacific Railroads and two shortlines in Pennsylvania) adopted the new "standard" time.[7]

The commendation of Allen's peers was expressed in an editorial in the *Railroad Gazette,* which read in part,

> To propose a uniform time was easy; to propose a practical system, like that with hour intervals between standards, did not require genius; to adapt one so that existing railroad systems might, for the most part, fall naturally under the different standards, must have taken much study and good judgment; to find a nomenclature which should not cause prejudice in communities as jealous of each other as some of ours are, demanded tact. . . . Seeing that all these various things needed to be done to make it possible to secure the favorable action of any considerable number of the managing officers who would have to decide on the adoption of the new time standards was, however, what more than anything else made the effort successful. . . . [Mr. Allen's] success, which is likely to identify his name for ever with a Time Standard affecting every person in the country, . . . shows what can be done by persistent effort and a careful adjustment of means to ends.[8]

His epitaph, inscribed on a tablet erected in his memory in 1915 reads, in part: "He devised and through the instrumentality of the American railway managers in 1883, put in effect, first in the United States, the system of standard time which has since been extended throughout the civilized world." That sentiment was a bit premature because time zone standardization for other than railroad use was not dictated on a national basis in the United States until 1919. By that time, most communities had already adopted railroad time as the standard. Unquestionably, they should thank William F. Allen, who, although he was not the first to develop a scheme for a uniform standard time, was an engineer of its introduction in the United States.[9]

# 20 The "Hoodoo" Trolley Car and Other Streetcar Tales (1887–1940s)

An earlier chapter in this book chronicles the invention of electric railroad vehicles and describes two New Jersey pioneers of their development, Thomas Edison and Leo Daft. Daft was also active in electric streetcar development. In 1887, one of his cars was in service at Orange, New Jersey. This car, on the Crosstown Line, collected electricity from two overhead wires that were spanned by a "troller" (the genesis of the word *trolley*). The troller ran freely on the wires and was pulled along by the movement of the car below. When the car stopped, the troller usually continued rolling along the wire until it was pulled up short by its tether, the electrical conductor bringing "juice" to the trolley motor.

Although the troller was a distinct improvement over the earlier practice of carrying current through the rails with the attendant danger of a serious electrical shock to people or animals, it had a tendency to tumble from its supporting wires. Rowsome tells of a newly hired Daft car conductor who fought an extended battle with his troller. Climbing up onto the roof of the car to replace the fallen troller, our conductor received a shock that threw him down. This act continued through five iterations until he finally managed to seat the troller properly. Within a city block, the troller fell again, and our hero made a significant decision: he resigned on the spot and retired to a nearby saloon.[1]

One source states that the Passaic, Garfield and Clifton Railway Company, beginning operation in Passaic in 1890, was the first streetcar line in New Jersey, but the Daft trolleys certainly predated that system. Two Daft lines were established in the state in 1887, the first in Asbury Park and the other in Orange. (The Asbury Park line operated continuously until it was abandoned in 1931, although not with Daft equipment throughout that time.) From this beginning, the proliferation of New Jersey trolley car systems during the 1890s was astronomical. By the end of World War I, the Garden State was crisscrossed by a spider's web of electric railways, dominated by the Public Service Corporation's lines. (Public Service was organized in 1903 by Thomas J. McCarter, a state legislator for whom McCarter Highway in Newark is named. PS soon had swallowed up over 100 trolley lines and was conducting traction operations with over 2,500 trolley cars on 900 miles of track.) Trolley ridership peaked in 1923, but the decline of the ubiquitous trolley soon began.[2]

There have been scores of trolley lines in the state of New Jersey, 162 according to one listing. These are too many to discuss within the limitations of this book. Rather than detail the history and fortunes of several, or even one or two, trolley car systems, a number of anecdotes are presented. While they may not provide a comprehensive picture of streetcar operation in the Garden State, they are interesting in themselves, and they provide a snapshot of operations. So hop aboard, drop your fare or token into the collection box, and find a comfortable seat, an oxymoron where trolley car seats were concerned, or grasp a dangling strap. Hang on tight because the unprepared are in danger of being spilled by a jerking start or sudden stop!

Figure 33. This trolley car, built by Leo Daft, was in service on the Orange, New Jersey, Crosstown Line in 1887. Electricity was collected from the overhead wires by a "troller," the four-wheeled contraption that rode along the wires. *Electric World.*

\* \* \*

In another instance of a frog war, this time between a railroad and a trolley car line, the South Jersey Street Railway Company was building from Red Bank to the shore. In Red Bank, the tracks of the New York and Long Branch Railroad (NY&LB) were in its path. The trolley company's franchise prohibited either tunneling under or bridging the railroad tracks, a "catch 22" situation because the railroad was adamantly opposed to having the trolleys cross at grade. The railroad stationed a locomotive at the projected crossing point and ran it back and forth to prevent the trolley construction crews from placing a crossing diamond there. The streetcar company took its case to court, and while awaiting a decision, its passengers had to alight from their streetcar at the NY&LB tracks, cross the tracks on foot, and board a waiting car on the other side. Finally, on 28 February 1898, a ruling was made in favor of the streetcar company. Almost immediately, construction crews were assembled, and they erected lights at the crossing point, the intention being that the crossing would be installed at night when there was less traffic on the railroad. The railroad's superintendent, Rufus Blodgett, was determined to prevent the crossing, and he ordered a freight train into the construction area to prevent further work. Now the locomotive that had been shuttling across the point of contention stopped for a moment, and Joseph Riley, a prominent Red Bank attorney who had been retained by the street railway, inserted a length of rail between the spokes of one of the driving wheels. Upon starting again, the rail prevented wheel rotation, and the main rod of the engine failed. Constable Stryker attempted to quell the ensuing fight and was attacked by a railroad employee who swung a crowbar at his head. Stryker was compelled to draw his pistol to defend himself. Ultimately, six railroad men were arrested but released on bail later that day. Although Blodgett stormed about and rallied his men to continue to defy the court order,

expecting that his management would obtain a stay (which they did not), he was finally compelled to accede to the demands of the elected officials of Red Bank to clear the area and permit the crossing to be accomplished. This was done quickly, and the first trolley car passed over the disputed section two days later. A few days later, to celebrate the occasion, the South Jersey Street Railway Company outfitted one of their cars with flags and bunting and, "with gongs clanging and whistles blowing," carried a group of distinguished guests to Asbury Park. Eid, who wrote of the incident, speculates that this affair must have "made Blodgett's face even redder. Rufus Blodgett was overheard to say that the biggest mistake in his life was that he never had his railroad fenced in so that he wouldn't ever see the dam trolley again."[3]

\* \* \*

One of the problems facing a streetcar motorman was the traffic with which he had to share the right-of-way. Horses and wagons moved no faster than a walk (albeit at a horse's pace), little boys darted in front of the car (when they were not perched outside on the back of the car), and autos raced along the trolley tracks (and often slid along the wet tracks to crash into the rear of the streetcar when attempting to brake during a rainstorm). Innumerable accidents have been reported over the years, but one was of special interest because it involved the "hoodoo car of the line."

The Public Service Company ran a trolley line between Somerville and Bound Brook, and on 16 June 1909 its eastbound car, number 524, which left for Bound Brook at noon, was struck at the Chimney Rock crossing by a ballast train emerging from a quarry. To prevent such an accident, PS had installed a derailer 40 feet before the crossing; the conductor of each trolley approaching that point was required to alight and throw a switch that enabled passage without derailing. In this instance, the procedure was followed, but for some unknown reason the car was tardy in clearing the crossing. At the same time, a Jersey Central ballast train was rounding a curve several hundred feet away, pushed by a switch engine that was still not visible because it was obscured by a grove of trees along the tracks. The railroad later insisted that a flagman was running ahead of the ballast train to warn of its approach, but, because of the curve, his signal could not be seen at once by the locomotive engineer. The train broadsided the trolley car, but most of the streetcar passengers, seeing the approaching train, had jumped off and escaped injury. However, five passengers who remained in the car were seriously injured, suffering contusions and cuts. They were rushed to the nearest hospital by special trolleys quickly dispatched to the scene. The conductor of the trolley car, Joseph Campbell, believed that number 524 was a jinxed car. It had been involved in a fatal collision the previous November when operating with a different crew. Campbell was certain that he was under the "spell of the hoodoo" because only a few days before the crash, a woman had died on a car that he was running between Somerville and Raritan. At that time, the woman "hailed a trolley car . . . and requested the conductor to assist her to the platform. She staggered into the car and was stricken with apoplexy as she sank into a seat. Conductor Campbell stopped his car in front of the residence of Dr. Seaman who promptly responded to a call for assistance. [The woman] expired shortly after the physician entered the car."

Despite experiencing these two traumatic incidents, Campbell was able to shake off his fears because car number 524 was removed from service after the Chimney Rock accident, almost totally destroyed, "overturned and crushed like an eggshell and left [in] a shapeless mass under the wheels of one of the ballast cars." A photograph, taken after the accident but before the remains of number 524 were removed, shows the overturned car resembling a pile of kindling wood.[4]

* * *

Another dramatic and tragic accident implicating a Public Service car occurred on 28 August 1905. Through cars ran along the "Fast Line" between Newark and Trenton, through Milltown. However, although passengers were not required to change cars, it was the practice that the PS crews coming from Newark ran no farther toward Trenton than switch number 1 near Dayton. At that point, south of New Brunswick, they were to wait for the next Newark-bound car so that a crew change would be made, and then they would take the northbound car back to Newark. This plan was in effect because the tracks south of New Brunswick were owned by the Trenton and New Brunswick Railroad, and PS operated on them under a lease arrangement.

On the fateful day, a PS interurban car, under the control of Motorman Whalen and filled with passengers, had already made the change at Dayton and was traveling toward New Brunswick. Just beyond a high trestle, a short distance from Milltown, Whalen's car was struck head-on by a Trenton and New Brunswick Railroad construction car that was towing a flat car. The construction extra, driven by Motorman Stoetelmyer, was trying to reach switch number 1. Stoetelmyer, having seen Whalen pass him at Milltown, heading southbound, and "guessing that the motorman [Whalen] of the car going toward Trenton knew he was following his car and would hold the car bound for Newark until he arrived." He guessed wrongly. Whalen later claimed that he "warned Stoetelmyer not to follow his car."

Now Whalen, seeing the construction train approaching, immediately applied his brakes. He managed to stop his car, and his conductor "shouted to the passengers to look out but before they could get out of the car the crash came." Stoetelmyer, running down grade at a high rate of speed, could not stop his car and in the ensuing crash 27 people were hurt, but there were no deaths. The "big, yellow car was telescoped for twelve feet by the big red car of the

Trenton line." Contributing to the horror was the electrical fire that ignited the debris and set the clothing of some trapped passengers afire. Relief cars with doctors on board were dispatched from New Brunswick and Trenton immediately after word of the accident was received.

One of the victims, Julius Gustafson, recounted:

I saw the motorman of the approaching car and another man jump, but before I had time to move the cars came together and the seat I was sitting on was driven back to the center of the car. A horrible scene followed, many were screaming in terror, others crying for help and others walking over the injured in order to reach an exit. Looking through the wreckage, I could see the little girl who sat with her mother all ablaze and thought she was burning to death. I never experienced such a sight.

Fortunately, although there were numerous injuries, there were no fatalities. The little girl that Gustafson saw "all ablaze" suffered burns on her hands and shoulders but recovered satisfactorily, as did her mother.[5]

Public Service disavowed all responsibility for the wreck, and according to some accounts, their crews attempted to discourage the investigators. Immediately after the crash, Detective Elwell, who happened to be nearby, was "starting for the scene of the wreck," but trolley line employees "tried to persuade him a car was merely off the track. 'Do you think I was born yesterday?' asked the detective." People with cameras were "ordered off," and the only photos were taken by PS's official photographer. Stoetelmyer, a novice motorman with only three weeks in that position, disappeared after leaping from his car, and detectives were charged with locating him.[6]

Strangely reminiscent of the Fast Line accident was another that involved two cars of the North Jersey Rapid Transit Company. Reported by E. J. Quinby, who had been a motorman at a later time, the accident took three lives, including a motorman who was working his very last trip. William Hutchinson had resigned a day earlier, but Superintendent Pilgrim convinced him to work one last run. Early on the morning of 21 July, Hutchinson rotated the controller of car number 20 and left the car barn at Ho-Ho-Kus; he was scheduled to work until 2:51 PM. About midday, a sudden electrical storm arose

and lightning affected several block signals. Orders were passed to continue operations while ignoring the damaged signals. Now Superintendent Pilgrim recruited John Frotaillio, a 21-year-old track worker, to accompany him on car number 12 to repair the signals. After fixing the signal at Ridgewood, Pilgrim reckoned that he would be able to reach a siding near Glen Rock and be safely off the northbound main line before the next car came along, an operation called "stealing a switch." As Pilgrim's "wildcat" car rounded the Prospect Street curve, he encountered Hutchinson's northbound car racing toward him! Hutchinson's car, coming from East Paterson, was loaded with passengers, including members of a Sunday school picnic. Hutchinson's car was "running downhill at about thirty miles per hour . . . [and] he had no reason to believe that the track was not clear. It was impossible for him to see far ahead, as on either side of the track are woods and the road curves a good deal." There was no time to avoid a catastrophic crash, and investigators determined that the controller handles of both cars were in the full speed forward position at the time of the mishap. Injured passengers on Hutchinson's car, some seriously hurt, were ministered to at the scene and removed to hospitals and nearby clinics; they all recovered. Hutchinson was "hurled to the top of his car" and was killed outright. The other two traction company employees were seriously injured, and despite being carried promptly to nearby hospitals, they died. Although their deaths were equally sorrowful, the most ironic circumstance was that the 40-year-old Hutchinson was killed only nine minutes before he was scheduled to retire from the job.[7]

* * *

There have been many stories written about runaway or hijacked cars, and one illustrative example involving a car of the Trenton and New Brunswick Railroad was described in the *Daily True American* as the car that "couldn't wait." At New Brunswick, one of the big trolleys "came rolling into town at a good rate of speed, without the assistance of a crew or the burden of a passenger. The car came down Throop avenue, turned into George street, and kept on in spite of the signaling of the people who wanted to board it, until it came to New street, when the trolley pole slipped from the overhead wire and the car came to a standstill through sheer exhaustion and a want of power." The crew had left the car at the local car barn without setting the brakes, and it moved out without attendants. As soon as they realized their mistake, the motorman and conductor boarded a second car and "strained every nerve to overtake the runaway."[8] The episode ended well because no one was hurt and the runaway was recovered.

Another incident, but not involving a runaway car, stands out in originality and humor. Regina Waldron Murray, in her delightful book *Profiles in the Wind*, tells the tale of "The Great Trolley Heist." This story concerns little Billy Moore, a 10-year-old who rode the Trenton Street Railway trolley to school every weekday morning. One day in the 1930s, perhaps a warm day, a few minutes into Billy's ride, the motorman decided to stop for a libation at Finney's Saloon. After a half-hour passed with no sign of the motorman, a woman passenger, fearing that she might be fired for being late, began to cry. Hearing her sobs, young Billy swung into action. He closed the trolley doors and rotated the controller arm, and the trolley resumed its journey. As it sped along, the pealing of the trolley's bell and the screams of the passengers attracted the attention of firemen lounging in front of Engine Company #6. However, before they could intervene, Billy brought the trolley to a stop, got off calmly, and walked into his school. That evening, the lad faced a tribunal consisting of his father, the trolley conductor, and a wrathful transit company official. His punishment was banishment from riding the trolley forevermore. An ironic postscript to the story is that Billy became Dr. William J. Moore, a respected and law-abiding physician appointed to minister to the New Jersey State Police. Ms. Murray told the author that many years later Dr. Moore received telephone calls "from friends in the State Police who laughingly told him that they were checking to see if the statute of limitations had run out on his crime."[9]

\* \* \*

One of the early streetcar lines in the state was the Bridgeton and Millville Traction Company, which was built during the period 1892–95 and relied on heavy summer traffic to its private amusement park. By 1902, park traffic of more than a half million riders on this small system accounted for over a third of its total patronage. It was on this road that a group

of four thugs boarded one of its cars, intending to rob the passengers. Unwilling to become victims, the passengers turned the tables on their attackers and forcibly ejected them from the car. In frustration, as the car resumed its journey, the would-be bandits showered the car with rocks. However, many crimes on streetcars were committed not by outsiders but by the company's employees.[10]

Trolley crews over the years were overwhelmingly honest, but, as in all human endeavors, there were a few who found or manufactured ways to "beat the system." The most commonly installed appliance designed to thwart such individuals was the register that sounded a loud "ka-ching" when it was activated by the conductor as he collected each fare. "Spotters" were hired to ride the trolley to ensure that each fare was registered, but some conductors developed an ability to shortchange the meter. One technique used during busy times was to collect a number of fares throughout the car and then ring them up at one time, one or two short. Technology also aided the would-be thief when a so-called "brother-in-law" became available. This was a device that could be worn under the conductor's jacket which, when activated by a concealed string, could be rung in imitation of the car register. The conductor could pretend to pull the register cord while simultaneously engaging the underarm device. In a crowded car, it was difficult for a spotter to establish the source of the sound. Ingenious as some of these schemes were, they were unnecessary when a sticky-fingered conductor was determined to steal fares.[11]

Nathan Cope described a continuing criminal conspiracy that took place in 1941 on the Five Miles Beach Electric Railway, a trolley line that ran through Wildwood, New Jersey. In the shore communities it was difficult to find sufficient workers to handle the great influx of visitors during the busy summer months; the regular trolley crews were too few to serve the necessary additional runs. The weekend schedule was accommodated by motormen and conductors who had regular jobs elsewhere and were recruited to work on Saturdays and Sundays, but the extra weekday trips posed a problem. Thus the trolley company felt fortunate to be able to hire and train a number of men to be assigned as motormen and conductors on the weekday runs. Little did they know that this group, all from South Philadelphia, were friends who had their own agenda. However, it soon became evident that something was amiss because the cash receipts did not come close to matching the traffic. Cars would roll along loaded with passengers, yet their fare registers showed only a dozen or so fares; the rest went into the crew's pockets. When their boss confronted one brazen crew, he was told that if any one of the group was discharged, all would resign. Such an action, akin to a strike, would have shut down the line during the height of the busiest season. The company manager retreated, but only to develop a plan to man all of the trolleys by asking former employees to return to the job full time and by authorizing overtime for others. With the means to keep the trolleys running in place, he brought his complaint and plan to the Wildwood Police Department. Police boarded cars along the line and removed the wrongdoers. An almost seamless transition between crews was made because as the police escorted the thieves from a car, their place was taken immediately by another crew and the trip continued. Some passengers were confused by the unfolding drama, but others were heedless of the arrests. When all of the suspects were in custody, the trolley company offered them a deal: leave town immediately or face charges. They accepted, and the company's revenues took a turn for the better for the remainder of the summer.[12]

This particular tale described a not uncommon situation when it was necessary to augment the operating crews during peak traffic periods. Robert Chew was superintendent (and general manager and treasurer) of the Ocean City Electric Railway in the days before World War I. His summer employees included many men who were on vacation from colleges; even high school students were occasionally hired when the need arose. Chew was aware that these temporary employees might be tempted to "skim fares." Consequently, he attempted to hire applicants living in the area who, he reasoned, would be less likely to steal. And he adamantly refused to hire those who wanted to be conductors rather than motormen. In Chew's eyes, they were men who intended to steal and had already worked out schemes for pocketing fares. Yet when a conductor was caught with his hand in the fare box, often by one of the "spotters" hired to police the conductors, Chew was generous enough to call him into his office and issue a stern warning to

desist or face dismissal. That threat was usually sufficient for a local offender to mend his ways rather than face embarrassment at work and at home.[13]

* * *

At a symposium several years ago, the author was treated to an amusing story about streetcars. The narrator, whom we will call "Joe," a motorman on a North Jersey line, described how company management stationed "checkers" at strategic points along the route. The function of these individuals was to monitor the adherence of individual cars to schedule. The unfortunate motorman who was consistently late in passing his checkpoints was certain to be reprimanded by management. It seems that one of the checkers, let's call him "Old Crabby," was a particular nemesis of all of the trolley crews, and he took exceptional glee in reporting deviations from schedule. One busy rush hour Joe was driving his car with a very short headway between it and the car following. When his car reached a switch where his route parted from another, for some reason he failed to set the switch in the proper direction. As a consequence, the car proceeded a few dozen feet along the wrong tracks. Realizing his mistake, Joe rectified it by backing up the car through the switch and onto his original route, a process that took some time. In the interim, another car had already passed the switch and continued on its way. When the wayward car proceeded along the avenue, it was now late but, more extraordinary, out of sequence. Uncertain as to how he would explain the discrepancy to Old Crabby, who would be waiting a few blocks away, Joe decided that a bold approach was best. As he drew near the checker, he called and waved a cheery "good evening" and rattled past. Old Crabby, astonished and speechless to find a car not only late but also out of sequence, jumped up and down and waved his hands, but the big car was now gone. Back at the car barn Old Crabby checked and rechecked the records of the departures of the cars before and after that of our narrator but could not explain the seemingly impossible fact that a car had somehow "leapfrogged" another along the route. Our hero laughingly related that this incident, one of the times when he certainly deserved censure, was never reported, probably because Old Crabby did not believe his eyes and couldn't explain how the cars had become rearranged.

In many cases, the last day of operation on an abandoned streetcar line was cause for celebration, not to mark a happy occasion but to memorialize years of faithful service. Many lines added special cars that were filled with fans, dignitaries, and just plain citizens wanting to be a part of the sunset of an era. Occasionally, the festivities deteriorated as souvenir hunters stripped the cars of parts and otherwise vandalized them, but Atlantic City's adieu to its streetcars in 1955 was unique. The traction company donated the last day's revenue to the local hospital, and in return the hospital arranged for its attractive nurses to ride the cars and present each passenger with a "last day" certificate. Usually there were teary farewells to the big cars, but there was rarely anticipation of better service to be provided by buses. Yet the time of the trolley had passed, terminated by the greater expense of its equipment and fixed plant, inflexible routing, traffic-choked streets, and the popularity of the private automobile.[14]

The trolleys in the Garden State were replaced long ago by buses, but it is possible to find some evidence of their existence. For instance, there is a "trolley park" in Secaucus, along the Hackensack River, at the west end of the Paterson Plank Road. Here in this "pocket park," a short section of trolley track remains, the last vestige of the Jersey City, Hoboken and Rutherford Electric Railway. In other towns around the state, one can still find rails buried in cobblestoned streets or other trolley artifacts either neglected by local authorities or felt to be not worth the money to remove them. A real treasure has been recovered by the New Jersey Transportation Heritage Center. A 100-year-old Stephenson-made trolley, one of 20 built in Elizabeth, New Jersey, for export to Lisbon, Portugal, in 1906, was acquired by the Center and returned to the United States. Permanent storage for this priceless car has not yet been arranged, but it will become a centerpiece of the Heritage Center.[15]

The streetcar played a major role in developing this state and others; it made possible longer commutes and thus the expansion of early twentieth-century communities. The promise that the electric cars delivered was expressed in the following lines from "The Song of the Trolley," a poem composed by Roy L. McCardell:

> I have harnessed nature's forces. I've freed the mules and horses.
> I have helped the toiling thousands to new ways to earn their bread.
> Then, as civilization's factor, I will laugh at each detractor
> And keep on doing business at the same old stand instead.
> Hear me whizzing through the highways—see me brightening up the byways,
> Annihilating distance as I merry speed along.
> I bring new life and faces to old sleeping towns and places
> And a million homes are brighter for the music of my song.[16]

# 21 A Pair of Majestic Railroad Terminals (1889 and 1907)

The demolition of Pennsylvania Station in New York City, while deeply distressing, resulted in at least one beneficial outcome: it aroused concerned citizens and emphasized the necessity to preserve rather than destroy many of the country's irreplaceable older monuments. Destruction of that great terminal, beginning in 1963, raised the visibility of the preservation effort nationwide and accelerated the drive to provide the city's Landmarks Preservation Commission with the legal authority to act on its decisions. Unfortunately, by the time that the Landmarks Law was enacted in 1965, Pennsylvania Station was almost completely demolished. Yet, without question, the preservation of Grand Central terminal in New York, Union Station in the District of Columbia, and other notable railroad stations nationwide, including two on the New Jersey shoreline, could be traced directly to the loss of Penn Station. The two Garden State edifices, the Lackawanna (DL&W) Hoboken terminal and the Jersey Central's (CNJ) Jersey City station, are the subject of this chapter.[1]

First, let it be said that there were five major terminals along the western shore of the Hudson serving the various railroads that reached the river. The CNJ and the Pennsylvania owned huge complexes at Jersey City; the Erie and the Lackawanna each had separate facilities (the Erie was also situated in Jersey City) but eventually merged operations at Hoboken. The West Shore Railroad operated a station at Weehawken. The terminals at Hoboken and Jersey City were chosen for this exposition because they still stand and are accessible to visitors: in the former case, as a working terminal serving Jersey commut-

ers, and in the latter, essentially as a museum, a prime attraction at Liberty State Park.[2]

## THE CENTRAL RAILROAD OF NEW JERSEY'S TERMINAL OF 1889 AT JERSEY CITY

Extension of its tracks to Jersey City was part of the CNJ's plan to meet competition from the Morris Canal and Banking Company, which carried enormous quantities of coal from Pennsylvania and which already had port facilities at Jersey City. Second, it was in response to complaints by passengers who had to transfer to New Jersey Railroad cars to reach Jersey City from Elizabethport. In the Communipaw section of Jersey City, Newark Bay was a vast shoal, at most four feet deep at high tide. The CNJ, operating under permission granted by the legislature in 1860 to extend its tracks, began to buy riparian rights to the waterfront from long-established families. In so doing, the CNJ became the defendant in a lawsuit brought by the Canal Company, one in which the courts ultimately found for the railroad.[3]

Now, in the early 1860s, although free to begin construction, the railroad had to cross the tidelands barrier, a project that necessitated the construction of a two-mile-long trestle across mudflats and Newark Bay. A pivot-drawbridge, which, when opened, provided two 75-foot-wide openings, was a impressive feature of the undertaking. A prodigious amount of fill was required, and despite the displeasure of local residents, New York City garbage was dumped endlessly and scores of oceangoing ships contributed their ballast to the project. Even scores of old Mor-

Figure 34. The two-mile long trestle and drawbridge across Newark Bay that brought the Jersey Central from Elizabeth to Bergen Point in Jersey City in 1864. Once there, the company built a train/ferry terminal to serve its patrons. An imposing new terminal replaced the original one in 1889. Kobbé, *Jersey Central*.

ris Canal boats were used to firm up the marsh. The final few feet of fill consisted of locomotive cinders and other "clean fill" obtained along the railroad's right-of-way. A view of this trestle was included in *Kobbé's Jersey Central*.

Invitees to the dedication of the bridge were fed and treated to a ride on the bay aboard the ferryboat *Central*, and Jersey Central president John T. Johnston recalled the occasion:

> I had arranged to have a blessing asked at each table, but before any such thing was possible all hands and mouths were hard at work, and it is very doubtful if twenty on board knew whether we went down the bay, or up the bay, or both. They found abundance of time, however, to praise the boat. She is universally admitted to be a beauty, even by those interested in running her down. The fifty baskets of champagne and forty baskets of claret began now to disappear with marvelous celerity, and though as a whole, the crowd behaved well, yet, as soon as we saw some beginning to get noisy, we stopped the wine, and kept the fun within bounds.

The *Central* was a brand-new boat, purchased to replace the *Kill van Kull*, which had been requisitioned by the government for wartime service.

Once the tracks reached Jersey City, a modest, three-track terminal was erected on Bergen Point; from there, a passenger could board a CNJ ferry to New York City. This station, built in sections at

Bound Brook, was carried by train to Jersey City and assembled on-site. Allegedly, this was the first instance of a prefabricated railroad station in the United States. However, within two decades, passenger traffic had outpaced the capacity of the waterfront station, and the railroad undertook the construction of a modern terminal that would replace the original one.[4]

A report in a local newspaper on 15 June 1885 stated that the three-story rail and ferry terminal being built in Communipaw would cost $400,000. It contained twelve tracks, each 512 feet long and protected by one-story train sheds. The terminal was "fitted with speaking tubes, electric bells and other modern appliances. At night it will be lighted with electric lights."[5]

The new station, completed in 1889, was designed by Peabody and Stearns, a Boston architectural firm. Everything about it was a superlative: it was the largest railroad complex on the waterfront; it boasted the largest collection of Bush sheds, covering the largest area, ever built; after Ellis Island opened (three years after the station was built), almost two-thirds of new immigrants processed at Ellis Island, a stone's throw away, made their way through the CNJ terminal en route to new homes. The headhouse was 215 feet wide and three stories high. The structure, made of brick and iron, was built upon piles. The waiting room in the center of the building was over 85 feet

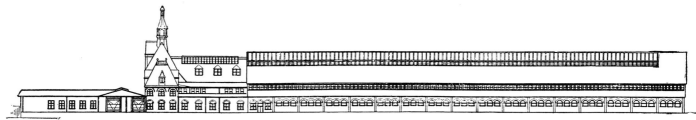

FIG. 680.—SIDE ELEVATION.

FIG. 681.—FRONT ELEVATION.

**Figure 35.** Front and side elevations of the Central Railroad of New Jersey's terminal at Jersey City. The side elevation shows the three distinct elements of the station: the low structure at the left leading to the ferry slips, the headhouse at the center, and the long train shed at the right. The front elevation shows the four ferry slips that faced the river with the headhouse behind them. This illustration was published in Walter G. Berg's classic book, *Buildings and Structures of American Railroads*. The original drawings were published in the 6 October 1888 issue of *Engineering News*.

long and more than 66 feet wide. A newsstand, restaurant, ticket office, private rooms, and upper-floor offices surrounded the waiting room. Natural light streamed in through the three large dormers and a room-length skylight. The train shed behind the building was 512 feet long, and it accommodated 12 tracks, separated by wide concrete platforms.[6]

The new CNJ terminal was in the planning stage at about the same time that the Statue of Liberty was dedicated (1886). The statue was the most prominent feature of the vista from the station's ferry slips, and its image was adopted for the CNJ's logo in 1944. Construction of the new terminal coincided with the heaviest immigration period in U.S. history, and many of those newcomers passed through the station on their way to western homes. Unfortunately, the railroad treated them as second-class passengers, relegating them to separate areas in the terminal and to uncovered platforms in the yard.

Two decades later, traffic demands necessitated an expansion of the terminal. The Baltimore and

Ohio and the Lehigh Valley railroads were tenants and contributed to the overcrowding. Upgrading was begun in 1912 and continued over the next 14 years. The number of tracks in the yard was increased to 20, served by 12 passenger platforms, and an extensive signaling system was installed. The train shed was removed and the more than 300,000-square-foot track area was protected from the elements by Bush sheds, the largest Bush installation ever constructed. (The Bush shed was a shed roof supported by columns at the center of a platform and extending upward at a shallow angle from the supports to a height of about 16 feet. Each module covered its adjacent track, but an opening of about 18 inches was left between modules for the smoke from an engine to escape. Skylights were built into the Bush shed roof to brighten the platform below. The economical Bush shed made it possible to do away with the huge, expensive, smoke-filled arched train sheds that had been a feature of most large terminals. Lincoln Bush, the inventor, was employed as an engineer by the DL&W.) The re-

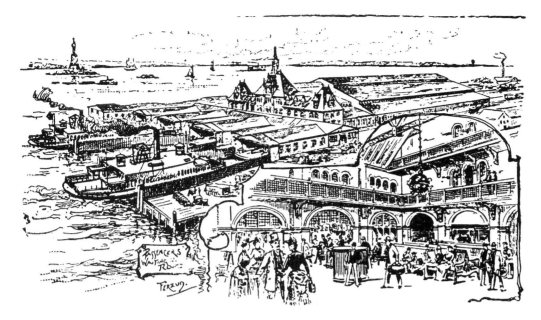

Figure 36. A bird's-eye view of the Central Railroad of New Jersey's Communipaw Terminal in 1893. The newly erected Statue of Liberty is evident at the top left. The inset at the lower right shows the elaborately finished waiting room with its room-length skylight. Author's collection.

maining bottleneck, the double-track bridge leading to the station, was finally rebuilt by 1922. The bridge rebuilding project was delayed by World War I and then by legal actions brought by the City of Newark and the newly organized Port Authority of New York. Those entities demanded that the new bridge be built at a more costly location. The CNJ eventually brought a suit to replace its bridge *in situ* and carried it all the way to the Supreme Court, where it received a favorable judgment.[7]

In 1937, the federal government opened a new gold depository at Fort Knox in Kentucky. Prior to that time, the nation's supply of gold bullion was stored deep below financial institutions on lower Manhattan. The gold transfer involved bringing it by truck and ferryboat to a heavily guarded train waiting on Track 20. The amount of bullion was so great that the movement took three years to complete. In later years, the station served as a location for the motion pictures *From the Terrace*, starring Paul Newman and Joanne Woodward, and *Funny Girl*, featuring Barbra Streisand and Omar Sharif. The peak year for terminal usage was 1929 when 21 million passengers used it. It was closed when the CNJ entered bankruptcy in 1967. At that time, the Aldene Plan, which ended all Jersey Central service between Newark and Jersey City over CNJ tracks, doomed the terminal. When Liberty State Park was created, the terminal was rehabilitated and, opened in 1980 without its ferry house and ferry slips, became one

of the triumvirate of historic attractions in the immediate area, the other two being Ellis Island and the Statue of Liberty.[8]

At the rededication of the restored terminal in 1989, Governor Thomas Kean said, "It stands as a spiritual gateway, where if we listen closely we can hear our heritage—the roar of the railroad, the babble of a dozen languages, the bark of the trainmen calling names of distant places soon to become hometowns of immigrants, and the feet of up to 50,000 commuters a day. And of course the melodic sound of the locomotive bell, ringing liberty and opportunity in a language common to all."[9]

## THE LACKAWANNA'S TERMINAL OF 1907 AT HOBOKEN

At Hoboken, a shed had been built to serve passengers on the Stevens' family ferryboats in 1862. The Lackawanna Railroad soon realized that something better was needed and built a 650-foot-long train shed at the ferry slip. Five years later, that "permanent terminal" burned to the ground, and its quickly built "temporary" replacement stood for 12 long years. Finally, in 1885, the DL&W threw up a cheaply constructed wooden structure that was no match for the other railroad terminals along the river. Although almost 100,000 passengers used the facility daily by 1900, the Lackawanna resisted all demands and entreaties for a better station. But in 1905, fate took a hand, and the terminal was destroyed by another fire. This

**Figure 37.** The Delaware, Lackawanna and Western Railroad's ferry terminal complex at Hoboken on 13 October 1913. Travelers arrived at the terminal by DL&W trains or by streetcars which used the two-level "barn" that is prominent in the central part of the photograph. North Jersey Chapter, National Railway Historical Society / North Jersey Electric Railway Historical Society, Deutsch Collection, Negative No. 566.

fire began on the ferryboat *Hopatcong*, which was berthed at a slip. Before the ship could be moved, the fire had spread to the terminal, and both were a total loss. A few months later, the Lackawanna lost its New York ferry terminal to fire also. To the great surprise of the road's many critics, rather than replacing its most recent terminal at Hoboken with another cheap structure, the Lackawanna management decided to build a station worthy of praise, one that incorporated improvements over the buildings of its rivals.[10]

The new Beaux Arts structure that was built in Hoboken by the DL&W after the disastrous fire of 1905 boasted a 225-foot-high bell tower housing a 2.25-ton bell, a 29,000-square-foot grand concourse, and a waiting room and ramps that could hold be-

tween 20,000 and 40,000 people. The waiting room was surmounted by a Tiffany glass roof, and the interior of the terminal was cooled by forced air that was passed over large blocks of ice, one of the first public buildings in the country to be so equipped. Because the building sat on piles in the mudflats along the shoreline, the architect who designed the building, Kenneth Murchison, opted for copper sheathing to cover his building, for brick or stone would have been too heavy. Much of the copper sheathing was embossed with various decorative shapes, such as fish, flowers, and shells.

A fine restaurant, with a balcony for al fresco dining, was established overlooking the Hudson River. From a practical point of view, dining in the terminal restaurant was the only way for local residents

Figure 38. The trolley loading platform at the Lackawanna's Hoboken terminal. In 1900, about 65,000 ferry patrons a day arrived at the terminal on foot or from trolley cars. The ladies' clothing provide a clue that this undated photograph was taken at about that time. North Jersey Chapter, National Railway Historical Society / North Jersey Electric Railway Historical Society, Deutsch Collection, Negative No. 93.

from Hoboken and Jersey City to view the river from the waterfront. The river's edge had become so developed that it was almost impossible to reach from the street. Over 100,000 passengers moved through the terminal each day, morning and evening. A jingle praising Murchison was composed and recited by the general passenger agent at the terminal's inaugural ceremonies. Written in the style of the Lackawanna's famous Phoebe Snow verses, but unfortunately lacking the same quality, the lines were dedicated

> To one whose art
> We look upon;
> It takes each heart,
> Murchison.[11]

Murchison took to heart the criticisms made in an editorial in the *Railroad Gazette* about terminal design in general. The editor who wrote that article complained that "we mass all passengers in one vast hall, and put here the ticket offices, the telegraph office, newsstand, chewing gum merchant and half a dozen other utilities or nuisances. We fill this hall with benches, and into it we turn the much enduring American crowd. . . . Passengers are passed through the waiting room as if it were an air lock through which one must go to get into a caisson." The architect produced a vast uncluttered space that Scull compared to the great Hall of Mirrors at Versailles. He separated the various classes of patron: train passengers were merged with the local passengers who arrived on foot or by trolley car, and all were removed from wagon traffic by dedicated walkways that avoided the huge waiting room. The walking passengers were routed to the upper level on the ferryboats with the wagons going to the lower level. Like its neighbor at Jersey City, the Hoboken terminal also served immigrants from Ellis Island, and one of the ferry slips was dedicated to the ferry shuttle that worked between the station and the island. Bush sheds (installed before the upgrading at the CNJ terminal) covered the 18 tracks in the yard behind the headhouse. An interesting postscript to the shed installation was that, within 10 years after completion, the train shed had settled in its pilings. The sinking was serious, as much as 17 inches below the original level. In 1919, the railroad's work crews raised the 9,000-ton structure by means of jacks adjacent to each supporting column. No change was made to the pilings, but additional concrete was poured to provide taller bases for the roof columns to sit upon.[12]

The Lackawanna Terminal, bounded by the Hudson River on the east, Observer Highway on the south, and Newark Street and River Street on the north and west, respectively, was saved from destruction by preservationists who managed to place it on the National Register of Historic Places in 1973. Ownership of the facility passed to NJ Transit in 1979, and that organization assumed control of commuter operations. Money became available for restoration, and although the dramatic bell tower is long gone (though there is a possibility that a replica will be erected), the grandeur of much of the building has been recovered. The terminal was rededicated in 1981 at a ceremony involving Governor Brendan Byrne and other state officials and is now a focus for many leisure activities and gatherings in addition to remaining a vibrant and viable transportation center. Parts of the films *Three Days of the Condor* with Robert Redford and *Voices* with Amy Irving were filmed on location at the Hoboken terminal.[13]

Unlike the center-city terminal which, according to Douglas, was a "place that should actually be integrated into city life, a transfusion point, a place where you were melded from one kind of environment—your home and office—to the world of travel," the Jersey Central and the Lackawanna terminals on the Jersey shore were designed to be efficient and effective conduits for transferring large masses of passengers from one mode of transportation to another. In their prime, the sheer number of travelers that passed through these edifices every working day was probably not exceeded anywhere in the country. That these monuments to superlative architecture and engineering remain standing is a testament to the quality of their construction and to the vision of those individuals who lobbied for their preservation.[14]

# 22  A Cape May Speedster (1895)

William Holman, a gifted promoter, conceived of a way to increase the speed of an ordinary locomotive without changing a single nut or bolt. He designed an engine that was intended to be run upon so-called speeding trucks. These speeding trucks were an undercarriage that was composed of two levels of wheels, the lower of which had three wheels that rested on the rails. The upper level of wheels, which Holman termed "friction wheels," supported the regular driving wheels of the locomotive. Each driver was cradled by two friction wheels, and each friction wheel, in turn, was supported by two wheels that rode along the track. For a locomotive with two drivers on each side (which was the case for the tests that were conducted), two speeding trucks, or undercarriage assemblies, were employed. No fastenings were used between the locomotive driving wheels and the speeding trucks; the weight of the locomotive was supposed to keep everything together.

Holman saw his invention as a means to increase the speed of the locomotive while reducing the piston speed; as stated in *Scientific American,* "the speed of the locomotive may be increased without . . . increasing the speed of the moving parts." It was his contention that the lineal distance covered with this arrangement was 75 percent greater than if the speeding trucks were not used. He achieved this increase by making each friction wheel with two treads of different diameters. The locomotive drivers rested on the smaller diameter treads, and the larger diameter treads engaged the lower, track-mounted wheels. According to the inventor, a secondary benefit of the use of speeding trucks was the mitigation of the hammering effect of the driving wheels on the rails.[1]

In 1894, Holman acquired a Soo Line Locomotive and mounted it on his speeding trucks. Initially tested on the Soo Line, Holman convinced the South Jersey Railroad (SJ) to conduct further tests of the machine on their trackage, too. Cook and Coxey speculate that because the SJ had experienced a severe shortage of motive power the previous year, the use of Holman's machine was seen as an opportunity to bring another locomotive to their rails. In any event, the SJ management were impressed by the test results (or by Holman's silver tongue), and they asked the Baldwin Works to add speeding trucks to a new engine that was being built for them. The engine was completed in July 1897 and put into local service that summer as road number 10.[2]

Figure 39 is a photograph taken on the occasion of the arrival of number 10 at Cape May City in mid-1897. It was remarked that a train of five cars hauled by this locomotive exceeded 105 mph speed! That speed may have been attained, but one observer noted that the Holman machine "rocked like a canoe in mid-ocean, and her crew were ready to jump whenever she took a curve."[3] However, the South Jersey Railroad's superintendent claimed that coal consumption was one-third less than with a conventional engine.

Encouraged by William Holman, the South Jersey road sought permission to run engine number 10 on the tracks of its neighbor, the Atlantic City Railroad. The latter road, concerned about the engine's high

**Figure 39.** The Holman locomotive, number 10, on the South Jersey Railroad's roster, upon its arrival at Cape May in mid-1897. Robert L. Long Collection.

center of gravity, denied permission. This was a wise decision, completely justified a short time later when the locomotive parted company with the speeding trucks as they roared along near Cape May Courthouse. The company soon discovered that when their Holman locomotive was not flying through the air, it was in the shops undergoing repairs. So they sold the machine, sans speeding trucks, to the Kansas City and Northern Connecting Railroad. This sale confirmed the opinion of one writer, who stated that "the one redeeming feature of the [Holman] arrangement was that the locomotive could be changed into a practical machine by simply lifting it off the speeding trucks."[4]

Angus Sinclair, a respected contemporary authority on locomotives, called Holman's invention an absurdity and, worse, a humbug. Sinclair was a particularly outspoken critic, and his comments, expressed in *Locomotive Engineering,* included his opinion that Holman was "densely ignorant of mechanics." He later corrected that opinion: "When we first heard of the Holman locomotive we supposed that it was the invention of some harmless crank who did not understand the elementary principles of mechanics, but we now believe that it has been, since its inception, an ostentatious machine designed to allure unwary capitalists into an investment which will be of the same real value as throwing gold coin over Niagara Falls." Sinclair contended that the machine's service on the West Jersey Railroad was "merely a stimulant to stock selling" that swindled many people. In his later book, *Development of the Locomotive Engine,* he described the experience of one poor woman who had an annual income of $750 derived from the interest on U.S. government bonds. "Some idiotic friends advised her to invest in the Holman Locomotive Company's Stock, assuring her that she would more than double her income without risk. Our washerwoman never loses a chance to ask me when the Holman Locomotive Company will begin paying dividends."[5]

Ernest Carter mentioned the Holman locomotive in his 1960 book, *Unusual Locomotives,* but only to express the prevalent opinion that "this idiotic machine was used as a basis for a nationwide share-pushing scheme designed to catch the unwary and lure them into an 'investment' which was utterly valueless."[6] More recently, Sinclair's opinion was supported by Paul Warner, who stated in *Railroad History* that "many unsuspecting persons invested their savings in it [the Holman Company], only to lose every cent."[7] Whether Warner was supporting Sinclair or was influenced by him is immaterial and does not change the fact that investors did lose money on Holman's venture.

From a technical point of view, Holman discounted the effects of friction throughout the train of wheels, and he devised an inherently unstable machine. As the authors of *The Atlantic City Railroad* mentioned, "Any person with mechanical training could see that 20 wheels with all of their bearings and associated friction made for a remarkably inefficient engine." Considering all of the obvious disadvantages, it is remarkable that the management of the South Jersey Railroad was persuaded to allow this creation to operate on their tracks, in regular service no less![8]

If Holman or his investors had considered the judgment of the editor of the *Journal of the Franklin Institute* concerning a patent issued to one Samuel Chapman Jr. in 1835, they would have been saved much abuse and money. Chapman proposed an apparatus that was strikingly similar to Holman's, even to calling the intermediate wheels "friction wheels." Chapman's invention produced this comment from the editor: "We are aware that the patentee is entirely erroneous in his views . . . but . . . he appeared to labor under a temporary hallucination, a certain cure for which, however, would be found in the attempt to put the thing into practical operation; whether or not this has been done, we have not heard; the news of its success, we presume, would have reached us."[9] Holman's invention *was* tried, but, all things considered, it would have been better left unbuilt.

# 23 The (Not So) Fast Line (1901–37)

Interurban railways, by definition, carried traffic between towns and cities. Generally, interurban cars were electrically powered and rarely operated as a train of more than one car. Historically, in this state, the demarcation between a trolley car line and an interurban line was blurred substantially because, unlike some other areas, New Jersey population centers often embraced numerous towns whose boundaries abutted each other. Sensibly, many streetcar lines ran slow trolley cars from town to town without regard for town limits. One wag disparaged them by pointing out that they ran "nearly as fast as the horse cars, which they succeeded." These street railway systems served local traffic primarily. On the other hand, interurban cars, those that we might call light rail cars today, were speedy and generally operated with limited stops over railroad quality roadbed laid mostly on private rights-of-way between distant towns. Although a case could be made that there were several early New Jersey interurban lines, two notable examples were the Camden and Trenton Railroad and the Newark-Trenton "Fast Line." The Camden and Trenton enterprise is mentioned here because its connection to the Fast Line at Trenton provided a trolley alternative between Camden and New Brunswick (and onward to Newark and Jersey City). However, this chapter is concerned mostly with the Fast Line because, in its relatively short life, it embodied lofty goals, political manipulation and maneuvering, construction and operating problems, and suspicions of ulterior motives, all described in detail and nourished by local newspaper accounts. It also furnished the last link in a trolley system that (except for major river crossings) extended from Philadelphia to Boston. With the completion of the bridge over Cass Street in Trenton in 1903, it became possible to ride by trolley between those two metropolises, a distance of 256 miles, for $3.15. The downside was that, at best, with many good connections, the journey took about 72 hours and required overnight stops at hotels along the way. Shorter "trolley vacation trips" like the one a Mr. Kennelly made from New York to Philadelphia in 9 hours were recommended for their "health and recreation" benefits. Despite a newspaper article that claimed "Long Trolley Rides Popular," not many travelers would forego the relatively fast steam railroad for the longer, though perhaps more picturesque, trolley trip.[1]

The Newark-Trenton "Fast Line" was the result of a series of railroad constructions, bankruptcies, and mergers. Its earliest ancestor was the Trenton and New Brunswick Railroad (T&NB), which was chartered in 1901 to build a standard-gauge railroad from Milltown Junction (near New Brunswick) to the state fairgrounds at Trenton. The T&NB was known as the "Fast Line" at the time of its inception, a name that stuck through its various rebirths. Even as early as the time of its incorporation, it was (wrongly) suspected that the T&NB was "a scheme of the Pennsylvania Railroad for a more direct route to its coal docks at South Amboy. The idea, it is said, is to do away with the coal traffic on main line." A few months later, the rumor mill had it that "the power behind the [Trenton and New Brunswick Railroad] is really the Philadelphia and Reading Railway, which has long manifested a desire to complete a direct and short connection with New York." The road was planned to operate on a private right-of-way laid out through mostly open country, without passing through a single village or town. It was reasonable to assume that it might become a link on a through interurban line from Philadelphia to New York City via the Jersey City waterfront or over a bridge to Staten Island, a plan that had been proposed earlier by A. L. Johnson, whose trolley company had run between Trenton and Princeton since 1901. Johnson's proposal would have bypassed New Brunswick, directed instead to Bound Brook. Although the avowed intention of the T&NB was to connect with the line to Camden, the Trenton terminal of the company was established at the state fairgrounds where a connection would be made to the Trenton Street Railway cars. This arrangement provided the trolley company with increased business during the annual fair, and despite the loss of tolls for wagons carrying people onto the fairgrounds, it also served the fair management well because of the additional traffic that the trolley would bring from New Brunswick. An early problem was that the company had neglected to obtain local franchises for their route. This was acceptable if only private lands were used, but as soon as the tracks crossed local and county roads, local governments had an interest in the matter. The situation was exacerbated by the trolley company contractors who, in their haste to reach early completion, acted quite high-handedly. In Mercer County, some local roads were crossed on a roadbed that was 18 inches higher than the road surface. In another instance, the trolley track emerged from a deep cut at such an acute angle with Edinburg Road that over 200 feet of road was taken over by tracks; the cut made it almost impossible for highway traffic to see an approaching trolley car. The issues were resolved through legal action.[2]

One of the highlights of construction involved the building of a bridge over the Pennsylvania Railroad tracks near Dayton. To minimize disruption of the railroad's operations, the company decided to erect the structure on a Sunday. Beginning at 10 AM on the appointed day in August 1902, two steel beams, each over 84 feet long and weighing more than 20 tons, "were raised from flat cars by two mammoth derricks and swung into place as neatly and easily as a carpenter would lay a floor beam." It appears that attendance at Sunday religious services suffered substantially on this day because "a large crowd was attracted by the work. Everyone within three miles who could get a bicycle seemed to be there." One spectator asked another, "What did you do with your Sunday school class?" The other replied, "I dismissed them. I didn't want to miss this sight."[3]

Originally contemplated to be powered from a third rail, the road began service on 3 November 1902 using six new 45-feet-long, 50-seat, carpeted, and illuminated cars, electrically powered from an overhead trolley wire and named for major New Jersey cities. The maroon cars were built by the Niles Car Manufacturing Company of Niles, Ohio, and were driven by four 50 horsepower motors. They were intended to operate at 35–40 mph over a line that was a little over 23 miles long. (Higher operating speeds might have been maintained if the line had been built with a third rail rather than a trolley wire. However, the third rail was not practical for a surface line that had to cross public roads, a condition that was impossible to consider from a safety viewpoint.) Arrangements were made with the Middlesex and Somerset Traction Company for the use of their tracks between Milltown and George Street in New Brunswick, but the initial trip along the city streets destroyed the newly laid brick pavements through which the rails were laid. Unfortunately for the trolley company, the mayor of the city was a passenger on that car, and he immediately prohibited T&NB cars from running along his city's streets until the problem (a question of oversized wheel flanges) was corrected. The remedy was a transfer to the local cars at Milltown, an unsatisfactory solution, especially since schedules were not coordinated. Poor judgment on the part of some crew members did not help; one conductor ordered passengers to leave his car at the end of the run during a storm late one evening. This thoroughly drenched, hapless group waited for an hour for a connecting car. Some months later in 1903, a local alderman complained that the Fast Line cars ran *too fast* along New Brunswick's streets. A local ordinance, adopted in 1896, had limited city speeds to 8 mph, but the big red cars regularly exceeded that limit.

Upon commencement of service, rumors of the

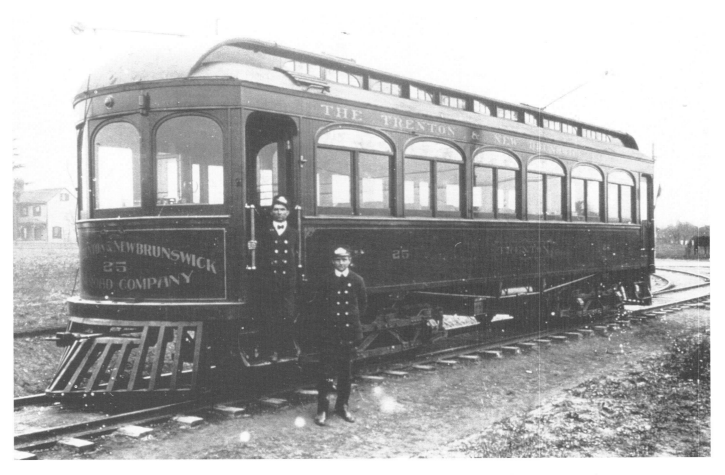

**Figure 40.** The *Trenton,* one of the six original cars furnished to the Trenton and New Brunswick Railroad in 1902 by the Niles Car Manufacturing Company. The cowcatcher that is shown was removed soon after receipt of the cars. North Jersey Chapter, National Railway Historical Society/North Jersey Electric Railway Historical Society.

line's ultimate disposition arose again. Some insisted that the Pennsylvania Railroad intended to acquire it (witnessed by the fact that PRR surveyors were operating in the area), while others brought the Gould interests into the equation, citing the clearing and grading work that was under way in Pennsylvania by a "line which seems to be without an owner." The T&NB, from early on, had been a puzzlement to observers who could not understand a railroad that "touches no villages or towns and passes through a country from which but a small amount of traffic can be drawn. . . . Back of all this mystery is a great certainty, which is manifesting itself more clearly every day. A great trunk line of railroad will eventually span the continent, under a single management. That

management, railroad men believe, will be Gould's." And again, the *Trenton Daily State Gazette* proclaimed, "There is abundant evidence that a great four-track steam railroad has been planned and is actually in an incipient stage of construction, that will cross the state in a direct line from Trenton to Staten Island sound, and will continue across Staten Island to a terminus on the New York bay." Gould's aspirations for the extension of the Wabash Railroad, both east and west, may have been real, but too much was made of the possibility that this short trolley line was a smokescreen for the tycoon's ambitions.[4]

In 1903, a prospectus was circulated by the New York and Philadelphia Electric Railway (NY&PER) that showed a through line between those two cities. It was obvious that this "mysterious" company, which filed charter papers in late 1904, had identified existing trolley lines and proposed merging them into a unified system. The consolidation of the T&NB and the Camden and Trenton Railroad (C&T) with the NY&PER was effected in March 1905. The Trenton Terminal Railroad, a 2,900-feet-long connector, had been completed in 1904, and it joined the C&T with the T&NB. But the connection at Trenton was not seamless because the C&T was a broad-gauge road (5'-0") and passengers from the standard-gauge Fast Line had to change trains where they met at Trenton. At about the same time, the Trenton and New Brunswick Company was rumored to be planning to extend its line to Jersey City, thus reducing the time of a trolley trip between Trenton and New York to possibly two hours, more nearly competitive with the steam railroad. Earlier, it had been possible, using local trolley tracks and making 12 changes of cars, to ride from Philadelphia to Jersey City, including a leg on the Fast Line, in about eight hours. At the New Brunswick end of the line, the New Jersey Short Line (NJSL) was projected to build to Elizabeth. Although there were accounts of construction contracts for the 36-mile road having been awarded in 1904 and 1905, a later article mentioned that the project was halted during the financial depression of 1907.[5]

Meanwhile, as early as December 1903, the newly organized Public Service Corporation (PS) revealed an interest in acquiring a route to Trenton and on to Camden by conducting an "experiment," an inspection trip of the lines from Newark to Trenton. Newspaper accounts "intimated that the principal object of the party's visit was to enter into negotiations for the purchase of the trolley lines of the Trenton Street Railway and the Trenton and New Brunswick Company." Public Service officials were circumspect in their public statements concerning the trip, but those of the local companies denied the report. However, in May 1904, PS, having acquired the Middlesex and Somerset Traction Company, whose lines centered in New Brunswick, made arrangements to utilize the tracks of the Trenton and New Brunswick Railroad to inaugurate through service from Trenton to Jersey City. The inaugural trip was made on Friday, 13 May, and five and a half hours were scheduled for the trip. Although a hot box delayed the first car to New York, it appears that the service was a success

initially because within a few weeks the schedule was augmented by the addition of cars to the run. When service was inaugurated in May, four round-trips were offered daily; by August, cars left Trenton every 30 minutes during the day. Now that PS's yellow cars were seen regularly on the T&NB tracks between Trenton and New Brunswick (and the T&NB's red cars were withdrawn), it was almost a foregone conclusion that rumors of a merger between the two companies would arise. The official response was that, since the New York service proved so popular, only through cars would be operated. Otherwise, further increasing traffic on the single track road by operating local cars also would have presented an exceedingly dangerous operation. But the popularity of the through service soon waned as patrons discovered that the trip "was evidently too tedious a journey to Trenton and Philadelphia for persons from Jersey City, Newark, and Elizabeth." By August 1905, Public Service admitted that the through line was "a failure" and that the headway between cars would be lengthened to three hours.[6]

Despite PS's admission that its through service to Elizabeth would probably be terminated, a new line extending the Trenton and New Brunswick began to take shape under the aegis of the New York and Philadelphia Electric Railway (NY&PER). Unlike the Public Service route, which utilized street railway tracks, the new line would be built on a private right-of-way. This would enable cars to be operated at high speed and thus shorten the trip between Trenton or New Brunswick and Elizabeth to a reasonable time. Because the line was to be constructed to a high standard and "built enormously heavy for a trolley line . . . and could be converted to a steam railroad simply by the placing upon it of the steam rolling stock," rumors questioning its true ultimate purpose arose for the umpteenth time. Some observers were certain that it would "become a link in a railroad company's scheme to secure a tidewater outlet."[7]

By early 1905, the NY&PER, a holding company, had acquired the stock of the T&NB and the NJSL. Only three years later, in February 1908, the three companies were in receivership, having been adjudged insolvent and without "quick" assets. On 3 May 1910, it was announced that the Fast Line and the Short Line were to be auctioned off. The sale, conducted at the Sheriff's Office in New Brunswick, realized only one bid, and the Fast Line passed into ownership of the bondholders for $200,000. The following day, the same group acquired the NJSL. Again, the rumor mill went into overtime, reporting variously that "Public Service means to take over the road" and then contradicting itself by noting once more that the 100-foot-wide right-of-way "dispels the belief that it was built for trolley purposes. It is expected that some railroad will soon show its hand in connection with this road."

A few days later, the assets of the T&NB and the NJSL were acquired by the Elizabeth and Trenton Railroad, which on 18 April 1911 was reorganized as the Elizabeth, New Brunswick and Trenton Railroad (ENB&T). The following month, the *New Brunswick Daily Times* announced that Public Service wanted to acquire the trolley line. On 29 July 1913, the Public Service Railroad (PSRR) was formed and commenced operations between Newark and Trenton, running on a schedule of two hours and 40 minutes. Under PSRR ownership, the through line was never an unqualified success. Several factors contributed to a decline in patronage, principal among which was the fact that conventional railroad service between the two cities (Newark and Trenton) was faster. The Fast Line between Trenton and Newark continued to be operated as the Public Service Railroad, but in 1924 the line was divided into two sections so that a through passenger required a transfer at New Brunswick. Connections could be made to the Trenton-Camden line, but because of the disparity of the gauges, passengers from the standard-gauge Fast Line also had to change trains at that junction.[8]

Although the Fast Line operated over private right-of-way like a steam railroad, almost all of its tracks were at grade level, making them accessible to pedestrians, animals, wagons, and carriages. But because people did not equate the two, believing that the interurban cars were not as fearful nor as fast as conventional railroad trains, they tended to ignore many of the dangers associated with them. Consequently, the Fast Line had its share of accidents. These ranged from head-on collisions to striking pedestrians, often small children who ran in front of the speeding trolleys and sometimes inebriated individuals found walking along or sleeping on the tracks. In one remarkable case, a man walking the track was caught upon a trestle by the arrival of a car. Hoping to escape injury, he lay down, thinking that the car might pass over him. Unfortunately, he was struck by a step on the car and tossed off the trestle; he fell 35 feet, yet survived. The victim must have been extremely hardy, and the severity of injuries may have been measured differently in bygone days, because the hospital reported that despite "a broken right arm, crushed right foot, and several other injuries . . . his condition is not serious."[9]

The most deadly accidents involved head-on collisions between two cars. One of these wrecks, which occurred on 28 August 1905, was detailed in chapter 20. That accident was sandwiched, timewise, between two others on the Fast Line of a similar nature. In August 1904, two cars loaded with passengers collided at the Trenton fairgrounds. The cause of the accident was an open switch, which allowed the westbound car to pass onto the eastbound track and smash into a car traveling at high speed. Two years later, on 6 May 1906, another head-on collision took place at Plainsboro. Eighteen people were injured when Conductor Laird, who was filling in for an ill Motorman Murphy, ran "a signal light warning him of another car approaching." The conductor of the other car, William Titus, who later became superintendent of the line, reported: "When we reached the switch I had a clear block and went through. The fog was thick and I could not see any car approaching. Suddenly I saw the form of the car loom up in the darkness and the light shining through one of the top windows. . . . I saw that a collision was inevitable and plugged the car. I jumped." A factor contributing to the accident was that the headlight on Laird's car was inoperative. Although 18 people were injured, all recovered. The monetary claims made by the 17 injured passengers (Laird, the conductor, was the eighteenth victim) were settled in the remarkably short time of five days, a scenario that would be impossible today. Titus was involved in two less serious accidents before the end of 1906.[10]

Of the many reports of accidents on Fast Line trolleys, one stands out for its humor tinged with sarcasm. Describing "an exciting time near Red Lion," a newspaper article told of encounters that two trolleys had with cattle on the same day: "One east bound car bumped a cow near Robert Askew's place and put her hors-combat, and the other, a west bound car, caught a bull on the trestle near Parson's Lane and both car and bull were put on the waiting list, the car having both trucks thrown off the track and the bull being so badly mangled that his mother wouldn't be able to identify him." Another type of accident that occurred with distressing frequency was collision with vehicular traffic. From horse-drawn teams when the Fast Line was initiated to an increasing number of unscheduled meetings with automobiles as the years passed, they took a sad toll of dead and injured.[11]

The recounting of these incidents highlights the dangerous nature of driving an interurban car. The motorman, occupying an extremely vulnerable position at the front of the car immediately behind a thin glass window, could be crushed or horribly cut by flying glass in a head-on collision or in the event of a derailment at high speed. But physical injury was only one of the hazards of operating the trolley car. In most accident cases, the crews were immediately arrested, charged with manslaughter, and held until a grand jury could sort out the facts—a case of "guilty until proven innocent." Fortunately for them, in the majority of cases, when the crew was acting in a reasonable, if not prudent, manner or was not violating company rules, either "no bill" was presented by the jury or they were acquitted at trial. In the cases of pedestrians being struck by the cars along the interurban right-of-way, one element of their defense was that the victims were trespassing on private property.

There were instances also of attempts to wreck Fast Line cars. In one, a Brooklyn resident, disgruntled because he had been ejected from a car for refusing to pay the fare, placed a long pole, large stones, and an iron bolt on the tracks in an attempt to derail the car. Found nearby, the man was arrested and jailed. A similar action was believed to have been taken by a farmer with a "grudge against the company." Seeing what he thought was a body lying on the track, Motorman Voight blew his whistle. Receiving no response, he braked immediately and discovered that what he thought was a body was, in reality, a heavy pole across the rails. "All trace of the culprit was gone, although efforts were made "to catch the miscreant." In many of these cases, it was adjudged that the wrongdoers were "demented," and some were remanded to an asylum. Another incident involved two brothers, 10 and 11 years old, who had often flattened pennies under the car wheels. One day they placed a horseshoe, a spike, and a block of wood upon the tracks hoping to see them mashed up. Their age and intent notwithstanding, the two boys were arrested and charged with attempting to wreck a Fast Line car. They were released on bail, and although there is no further account of the disposition of the legal action, it is likely that they received adequate punishment at the hands of their father.[12]

On a more pleasant note, there were occasions when people demonstrated their better nature. After a late spring snowfall stalled two Fast Line cars near Dutch Neck one Sunday evening in 1914 and stranded 30 passengers, George Conover, a farmer, rose to the occasion. He walked to the cars and invited all aboard to spend the night at his house. Most of them stayed on until Wednesday, when teams were able to reach Conover's home and bring his visitors to nearby railroad stations. Conover was not the only hospitable homeowner in the vicinity. Other nearby trolleys were blockaded by the snow, and their passengers were accommodated at the homes of several farmers.

In a romantic vein, the *New Brunswick Times* of 15 April 1913 reported the elopement of Miss Lillian Chamberlain, a 16-year-old girl, with Edward Kercado, a conductor on the Trenton–New Brunswick run. They were childhood friends, having met when Kercado worked on her grandfather's farm. They met frequently during trips Miss Chamberlain took to Trenton on the trolley. Missing from home, she was tracked down "by the irate father," and their bridal breakfast, which had been arranged by the groom's mother, was interrupted by two "burly" policemen who brought the newlyweds to the Trenton police station, "where Raymond Chamberlain, father of the bride, was waiting to take his daughter back home" for "a talkin' to." Upon learning that the couple had been legally married in Delaware, Chamberlain relented somewhat and gave the girl his blessing, if not his unqualified approval. Because of her age, the girl was compelled to return home with her father, but later was permitted to reside with her husband at her mother-in-law's home. In a sad postscript to this story, a few months later Kercado was arrested after the trolley car which he was driving struck a small boy in Highland Park.[13]

Throughout the country, wherever interurban

lines operated, transportation of freight was almost always an important element of their business. Although incorporated under a steam railroad charter that permitted the transportation of freight, the Fast Line mostly carried passengers for several years after commencement of service. (In New Jersey, electric railways incorporated under the steam railroad act were allowed to carry freight, but that privilege was prohibited if they were incorporated as traction or street railway companies. In 1906, the New Jersey legislature passed a bill that permitted goods to be carried by traction companies, and that right was extended to local trolley lines in 1909.) The management of the Fast Line eventually realized that the transport of fresh milk represented an important revenue source and that individual dairy farms along the route would provide substantial business. They were prepared to capitalize on this business because two of the original six cars that they had purchased from Niles were combination cars, suitable for carrying passengers or freight. Although a major milk producer, the Walker Gordon Company, was located about a mile from the electric railway's tracks, it probably contributed little freight business because it was served by the Pennsylvania Railroad on its own siding. Incidentally, the fact that the Fast Line was incorporated under a steam railroad charter probably had as much to do with the endless rumors about its ultimate purpose as any other single fact.[14]

At the end of the 1920s, the right-of-way was leased to Public Service's sister organization, the Public Service Electric and Gas Company, for the erection of a high voltage electric power line. To this day, the power line, which still stands, marks the trace of the trolley. By the end of 1930, the Fast Line was down to one round-trip a day on the New Brunswick–Trenton segment, sufficient to maintain the franchise but not to encourage or sustain ridership. The gas-electric cars in use by that time were replaced by rail-buses that could run on rails or highway. A major reason for their adoption was the fact that the trestle near Dayton was deemed unsafe. It was avoided through the use of the rail-bus vehicles that rode the tracks at either side of the trestle but detoured around the trestle on local roads. Finally, the Fast Line was abandoned on 11 May 1937.[15]

Although there is no question that the demise of the Fast Line was due, in large part, to the ascendancy of motor vehicles for the personal transportation needs of the population for short and medium distance trips, other considerations involved its location and scheduled speed. These considerations were mutually exclusive; a private right-of-way with limited stops ensured high average speed but reduced the traffic potential. Furthermore, reviewing the history of the Trenton–New Brunswick Fast Line, one might be advised to consider the approaches taken by early conventional railroads when they were sited. Most of those enterprises sought to touch as many towns along their way as possible in order to maximize passengers and freight traffic. Not so with the Fast Line, which had curtailed its revenue potential drastically by avoiding village centers along its route. This fact ensured that the line's income would be obtained almost exclusively from travelers who wished to make the trip between the two cities at a relatively high speed. It also was a major contributor to the persistent and endless rumors that there was a sub rosa reason for the Fast Line's existence. Despite denials, it is reasonable to assume that the Fast Line management had always intended it to be an important link in a trans-Jersey high-speed trolley line. A connection with the Camden and Trenton Railway was touted during early planning and construction, and continuation of the route beyond New Brunswick to Elizabeth or Jersey City was proposed. The Fast Line would be one leg of a high-speed interurban trolley network that was to extend from Camden to Elizabeth (read Philadelphia to New York). The fallacy in this plan was that the other legs of the system—the Camden and Trenton Railroad, the New Brunswick Traction Company, the Middlesex and Somerset Traction Company, and others at the ends of the Fast Line tracks—were speed-limited as a result of running through numerous towns and cities. The New Jersey Short Line, using a private right-of-way to Elizabeth, was proposed as a remedy, but the plan died before it could be implemented. At the Trenton junction, the C&T was of a different gauge, making a change of cars unavoidable. Now when the Public Service Corporation appeared on the scene, it began the wholesale acquisition of street railways in the state. It then introduced its own vision for a trans-state trolley system using the T&NB Fast Line and existing properties that it controlled, almost all of which were street railways, not private right-of-

**Figure 41.** Toward the end of its life, the Fast Line employed gasoline-powered rail-buses. This photograph, taken in April 1935, shows one of these vehicles, number 1011, crossing the trestle across Lake Farrington near New Brunswick. North Jersey Chapter, National Railway Historical Society/North Jersey Electric Railway Historical Society.

way interurbans. Although the Fast Line leg between Trenton and New Brunswick ran at an average speed of about 30 mph, competitive with the Pennsylvania Railroad's scheduled time between the two cities, the entire trip was conducted at a considerably slower average speed. When Public Service began operating it as a through line, the Fast Line was reduced to being part of a system that was a not-so-fast line, which doomed it to being a regional carrier serving a limited market.

\* \* \*

Postscript: The Trenton-Camden "Riverside Line," named earlier in this chapter as the Camden and Trenton Railroad, began in 1898 as the Monmouth Traction Company. The company's plans were

to build an interurban line from Camden to Atlantic Highlands by way of Trenton. During the following year, this plan was scaled back, and the trackage from Trenton to the seashore was eliminated and never built. Along with new goals, the company acquired a new name, the Camden and Trenton Railroad. As was often the case, the traction company experienced delays at points of crossing at grade with conventional railroads. It took months to resolve the issue at one such crossing in Burlington, but at least in this instance, unlike the various crossing incidents described elsewhere in this book, there was no resulting "frog war." When the line was opened between Trenton and Camden, the big green cars took three hours to make the trip. Three hours was not acceptable for an approximately 35-mile trip, especially for a line purporting to provide rapid service. Within three years, the line was bankrupt. Reorganized in 1910 as the Riverside Traction Company, another setback was experienced in 1911 when one of its bridges failed under the weight of a car; service was reinstated in two days, but the damage to the line's reputation was permanent. In 1912, the Riverside line was acquired by Public Service Corporation un-der a long-term lease. As automobile usage increased, trolley ridership fell off, and PS replaced the trolleys with buses. Rails were removed, but some buses still follow the original route of the trolley line. Interurban rail service between Camden and Trenton was reestablished in 2004, operated by NJ Transit as the River LINE.[16] A description of the River LINE is provided in chapter 27.

# 24 Catastrophe at the Thoroughfare (1906)

Miss Ida May Dubell left her home in Florence, New Jersey, on the morning of 28 October 1906, intending to spend a pleasant Sunday on the Jersey shore with her fiancé, William Edwards. She boarded a streetcar to the railway station where she would catch a train to Camden. As it approached the Pearl Street bridge in Trenton, the streetcar derailed and narrowly missed plunging into the stream below. Such a happening might have persuaded other young women to amend their plans, but Ida decided to continue on. Upon reaching Camden and meeting Will, the two boarded the new electric train to Atlantic City.[1]

The West Jersey and Seashore Railroad (WJ&S) was the result of an 1896 consolidation of the Pennsylvania Railroad's south Jersey holdings.[2] It had been electrified only a few weeks earlier and had promised quick, clean service to the shore resort. The 1 PM train, consisting of three cars, left the Camden station promptly, made a stop at Pleasantville, and then proceeded, via Newfield Junction, across a salt marsh near Atlantic City. Its motorman, Walter Scott, had been pushing along at 50–60 mph, and the train was three minutes ahead of schedule when it reached the Thoroughfare, a tidal creek that forms the northwest boundary of Atlantic City. The railroad crossed the salt marsh and water via an open trestle with a draw at the creek. Moments before the train arrived, the drawbridge had been opened to allow the yacht *Sinbad* to pass through. As Scott approached the draw, all appeared to be normal, but he slowed to 20 mph, the usual speed across the bridge. Accounts of the accident mentioned that the first car "stubbed its toes" and plunged over the side of the trestle.[3]

Upon "hearing the grinding of the car wheels," Miss Dubell "looked out and saw the first car take its plunge." Falling back into her seat, which was in the second car, she felt the car tip and begin to follow its leader off the trestle. According to the *Trenton Times,*

> Edwards seized her and shouted, "Hang on! For God's sake, hang on!" At that moment the car hit the water and, thanks to its 32 tons of motorized trucks, was immediately submerged. Edwards succeeded in pushing Ida through the open window whereupon "it seemed an hour before I rose to the surface. . . . Will's face was bleeding terribly while he was trying to save me. He dropped out of sight as I arose to the surface."

When she reached the surface, her foot struck the car roof, and she found that she could stand on the roof until help arrived. While still underwater, Ida saw two men pull a little girl out through another window, but very few passengers managed to escape from the first two cars.[4]

Providentially, as the third car began to follow the others, its rear truck snagged the trestle and the car hung for a short time, suspended from the bridge. Its brakeman, Ralph Wood, made his way to the rear door and held it open so that passengers could escape. (All of the side doors on the cars had been locked by levers and could not be opened by the travelers inside.) Some of the passengers in this car were musicians who were booked for a performance at Young's Pier. Also in that car were seven members of an Italian band, all of whom died in the wreck. (Fourteen very lucky passengers had left the train a few minutes earlier when it stopped at Pleasantville, five miles away.)[5] After a minute or two, the third car lost its purchase on the trestle and slipped into the creek.

Early reports on the day of the tragedy estimated that nearly 80 people had died in the wreck. This number, if it held, would have made the Thoroughfare accident the most costly in human life in the history of railroading in the state to that time. By the following day, the death toll had been revised downward to 66, still a record because that number edged out the 42 people who had died in a railroad accident near Atlantic City 10 years earlier. The final number was still a substantial toll, numbering 57 victims, greater than the casualties at an accident in Mays Landing in 1880.[6] In terms of deaths, these three accidents, all involving trains of the Pennsylvania-controlled West Jersey Railroad, were to remain the worst in New Jersey until they were surpassed by the wreck of a Pennsylvania Railroad commuter train at Woodbridge in 1951 that killed 85. The Thoroughfare calamity was compounded by the fact that the tide was coming in, and many of the victims who did escape the cars were engulfed in surging, swirling water. Although the exact number of passengers on the train was unknown, only about half escaped alive. William Edwards was not a survivor.[7]

Newspaper accounts stated that "within half an hour after the cars had plunged into the water, the draw was surrounded by thousands, all anxious and willing to risk their lives to help." Survivors were picked up by the many boatmen who arrived, and some were transported to the Atlantic City hospital. The dead were brought to an improvised morgue at the Empire Theater in Atlantic City. According to the same accounts, the water at the time of the accident was 20–25 feet deep, and raising the cars from the muck at the bottom remained a problem even at low tide. In particular, the heavy trucks, which included traction motors and gearing, could not be salvaged as a unit. Divers were called from Philadelphia to place explosive charges to break up the trucks into manageable pieces. Over two days, divers were also employed in searching the underwater wreckage for victims.

An intense investigation and coroner's inquest into the cause of the accident were undertaken. One speculative reason was advanced by the chief of police in Atlantic City. Chief Maxwell determined that the bridge tender, Daniel Stewart, had recently been assaulted by "river pirates" because of his "warfare" upon them. The chief theorized that the pirates, or "wreckers," had sabotaged the bridge in retaliation. He immediately began a search for three members of this "rough element." However, the coroner's jury, convened immediately and composed of six prominent Atlantic City residents, determined that the accident was caused by a rail on the draw that failed to lock in place properly after the span had been opened for the *Sinbad*. Instead, the end of one rail mismatched the end of its mate, and "when the wheels of the speeding train struck the elevated section of track at [that] point the train got such a jolt as to cause the train to leave the track." The mismatch was determined by the jury to have resulted when a mechanism called an "elevator" failed to seat the rail securely.[8]

The Pennsylvania Railroad's general manager, William Wallace Atterbury, disagreed vehemently with this assessment. He attributed the wreck to a broken car wheel or flange. He had the inquest members interview the bridge tender and the towerman on duty at the time. After explaining the fail-safe features of the interlocking arrangement between the rails and signals and the normal operating procedure at the junction of the rails, it was the opinion of Atterbury and the bridge attendants that the rail/signal/latching system could not break down. However, under sharp questioning by members of the jury, the towerman "admitted that the operation of his lever would not insure the rails coming together flush at the point of union." The jury's verdict agreed with Atterbury's conclusion, but there were some skeptics who continued to attribute the accident to a failure of the drawbridge rail alignment.[9]

Based on Atterbury's assessment, Daniel Stewart was charged with criminal negligence and involuntary manslaughter and jailed. However, three months later, he was vindicated when a grand jury sitting in Atlantic City made an unannounced visit to the drawbridge site, where they ordered the bridge tender to operate the draw several times. After each movement, the rails were inspected and found to be misaligned, although the signals displayed a clear indication. That jury recommended that Stewart be released and pronounced that the motorman, Walter Scott, was blameless since the signals showed a clear track at the time of the accident. Charges were

**Figure 42.** Coach number 6704, the first car in the train that was wrecked on 28 October 1906, being recovered from the tidal waters of the Thoroughfare near Atlantic City. It and its following neighbor plunged off the trestle, but providentially the third car snagged on the trestle and did not follow the others immediately. Although not readily evident, the very edge of the tower that controlled operation of the draw is visible above the wrecking car. Robert L. Long Collection.

then filed against officials of the WJ&S for operating an unsafe bridge. A permanent speed restriction of 8 mph was then imposed on subsequent bridge crossings.[10]

In days past, songs and poems were often written to commemorate tragic events. This accident was no exception and was memorialized in "The Wreck at the Thoroughfare." Sung to the music of the hymn "Safe in the Arms of Jesus," its refrain lamented,

> Wildly the cries of anguish
> Fall on the Sabbath air,
> Hopes of a life-time lying
> Down in the Thoroughfare.[11]

The 1906 Atlantic City catastrophe was the last major drawbridge accident in the United States until 15 September 1958, when a Jersey Central commuter train plunged from a drawbridge spanning Newark Bay at Bayonne. The circumstances of this accident were eerily similar to that at Atlantic City. The draw had been opened for a small ship, and the train, disregarding stop signals, continued at speed into the gap. The engine and two cars dove into the Bay, but the third car snagged on the bridge and rested there for about two hours before it too fell into the water. Fifty-eight people lost their lives.[12]

# 25 Making Tracks in New Jersey (1914–Present)

Arguably, during the mid-twentieth century, there were probably more trains produced per capita in northern New Jersey than any other place in the world. In 1939, Earl Chapin May, who wrote about model trains, reported, "During one recent year a single . . . railroad manufacturer produced in America 400,000 locomotives, 1,200,000 railroad cars, and 3,000,000 feet of steel track." But these were not trains that were to be operated by prominent railroads, carrying passengers through New Jersey to the far corners of the country. Rather, they were model trains—May said "toys"—manufactured by the Lionel Corporation at its plants in Newark, Irvington, and Hillside.[1]

The Lionel Corporation was founded by Joshua Lionel Cohen (later changed to Cowen) in 1900 in New York City. His first model train offering was the Electric Express, a wooden gondola car driven by an electric motor mounted beneath the deck. Cowen visualized the car, running on a track that he furnished, as an advertising gimmick, an attention-getter for show windows in retail stores. But when larger orders began arriving, he realized the true potential of the product as a child's toy and organized the Lionel Manufacturing Company. Lionel's first toy train catalog, published in 1903, displayed a derrick car and a gondola car. Also included was a reproduction of the locomotive from the Baltimore and Ohio Railroad's *Royal Blue* train, a popular prototype at the time. This tinplate engine was powered by a wet cell battery, but Cowen, a talented designer, understood the limitations of battery-driven toys and soon developed a safe transformer to operate his trains off

house current. In turn, this advance required a third rail for an efficient electrical system. That feature, a three-rail track, simplified and ensured the adoption of Lionel trains, even in households without a basic knowledge of electrical application. Lionel's innovations contributed to a rapid growth. Whereas the 1906 catalog offered but one engine and about a dozen cars and trolleys, four years later Cowen's offerings had expanded to several locomotives, 11 trolleys, and many more cars. Lithographed tinplate structures were also provided for sale.

Seeking larger quarters, he moved his factory to New Haven, Connecticut, in 1910 and then to Newark in 1914. Three years later, the company relocated to Irvington and finally, in 1929, to Hillside, its last New Jersey venue. Lionel prospered in the 1920s, but suffered substantially through the Great Depression, its situation made worse because its product, a toy, relied upon discretionary spending, i.e., money left over after the essentials had been budgeted. There was little of that, and the company entered receivership in 1934. But, after reorganizing, success overtook Cowen again, and he went on to become the predominant toy train manufacturer in the United States.[2]

There were several reasons for Lionel's success. First, their trains were substantial and rugged, able to withstand rough treatment from small hands. Second, as mentioned, their equipment was easy to assemble into a layout and, once installed, usually ran flawlessly. Third, the company offered a well-rounded line of trains and accessories; their market research targeted their audience's wants in the model railroad line. Fourth, although a relatively expensive toy, Lionel's offerings were competitively priced. Fifth, although Lionel trains were not scale models in the sense that they were faithful miniature representations of real trains, they were more accurate than their competitors. Finally, if a train or locomotive or accessory did break, Lionel maintained an extensive network of repair shops that provided quick and reasonably priced service.

From its earliest days, Lionel faced formidable competitors. Several firms had made pull-type or friction or windup (with clock motors) toy trains before 1900. In 1905, Voltamp began making electric trains. Lionel's major competitors were the Ives Corporation (founded in 1886) and American Flyer, which later became an A. C. Gilbert (of Erector set fame) company. However, Cowen's innovative management introduced strong marketing and design teams, led by very capable individuals. He outsourced some products to a high-quality Italian stamping and die-casting firm. He constantly improved his products and opened a large factory showroom in New York City. Lionel was a strong competitor, and Ives became a casualty of the competition, bankrupted in 1928. Lionel joined with its other major rival, American Flyer, to buy the bankrupt company, and Ives's assets were divided between them. In 1930, Lionel bought out American Flyer's interest and shuttered the Ives plant in Bridgeport, Connecticut.

It is important to note that the toy and scale model train industry encompasses many sizes, expressed as "scale." Technically, the word *gauge,* for prototype as well as miniature trains, is used as a measurement of the distance between the track rails. However, in referring to model trains, the distinction is sometimes lost. *Gauge* is often used to denote the relative size of model train. Before 1900, toy train manufacturers paid little attention to scale sizes, and there was no track gauge standardization. When Lionel entered the field, it made its product to a gauge that measured 2.875 inches between the rails. However, by 1907, it was making "standard gauge" products (2.125 inches between rails). In 1910, Ives and American Flyer began producing trains to the smaller "O" scale (1.25 inches between rails), and Lionel followed suit in 1915 while continuing to produce "standard gauge" trains. The company introduced "OO" scale in 1938. It discontinued making trains during World War II and never resumed production of OO scale products after the war. (It should be mentioned that trains larger than "standard gauge" are also used, notably outdoors where the result is called a "garden railway." Again, live steam modeling, where the locomotives burn fuel and operate from the steam that is generated in a boiler just like the "big boys," is another branch of the hobby.)[3]

In this chapter, the words *toy* and *model* are used somewhat interchangeably, but in 1939, William K. Walthers, a prominent leader in the model railroad industry, attempted to explain the difference between a toy railroad and a model railroad. He concluded that "a toy railroad is laid down once or twice a year and operated for amusement, just to watch the trains go round. A model railroad has a definite location, a plan for its continuation, and is operated with a purpose." The last sentence was buttressed by the leader in toy trains, Lionel itself. In their *Handbook for Model Builders,* the company's writers warn, "To begin a model railroad calls for a set of trains and space where a table or bench may be built and on which track may be fixed permanently."[4] Obviously, Lionel was trying to dispel the image of itself as a toy train manufacturer exclusively and saw no contradiction in using its products in a permanent model railroad.

Another distinction centers around the material used to make the train. Toy trains had long been made of stamped, tin-plated steel, whereas the more recent scale models (1930s forward) were machined (and/or cast) masterpieces. Of course, scale modelers would scorn the tinplate trains, whose track had a center third rail, as being unfaithful to prototype, but it was Lionel and similar companies that instilled a love of trains in many boys (and a few girls). Many of these youngsters would "graduate" from their tinplate "toys" to become dedicated scale modelers. Lionel made a notable departure from tinplate when they introduced a highly detailed scale model of a New York Central Railroad "Hudson" (4-6-4) type locomotive in 1938. This prized model retailed for $75 and was a faithful reproduction of its real-life forerunner, except for oversize wheel flanges designed to run on tinplate track. It is noteworthy also that, after World War II, some railroads contributed to the cost of tooling for Lionel models of their prototype locomotives.[5]

In 1948, Lionel introduced plastic parts in its trains and made other innovations to their lines. The 1940s and 1950s were the halcyon days of model railroading, and the Lionel Corporation was the preeminent manufacturer of toy trains. In the early 1950s it was the largest toy company in the world, and it recorded its best year in 1956. It employed 2,000 people in 1953.[6] Scale model railroading played a substantial part in the beginning of the downward spiral of Lionel's fortunes. Before and after World War II, a number of scale model manufacturers offered kits and finished products that reproduced exactly, in miniature, their prototypes on the real railroads. Scale model railroads were originally built in "O" scale, but the desire to "pack" more layout into a smaller space and improved miniaturization techniques, especially the development of smaller motors, accelerated the acceptance of "HO" (essentially, half-O) scale models. The trend toward smaller and smaller models continued, and then even tinier trains became widely available. Dozens of producers of HO scale equipment sprang up and captured much of the adult market. By 1950, 69 percent of railroad hobbyists were working in HO scale.[7]

Serving the scale model community were numerous manufacturers, two of which were prominent in New Jersey. The Atlas Tool Company was also located in Hillside and was a well-known maker of track and HO models. (Atlas briefly competed against Lionel in O scale.) Another prominent HO train maker was Mantua Metal Products Company, founded by John N. Tyler in 1926 and originally established at the town of Mantua in South Jersey, then relocated to Woodbury Heights. In 1947 the original partnership was dissolved, and John Tyler became the sole owner; he later changed the name of the concern to TYCO Industries, Inc. (There is no relationship to the similarly named conglomerate Tyco International.) The company diversified its toy lines beyond model trains, and in 1970 the business was sold to Consolidated Foods and production was gradually shifted to the Far East. Encountering financially difficult years in the 1990s, the company recovered and was sold again in 1998 to Mattel. At that time, TYCO was the third largest toy company in the United States. Unfortunately, in 2001, its seventy-fifth anniversary, "market conditions" had impacted the company, and it discontinued its model railroad lines.[8]

Lionel attempted to become a factor in HO scale; in 1957 it introduced a line of HO trains made by outside suppliers. This line was continued until 1967, at which time it was evident that the entire market

for toy trains had declined precipitously. The company's founder passed away in 1965.

Between 1959 and 1963 Lionel was sold three times, and its fortunes declined. It purchased American Flyer, its longtime competitor, in 1967, but that acquisition did not help, and the company spiraled into bankruptcy in 1969. Under a forced reorganization, General Mills purchased the rights (along with tools, dies, plans, and patents) to manufacture Lionel trains. However, Lionel had begun to phase out the Hillside, New Jersey, plant and had sold some of its manufacturing equipment, so the General Mills management relocated the Lionel production line to Mexico. That decision was flawed: the Mexican facility could not meet schedules, and the manufacturing line was reestablished at Mt. Clemens, Michigan, in 1975. In 1985, General Mills decided to divest itself of its toy businesses and sold the Lionel division to a private investor who established it as Lionel Trains, Inc. The company was sold again in 1995 to an investment firm that included rock singer Neil Young as a member. That latest reincarnation, Lionel L.L.C., resurrected many old Lionel favorites.[9]

An early book on model railroading, published in 1942, asserted "that no man outlives his boyhood love of locomotives."[10] That sentiment may have been true once, but the disappearance of real steam locomotives and the decline of railroads in general in this country have made the statement an anachronism. There are many men today who have never seen a steam locomotive, much less been enamored of them. (For many railroad fans, it is difficult to exhibit the same degree of affection or delight in the sterile outlines of electric and diesel locomotives.) Furthermore, many other distractions have intruded upon our lives and occupy the time that might have been spent enjoying a model railroad. However, there are dedicated modelers who enjoy the hobby and who have, singly or in groups, built impressive model railroads. They carry on a tradition begun by Ives, American Flyer, and others, but most notably the Lionel Corporation. Their works are often on display, available for the enjoyment of young and old alike. A large Lionel layout is on display at the South Jersey Railway Museum in Tuckahoe, N.J., and there are several large scale-model layouts in operation (available for public viewing during limited periods) around the state. The Model Railroad Club, a long-established group, operates one of these in Union, New Jersey, in

**Figure 43.** The Pacific Southern Railway is a large HO scale-model layout that incorporates many detailed features of the American landscape—towns, ports, farms—all joined by extensive railroad tracks. Here Tom Lavin, a member of the railroad club, is shown arranging buildings in a town that overlooks one of the miniature masterpieces of the layout, the Pate Brothers three-ring circus, built by Carl Pate and complete with "big top." Photo by Cliff Moore. Used with permission of the Pacific Southern.

affiliation with the Union County Division of Parks and Recreation. There they have assembled 1,600 square foot HO gauge and 400 square foot N scale (much smaller than HO) railroads. Another impressive layout is the Pacific Southern, located at Rocky Hill, New Jersey.[11]

A most unusual and notable model railroad was built by Bruce Zaccagnino for Northlandz, a children's attraction on Route 202 near Flemington that also features a doll museum, a 94-room dollhouse, and a 2,000-pipe organ, Zaccagnino advertises it as "the world's largest miniature railway" with 125 trains on eight miles of track. The layout incorporates 500,000 trees, 75,000 pounds of plaster, and wood sufficient to build five full-size houses. The builder has cleverly arranged the model railroad display so that a visitor wends his way over a mile-long tour in which only a limited portion of the entire layout is visible at any one time. Zaccagnino was especially lavish in his creation of mountains (some 35 feet high) and gorges and hundreds of trestles and bridges, one of which is 24 feet long, over which the trains operate. Miniature buildings and features range from the elaborate to the quixotic. One can find "the world's steepest cow pasture" and "the world's longest invisible bridge" here.[12]

Finally, another group of railroad enthusiasts has emerged fairly recently. These are collectors, less interested in model railroad operation than in admiring and exhibiting old train models. The successors to the original Lionel Corporation recognized this segment of the market and courted them with new releases of old favorites.

The Hillside Lionel manufacturing complex became the Hillside Industrial Park, home to many operations, but none associated with railroading. It was destroyed by fire in 2004.[13]

# 26 The Outlaw Railroad Strike and the "Indignation Specials" (1920)

As a general rule, the railroad unions—which were called "Brotherhoods" and consisted of the operating employees, such as engineers, conductors, and firemen—were slow to strike and maintained close relationships with the railroad management. Nevertheless, there were instances of railroad labor unrest, some serious, such as the "Great Railway Strikes of 1877," that employed the use of federal troops to quell the subsequent rioting. A consequence of the 1877 insurrection was the emergence of "alternative" labor organizations. The Knights of Labor and the American Railway Union, which drew their members from workers with lesser positions—shop workers and track, yard, and station workers—were more radical and more militant than the Brotherhoods. These groups were willing to challenge management and to strike, but after some defeats they disappeared from the scene. For the most part, railroad labor peace prevailed up until the United States entered World War I. But then the operation of railroads was assumed by the federal government. Labor was in short supply during the war, and the Railroad Administration allowed labor unions (apart from the Brotherhoods) to recruit members into rail unions. Again, these unions were more militant, a situation that led to a nationwide railroad strike in 1922. But before that widespread action, some of the more aggressive union members, arguing that prices had seriously inflated during the war but that wages had not kept pace, triggered an outlaw strike. (A strike by organized labor that is not sanctioned by the union is called a "wildcat" or "outlaw" strike.)[1]

The outlaw strike of 1920 was alleged to have been started at Chicago in early April 1920 by James O'Gara of the Yardmen's Association. Yardmen president John Gruneau was also identified as an "outlaw leader." Other wildcat strikes were begun at the Camden engine shops and among marine employees of the Erie Railroad at New York Harbor on 1 April 1920.[2] Within days, the Yardmen's outlaw strike had spread through much of the Midwest, and on 9 April organized railroad labor, fearing a total loss of control within its ranks, took an unprecedented step and appealed to the "government to take drastic steps to quash the strike." By the following day, the strike's effects were beginning to be felt in New Jersey. Trains running between New York and Philadelphia were canceled due to crew shortages, some Erie Railroad firemen at Jersey City walked out, causing confusion and delays to the morning commuter rush, "ferries ran spasmodically" because harbor workers failed to report for work, and headlines trumpeted an impending food crisis due to freight tie-ups and the walkout by marine employees who operated tugboats between New York and New Jersey. According to the *Trenton Evening Times*, "The unauthorized strike of radical railroad workers in Chicago, which spread rapidly over this vicinity yesterday, grew to alarming proportions during the morning hours. Freight transportation was at a standstill, threatening the city's food supply; passenger trains on many lines moved haltingly . . . and Manhattan was nearly isolated from New Jersey by the strike this morning of employees of the "tubes" running under the Hudson River."

With the loss of Hudson Tubes service, thousands of New Jersey commuters were unable to reach their jobs in Manhattan; the few ferries that still operated were jammed to stated capacity and beyond. A rush hour ban on the carrying of vehicles was imposed, and people stood in the spaces ordinarily filled with cars. The city of Trenton was left almost completely without rail service, and railroad spokesmen were unable to state when, or if, trains would reach the city. The local yard men were "on fire" and threatening to quit momentarily. Only the Philadelphia and Reading Railroad (P&R) was running normally, but its management placed an embargo on freight in anticipation of curtailed service. It was suggested that Trenton area commuters might make use of trolley lines to travel to New York or Philadelphia. The Public Service Company had a well-integrated system of trolley lines that might have functioned as an alternative means but only with a substantial increase in travel time.[3]

On 10 April, Brotherhood officials declared the strike to be "leaderless, unlawful and unwarranted, and an attempt by radical elements to gain control of the brotherhood." They further stated that the unauthorized work stoppage would end quickly and the "strike fever [would] burn out." This position proved to be overly optimistic because on the same day, the insurgents proclaimed that, far from being broken, the strike would spread because they had issued 20 charters, accounting for 25,000 members, in their "rump" union. At this early time, the situation was murky, and railroad officials were at a loss to determine the cause of the walkout. When asked, "Many of the men asserted that they did not know what the grievances were but there were muttered complaints of 'starvation wages' and 'unsatisfactory conditions.'" The best explanation was that the men "struck in sympathy with other men that are on strike in other parts of the country." In New Jersey, strike orders were spread by unknown men who traveled from yard to yard imploring the workers to quit and assuring them that the Brotherhood leadership supported them. No one could name these messengers. As a result of these excursions, it was generally believed that the legitimate union officials were involved. To dispel that impression, Brotherhood officials addressed the strikers and worked diligently to advise all that they were not in sympathy with the walkout.

By Monday, conditions had deteriorated further. At Penn Station in New York, 3,000 people fought to board a five-car Pennsylvania Railroad (PRR) train, one of the few that would leave for New Jersey and Philadelphia that day. Specialized electric locomotive engineers who drove trains from Manhattan Transfer through the Hudson River tunnel left their posts, and the PRR made plans to terminate trains at Newark and Jersey City. The Central Railroad of New Jersey suspended all service in the state, an action that affected 55,000 commuters and also eliminated P&R service east of Bound Brook. False inflammatory rumors were widespread: one stated that a Jersey City yardmaster had been killed when he reported for work and a telegraph operator had been driven from his tower by a group of armed men; another threatened that the barracks where employees waited for their assigned trains would be blown up and that locomotive cabs would be "fixed" if engineers and firemen attempted to work.

Investigators working for the railroads "discovered" the existence of a "secret committee," "well equipped with money and commanding hundreds of experienced agitators," directing the strike. Another rumor had the New Jersey National Guard summoned for strike duty. One true, ominous development was the discovery of a stick of dynamite on a Lackawanna ferryboat, and in Jersey City an iron bar, hurled through the window of a passing Jersey Central train, struck and injured a passenger. Although the mails were delayed, there was a bright spot in the news: the anticipated crisis in food supplies did not materialize (although prices did rise).[4]

Tuesday, 13 April, saw a widening of the strike, both nationally and in New Jersey. Most of the crews of the Central Railroad of New Jersey deserted their trains as they arrived at Jersey City that morning. Since those commuters who arrived on those trains would have no trains to take them home that evening, the president of the road "hastily crossed the river and pleaded with the strikers, who had remained near the railroad yards, to postpone the strike until the commuters . . . had been taken home. This plea was effective, and enough men stayed on the job to take return trains . . . over all the lines of the Jersey Central." President Besler's efforts notwithstanding, thousands of commuters *were* stranded in New York City; hotel rooms were sold out, and many hotels pressed their ballrooms and banquet halls into use as makeshift dormitories. The last link in freight service into Trenton was severed when the P&R employees joined the work stoppage. Pennsylvania Railroad workers at the Trenton shops also joined the strike after meeting at the Moose Hall. This day saw the emergence of volunteers, military personnel, students, and ordinary citizens who offered to man the trains. In some towns, Boy Scouts were dispatched to distribute recruiting flyers to all the homes, and similar word was broadcast at movie theaters and restaurants. Indicative of another time (can the reader imagine that such offers would even be considered today?), many of these offers were accepted, and those with previous railroading experience were especially prized. Thus were born the "Indignation Specials," those trains which were run by volunteers during the strike.[5]

Samuel Gillespie, a well-to-do businessman and regular commuter on the Delaware, Lackawanna and Western Railroad (D,L&W), along with former Navy lieutenant Henry Rawle, a vice president of the Celluloid Company, John Stedman of the Prudential Insurance Company, and F. E. Van Auken and Alfred Maury, also veterans, "virtually took possession of a train" in Morristown. With a regular locomotive engineer at the throttle, Rawle served as fireman and the others became conductors for the day. Along with William Ayres, the regular conductor, this group of businessmen brought the "Gillespie Special" into Hoboken.[6]

That same day, Tuesday, a group of Princeton University students "offered themselves as railway strikebreakers." The article describing this development went on to say,

> Samuel Rea, president of the Pennsylvania Lines, has notified President Hibben [of Princeton University] that, while he cannot use volunteers at this time, he will not hesitate to call on the students if they are needed.
>
> Independent groups of students left Princeton yesterday [Monday] afternoon to help break the strike. A number of them, including several members of the football team, have gone to aid the Erie and Lackawanna until Sunday.[7]

Although the PRR initially declined the students' offer, by Thursday it reconsidered and recruited more than a score to help with the movement of freight trains. When a call for strikebreakers was issued at the college, the registrar's office was swamped with volunteers. The scene was described graphically in the *New York Times*:

> A line was rapidly formed stretching from the registrar's office on the second floor of Nassau Hall down a spiral staircase and half-way across the intervening space between Old Nassau and the library. The men were so eager to see to it that their names would get on the list that it was necessary to summon "Chuck" Carpenter, captain of the wrestling team and the biggest man in college, to act as sergeant at arms. He was actively engaged in preserving order throughout the period of signing up.

Nearly 200 students signed up and were deployed to various sites. Eighty-seven Princeton undergraduates arrived at the yards in Jersey City to work; 45 were assigned to the Lackawanna, and they were quartered at Hoboken. Two acted as firemen on the Princeton Branch, another two worked on the Rocky Hill Branch, and a few were brought to Point Pleasant. The greatest number left New Jersey to take up jobs at Pittsburgh. Other Princetonians were brought to the West Morrisville, Pennsylvania, and Coalport, New Jersey, yards for training as brakemen and firemen. Their departure from Princeton the preceding evening provided an excuse to celebrate and party at the college, resulting in "a demonstration that has not been rivaled in Princeton since the signing of the armistice." W. W. Atterbury, a Pennsylvania Railroad vice president, wrote a personal letter of thanks to the Princeton men, even though he was a Yale graduate.[8]

The Hudson Tubes spent most of Tuesday running "instruction" trains over their lines to teach their operation to new recruits, in accordance with a requirement of the Interstate Commerce Commission that new trainmen must make several supervised runs before running independently.[9]

By Wednesday, 14 April, the volunteer movement was in full flower. Offers to help came from many sources, including local high schools. It was reported that "civilian volunteers to break the strike of rebellious railroad workers here were drilling in New York and New Jersey terminals today and railroad officials announced services of several hundred men probably would be utilized to operate suburban trains." The first trains on the Erie Railroad manned by volunteers were greeted at stations along the line by exuberant crowds who cheered and waved flags. The mayor of Westwood fired one engine, and wealthy residents of

**Figure 44.** This cartoon detected progress in settling the outlaw strikes when it was announced that the Railroad Labor Board would mediate the dispute. *Philadelphia Record*, as reprinted in the *Trenton Times*, 15 April 1920.

HOPEFUL SIGN OF MOVING.          —Philadelphia Record.

the town crewed the train. The "Millionaire Special" from Upper Montclair sped into the Erie terminal at Hoboken in good time. Although there were some reports of a weakening of the walkout, commuters took no chances. Many boarded the trains carrying suitcases in preparation for spending the night in New York City, if necessary.[10]

Students from Rutgers and Stevens Institute of Technology also stepped forward and helped operate trains over the Erie and Lackawanna Railroads. About 100 Stevens men appeared unbidden at the Erie's Jersey City yards "dressed in overalls, caps and old shoes and many of them carried tin dinner pails." Others "wore sneakers and suffered severely from standing on the coal-strewn platforms of the locomotive tenders. Many wore sport suits and sophomore neckties, but the strangeness of their attire did not minimize the respect which the old-time railroaders gave them for their enthusiastic work." The Stevens undergraduates were quartered in eight Pullman cars at Jersey City. Before the end of the week, the two roads were each operating about 25 trains each way daily accommodating about half of their normal traffic. Thankfully, there were few incidents of violence directed toward the volunteers. One unprovoked attack by three strikers upon a volunteer crew in a locomotive cab at Hoboken resulted in the arrest of the attackers. Several of the outlaw leaders appeared at the police station and deplored the incident and pledged to restrain their men from further violence. Many New Jersey towns held "indignation" meetings and established "Transportation Committees," the intent of which was to organize local citizens for potential volunteer duty on train crews. Subsequently, over 5,000 individuals signed up.[11]

It took several more days before the outlaw strike could be considered ended in New Jersey. On Friday, there were predictions that the strike on the PRR would spread still further, but it may be that the volunteer efforts forestalled a more widespread work stoppage. Over the weekend, more and more of the regular railroad workers returned to their jobs

as word was received from the strike leaders at Chicago that the strike had ended. By Monday, 19 April, newspaper headlines blared "Union Decides to Call Off Strike" and "Men Return," but conclusion of the stoppage was deferred when some regular crews expressed fear of taking their trains into the Jersey City yards where some recalcitrant strikers pelted the trains with rocks. Hudson Tube service, critical for commuters, returned to daylight operation, under heavy guard, on Tuesday. In subsequent days, as indicated by the decline in space allotted to the outlaw strike story by newspapers, the outlaw strike was abated but was not fully quelled, insofar as freight traffic was concerned, until mid-May. In fact, sporadic walkouts continued to affect railroad operations until July 1920, when wage improvements were granted.[12]

The catalyst for ending the wildcat strike was President Woodrow Wilson's action on 13 April in staffing a railroad labor board that was designed to mediate labor disputes. The *Philadelphia Record* recognized this "hopeful sign of moving" with a political cartoon. The Railroad Labor Board had been constituted under the Esch-Cummins Law, which had been enacted earlier that year, but its membership had not been designated.[13]

The causes of the outlaw strike were variously attributed to "radicals" and "Bolshevists," to a plot to

**The Outlaw Railroad Strike and the "Indignation Specials"    135**

bring the railroads back under government control, and to inadequate wages. No less an authority than the attorney general declared that the strike was "a revolutionary movement designed to overthrow the Government." More likely, the move was intended to overthrow the management of the Brotherhoods; at least that was the avowed purpose of the Tube workers who struck, asserting that they (the union leaders) "had misrepresented the men."[14]

Although it was generally agreed that the leftist organizations had no part in inciting the strike, the Communist Party of America took advantage of the fait accompli and promulgated a leaflet designed to agitate the insurgents and inflame the situation further: "Sweep aside the traitors to the working class in your organization," it read, referring to the leadership and loyal members of the Brotherhoods, the American Federation of Labor, and the Trainmen's Union. "Throw them out of your organization, making your organization the militant expressing of the workers. . . . Make it a real fighting organization against low wages, bad working conditions, MORE IMPORTANT, AGAINST THE CAPITALISTS AND THE WHOLE CAPITALIST SYSTEM."

William D. Haywood, leader of the International Workers of the World, an organization with an anarchist and Marxist reputation and dedicated to the overthrow of capitalism, also denounced the American Federation of Labor and expressed sympathy for the strike. This position might have been expected from him, but he added fuel to the fire by exclaiming, "New York is only five days away from starvation."[15]

However, it is certain that the trigger for the action was a low wage scale exacerbated by an infla-tionary cost of living after the end of the war and the procrastination of the government in remedying the situation. Conductors received $6.00 for 12 hours of work, and passenger engineers were paid $6.05 for 10 hours and 40 minutes. A freight engineer could max out at $6.80 for 8 hours. Brakemen received $4.05 for 10 hours. To emphasize the prevailing low wages, one trainman produced a small notebook that showed his monthly income was $102.50. On this he supported a wife and four children. Even though his expenditures included no medical or entertainment expenses—he couldn't afford them—he was $3.27 "in the hole" at the end of the month. The Railroad Labor Board, with members representing railroad management, railroad unions, and the public, finally agreed to increase wages about 20 percent.[16]

The conclusion of the outlaw strikes coincided with the beginning of another movement directed against the high cost of living. Congressman William D. Upshaw of Georgia, the self-proclaimed "President of the Congress Overall and Old Clothes Club," protested the high cost of clothing and appeared in Congress dressed in a one-piece bib overall. Overall clubs quickly sprang up all over the country, and a few days later, congressional secretaries took to the new fashion. When four secretaries, with overall legs rolled up to midcalf, passed a group of Daughters of the American Revolution who were touring the Capitol, the latter decried the "horrifying spectacle." Although the overall movement caused only a few retailers to lower clothing prices, it, like the outlaw strikes but in a more benign fashion, highlighted the wage-cost issue and brought it closer to a resolution.[17]

# 27 Modern Light Rail in the Garden State (1929–Present)

New Jersey has three modern light rail systems in operation, descendants of the interurban railways that carried passengers throughout the state.

## NEWARK LIGHT RAIL (NEWARK CITY SUBWAY)

The Newark City Subway was built mostly on the bed of the Morris Canal over a period of 13 years. The first phase, begun in November 1929, involved covering over the downtown Newark portion of the canal (which created a new street, Raymond Boulevard) and preparing separated crossings over the remainder of the right-of-way. Service began between Warren Street in Newark and Heller Parkway on 16 May 1935. Further extensions took the line to Pennsylvania Station in 1937 and to Franklin Avenue at the other end in 1940.

The tracks were shared by a number of trolley car lines that were rerouted from their original streets and by a new route, the number 7-City Subway line, which ran the entire length. The trolleys in use on those lines were steadily retired and replaced by buses until, by 1952, only the City Subway survived. The line was operated by Public Service Corporation (PS) from its inception until Transport of New Jersey acquired it around 1980. Shortly thereafter, along with other rail properties, it was ceded to New Jersey Transit (NJT), the present operator. In 2002, the line was extended northward from Franklin Avenue through Belleville to Grove Street in Bloomfield. Additions to the system continue to be made; in Newark, a con-nection between Penn Station and the Broad Street Station, about one mile distant, was completed as a branch of the original system.[1]

This 5.1-mile light rail system began as part of a trolley car network and still shares many of the characteristics of a street railway. For most of its life it employed trolley cars on the number 7 line, albeit top-of-the-line PCC cars, those cars which were specially designed by an Electric Railway President's Conference Committee and intended to halt the trolley car's march into oblivion. The first of the PCC cars entered service on the Brooklyn and Queens Transit line in New York City in 1936. Cars used by the Newark system were obtained from Minneapolis in 1954 when streetcar transportation was abandoned there. Those cars, built in the late 1940s, remained in service in Newark until 2001—over 50 years later! The Newark Light Rail System still makes numerous stops on its short journey. However, the system also displays characteristics more closely associated with an interurban line: it operates on a private right-of-way, it travels between cities (Bloomfield, Belleville, and Newark), and it has more recently been equipped with true light rail vehicles of the type used by Hudson-Bergen Light Rail (HBLR), using pantographs instead of the trolley poles. Still visible today are some of the beautiful tile murals, depicting life along the old Morris Canal, that were installed by WPA workers at various stations when the line was built.[2]

## HUDSON-BERGEN LIGHT RAIL

The HBLR system has three branches. One connects Bayonne with Exchange Place and Hoboken Terminal, points from which passengers can transfer to New York City via the PATH. At Hoboken, connections can also be made to several other NJ Transit lines that carry commuters deep into New Jersey. Liberty State Park is also served, although the old Central Railroad of New Jersey terminal is some distance removed from the light rail station. The line from West Side Avenue in Jersey City extends to Tonnelle Avenue in North Bergen. Another branch runs between Hoboken Terminal and the North Bergen terminus.[3]

The HBLR system is owned by New Jersey Transit but is operated by an independent contractor, 21st Century Rail Corporation, which designed, built, and maintains the system. It uses Japanese-made vehicles. The first phase of the system was opened in the spring of 2000, and subsequent additions enlarged the system to its current length. When construction is completed, the line will be almost 21 miles long. Its name, Hudson-Bergen Light Rail, is a misnomer. It was originally planned as a more ambitious undertaking extending into Bergen County, but escalating construction costs and changing priorities curtailed that plan, and the current system lies wholly within Hudson County. However, even in its abbreviated form, it does provide service through one of the most densely populated parts of the state. HBLR employs some abandoned railroad rights-of-way, spliced together from former Jersey Central, Lackawanna, Conrail, West Shore, and New Jersey Junction Railroad tracks. In downtown Jersey City, HBLR shares city streets with auto traffic. In 2006, the system enjoyed a patronage of 27,000 riders per day, a number that is expected to increase to 100,000 when the HBLR lines are fully built. The system is meeting one of its early objectives, namely, reducing vehicular traffic in the Hudson River shoreline region that it serves.[4]

Under consideration are plans to extend rail service from NJ Transit's Pascack Valley Line to the Meadowlands Sports Complex. In addition, a less likely to be implemented proposal to bring HBLR tracks to the Meadowlands has also been floated. Whether these projects, or the construction of the long-planned Bergen County branch of HBLR, will reach fruition remains to be seen.[5]

## THE RIVER LINE

NJ Transit (NJT) inaugurated service on its River LINE on 14 March 2004. The first train left Pennsauken at 5:27 AM and carried more than 20 paying passengers on its short trip to the Entertainment Center station at Camden. The River LINE is 34 miles long and serves 20 stations along its route from Trenton to Camden. It is the first light rail system to be built in the United States using diesel-electric motive power.[6]

Much of the trackage between Camden and Trenton is laid over the nearly-abandoned Camden and Amboy Railroad (C&A) right-of-way along the east side of the Delaware River. (Amtrak's Northeast Corridor follows the west bank of the river from Philadelphia to Trenton.) Pennsylvania Railroad (the C&A's inheritor) passenger service had been phased out in 1963, but freight service continued at a minimal level and is maintained even today by Conrail Shared Assets. NJ Transit purchased the right-of-way in 1999 for $67.5 million, along with exclusive access from 6 AM to 10 PM and Saturday nights and Sunday mornings. Conrail Shared Assets enjoys access for freight at other times. A division of time slots was mandated by the Federal Railroad Administration, which prohibits the light rail cars to be run with ordinary railroad cars. The rolling stock was built by Bombardier Transportation in association with Stadler Rail AG, and the Bechtel Corporation designed the overall project. The firms share in the operation and maintenance of the system, whose first cost was about $1 billion. None of that cost was borne by the federal government, which questioned the need for the system.[7]

Completion was delayed for more than a year beyond the target date by a number of small problems and one major one. A new double-track bridge, intended to replace an aged, low-level, movable bridge, was required to cross Rancocas Creek between Riverside and Delanco. The new bridge was floated into position in April 2001, but the barge upon which it was carried capsized before the bridge was in place. It took four months to recover the bridge and position it so that it could be properly installed.

The River LINE follows a path that has many reminders of New Jersey's manufacturing heritage. From Trenton, where a bridge crossing the Delaware still sports an illuminated sign bragging, "Trenton Makes, the World Takes," a passenger can see the historic Roebling Works, where John Roebling made wire rope that supported many of the country's early suspension bridges, including the famous Niagara railway bridge. At Burlington City, reminiscent of early twentieth-century interurbans, the train passes along the city's streets. It returns to its dedicated right-of-way until it approaches downtown Camden, where again street-laid tracks carry the train into the Walter Rand Transportation Center and finally to the Aquarium and the Tweeter Entertainment Center.

The River LINE, which initially charged adults only $1.10 for a one-way ticket good over the entire line, was touted by its supporters as a means to reinvigorate many of the small towns along its route and to provide low-cost commutation for residents of those towns, either north to Trenton with its many state offices or south to Camden where connections could be made with PATCO trains that brought one to downtown Philadelphia. On the other hand, the River LINE never lacked critics, some of whom named the enterprise the "Boondoggle Express." Most critics insist that the light rail system was a poor investment for this area. The low fare, combined with low patronage, was expected to make it the poorest performing (economically) rail line in the country. Fares were anticipated to cover only 5 percent of the operating costs. There is evidence that politics played a large role in the project. South Jersey legislators had complained that much of the improvements made by NJ Transit occurred in the northern part of the state, and they insisted upon a light rail system serving the southern counties. NJT attempted to comply but experienced substantial opposition to its first choice of route; it was compelled to accept the present route, which had lower ridership potential.[8]

Two years after inauguration of service, the River LINE is still not economically viable. Although fares have increased nominally and ridership has increased beyond the original estimate of 6,000, fare receipts do not even begin to cover operating costs. NJ Transit believes that the system has demonstrated its effectiveness through improvements in business development along its route. Although changes are still minimal, NJT can point to new residential development and business opportunities along the line. According to the *Trenton Times*, "As a traffic reliever, it probably is not the best use of scarce capital, but as an economic development engine, it will be an extraordinarily successful investment that will pay off over the long term. . . . The line is already boosting the commercial, retail, and residential markets in the towns that it serves." A possible future connection to NJ Transit's Atlantic City line might be built, funds permitting. On a positive note, unlike the old Riverside Line between the two cities, the River LINE makes the trip in about an hour, beating the 1905 time by two hours![9]

NJ Transit produced what it terms a River LINE "owner's manual," which is a compact brochure that describes the system in detail. It includes a list of all stations and their parking capacities (parking is free at all, except for Trenton). All connecting services—to Amtrak, PATCO (Port Authority Transit Company), SEPTA (Southeastern Pennsylvania Transit Authority), BurLink (a Burlington County shuttle bus), and the CCIA (Camden County Improvement Authority) shuttle bus—are shown.[10]

It appears at this time that the principal advantage of the Newark and Hudson-Bergen Light Rail systems is the reduction of vehicular traffic in the densely populated areas of North Jersey. That benefit is not particularly applicable to the River LINE, which can claim instead its potential for developing the riverside corridor through which it runs. For over 175 years, since railroads were introduced into this country, there has been a consistent pattern of development along their routes, and there is no reason to believe that the River LINE will not follow that model. Economic benefits apart, a ride on any of these systems, especially during off-peak hours, is a pleasurable experience for a rail fan. Take the HBLR and travel through the heart of early railroad installations along the Hudson River waterfront or ride the River LINE through numerous industrial towns along the Delaware to the last stop at Camden where several attractions—the battleship New Jersey, the Tweeter Center, a minor league ball park, and the State Aquarium—await you. All of this without concern for traffic!

# 28 The Dirigible Railroad at Lakehurst (1932–37)

Before the age of practical heavier-than-air flying machines, man soared into the sky in balloons. Jean Pilâtre de Rozier made the first flight on 21 November 1783 in a Montgolfier balloon. The earliest balloons relied on heated air to lift them, but it was not long before the advantages of a balloon filled with a lighter-than-air gas was recognized and exploited. In fact, de Rozier employed just such an apparatus, a hot air balloon attached below a gas-filled balloon, to attempt an English Channel crossing in 1785. He and a passenger were killed when the upper balloon exploded, and they fell from an altitude of 3,000 feet onto the rocky shore of France. Unpowered lighter-than-air craft remained the sole vehicles available for aerial flight for many years, and almost a century passed before steam engines small enough to carry aloft were applied in 1852. Now, for the first time, it was possible to fly and direct a flying machine along a desired course.[1]

But these early airships were nonrigid, that is, their gas container had no supporting elements except for the gas itself. The first rigid airship, *La France*, a craft with a skeleton, the definition of a dirigible, was flown in 1884 in France by Charles Renard and Arthur Krebs, captains in the French Army Corps of Engineers. Ferdinand von Zeppelin, the inventor who is most closely associated with dirigible development and who lent his name to the genre, ascended in his first craft in 1900. Dirigible development both literally and figuratively "took off" from that point; heavier-than-air craft (airplanes) were crude and dangerous, with limited payloads for many years to come. Dirigibles were hailed as the only aircraft that promised to carry large loads, passengers and freight, over long distances. But they were not without safety problems. Early American dirigibles fell from the sky: one carrying 16 passengers crashed in California in 1908, and a more dramatic and more deadly incident occurred when a dirigible flying above the Loop in Chicago in 1919 fell in flames through the glass roof of a downtown bank; 11 people died.

Thanks to von Zeppelin's persistent promotion of rigid airships, Germany became a leader in their development and production. After World War I (during which dirigibles had been used by Germany as offensive weapons with indifferent military outcome), the U.S. Navy acquired a German airship. The ZR-3, obtained as part of a reparations agreement, arrived at Lakehurst in October 1924 and was renamed *Los Angeles*. The Navy established an extensive base for lighter-than-air craft at Lakehurst, New Jersey, beginning in 1919, and this base figured in dirigible exploits during the 1920s and 1930s. Another lighter-than-air craft base was established at Sunnyvale, California.[2]

A railroad connection existed before the Navy acquired the base. A Baldwin Locomotive Works subsidiary won a contract in 1915 for the production of artillery shells for the Russian government. That company established an ammunition proving ground near Lakehurst in that year. The base passed into U.S. Army ownership after the country entered World War I, and at the end of that conflict, the U.S. Navy purchased the land.[3]

One of the unique features of dirigibles is their massive size, required to contain sufficient gas to pro-

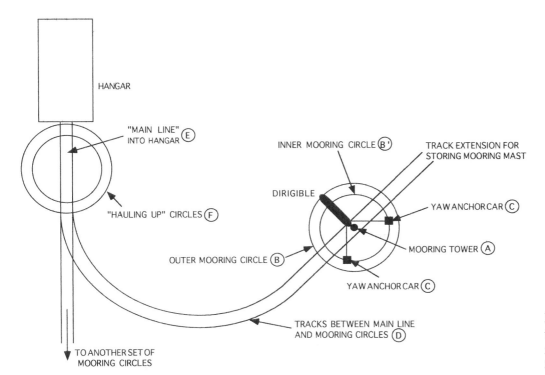

**Figure 45.** A plan view (not to scale) of the dirigible railroad at Lakehurst Naval Air Station. Author's drawing.

Labels in figure:

HANGAR

"MAIN LINE" INTO HANGAR (E)

"HAULING UP" CIRCLES (F)

INNER MOORING CIRCLE (B')

TRACK EXTENSION FOR STORING MOORING MAST

DIRIGIBLE

YAW ANCHOR CAR (C)

MOORING TOWER (A)

OUTER MOORING CIRCLE (B)

YAW ANCHOR CAR (C)

TRACKS BETWEEN MAIN LINE AND MOORING CIRCLES (D)

TO ANOTHER SET OF MOORING CIRCLES

vide adequate lift. One downside of the huge external surface areas presented by a dirigible is that substantial wind forces act against them. In flight this is a problem, but one that is controllable in part by maneuvering and steering devices and surfaces. However, dirigibles always had to avoid storms and high winds. On the ground, the problem can be deadly if the machine is tossed around with little room to recover. The original method for landing an airship involved dropping lines from the ship to a ground crew below as the ship approached for a landing. Each member of the ground crew was expected to grab a rope and haul the ship down. (The author recalls participating in such an operation at an Air Force base in Florida that involved landing a much smaller "blimp," rather than a dirigible.) Once at, or close to, the ground, the airship was "walked" to a tie-down location and secured. However, this method was inadequate for large airships. The Navy craft *Los Angeles* was 658 feet long, and the *Akron* was 785 feet, so a new procedure and equipment were devised. These included a 162-foot-high mooring tower, to which the airship was secured by a ball and socket joint in the ship's nose. The system allowed the airship to swing around the tower when it was buffeted by light winds, and it worked well enough until a

day in 1927 when the *Los Angeles* was caught by a capricious wind that brought the ship into a vertical attitude, standing straight up, with nose down, still tethered to its tower. Although no one was injured, this underscored the importance of finding a better way of handling the large ships on the ground at Lakehurst. The solution was the "dirigible railroad," which provided the means to safely handle dirigibles during docking and housing operations under most weather conditions. However, before the dirigible railroad was constructed, on the momentous occasion of the *Graf Zeppelin*'s arrival at Lakehurst in 1928 after completing its maiden voyage to the United States, it had to be manhandled to the ground by 160 sailors and then fastened to a 70-foot-high "stub mast." Removal to the prepared hangar was delayed until ground winds subsided. The *Los Angeles* was already under cover and had been moved to one side of the enormous hangar to make room for the newcomer.[4]

The dirigible railroad drawn in figure 45 envisioned a melding of established techniques for mooring an airship with railroad technology that improved safety and eliminated the need for a large ground crew. Central to the plan was a mooring tower, a short stub mast, to which the nose of the ship was attached (A). A shorter tower was installed to anchor the tail of the craft close to the ground (thus eliminating a recurrence of the *Los Angeles* fiasco). The tail was fastened to a four-wheel railroad car, called a "riding out car" (not shown in my drawing) that ran on a circular track, a "mooring circle" (B and B') that extended completely around the mast. Suitable, free-running clamps on the car allowed it to move along the track yet restrained it from being raised from the track in the event of an updraft acting against the airship. Two concentric mooring circles were installed so that large or small dirigibles could use the system.

Landing a dirigible using the new system, while not simple, required fewer hands on the ground. As the craft approached the short mooring mast, it had to travel slowly because it was so low and even the slightest miscalculation might dash it against the ground. Lines were dropped from just behind the nose of the ship, and ground crews would attach these lines to two locomotives, called "yaw anchor cars" (C), positioned on the mooring circle tracks. These locomotives drew the ship forward to mate with the socket on the tower to which it would be fastened. The technique was similar to, though more demanding than, the method used to draw ships through the locks of the Panama Canal. At Lakehurst, the yaw anchor car operators had to pull the ship forward while compensating for sideways movement (yaw) and simultaneously avoiding damage to the fragile envelope.

In addition to the improved mooring method, the dirigible railroad was expanded to allow a small ground crew to move an airship into the cavernous hangar. To do this, the riding out car was removed so that a swiveling tail wheel, installed at the stern of the ship, was free to travel along the ground. The mooring tower was made with a four-legged base, and each leg was mounted on a standard gauge railroad truck. The trucks were moved along parallel railroad tracks (D and E) by a small locomotive coupled to one of the trucks. The tracks extended from the mooring circle via a large curve to and into the hangar. On its trip to the hangar, the airship would cross over the concentric mooring circles and then over another set of concentric, circular tracks installed in front of the hangar. These tracks were known as the "hauling up circles" (F). Once the mooring tower was close to the hangar, it was positioned in the center of the hauling

up circles. At this time, the tail wheel of the dirigible would be located over one or the other of the hauling up circles, although it most likely would be angularly displaced from the parallel mooring mast tracks. Now the tail wheel was removed, and the stern of the airship was secured to a second riding out car. A locomotive, coupled to the riding out car, now pulled the stern around to orient the ship along the line of tracks leading into the hangar. Since the riding out car was now positioned at a right angle to the desired line of travel, the locomotive was detached from the car, which was then jacked up, rotated 90 degrees, and rerailed onto a track leading into the hangar. Finally, the mooring mast locomotive pushed the dirigible into the hangar. Once it was located in the calm interior of the hangar, the mast was withdrawn; attachment to the riding out car was sufficient to provide stability to the craft.

Gas-electric locomotives were used for the dirigible railroad, and they included a 35-ton Plymouth engine that was employed at the mooring tower. The 0-8-0 locomotives built by the Porter Locomotive Works and weighing 132 tons were used as yaw anchor cars. Power was transmitted to their wheels via a driveshaft and side rods. Other locomotives were used for the system, but all disappeared after dirigible operations ceased at Lakehurst. Although no mention of them is made in accounts of the *Hindenburg* disaster, it is likely that one or both of the yaw anchor cars that were being used to dock the airship were destroyed as well.[5]

It should be noted that extensive rail facilities existed at the naval base at Lakehurst long before the dirigible railroad was constructed. Miles of tracks on the base served the hangars, power house, helium production facility, and the various storehouses. The Central Railroad of New Jersey (CNJ) provided service to Lakehurst (the town and the naval base). Lakehurst service facilities, gone now, included a turntable, engine house, and shops, and it was a regular stop for daily passenger and freight trains, including the *Blue Comet* (see chapter 9). The railroad occasionally provided special trains for events such as the arrival of the ZR-3 from Germany on 15 October 1924. On that occasion, the Jersey Central heralded "See the ZR-3 at Lakehurst" in newspaper advertisements that listed excursions the following weekend.

When the *Graf Zeppelin* was scheduled to arrive at Lakehurst on 14 October 1928, 65,000 people

**Figure 46.** The *Hindenburg*, tethered to its mooring mast, during its second visit to the United States in May 1936. Elements of the dirigible railroad and the huge hanger are clearly evident. Note that the tail of the craft is supported at the outer mooring circle. Courtesy of Hagley Museum and Library, accession number 70.200.9022.

came to watch. Many traveled by car and bus, and others came via the Jersey Central. "The scene about the hangar suggested a fair. A number of stands were erected for the sale of 'hot dogs,' pop and ice cream. One man did a great volume of business selling waffle and ice cream sandwiches. . . . [There were] all the catch-penny salesmen known to football and world series throngs."[6]

Coincident with that date (14 October 1928), the American Zeppelin Transport Company contracted with the Jersey Central to carry passengers and mail from New York City (via ferry to Jersey City, then by rail to Lakehurst). On these trips, trains originating at Jersey City were brought into the Navy base via a spur that led to a hangar on the field. The run from

Jersey City took 85 minutes. Perhaps the best remembered trip was that of a train that left New York City from Pennsylvania Station in October 1936. The train carried two cars filled with leaders of the industrial, financial, and aviation worlds to the "Millionaire's Flight." That sightseeing flight was a 10-hour round-trip over six northeastern states on the *Hindenburg*, which was organized by the Goodyear-Zeppelin Company, a joint venture between Germany and the United States, before the celebrated airship made its last Atlantic crossing of the year. (The railroad had also run a special train to Lakehurst for patrons to see the *Hindenburg* after its first transatlantic crossing earlier that year.) The train moved over tracks that were jointly owned by the Pennsylvania Railroad and the Jersey Central and was then brought to Lakehurst by the CNJ. But by 1936 the special railroad trips to meet the dirigibles were few, and most Zeppelin passengers were brought by bus or auto to New York or, in some cases, via airplane from a specially constructed runway at the Lakehurst base to Newark Airport.[7]

The Navy built the first American dirigible, the *Shenandoah*, at Lakehurst. It was followed by the *Akron* (1931) and the *Macon* (1933), which were built by Goodyear-Zeppelin. All three ships were lost in accidents: the *Shenandoah* in 1925, the *Akron* in 1933, and the *Macon* in 1935. Only the German-built *Los Angeles* survived that fate, but it was decommissioned in 1939 and scrapped. Dirigibles were "written-off" by the Navy, but its lighter-than-air experience continued in the shape of "blimps." These smaller, nonrigid airships proved to be valuable adjuncts to naval aircraft and surface ships in helping to patrol the sea lanes along the coast during World War II. Although the Navy dirigible program ended, the Lakehurst lighter-than-air facility remained to serve airships of the German Zeppelin Company. But two years after the loss of the *Macon*, disaster struck the *Hindenburg*. While landing at Lakehurst in May 1937, the gigantic airship, the largest object ever to fly and only 78.5 feet shorter than the steamship *Titanic*, burst into flames; 36 died in the accident. (The United States controlled the supply of scarce helium gas, and as a consequence other countries relied upon a more effective lifting agent, hydrogen, which unfortunately is flammable.) This incident provided the final chapter in the history of rigid airships, although there have been periodic renaissances that, so far, have not been productive. No longer did the sleek and awesome ships glide through the sky, their glamour put aside in the interest of safety. Already, in 1937, it was evident to knowledgeable airmen that airplanes would assume their role.[8]

There are some who believe that a ghost, or ghosts, of the *Hindenburg* survivors can be seen and heard in Hangar #1. In her book *It Happened in New Jersey*, Fran Capo relates that naval personnel at the base have seen a ghostly figure in the hangar, a shape that disappears when one approaches it. She describes the experience of Alan Gross, an airship historian, when he was alone in the hangar during the small hours of morning. He claimed that he often heard "murmurs and whispers," but could not determine their location. He walked through "cold spots," an indication of paranormal activity, he was told. Others have heard engine sounds and voices during the daylight hours, perhaps, they say, of the victims who perished in the accident, shouting "away the lines" or "she's on fire." But, ghosts or not, it is unlikely that Lakehurst will ever again participate in the thrill and excitement of a dirigible arrival or departure.[9]

Today, the Naval Air Engineering Station (formerly Lakehurst Naval Air Station) on County Route 547, north of Route 70, features a "Welcome Center" where a visitor may view photographs and displays pertaining to the base's mission, past and present. Tours of the base are provided regularly. Hangar #1 has been named a National Landmark, and a monument marks the spot where the *Hindenburg* crashed. Within Hangar #1 one might still find a few embedded rails from the tracks that were part of the dirigible railroad.[10]

# 29  Calamity at Woodbridge (1951)

The Pennsylvania Railroad (PRR) holds the dubious distinction of involvement in four of the six railroad accidents with the highest death tolls in the state of New Jersey. Furthermore, if one considers that the Camden and Amboy Railroad (C&A) was the direct predecessor to the PRR, the Pennsylvania's accident listing would also include the first railroad accident in the state and, a few weeks later, the first fatal railroad accident. In September 1833, on its maiden trip, the *John Bull,* the C&A's pioneer locomotive, struck a hog. The hog was decapitated, and the train jumped off the rails, "causing a male passenger to turn a summerset out of the window." A much more serious accident occurred at Hightstown, New Jersey, on 11 November 1833 when a broken axle caused the derailment of a train carrying 24 passengers. Two were killed, and others, including Cornelius Vanderbilt, were injured. Former president John Quincy Adams was also a passenger on this train, but he suffered no injury.[1] But the worst railroad accident in the history of New Jersey occurred in 1951 on the Pennsylvania Railroad near Woodbridge, New Jersey. Eighty-five people died, and hundreds were injured in that accident.[2]

Part of the story about the 1906 railroad accident at the Thoroughfare (see chapter 24) is told through the eyes of a survivor, Ida May Dubell, who was traveling on the train with her fiancé. Forty-five years later, another engaged young lady, Pearl Goldsmith, was a survivor of the Woodbridge tragedy. Unlike Ida, Pearl did marry her fiancé, Jerry Selinger, although years later, with a smile, she blamed him for her presence on the train. That fateful evening, awaiting a telephone call from Jerry, she had delayed her departure from her office, thereby missing her usual train.

The wreck of the commuter train at Woodbridge was precipitated, and its effects were compounded, by a number of factors. The *Broker,* a train so named because it typically carried Wall Street employees, was particularly crowded on 6 February 1951 because the road's competitor, the Central Railroad of New Jersey, had been hit by a strike. The 11-car PRR train departed Jersey City at 5:10 PM after receiving passengers from a connecting Hudson Tubes train. It stopped at Newark and then accelerated toward its next stop at Perth Amboy. About a third of a mile beyond the Woodbridge station and close to the business district, the steam locomotive swung through a sharp curve and entered a temporary timber trestle that had been erected to carry the tracks over Legion Place and around some improvements that were being made while the New Jersey Turnpike was under construction nearby. Recognizing the hazards involved in passing over the temporary rails, railroad management had notified all engineers eight days earlier that, effective at 1:01 PM on 6 February, train speeds could not exceed 25 mph through that area. (Normal operating speed was 60 mph.) No signal lights had been installed at the bypass.[3]

Despite the speed order, the *Broker* thundered onto the trestle at 50–60 mph. Early reports indicated that the engine and the first five cars passed safely over the trestle, but then "something appeared to give way" below the sixth car, which fell but came to rest on the concrete abutments. When the sixth car dropped, it precipitated a whiplash effect through

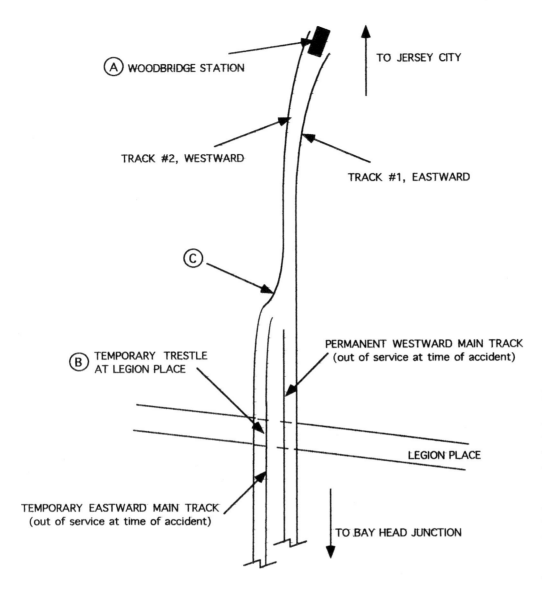

**Figure 47.** Track diagram of the Pennsylvania Railroad tracks near Woodbridge, N.J., on 6 February 1951. The *Broker* had passed Woodbridge station (A) and a sharp curve (C) before it plunged from the temporary trestle (B) onto Legion Place below. Author's drawing, adapted from Interstate Commerce Commission investigation report.

the cars ahead that caused the engine to fall on its side. The tender and the first four coaches tumbled down the embankment, the first two tilted but not overturned. The third and fourth cars, the most seriously damaged, went farther down the embankment, and most of the dead and severely injured passengers were in these cars. The seventh and eighth cars continued past the sixth car; their sides were ripped off, and they fell near the third and fourth coaches. The last three cars remained upright on the rails; most of their occupants received only minor injuries. The very last car, a "club lounge," was a private car rented by a commuter club of Wall Street executives.

Fifty years later, Pearl Selinger, remembered it "like it was yesterday":

The train was extra crowded. Everything was going along fine. I was sitting with friends from my block when all of a sudden the train was rocking. My feet flew in the air, my shoes flew off. When I woke up dead people were lying on top of me. Blood was all over me. My collarbone was broken, my left arm was broken. There was so much smoke in the air, I thought the train was going to catch on fire. I climbed through a window and sat down in the mud. A man from the neighborhood brought me into his house and took me to Perth Amboy Hospital.[4]

Frank LaPenta, one of the first of the local people to arrive on the scene, discussed the accident with the author in November 2006. His most vivid recollection was of the eerie silence—no crying, no shout-

**Figure 48.** The aftermath of the tragic accident at Woodbridge, N.J., on 6 February 1951. The temporary trestle over Legion Place is evident at the center of the photograph. The *Broker* left the rails at this point while traveling at 50–60 mph in violation of the 25 mph speed restriction over the temporary trestle. Popperfoto / Classicstock.

ing, no noise at all except for the hissing of escaping steam. A large crowd of onlookers quickly gathered at the crash site and impeded the efforts of the emergency personnel. Since police officers and firemen from a dozen nearby communities were aiding in the rescue operation, the mayor of Woodbridge requested troops to clear the area. Soldiers from nearby Camp Kilmer and local National Guardsmen moved the spectators away from the immediate scene. Firemen erected ladders against the upset coaches to remove the injured, who were brought to nearby houses for first aid treatment or, in the case of the more seriously wounded, to hospitals. The emergency personnel were hampered further by the mix of ice and mud on the embankment and the streets below.[5] Rescue efforts continued throughout the night, and temporary

morgues were established in Middlesex County. It was later determined that 345 persons had received treatment for injuries at medical facilities in New Brunswick, Rahway, and the Amboys.[6]

Despite the early protestations of the *Broker*'s engineer, James Fitzsimmons, who claimed he was not speeding when the train entered the trestle, he later admitted that he was doing about 50 mph. The conductor, John Bishop, testified that "the train's speed was so excessive that he was just about to pull the emergency cord for a slow-up when the train leaped the rails." Bishop also mentioned that he had discussed the speed restriction at Woodbridge with Fitzsimmons before the train left Jersey City. Fitzsimmons told investigators that there was no signal at the trestle and inferred that this was the cause of the accident because he would have reduced speed accordingly if he had been warned by a signal. The railroad's division superintendent admitted that the trestle was not tested before it went into operation that day. It was designed with a safety factor of six, meaning that it was expected to support up to six times the maximum load that it would be subjected to. All agreed, however, that the structure appeared to be sound and that six trains had crossed it earlier in the day. One disturbing note that a member of the Interstate Commerce Commission thought "might have some significance" was that the railroad ties on the temporary bridge were never fastened down.[7]

The Middlesex County prosecutor, Alex Eber, the chief investigator, castigated the railroad for its "complete and indifferent disregard for human life." He attributed the wreck to the lack of a signal at the trestle and to the railroad's alleged failure to ensure that the speed restriction order had been delivered to, and acknowledged by, the engineer. The high speed passage over the trestle was fixed officially as the cause of the accident.[8] Eber brought charges before a Middlesex County grand jury, which on 20 February 1951 delivered a verdict that the Pennsylvania Railroad "did feloniously kill and slay" 84 individu-als and then returned 84 manslaughter indictments against the road. Upon appeal, a New Jersey superior court dismissed the charges. The railroad did, however, become the defendant in numerous civil suits and was required to provide substantial monetary settlements. One positive action resulting from this tragedy was the adoption of recommendations made by the Interstate Commerce Commission and the N.J. Public Utility Commission. New rules were signed into law that provided much stronger safety measures and more frequent medical examinations for railroad crew members.[9]

In 2001, on the occasion of the fiftieth anniversary of the accident, a memorial ceremony was held at United Methodist Church in Woodbridge. Some survivors, Pearl Selinger included, and local politicos recalled the disaster. New Jersey Transit prepared a plaque commemorating the incident that was then mounted at the Woodbridge railroad station. Legion Place, the street spanned by the temporary trestle, is not far from exit 11 of the New Jersey Turnpike. The route taken by the *Broker* on that fateful day is presently used by New Jersey Transit and Conrail Shared Assets lines.[10]

# 30 Railroad Retreat and Renaissance in the Garden State (1950–Present)

Because New Jersey is small, railroads offered abundant service to many communities. Some towns were served by two or more railroads, a potentially unprofitable situation. For many years, when railroads were the major provider of transportation services, that situation could be tolerated. But as railroad patronage declined, it became evident that some belt-tightening in the form of service reduction was required. Ultimately, abandonment or the threat of abandonment became widespread until various governmental entities undertook to subsidize some of the remaining routes. The situation of railroads in the Garden State can best be evaluated by dividing operations into three components: freight, long-distance passenger travel, and commuter service. In the 1950s, there were only a handful of major railroads operating in the state, and their decline had already begun. Freight service was provided by all of these roads to a greater or lesser degree, depending upon competition and the customers that they served, and several of them also ran long-distance passenger trains. The deterioration of these two components of the railroad equation were addressed early on throughout the East, by the formation of the Consolidated Rail Corporation (Conrail) and Amtrak, the former to handle freight service, the latter to handle long-distance passenger travel nationwide.

"Long-distance" rail travel between New Jersey cities was not significant. Intercity passenger trains were operated by several roads, including the Pennsylvania Railroad (PRR), which later became the Penn Central. But these were trains whose mission was to carry people through the state, not within

it. Yet the New Jersey railroads were subject to the same influences and pressures as others were nationwide. In 1920, railroads nationwide carried 1.2 billion passengers; by 1964, annual railroad ridership had declined to less than 300 million. The decline has been attributed to many factors, including the popularity of the automobile, an explosive growth in paved roads culminating in the interstate highway system, the Great Depression, restrictive government policies, and the ascendancy of the airplane for long trips. Between 1920 and 1964, there were some periods of rail resurgence due to the introduction of streamlined trains and World War II, a period when auto fuel for civilians was rationed and when millions of troops were carried over the rails. By 1970, however, the situation was grave and rail passenger traffic was dying.

Amtrak, officially identified as the National Railroad Passenger Corporation (NRPC), was created in 1971 by Congress to "subsidize and oversee the operation of intercity passenger trains." Under the terms of the Rail Passenger Service Act of 1970, any railroad that provided intercity passenger service could elect to join the NRPC and be relieved of its responsibility to continue passenger service. The members contributed rolling stock or cash to the NRPC and were compensated in turn with shares of NRPC stock. At inception, 20 of the 26 railroads that were eligible opted to join, but only the Penn Central was a factor in passenger travel in New Jersey, and the original Pennsylvania Railroad tracks through the state (part of the so-called Northeast Corridor) are still the sole Amtrak presence. It is along this corridor that the fastest train in the United States, the *Acela Express,* operates. The *Acela,* capable of a maximum speed of 165 mph (although in service it is not pushed to that speed), reduces the New York to Washington run time by 15 minutes. This is significant because the time reduction is an improvement over 125 mph Metroliners, and *Acela's* speed is limited more by track conditions than by capability. Incidentally, the brand name Acela was chosen to signify high acceleration and general excellence.[1]

The creation of Amtrak and its assumption of intercity passenger traffic eliminated that burden from American railroads. However, most railroads continued to operate in a deficit mode, and New Jersey railroads were no exception. The Penn Central operated for only two years before it declared bankruptcy in 1970. In anticipation of a general collapse of rail service, Congress proposed nationalizing the American railroads, a position that was opposed by the Association of American Railroads. The AAR proposed a federally funded private company instead. Following that suggestion, the Regional Rail Reorganization Act of 1973 was passed. Under its provisions, Conrail was incorporated in 1974, and several northeastern roads were brought under its umbrella, including the Penn Central, Erie-Lackawanna, Lehigh Valley, Reading Company, Central Railroad of New Jersey (CNJ), Lehigh and Hudson River, and others controlled by the major players. Conrail operations, intended to restore profitability to freight operations, began in 1976.

A major problem remained: Conrail, like the Penn Central before it, was subject to government regulation, a situation that prevented it from implementing many cost reduction programs. The Staggers Act, which deregulated the industry in 1980, finally permitted Conrail to reorganize its routes and eliminate many unprofitable ones. It began turning a profit, and its shares were floated on Wall Street. In 1998, CSX Corporation and Norfolk Southern, two giant private operators, purchased Conrail and divided its assets according to their spheres of interest, and operation of the system under their control began on 1 June 1999. There were also some areas of joint interest, and these were maintained as "Conrail Shared Assets." The latter segment, the last remaining part of Conrail, provides freight services in the New York/North Jersey and Philadelphia/South Jersey terminal areas.[2]

Commuter traffic in New Jersey was extensive and an important element of the state's rail functions. Carrying workers between New Jersey cities and to New York City began almost as early as the introduction of railroading. By 1840, more than 700 workers were commuting to the New York metropolis by train and ferryboat. In short order, a network of rail lines were established to serve commuter needs in the various towns in the northern part of the state, and gradually this network was extended to cover some of the rest of the state, notably in the Philadelphia area. The network prospered, and thousands of workers were carried from home to job every day. When the system collapsed in the 1970s and was succeeded by New Jersey Transit (NJT), it was gradually rebuilt (somewhat) to offer safe, quick, and reasonably convenient service. This is one of the brightest spots in the current railroad picture in New Jersey. NJT has steadily improved commuter service, rehabilitated the physical plant, and conducted a commendable preservation effort of many of its worthy historic structures.[3]

In the 1950s, the financial situation of railroads became desperate, and hoping to salvage some measure of solvency, they began to petition the New Jersey Public Utility Commission (PUC) for permission to abandon passenger service. The trickle of applications became a flood after the federal Transportation Act of 1958 became law. That legislation empowered the Interstate Commerce Commission to permit railroads to abandon their passenger service over the objection of state agencies such as the PUC. In 1959, as passenger train schedules were shortened (and eliminated in some cases), the State of New Jersey established the Division of Rail Transportation within the Highway Department. It was charged with ensuring the continuance of commuter service in the state and seeking a long-term solution to the problem. It addressed the situation by distributing subsidies to affected railroads on an annual basis to keep the trains rolling. At best, this was a stopgap measure with the funds coming from budgets within the Highway Department, an obvious competitor for patrons as well as money. Railroads were encouraged to save money by merging, but railroad service recovery in New Jersey began around 1966.[4]

The Transportation Act of 1966 was the catalyst for the establishment of the New Jersey Department of Transportation (NJDOT), the first state department of transportation in the country. It promptly became involved in the operation of the remaining private commuter railroads. The NJDOT implemented the Aldene Plan, a strategy that cut costs yet preserved, even improved, passenger convenience. Under the plan, the Central Railroad of New Jersey was compelled to abandon its Jersey City terminal in favor of using Lehigh Valley and Northeast Corridor tracks from Cranford to Newark. It could no longer access its ferryboats, and its Broad Street station in Newark was shuttered. Penn Station in Newark, where a connection could be made to Port Authority Trans-Hudson (PATH) or Amtrak trains, became the end of the line for CNJ trains.[5]

By the early 1970s, five private railroads still provided commuter service in the state: the Central Railroad of New Jersey; Erie-Lackawanna (the two roads had merged in 1960); Penn-Central (a union of the Pennsylvania and New York Central railroads in 1968); Pennsylvania-Reading Seashore Lines (PRSL), a long-time melding (since Depression days) of the PRR and the Reading assets serving the Jersey shore; and the Reading Company. (Parts of these railroads formed the foundation of NJ Transit.) When Conrail was established in 1976, it continued commuter service in New Jersey under contracts negotiated with the NJDOT. This was still an unsatisfactory solution because Conrail's principal interest—indeed, responsibility—was to freight service. But New Jersey commuters had to suffer through a number of bad years with atrocious service before a happier situation emerged.[6]

The Commuter Operating Authority (COA), a creation of New Jersey's Transportation Act of 1966, established the New Jersey Transit Corporation on 17 July 1979. NJT was expected to "acquire, operate and contract for public transportation in the public interest" using commuter trackage and many of the stations along the rights-of-way purchased by COA. The 1979 act enabled the New Jersey Transit Corporation to undertake rail operations directly. A few years passed before the most expeditious way to accomplish this was determined. Driving that determination was the decision by Congress to direct Conrail to end its passenger business by 31 December 1982. The consequence was that, effective 1 January 1983, NJ Transit Rail Operations, a subsidiary of NJT, began offering commuter service.[7]

When NJ Transit assumed control of the state's

commuter rail operations, they were in deplorable condition. Decades of neglect left the new agency with obsolete rolling stock, unreliable motive power, and structures in wretched condition. The few years of subsidies had done nothing more than apply bandages to the bleeding system. The new organization was tried sorely during its first few months of operation. The first train controlled under its auspices left Hoboken Terminal on time on 1 January 1980, but before spring had arrived, NJT had been hit by an all-day blizzard and then a 34-day strike that halted all service. However, the agency moved swiftly to rehabilitate its system. New rolling stock and motive power were ordered, and structures were upgraded. Track and signals and power distribution systems were improved, and bridges and tunnels were repaired.

A glance at NJT's route map shows lines centered around Hoboken and Newark that fan out to Spring Valley and Port Jervis, New York (the Pascack Valley, the Main, the Bergen County, and the Port Jervis Lines), to Hackettstown via the Morristown or Montclair-Boonton Lines, to Gladstone on the Gladstone Branch, and to High Bridge on the Raritan Valley Line. NJT's Northeast Corridor Line provides "Midtown Direct" service to Penn Station in New York City via the tunnel through Bergen Hill built by the Delaware, Lackawanna and Western in 1877 and then through the Hudson River tunnels built by the Pennsylvania Railroad early in the twentieth century. Brief histories of these various spokes in NJT's network of commuter rail lines are provided below.

In 1856, the Hackensack and New York Railroad was chartered, and two years later it began operating between Hackensack and Jersey City. After it was granted permission to build northward, it reached Hillsdale in 1869 and was acquired by the Erie Railroad. After the Erie's bankruptcy in 1882, the road became the New Jersey and New York Railroad (NJ&NY), although it was still controlled by the Erie. Passengers continued to be carried by the NJ&NY through good times and bad, after the Erie-Lackawanna merger, and into state ownership. In 1969, timetables began to identify the NJ&NY as the "Pascack Valley Line," a name that continued after NJ Transit became its operator. The line extends from Hoboken to beyond the state line to end in New York State.

NJ Transit's Main Line and the Bergen County

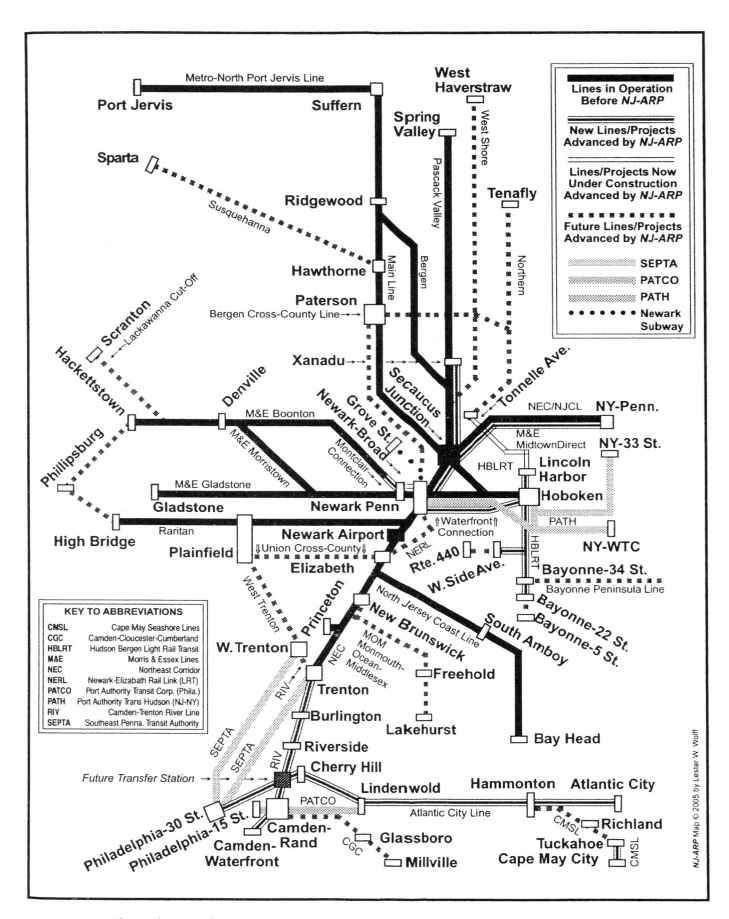

Line are composed of Delaware, Lackawanna and Western (DL&W), and Erie trackage. The Erie Railroad's original charter limited its route to New York State, but it later entered New Jersey because its passengers objected to terminating their trip at Piermont, New York, some distance, 90 minutes by steamboat, up the Hudson River from New York City. To avoid this inconvenience, many travelers left the Erie at Suffern, New York, and changed to New Jersey carriers at that point to reach Jersey City, a short boat ride to the city. To eliminate that situation, the Erie purchased the two competitive carriers, the Paterson and Ramapo and the Paterson and Hudson River railroads, and was able to offer through service into Jersey City. Traffic increased to such an extent that, in 1880, the Erie decided to bypass bottlenecks at downtown Passaic and Paterson. The Bergen County Railroad was the result, stretching from Rutherford to Ridgewood; it is now NJ Transit's Bergen County Line.

The Port Jervis Line is a continuation of the Main Line, and it runs exclusively in New York State over ex-Erie tracks. NJ Transit operates this branch between Suffern and Port Jervis under contract to Metro North Railroad, a New York State agency.[8]

The Morristown Line is one of the three routes that were collectively identified by NJ Transit in 1987 as the Morris and Essex Lines. The other two were the Montclair Branch and the Gladstone Branch. The Montclair Branch was later made part of the Montclair-Boonton Line, and the Gladstone Branch is now identified separately from other NJ Transit Lines.[9]

The Morris and Essex Railroad (M&E) was built between Newark and Morristown in 1838. It was chartered in 1835 and operated between Newark and Madison by horsepower until 1837; steam power was introduced that year. Passengers were carried in an eight-wheel car with a capacity for 70 to 100 passengers. The road was then continued westward to Dover (1848), Hackettstown (1854), and Phillipsburg (1866). Meanwhile, the M&E pushed into Jersey City, first through the Palisades using the New York and Erie Railroad tunnel and then, later, after

the M&E had been purchased by the Lackawanna, through a new tunnel under Bergen Hill. The M&E was not officially merged into the Lackawanna system until 1945, when it became part of the Erie-Lackawanna Railroad, then Conrail, and finally the Morris and Essex Lines of NJ Transit.[10]

The Montclair Branch of the Morris and Essex Railroad, chartered in 1852 as the Newark and Bloomfield Railroad (N&B), made a connection to the main line of the M&E. The Morris and Essex assumed control of the branch from the N&B in 1868, the same year that the M&E was bought by the DL&W. At one time, this short branch, about four miles long, was the busiest commuter railroad in the country.

NJT's Montclair-Boonton Line is composed of the Montclair Branch and its extension to Boonton over former Erie-Lackawanna tracks. Originally part of the Morris and Essex Railroad, the Boonton Branch bypassed M&E's Morristown route to bring coal and iron products to and from the Denville-Dover-Hackettstown area. Another part of the Boonton Line was Erie right-of-way, used by the Erie-controlled New York and Greenwood Lake Railway. Access to Hoboken terminal is over part of the Erie main line tracks.

The Gladstone Branch of NJ Transit began as the Passaic Valley and Peapack Railroad in 1872, running from Summit to Bernardsville. This short railroad soon failed and was acquired by the DL&W and renamed the Passaic and Delaware Railroad. Under this flag, construction continued from Bernardsville to Gladstone and stopped there. The ambitious goal of reaching the Delaware River, expressed in the road's name, was never achieved. As the hilly country surrounding the road was populated by people who worked in Newark and New York, the branch became an important commuter factor.[11]

The antecedents of the Raritan Valley Line are to be found as early as 1831. The Elizabethtown and Somerville Rail Road, chartered in 1831, was one of the earliest roads to be built in the state. Begun at Elizabeth, it built westward in easy steps. This railroad, described in chapter 9, grew into the Central Railroad of New Jersey. The CNJ was one of the roads that were melded into Conrail and then brought into the NJ Transit family. Identifying logos are used for each of the several NJ Transit lines, and the one used with the Raritan Valley Line is the Statue of Liberty head, the longtime symbol of the Jersey Central Railroad.[12]

The Northeast Corridor Line, which operates from New York City over Amtrak's Northeast Corridor right-of-way, reaches out to Central New Jersey, terminating at Trenton. Part of the trip is made over the New Jersey Railroad and Transportation Company right-of-way that ran from Jersey City to New Brunswick in 1835. The leg from New Brunswick into Trenton was completed by the Philadelphia and Trenton Railroad (described in chapter 2). During its first year of operation, the NJRR carried 126,485 passengers. This route, from Trenton to Jersey City, replaced the original Camden and Amboy Railroad (C&A) alignment, and when the C&A was sold to the Pennsylvania Railroad, it passed to PRR (then to Penn Central) ownership. NJ Transit uses the old PRR tunnels to bring its trains directly into Manhattan.[13]

Leaving New York City aboard a Northeast Corridor Line train, one travels south toward Trenton. Connections to Amtrak can be made at several stations along the route. Before reaching Trenton, one can connect at Rahway with North Jersey Coast Line trains that terminate at Bay Head on the Jersey Shore. Although NJT's Northeast Corridor Line ends at Trenton, connections with Southeastern Pennsylvania Transit Authority (SEPTA) cars make a run into Philadelphia possible. Trenton is also a terminus for the new River LINE, a new light rail system that, along with two other light rail lines operated by NJ Transit, is described in chapter 27.

The North Jersey Coast Line was derived from New York and Long Branch Railroad tracks. Construction of the NY&LB, which was controlled by the Central Railroad of New Jersey, proceeded in steps from Jersey City to and through the North Jersey shore communities; service began in 1875. The line, crossing several rivers, bays, and streams, required a multitude of bridges, one of which, the trestle and drawbridge across the Raritan River, had one of the longest movable spans ever built up to that time. This bridge, with a 472-foot-long swing section, was designed by J. Linville, and the movable swing section was supported on a "pier by a central drum, the load being transferred either to a central anti-friction cone-bearing pivot or to a series of 30 bearing-wheels under the drum." Hydraulic cylinders raised the swing section four inches before the bridge

was moved from the closed position. The NY&LB terminated at Bay Head, where it met the Pennsylvania Railroad. Since the PRR was also interested in the shore market, it made an agreement with the CNJ to share the NY&LB tracks. Both railroads touted seashore service and operated amicably over the same rails for years. The final stake was thrust into the heart of post–World War II rail service to the Jersey shore by the building of the Garden State Parkway. This modern toll road made shore travel by automobile more convenient (and stressful, considering the weekend traffic jams). The Brielle drawbridge, connecting Monmouth and Ocean counties, is the southernmost Coast Line movable bridge.[14]

Until recently, with the advent of casinos and frequent bus service, Atlantic City was mainly a beach resort area for Philadelphians and New Yorkers. Most of the early visitors from New York City arrived by boat. Several pioneer railroads built to the shore city from Camden, carrying their patrons to that city from Philadelphia by ferryboat (see chapter 8). The first of these was the Camden and Atlantic Railroad, which passed into PRR control in 1885. Two years earlier, the Philadelphia and Reading Railroad had taken over the Philadelphia and Atlantic City Railroad, the second road built to Atlantic City. The Reading then cobbled a few of its other holdings to the P&AC and named the new entity the Atlantic City Railroad. The West Jersey and Atlantic Railroad was the third road built into Atlantic City, and it merged with the Camden and Atlantic to become the West Jersey and Seashore Railroad. Eventually this confusing series of mergers and acquisitions was sorted out when the Pennsylvania and Reading interests were joined as the Pennsylvania-Reading Seashore Lines in 1933. PRSL was folded into Conrail, which then abandoned all South Jersey rail services to shore points in 1982. Resurrected in 1989, Philadelphia–Atlantic City service was operated by Amtrak and NJ Transit for three years before Amtrak withdrew from the arrangement and turned the Atlantic City Line over to NJ Transit.[15]

Connections are made to PATH trains at Hoboken. Secaucus Junction, a new facility in the Jersey Meadows, in the shadow of the New Jersey Turnpike, facilitates transfers between the various NJT lines. In 2001, service was extended to Newark Airport, and NJ Transit acquired "Clocker" (New York–Philadelphia) service from Amtrak in 2005. The Clockers

Figure 50. NJ Transit's eastbound North Jersey Coast Line train crosses the Manasquan River drawbridge at Brielle on 13 October 2004. Reproduced with permission of NJ TRANSIT / Michael Rosenthal—Photographer.

had previously been part of Amtrak operations; after NJT assumed their operation, service was terminated at Trenton. A postscript to this fact was that a commuter group's private club car was included as part of the Amtrak Clocker consist. A farewell party was held during the last Amtrak run, the club was disbanded, and its members now ride on NJ Transit's Clocker *sans* club car.

An integral part of this pattern is the surface transportation network operated by NJ Transit. The largest bus operator in the state, Transport of New Jersey (earlier Public Service Coordinated Transport), was melded into NJ Transit operations, which established New Jersey Transit Bus Operations to run its large bus fleet. After many, many years, a coordinated inter-modal transportation system has finally been achieved. New Jersey Transit is not resting on its laurels, however. It has an extensive list of projects for future funding and construction. Periodically there is talk of reviving the West Trenton line, the ex-Reading right-of-way that ran from West Trenton

to join with the present Raritan Valley Line, and extending the Boonton Line to Phillipsburg. The inclusion of a program to consider a Perth Amboy/South Amboy ferry to New York is sure to evoke memories of the granddaddy of them all, the Camden and Amboy Railroad.

But perhaps the most ambitious of the plans is the digging of a new Hudson River tunnel, identified as THE (Trans-Hudson Express) Tunnel, a multibillion-dollar project to enhance safety and relieve bottlenecks experienced in the 100-year-old bores (see chapter 7). According to a brochure published by NJ Transit that defines the economic benefits of THE Tunnel, it will immediately double commuter rail capacity and, within 10 years, will add 44,000 permanent jobs to the region. Additional benefits would accrue to the subregions, those counties in New York and New Jersey that lie somewhat farther from the Hudson River. Despite the obvious desirability of additional tunnel capacity under the Hudson River, some have already begun to criticize the undertaking.

The Lackawanna Coalition is concerned that "the project has been scaled back considerably from its inception" and that some Midtown Direct trains will be pulled from rush-hour service, costing their riders seven additional minutes. However, as of 2006, the federal government has advanced the project to the preliminary engineering phase, a hopeful sign that the enterprise will advance.[16]

Unlike many histories of bureaucratic organizations, the NJ Transit story is a shining example of excellent management and efficient operations. However, a threat to NJ Transit's continuing outstanding performance is the financial health of the state. By the year 2006, the state's Transportation Trust Fund was essentially exhausted, with all of its income pledged to pay interest on bonds that it had issued. Steps are being taken to restore New Jersey's economic viability, but it remains to be seen whether NJ Transit is adequately funded to build upon the remarkable renaissance that it generated in New Jersey railroad commuting.[17]

Another element in the NJ Transit story that is narrated in more detail in the next chapter is the agency's devotion to the preservation of historical artifacts. Although this responsibility may have been thrust upon a less than willing NJT, it has done a commendable job in saving stations, bridges, signal apparatus, and other railroad memorabilia from deterioration or destruction.

An excellent reference source, though dated, regarding NJ Transit is Joel Rosenbaum and Tom Gallo's *NJ Transit Rail Operations*. In addition to a detailed description of the system, historical and current (as of 1996), the book is profusely illustrated with superb color photographs of sites and equipment.

# 31 Preserving the Railroad: A Little Paint, Some Elbow Grease, and a Lot of Love (1980–Present)

After the enormous outcry resulting from the 1964 demolition of Pennsylvania Station in New York City, preservation and restoration efforts experienced a nationwide impetus. Happily, New Jersey preserved many of its historic sites and buildings, including railroad structures. These consisted mostly of neglected or abandoned stations and bridges. Early efforts were undertaken by Amtrak, which, following federal guidelines, rehabilitated 13 stations between Boston and Washington, D.C. Private developers recycled many others, but in New Jersey much credit must be awarded to New Jersey Transit (NJT), which, despite some early misguided attempts, has rehabilitated many railroad stations along its lines.

In the late 1970s, Congress authorized Conrail and Amtrak to sell railroad lines and 130 railroad stations along those tracks. After rehabilitating the stations, the plan was to give them to local municipalities, who would then be responsible for continued maintenance. When New Jersey Transit was established, it acquired 144 stations from Conrail, the successor to the Penn Central. Over 50 of the stations are listed on the National Register of Historic Places. One of the requirements of NJT's founding was that it adhere to federal preservation policies. At first, lacking a clear vision, the agency did more harm than good, spraying antique wooden walls with stucco and taking other equally insensitive steps. Fortunately, a full-time preservation expert was hired, and a truly notable restoration program was begun. In many instances, stations were given to municipalities or leased to private investors who had to maintain strict standards regarding appearance and appropriate use. Many of these stations are available to be seen in their original glory (mostly), a tribute to an enlightened program of restoration and renewal.[1]

A few examples of restoration are listed below.

Whitehouse Station is a tiny hamlet that sits astride the Central Railroad of New Jersey's tracks in Readington Township, Hunterdon County. Its original depot had deteriorated substantially by 1873, and the *Hunterdon County Democrat* lamented that "Whitehouse Station citizens are getting up a great hue and cry at the dilapidated condition of their depot. It is a disgrace to that growing village and not fit to confine a good rat dog in." Fortunately, its replacement, located on Main Street and erected in 1892, was a more substantial and architecturally pleasing Richardson Romanesque structure. By the late twentieth century, the station was decaying and a target for demolition when a group of community volunteers restored the small building and adapted it for use as a public library serving the local community. When these volunteers began work, the station "was cold, dank, and dark. The roof was a mess. But the original stained glass remained." An inspired touch was that, in its reincarnation, the library was opened at 6 AM to accommodate commuters waiting for early morning trains. Although this early-opening practice has ended, the structure continues as the Readington Township Public Library and is exceptionally well maintained.[2]

The Park Ridge Carpenter Gothic depot at Hawthorne and Park Avenues was rescued from the demolition bulldozer by a concerned citizen and a willing crew of volunteers who, contrary to expert opinion, believed that it could be saved. The station was built in 1871 by citizens of the town who donated it to the Erie Railway with the proviso that Park Ridge be made a stop on the line. It has been restored to its former gingerbread glory and is used as a community meeting place.[3]

In three instances, private and public interests have converged to the delight of gastronomes. A Philadelphia and Reading Railroad (P&R) station at Bound Brook was renewed by a restaurateur who, aided by grants, turned the 1913 Classical Revival structure into a popular restaurant. A historic district was formed in the adjacent area. Built by the Delaware, Lackawanna and Western Railroad in 1901, a restored Richardson Romanesque Bernardsville depot has become a coffee shop and gourmet delicatessen. The 1901 station replaced an earlier frame structure with a "pagoda" roof, a common feature on Lackawanna stations at the time. The old depot was moved closer to the town center in 1900 and still stands, serving as a newspaper office.[4] In Lambertville, the depot built by the Belvidere Delaware Railroad (Bel-Del) in 1867 has been restored and has functioned as a fine restaurant since the 1980s. Located on Bridge Street near the Delaware River, this 2.5-story stone station was designed by Thomas U. Walter, who also designed the dome of the Capitol in Washington, D.C. The cupola surmounted by an obelisk remains. The gable ends and the dormers are "clipped." This architectural distinction, known as "jerkinhead," gives the roof the appearance of an abbreviated hip roof. The upper floors originally served as Bel-Del division offices.[5]

In Somerville, the Central Railroad of New Jersey Queen Anne style station was designed by Frank V. Bodine and constructed in 1890 at a cost of $15,000. This, the fourth depot at the site, had a general waiting room, a separate ladies' waiting room, a smoking room, and a baggage room. A ticket and telegraph office was situated in the end tower of the building. A newspaper account, written at the time of completion, described the ladies' waiting room as "containing a number of easy chairs, instead of the usual hard benches, and as one peeps in through the windows at the occupants, there is an air of comfort suggestive of a feminine club. The room appears to be so

Figure 51. Restored stations representing four New Jersey railroads. Clockwise from upper left: Central Railroad of New Jersey depot at Whitehouse Station is now a public library; Philadelphia and Reading station at Hopewell is now used for community meetings, and the upper floor is rented to businesses; the Belvidere-Delaware depot at Lambertville now houses a fine restaurant; and the Erie-Lackawanna Railroad station at Bernardsville offers a delicatessen. Author's photos.

exclusively for ladies that a mere man hesitates to look upon its sacred precincts." However, destruction of the fine structure was narrowly averted. Around 1970, when the area was being redeveloped, the station lay directly in the space allocated for an arterial street and a parking lot, and according to Louis Sylvain, Somerville's urban renewal director, "It would also be a poor companion to the modern style architecture which the developer proposes." Fortunately, others disagreed: the street was curved around the structure, and the building was saved. Today the restored building, which is located on Veterans Memorial Parkway, serves as a law office.[6]

The P&R station at Hopewell had fallen into disrepair when the Borough of Hopewell acquired it, using municipal and privately donated funds. Federal and state grants provided funds for restoration. The Second Empire red brick station was built around 1880 after the P&R had formally leased the Delaware and Bound Brook Railroad. Station staff lived on the upper floors; the station complex included a frame freight house and a passenger shelter. The freight house has also been restored, a project undertaken by a local Boy Scout as a requirement for Eagle grade. The depot and freight house, located on Railroad Place, are now used for meetings of community organizations. The upper floor of the station has been refurbished for rental to businesses.[7]

More expensive and extensive rehabilitation was undertaken at two large terminals at Newark and Hoboken. Newark's Pennsylvania Station, which was the last major architectural project of the famed firm McKim, Mead and White, became the centerpiece of the effort to revitalize and redevelop the city center. An even more expensive restoration involves the Erie-Lackawanna Terminal at Hoboken. This program, like many of the others, will be at the heart of an area that was rescued from neglect and general decay.[8]

One of the crown jewels of the New Jersey railroad preservation movement is the Central Railroad of New Jersey terminal at Jersey City. Within the borders of Liberty State Park and directly opposite the tip of lower Manhattan, the water view from the park includes the Statue of Liberty and the newly restored Ellis Island immigration facility. But for railroad aficionados, the undisputed attraction is the restored CNJ terminal. When it was erected, the Gothic revival building, resembling a great French chateau with dormered mansard roof, cupola, and clock tower, dominated the waterfront at the Communipaw section of the city. Railroad commuters from Hunterdon and Somerset counties and from shore points arrived at the track sheds behind the structure, then passed through it to reach their ferryboats for the final leg of their journey into New York City. Immigrants newly landed from Ellis Island (which opened as a processing center in 1892) entrained here for destinations nationwide, although they were carefully segregated from the road's regular customers. The luxuriously furnished ladies' parlor of earlier years, located in a corner of the waiting room, has been converted into an auditorium. The two terminals, the CNJ at Jersey City and the Lackawanna at Hoboken, are described in greater detail in chapter 21.[9]

Although the lion's share of the restorations in New Jersey involve old stations, other railroad artifacts have also been included in renovation programs. For example, the Erie Railway interlocking tower at Waldwick was purchased by the Borough of Waldwick in 2000. Planning and fund-raising occupied the next several years, but exterior restoration was completed in time for its dedication in 2005. Work continues on the interior, including the installation of a signal interlocking machine that had been a fixture of the original tower.[10]

Other railroad preservation efforts have been completed or are ongoing, too many to describe here. The reader is directed to the *New Jersey Register of Historic Places,* which may be found in most public libraries. The *Register* lists signal towers, bridges, trackwork, and entire rail corridors and districts throughout the state.

In addition, several counties support cultural and heritage commissions that catalog and describe historic sites and districts, including those with railroad connections, within their county.

# 32 Reliving the Past: Riding the Golden Oldies (Present)

One of the pleasures of modern life is to travel speedily from place to place in comfort. Superhighways accommodate our personal vehicles, and for longer trips, air travel can move us across and between continents almost as fast as the sun. Alas, except for some special cases (e.g., subway service), traveling by railroad has deteriorated substantially over the past half century. While freight is still a staple of rail movement, passenger traffic has been a casualty. Trains reach fewer destinations, and except in a very few instances, their average speed has not improved. Comfort aboard, while not worse, certainly is not better than it was 60 years ago. Arguably, safety has improved, but even that attribute depends upon the measurement parameters. In fact, unless the national perception and will are radically changed, it is possible that most passenger rail traffic will suffer further declines in the next few decades. So, we must ask, how will rail fans and the coming generations of children experience the thrill of a hissing steam engine, the scream of a train whistle, and the rattle of a train car as it rounds a curve or struggles upgrade with its load? Yes, there will be a few museum exhibits that, through the magic of audiovisual effects, can offer a pale image of the real thing, but the best and most authentic experience will be a ride on one of the several so-called tourist trains. Fortunately for New Jerseyans and visitors to the state, there are several such experiences that can be savored. Furthermore, although the last steam locomotive to operate in New Jersey in common carrier service (1958) was a switching engine on the Union Transportation Com-

pany's rails, there are several working museums that have steam locomotives on their roster.

The Black River and Western Railroad (BR&W), a shortline, was incorporated in 1961, named after the Black River in Chester. Organized by a group of rail fans, the road leased the Flemington Branch of the Penn Central Railroad (ex-Belvidere and Delaware River Railway) in 1964 and began to run excursions from Ringoes to Flemington the following year. In 1970, the BR&W bought the Flemington Branch and began operations as a shortline railroad. The tourist operations are conducted on the same tracks that serve a number of freight customers. Black River and Western steam locomotive number 60 originally hauled sugar beets in Colorado. The BR&W is accessed from either the Flemington Station, off Route 12 in Liberty Village, or at Ringoes, on County Route 579, about three-quarters of a mile from Highways 202 and 31. The station at Ringoes dates from 1854 and has been restored.[1]

The Cape May Seashore Lines (CMSL) is a regional railroad that also offers tourist rides. Founded in 1984, it is privately owned and was organized to provide rail service on the NJ Transit's Cape May Branch between Tuckahoe and Cape May City, 27.4 miles distant. CMSL operates over tracks rich in history. Incorporated in 1890 as the Tuckahoe and Cape May Railway, the road was completed in 1894. In 1901, along with others, it was merged into the Atlantic City Railroad, a subsidiary of the Philadelphia and Reading Railroad. Subsequent mergers involved the Cape May Branch: the formation of the Pennsyl-

Figure 52. This friendly conductor on the Black River and Western Railroad shared his badge of office, his cap, with a young passenger on a sunny summer day in 1996. Author's photograph.

vania-Reading Seashore Lines (P-RSL) in 1933; the incorporation of the P-RSL into ConRail in 1976; and finally the acquisition by NJ Transit. NJ Transit discontinued passenger service on the branch in 1981. In 1996, passenger service was inaugurated by CMSL between Cape May Courthouse and Cold Spring, and three years later that service was extended to Cape May City, the first time in 18 years since the latter town had enjoyed rail service. For passenger service, CMSL uses Budd-built RDC cars obtained from the former Pennsylvania-Reading Seashore Lines and from the Boston and Maine Railroad. Alternatively, a passenger consist may be hauled by a diesel-electric locomotive. The site address for the CMSL is given as Rio Grande, New Jersey, but stations are also located at Cape May City, Cold Spring, Cape May Court House, Dennisville, Woodbine, and Tuckahoe. Incidentally, the Philadelphia and Reading station at Tuckahoe, built in 1894, has been lovingly restored, inside and out.[2]

The Morris County Central Railroad operates out of the Whippany Railroad Museum, which occupies a restored freight house of the Morristown and Erie Railroad dating to 1904. Originally established at Whippany, the museum and train were moved in the early 1970s to Newfoundland, New Jersey, where the train operated on New York, Susquehanna and Western tracks. There it ran its last train in 1980, but several years later it reestablished a base at Whippany. An historic 0-6-0 steam locomotive built for the U.S. Army in 1942 is one of the locomotives used to carry passengers on a 10-mile, 45-minute excursion. The Whippany Railroad Museum is located at the intersection of Route 10 West and Whippany Road near the town of Whippany.[3]

The first operating steam train exhibit in the Garden State and one of the first in the United States is located at the New Jersey Museum of Transportation, where train rides are available daily in July and August and on weekends from April through October. The roster of the Pine Creek Railroad, founded

in 1952, included several old steam locomotives, one a Shay-geared logging engine, but there have been issues with ownership and with maintenance of the old steamers. A train from Ireland, consisting of a locomotive and three coaches, and rolling stock from Newfoundland and Hawaii are located there. A diesel-electric locomotive is available for excursions within the park on the three-foot gauge track, and a number of cars are to be found at the museum, including an 1874 caboose from the Central Railroad of New Jersey. Several historic railroad structures from nearby towns were relocated to the grounds. The museum is privately owned and leases space from the state. It is located at Allaire State Park, 4265 Route 524, in Wall Township (Monmouth County), New Jersey.[4]

Another railroad venue is a work in progress. The New Jersey Transportation Heritage Center is an ambitious undertaking whose mission is to preserve the images and artifacts of New Jersey's transportation heritage. Although it embraces all forms of transportation from canals to streetcars to trucks and buses, a major element of the Center's collection involves railroads. Springing from the United Railroad Historical Society (formed in 1987 by 17 historical and railroad societies to preserve New Jersey railroad artifacts), the Heritage Center has become a major repository of transportation memorabilia and historic items. Many such items have already been acquired, and the jewel of the collection at this time is a three-foot gauge, 100-year-old trolley car built in New Jersey (see chapter 20). Part of the vision of the Center involves the employment of the streetcar for rides on the grounds. It was proposed that the Center would be permanently located at Phillipsburg, at a site rich in railroad history. Although much of the collection is located there at this writing, its permanent location is still in question. The volunteer organization maintains an exhibit in the Phillipsburg railroad station that is open to the public at specified times, and it fully expects to run train excursions from there to a nearby point.[5]

In 2004, the New York, Susquehanna and Western Technical and Historical Society acquired a Chinese-built coal-fired steam locomotive that operates on Belvidere and Delaware River Railway tracks out of Phillipsburg. A self-propelled, Brill-made railcar, popularly called a "doodlebug," also operates in that venue.

It should be noted that there are many small-scale railroads in New Jersey, usually found in amusement parks, malls, and local parks. Many use a two-foot gauge (or smaller) track, and their trains are drawn by gasoline–powered locomotives. Only one is mentioned here and then only because of its history and proximity to the New Jersey Transportation Heritage Center. The Centerville and Southwestern Railroad (C&SW), located at Cross Street and Pine Alley in Phillipsburg, provides rides from May through September on 9⁷/₁₆-inch gauge track. Owned by the town of Phillipsburg and operated by the Phillipsburg Railroad Historians, who have a diesel-electric locomotive and a number of cars, the C&SW was transplanted from the Becker Dairy Farm at Roseland (which was originally named Centerville), where it operated for many years.[6]

Most of the railroads mentioned in this chapter offer special excursions on major holidays, including Easter Bunny, Halloween, and Santa Specials. At some locations, entire trains may be chartered for school, business, or rail fan groups.

Although there are rail fans who, individually or in groups, lobby for a railroad renaissance, their appeals have fallen mostly on deaf ears. One can only hope that the tourist attractions offering train rides may reawaken an interest in train travel. The magic of train rides could be the tipping point that might influence a sufficiently large lobby to press for a railroad or a light rail installation instead of, or in addition to, another highway. Further, let us hope that such a railroad revival occurs in one of the most logical of all areas—the densely populated Garden State.

# 33  And, in Closing . . .

. . . there are many, many more railroad tales of New Jersey people and incidents that have played a part in railroading history, such as the following:

*Ross Winans.* One of the most talented of the early American locomotive builders was Ross Winans, although his creations were strange. Winans designed and built his early locomotives for the Baltimore and Ohio Railroad (B&O), and his works was located adjacent to the B&O facilities in Mount Clare, Maryland. Made famous by the unconventional yet rugged engines he produced there, many do not realize that Winans was a New Jersey native. Winans was born in 1796 on a farm in Vernon Township in Sussex County. When he was seven years old, the family moved into town and lived for a few years in the building that his father operated as a tavern. (Circuit ministers held services at Winans's tavern on Sundays. The tavern building was recently relocated, and a Burger King was built on the site.) Married in 1820, Ross and his bride lived on a nearby farm. A tinkerer at heart, Winans made several inventions and then became interested in the new technology of railroading. Meanwhile, his father had occupied a house known as the "Sea Captain's House" (now used as a Coldwell Banker real estate office on County Route 515). Here, in a spacious garret, Ross Winans built a model railroad that enabled him to study and conduct experiments on railroad devices and appliances. Probably it was here that he perfected the "friction wheel," a railroad wheel bearing, or mounting, that reduced the frictional forces generated by a heavily laden car. His public demonstration of that arrangement at Baltimore in 1828 was heralded by one au-

thority as "so great a discovery [that] There will be no use for Locomotive Engines where one horse can draw so much." That observer was overly optimistic, because Winans's friction wheel was effective (as an *anti-*friction wheel), but it was subject to excessive wear and was soon replaced by other designs. Yet Winans's reputation as an original thinker had been established, and he went on to become an important designer of locomotives and one of the country's first multimillionaires.[1]

*On How an Opossum Crashed (and Trashed) the Ladies' Car.* Tom Taber offered a charming story in his unpublished manuscript about a 'possum that (unwillingly and unwittingly) took a ride in a railroad car reserved for ladies. The following is the transcript that he provided, taken from the *True Democratic Banner:*

> This morning, October 24, 1872, as the morning train on the Chester Railroad was nearing Horton's Station, an accident occurred, the like of which was never heard of before. An opossum, desiring to cross the track because he wanted to get to the other side, was struck by the pilot of the locomotive, and thrown up into the air a considerable distance. In his downward flight, he passed over the locomotive and tender, and entered the ladies passenger car through the thick glass light in the door, smashing it to atoms, and landing in the middle of the car near the stove. The train was immediately stopped, when the damage was ascertained to be as follows: One pane of glass completely smashed, and pieces scattered over everybody and everything in the car; all therein terribly frightened and put to their wits' ends to know what was the matter; and Mr. Opossum

163

standing uninjured in the aisle, and wondering why the train did not slow up to let passengers get aboard. The gentlemanly conductor, Mr. Frank B. Eldridge, and Mr. Theo. P. Skellenger, a passenger, soon cleared away the wreckage, and the train sped on her way to Dover, the bearer of the most remarkable passenger that ever patronized a railroad. We are happy to state that Mr. Marean, Engineer, and Mr. Roach, Fireman, stood undaunted at their posts, amid the wreck of matter and the crash of worlds! The opossum was forwarded at once by Charley Holmes' train to Hoboken, consigned to A. Reasoner, Esq., Superintendent of the D.L.&W.R.R., charged with the crime of breaking and entering; to be dealt with as the law directs.[2]

*The Great Canal Boat and Train Wreck.* Not every day do a train and a boat collide! On 12 June 1905, a Jersey Central train, pushed by locomotive number 410, was backing up toward North Sussex Street in Dover. Unfortunately, the drawbridge over the Morris Canal, which lay between the train and its objective, was open and a canal boat loaded with coal was stopped in the lock below the bridge. When the train's brakes failed, the lead car of the train, a gondola car, tumbled from the rails onto the boat. The locomotive, still pushing, drove the car against the far wall of the lock; at the same time the locomotive tender jackknifed into a vertical position. Although the boat, bridge, and gondola were severely damaged, there were no human casualties. Most fortunate were the canal boat captain, George Meyers, and his wife and small daughter, who were on the boat at the time. The site of the accident lies behind the present-day *Laughing Lion* restaurant.

Surprisingly, this unusual accident was not a singular occurrence in the state of New Jersey. On 30 August 1858, a similar incident happened on the Morris and Essex Railroad. The drawbridge over the Morris Canal at Dover was regularly left open at night to allow the free passage of canal boats. Any train approaching the crossing was required to signal for the bridge to be closed. That fateful evening, the engineer of the locomotive *Pequest*, which was not attached to a train, neglected to call for the closing, and the engine tumbled into the canal, hitting a boat that was passing below. The boat was destroyed, but its occupants and the engine crew were unhurt.[3]

*Johnny Corter.* Some folks have witnessed a dramatic motion picture rescue where the hero sees a child on the tracks in front of a speeding train, races to the cowcatcher, and at the last moment snatches the child from certain death. This fictional presentation was played out in real life in the 1920s. Johnny Corter was a locomotive engineer who worked on the New York and Greenwood Lake Railroad. His regular run took him through Mountain View, Carlton Park, and Singac and past his daughter's home. Frequently his little granddaughter would wave to him from the large window at the front of her house. One day she was not at her usual observation post. She was standing on the tracks directly in front of his train! Leaving the operation of the train in the care of his fireman, Corter ran along the running board of the locomotive and onto the cowcatcher. He reached for the little girl, caught her, then slipped and fell from the engine. He and his granddaughter rolled down an embankment; neither was seriously hurt.

Another rescue of a child from the tracks is almost beyond belief. Certainly only a motion picture, perhaps one starring Lassie, might dare to present it, yet it happened. The *Newark Daily Mercury* headlined their story of 11 November 1851 "Extraordinary Sagacity." It reported, "Yesterday afternoon as the Morris & Essex Railroad train was returning to Newark, when within a mile of the depot, an infant was discovered lying or crawling on the track. A large Newfoundland dog belonging to James Bishop, Esq., rushed forward, and seizing the child, bore him to a place of safety, the locomotive almost grazing the dog."[4]

*The Hookerman, a Bona Fide New Jersey Ghost.* The tale of the Hookerman has been recounted for many years with many variations. The common thread is a railroad worker, Lester Clemmons, who lost an arm along the railroad tracks near Flanders. Lester's job was to walk the tracks over his assigned section to ensure that all was well and that there were no faults in the rails, spikes, or ties. One version of the story is that Lester was mentally unbalanced before his deadly encounter; another is that he was driven insane by the loss of his arm. One version has Lester dying at the scene of the accident, but in another version he was institutionalized and his missing limb was replaced by a steel hook.

The more detailed and more interesting version, which asserts that Lester was mentally unbalanced, discusses his propensity for arguing with himself. He always saw two sides of any argument and consequently had difficulty reaching a conclusion. In any event, after returning one evening from an inspection tour and preparing for bed, he thought about a potential problem that he had encountered. He had noticed several loose ties, but being without tools at the time, he had decided to undertake repairs later. At home, he argued with himself:

"Should I return immediately?"
"No! No trains are expected until tomorrow."
"But suppose an unscheduled train should arrive? Would I want to be responsible for an accident?"

Faithfulness to duty won the argument, and Lester set out to make repairs. Accomplishing the task took some time, and since he had been tired even before he started out, fatigue overcame him, and he fell asleep on the track. He was awakened by a vibration through the rails, but when he attempted to rise, he discovered that his arm was caught below a rail. Try as he might, he could not free himself! Rather than be killed on the track by the approaching train, Lester amputated his own arm using a saw from his tool kit. However, his effort was in vain because, although he got off the track, he suffered an extreme loss of blood, collapsed, and died a few feet away.

The tale asserts that since that fateful night, Lester roams the tracks in the Flanders area, searching for his lost arm. Witnesses on the hunt for the Hookerman (many of whom are of questionable reliability) have seen strange lights, supposedly Lester's lantern, along stretches of track in Flanders on North Four Bridges Road. He has even been encountered on dark nights far afield in Washington Township near Naughterton Road and in Hillsborough Township off Roycefield Road. A scientific study was conducted in 1976 with extensive detection equipment, and the experts noted changes in their readings when a light appeared above the tracks. One explanation attributes the phenomenon to stresses on the rock below the surface that produced an electrical signal and

a sudden light. True or false, explainable or not, New Jersey's railroad ghost provides an intriguing yarn.[5]

*Build Your Own Station.* It was not unusual for wealthy individuals to locate their homes in sparsely settled areas. Long ago, it was possible to "flag" a train, waving it to a stop by vigorously displaying a scarf or other indicator, almost anywhere along the tracks. But by the waning years of the nineteenth century, railroads had become less compliant, maintaining schedules and fixed stopping points. Thus, if a wealthy commuter desired the convenience of a station near his home, he might have to build it himself. In one such instance, at Glen Ridge, A. G. Darwin had a charming station built above the tracks of the Montclair Branch of the Delaware, Lackawanna and Western Railroad. The *Railroad Gazette* commented that the cost of building the station was shared by Darwin and by the railroad. This station, built of blue-black traprock, resembled a large private house, conforming to the architecture of the surrounding residential community. Because the railroad at this point passed through a deep cut, the second story of the station was at street level, 18 feet above the rails. Darwin deeded the station to the railroad, and it served as both depot and post office. In the 1870s, Stewart Hartshorne was taken with the beauty and tranquillity of the area that is now Short Hills. Believing that the region would become a country retreat for well-to-do New Yorkers, he had a station constructed there. Hartshorne arranged with the Lackawanna to provide daily service for commuters at that station.[6]

It is always difficult to bring a book to a close, particularly when there are more stories to be told. The reader will find in these pages some tales that are familiar and others that are not. It cannot be said that all of these are important tales of New Jersey railroading, but they are interesting and may stir the reader to seek out some of the sites mentioned and to enjoy some of the pleasures of railroading in the Garden State.

# Notes

## Introduction

1. Kobbé, *Kobbé's Jersey Central*, 34; Lane, *From Indian Trail to Iron Horse*, 406–7; Cunningham, *Railroads in New Jersey: The Formative Years*, 295.

2. Cranmer, *New Jersey in the Automobile Age*, 24–29.

## 1. The Colonel Takes to the Rails (1825)

1. *Newsletter of the Society for Industrial Archeology*, Spring 2005, 1, 2; Kirby and Laurson, *The Early Years of Modern Civil Engineering*, 94; Pangborn, *The World's Railway*, 22, 23; Sinclair, *The Development of the Locomotive Engine*, 19; *Scientific American Supplement*, 24 April 1897, 17,770; Turnbull, *John Stevens, an American Record*, 477.

2. Watkins, *The Camden and Amboy Railroad: Origins and Early History*, 13, 14.

3. Dunbar, *A History of Travel in America*, 883–84.

4. Myers, *The Story of New Jersey*, 285.

5. Turnbull, *John Stevens*, 363, 473; *American Railroad Journal*, 13 September 1851, 578.

6. *American Railroad Journal*, 24 February 1851, 578; Cunningham, *Railroading in New Jersey*, 3.

7. Turnbull, *John Stevens*, 373.

8. Lane, *Indian Trail*, 282; Pangborn, *World's Railway*, 27; Comstock, *The Iron Horse*, 18.

9. Cunningham, *Railroads in New Jersey*, 29, 30.

10. Watkins, *Camden and Amboy Railroad*, 14; Honeyman, *Northwestern New Jersey*, 275; Raum, *The History of New Jersey*, 340; Lane, *Indian Trail*, 282–83.

11. Beck, *Tales and Towns of Northern New Jersey*, 184; Comstock, *Iron Horse*, 18; Holbrook, *The Story of American Railroads*, 22; Phillips, *Yonder Comes the Train*, 43.

12. *Scientific American*, 13 November 1875, 307; Armytage, *A Social History of Engineering*, 125; Turnbull, *John Stevens*, 473.

13. *Scientific American Supplement*, 24 April 1897, 17,770; Douglas, *All Aboard*, 20; Turnbull, *John Stevens*, 477–78.

14. Turnbull, *John Stevens*, 478.

15. *Stories of New Jersey*, 395.

16. Myers, *Story of New Jersey*, 286; Lane, *Indian Trail*, 283; Watkins, *Camden and Amboy Railroad*, 15.

17. *Stories of New Jersey*, 396.

18. Cunningham, *Railroading*, 3.

19. *Proceedings of the New Jersey Historical Society*, July 1925, 274–75.

20. Lane, *Indian Trail*, 281–82.

## 2. From Camden to Amboy by Rail in Seven Hours

1. Burgess and. Kennedy, *Centennial History of the Pennsylvania Railroad*, 243, 245; Cunningham, *Railroads*, 35; Cunningham, *Railroading*, 6; Watkins, *Camden and Amboy Railroad*, 20, 21; Turnbull, *John Stevens*, 499; Raum, *History of New Jersey*, 340; *Acts Incorporating the Delaware and Raritan Canal Company, the Camden and Amboy Railroad and Transportation Company, and the New Jersey Railroad and Transportation Company*, 5, 17; *Charters of Rail Road and Other Companies between New York and Philadelphia*, 1, 7.

2. Cunningham, *Railroading*, 6, 7; Watkins, *Camden and Amboy Railroad*, 25; Douglas, *All Aboard*, 25.

3. Menzies, *Passage between Rivers*, 32; Watkins, *Camden and Amboy Railroad*, 77; Cawley and Cawley, *Along the Delaware and Raritan Canal*, 42; MacAdam, *West Windsor, Then and Now*, 34; Stover, *American Railroads*, 16.

4. Burgess and Kennedy, *Centennial History*, 250–52; Cunningham, *Railroading*, 7; Menzies, *Passage between Rivers*, 36; *Acts Incorporating the Delaware and Raritan Canal Company, the Camden and Amboy Railroad and Transportation Company, and the New Jersey Railroad and Transportation Company*, 27–32; *Charters of Rail Road and Other Companies between New York and Philadelphia*, 12–18.

5. Raum, *History of New Jersey*, 341.

6. Carey, *Beauties of the Monopoly System of New Jersey, by a Citizen of Burlington*, 7–20; Stockton, *Defence of the System of Internal Improvements of the State of New Jersey*, 7–8, 20–21, 46.

7. James P. Snell, *History of Hunterdon and Somerset Counties*, 114; *New Jersey History*, October 1927, 405, 412.

8. *Engineering*, 10 June 1892, 734; Vance, *North American Railroad*, 53.

9. Bianculli, *Trains and Technology*, 3:95–97; Turnbull, *John Stevens*, 509; Watkins, *Camden and Amboy Railroad*, 29–31; Burgess and Kennedy, *Centennial History*, 246.

10. Jacobs, *History of the Pennsylvania Railroad*, 12; *New Jersey History*, July 1925, 276.

11. *New Jersey History*, July 1925, 273–74; Vance, *North American Railroad*, 105.

12. *New Jersey History*, October 1927, 410.

13. Watkins, *Camden and Amboy Railroad*, 22.

14. Watkins, *Camden and Amboy Railroad*, 71.

15. Cunningham, *Railroads*, 35.

16. Pangborn, *World's Railway*, 86; Burgess and Kennedy, *Centennial History*, 247; Watkins, *Camden and Amboy Railroad*, 42; Lane, *Indian Trail*, 287.

17. *New Jersey History*, July 1925, 279; Watkins, *Camden and Amboy Railroad*, 43.

18. Stover, *American Railroads*, 16; Jacobs, *History of the Pennsylvania Railroad*, 26.

19. "Travelling in America Sixty Years Ago," *Scientific American*, 14 January 1893, 26.

20. Turnbull, *John Stevens*, 508; Burgess and Kennedy, *Centennial History*, 247.

21. Cunningham, *Railroads*, 40.

22. Cunningham, *Railroads*, 43, 45; Jacobs, *History of the Pennsylvania Railroad*, 26; *New Jersey History*, October 1927, 411; Watkins, *Camden and Amboy Railroad*, 44–47; Burgess and Kennedy, *Centennial History*, 249–52; John H. White, *The John Bull*, 90.

23. Watkins, *Camden and Amboy Railroad*, 49; Burgess and Kennedy, *Centennial History*, 242; Billington, *The Innovators*, 113; PRR Chronology, 1839, www.prrths.com.

24. *First Joint Report of the Associated Delaware & Raritan Canal Co., Camden & Amboy R.R. & Transportation Co., and New Jersey R.R. & Transportation Co. to the Stockholders*, April 1867, 3.

25. MacAdam, *West Windsor*, 26, 27; White, *The John Bull*, 93.

26. *Lease and Contract Dates June 30th, 1871, between the Delaware and Raritan Canal Company, the Camden and Amboy Railroad and Transportation Company, and the New Jersey Railroad and Transportation Company, Philadelphia and Trenton Railroad Company, Parties of the First Part and the Pennsylvania Railroad Company, Party of the Second Part*, 31 June 1871.

27. Watkins, *Camden and Amboy Railroad*, 59; Hunter and Porter, *Hopewell: A Historical Geography*, 180; Jacobs, *History of the Pennsylvania Railroad*, 26.

28. *West Jersey Rails*, 1999 reprint of the 1983 edition, 4.

29. *New Jersey History*, July 1925, 281, 282; Watkins, *Camden and Amboy Railroad*, 3, 4, 66; Treese, *Railroads of New Jersey*, 10, 41–42.

30. MacAdam, *West Windsor*, 26–28.

## 3. Isaac Dripps and the *John Bull* (1831)

1. *Proceedings of the New Jersey Historical Society*, July 1925, 276–77; Watkins, *Camden and Amboy Railroad*, 3, 36, 37; Cunningham, *Railroads*, 39; Jacobs, *History of the Pennsylvania Railroad*, 12; *New Jersey Almanac, 1964–65*, 313–14; Turnbull, *John Stevens*, 504; White, *The John Bull*, 22–23; *Stories of New Jersey*, 397; Treese, *Railroads of New Jersey*, 41.

2. Turnbull, *John Stevens*, 506; Cunningham, *Railroads*, 37.

3. *Stories of New Jersey*, 398–99; *Proceedings of the New Jersey Historical Society*, July 1925, 279; Watkins, *Camden and Amboy Railroad*, 37, 38; Cunningham, *Railroads*, 39.

4. *Proceedings of the New Jersey Historical Society*, July 1925, 279; Turnbull, *John Stevens*, 506.

5. Watkins, *Camden and Amboy Railroad*, 39–40.

6. Cunningham, *Railroads*, 41; Lane, *2 Indian Trail*, 89.

7. Stevenson, *Sketch of the Civil Engineering of North America*, 163.

8. *Proceedings of the New Jersey Historical Society*, July 1925, 281; Bianculli, *Trains and Technology*, 1:47, 49; Watkins, *Camden and Amboy Railroad*, 40, 41; Cunningham, *Railroads*, 38.

9. Jacobs, *History of the Pennsylvania Railroad*, 26, 27; Bianculli, *Trains and Technology*, 1:86; Cunningham, *Railroads*, 44; Watkins, *Camden and Amboy Railroad*, 2, 34; Stover, *American Railroads*, 25; *New Jersey Almanac, 1964–65*, 314; White, *The John Bull*, 57–74; White, *A Short History of American Locomotive Builders in the Steam Era*, 99; Raum, *History of the City of Trenton*, 351.

10. Bianculli, *Railroad History on American Postage Stamps*, 19; *Stories of New Jersey*, 400–401; *Proceedings of the New Jersey Historical Society*, October 1927, 410; White, *The John Bull*, 32, 34; Bulletin 19 of the Friends of the Railroad Museum of Pennsylvania; Bailey, *John Bull, a Replica of the Past*, 1–4; Cudahy, *Over and Back: The History of Ferryboats in New York Harbor*, 60; John H. White, "Resurrection: The *John Bull* Steams Again at 150 Years of Age," *Railroad History*, 144: 9–28; Treese, *Railroads of New Jersey*, 16.

## 4. Ashbel Welch, Railroad Man (1836–74)

1. J. Roscoe Howell, *Ashbel Welch, Civil Engineer*, 8, 10; Menzies, *Passage between Rivers*, 36, 40; Burgess and Kennedy, *Centennial History*, 247, Snell, *Hunterdon and Somerset Counties*, 289; *Biographical Encyclopedia of New Jersey*, 420.

2. Watkins, *Camden and Amboy Railroad*, 44–45; Burgess and Kennedy, *Centennial History*, 251, 264.

3. Howell, *Welch*, 14–17; Menzies, *Passage between Rivers*, 101; Snell, *Hunterdon and Somerset Counties*, 289; *Biographical Encyclopedia of New Jersey*, 420.

4. Howell, *Welch*, 19, 21; Burgess and Kennedy, *Centennial History*, 264, Snell, *Hunterdon and Somerset Counties*, 115, 290; *Biographical Encyclopedia of New Jersey*, 420.

5. Watkins, *Camden and Amboy Railroad*, 58–59.

6. Howell, *Welch*, 22; Snell, *Hunterdon and Somerset Counties*, 289.

7. Cunningham, *Railroading*, 7; Bianculli, *Trains and Technology*, 4:127; Stover, *American Railroads*, 147.

8. Snell, *Early Railways*, 55–56.

9. Welch, *Report on Safety Signals*, 6–7.

10. *American Practice in Block Signaling*, 3.

11. Welch, *Report on Safety Signals*, 6; Cunningham, *Railroading*, 44; *Biographical Encyclopedia of New Jersey*, 420; Burgess and Kennedy, *Centennial History*, 253–54; Snell, *Hunterdon and Somerset Counties*, 290.

12. Menzies, *Passage between Rivers*, 100, 104; Burgess and Kennedy, *Centennial History*, 236, 240; Snell, *Hunterdon and Somerset Counties*, 289–90; *Biographical Encyclopedia of New Jersey*, 420.

13. Howell, *Welch*, 25.

14. Howell, *Welch*, 18, 21; Beers, *Atlas of Hunterdon County, New Jersey*, 70, 74; Warren F. Lee and Catherine T. Lee, *A Chronology of the Belvidere-Delaware Railroad Company*, 318; author's conversation with William McKelvey, D&R Canal historian, 11 August 2005; Black River and Western Railroad, www.brwrr.com; Hunter and Porter, *Hopewell*, 180; *D&R Canal State Park*, undated brochure of the New Jersey Department of Environmental Protection, 3.

## 5. Locomotives

1. White, *American Locomotive Builders*, 31–32; Cunningham, *Railroads*, 140; Pierson, *Narratives of Newark (in New Jersey)*, 258–59; Works of Karl Gerhardt, www.twainquotes.com/Gerhardt/kgworks1890.html; Karl Gerhardt in *New Orleans Times Democrat*, www.twainquotes.com/Gerhardt/NOTD.html.

2. White, *American Locomotive Builders*, 31–32; Cunningham, *Railroads*, 140.

3. Raum, *History of the City of Trenton*, 351.

4. White, *American Locomotive Builders*, 49–50, 99.

5. Murphy and Murphy, *Paterson and Passaic County: An Illustrated History*, 12–13, 59, 60–63; Cunningham, *Railroads*, 142.

6. Murphy and Murphy, *Paterson and Passaic County*, 71–72; L. R. Trumbull, *A History of Industrial Paterson*, 114–18; Bianculli, *Trains and Technology*, 1:78–79; Cunningham, *Railroads*, 128; *Rogers Locomotive Catalog*, 1876, 6–8;

Peter Moshein and Robert R. Rothfus, "Rogers Locomotives: A Brief History and Construction List," *Railroad History*, Autumn 1992, 167: 13–16.

7. Cunningham, *Railroads*, 132; Trumbull, *History of Industrial Paterson*, 115, 120, 123; Murphy and Murphy, *Paterson and Passaic County*, 73; *Rogers Locomotive Catalog, 1876*, 5.

8. Murphy and Murphy, *Paterson and Passaic County*, 72; White, *American Locomotive Builders*, 69, 95; Trumbull, *History of Industrial Paterson*, 128–9; Bianculli, *Trains and Technology*, 1:120–21; Cunningham, *Railroads*, 132; *Locomotive & Railway Preservation*, May/June 1995, 26; *Railroad History*, 104: 54.

9. Cunningham, *Railroads*, 172.

10. Jones, *The Pascack Valley Line*, 23–25.

11. White, *American Locomotive Builders*, 49; Bianculli, *Trains and Technology*, 1:117, 187–89; Carter, 53–4; *Railroad History*, 104: 58–59.

12. White, *American Locomotive Builders*, 38; Trumbull, *History of Industrial Paterson*, 119, 125, 139–40; Cunningham, *Railroads*, 138.

13. Murphy and Murphy, *Paterson and Passaic County*, 68, 72; Bianculli, *Trains and Technology*, 1:118–20.

14. Cunningham, *Railroads*, 133, 138–40; Trumbull, *History of Industrial Paterson*, 148; *Rogers Locomotive Catalog, 1876*, v.

15. Bianculli, *Trains and Technology*, 2:170–71; Cunningham, *Railroads*, 139.

16. *Scientific American*, 16 August 1851, 388, White, *The American Railroad Passenger Car*, 117, 120; *Railroad History* 4:31–34 and 46:11; *American Railroad Journal*, 22 October 1853, 679, 31 March 1855, 201, and 20 October 1855, 664; *Railroad Car Journal*, February 1895, 25; *American Railway Review*, 14 March 1861, 150; Jones, *The Pascack Valley Line*, 10, 11.

17. Murphy and Murphy, *Paterson and Passaic County*, 73; author's conversation with Jack DeStefano, director, Paterson Museum, 4 January 2006; flyer regarding the Historic Homecoming of the 1910 Alco-Cooke Locomotive, Paterson, N.J., 1978.

18. Frank T. Reilly, locomotive listing, 1 February 1982, Stirling, N.J.

## 6. Piercing the Palisades (1838–1910)

1. *Science Record*, 1876, 382–83; Answers.com, s.v. "Palisades."

2. Cunningham, *Railroading*, 14.

3. Cunningham, *Railroads*, 60; *Railroad History*, 88:123.

4. *Midlander* 5, no. 3 (n.d.); *Railroad History*, 88:131.

5. *Scientific American*, 13 October 1883, 227; Answers.com, s.v. "Palisades" and "Erie Railroad"; Wikipedia, s.v. "Conrail"; *First Joint Report of the Associated Delaware & Raritan Canal Co., Camden & Amboy R.R. & Transportation Co., and New Jersey R.R. & Transportation Co.*, 3.

6. Edward H. Mott, *Between the Ocean and the Lakes: The Story of Erie* (New York: Ticker, 1908), 360; John Houston to Joseph Bennett, 1 December 1860, as reported in the *Journal of the Franklin Institute*, February 1861, 87, 88.

7. Thomas McConkey, "History of the New York & Erie Bergen Tunnel," *Midlander* 5, no. 3 (n.d.): 1, 3; Mott, *Between the Ocean and the Lakes*, 360.

8. *Civil Engineer and Architect's Journal*, December 1856, 404; Cunningham, *Railroads*, 165; *Science Record*, 1876, 383; Cunningham, *Railroading*, 38.

9. *Scientific American*, 26 May 1877, 319; *Midlander* 5, no. 5; Cunningham, *Railroads*, 200; Bianculli, *Trains and Technology*, 4:97; Cunningham, *Railroading*, 38; Thomas T. Taber, "Commuter Railroad," 289–92.

10. Bianculli, *Trains and Technology*, 4:97, 98, 103; *Science*

*Record*, 1876, 383; *Scientific American*, 26 May 1877, 319–24; *Scientific American Supplement*, 24 March 1894, 15,193; Taber, *The Delaware, Lackawanna & Western Railroad in the Nineteenth Century, 1827–1899*, 86.

11. Thomas T. Taber to author, 18 August 2005; Answers.com, s.v. "Palisades."

12. *Newark Star-Ledger*, 28 July 2005, 16, *Trenton Times*, 30 September 2005, C8.

13. *Train Sheet*, Railroadians of America, Roselle, N.J., Summer 1995, 2; *Scientific American Supplement*, 15 July 1882, 5,436 and 24 March 1894, 15,193; Answers.com, s.v. "Palisades"; Cunningham, *Railroads*, 252.

14. *Scientific American*, 23 December 1893, 410; *Scientific American Supplement*, 24 March 1894, 15,193.

15. Taber, *Delaware, Lackawanna & Western Railroad*, 88; history of the Bergen Arches, www.jerseycityhistory.net/bergenarches .html, 2, 4; Scott E. Randolph, curator of the Erie-Lackawanna Historical Society, to author, 7 February 2006.

16. Myers, *Story of New Jersey*, 296–97; Burgess and Kennedy, *Centennial History*, 469.

17. *Scientific American*, 31 October 1891, 279, and 21 April 1894.

## 7. The Final Barrier

1. *Collier's Encyclopedia*, vol. 12, s.v. "Hudson River"; Jacobs, *History of the Pennsylvania Railroad*, 82.

2. Cunningham, *Railroads*, 24–25; Scull, *Hoboken's Lackawanna Terminal*, 9; Smith, *Romance of the Hoboken Ferry*, 27; Cudahy, *Over and Back*, 30, 32; Burgess and Kennedy, *Centennial History*, 464–65; Jacobs, *History of the Pennsylvania Railroad*, 83.

3. Cunningham, *Railroads*, 62, 63; Hudson River Bridge (unbuilt), www.nycroads.com/crossings/hudson-river-bridge, 1, 2.

4. Cunningham, *Railroads*, 23; *Cassier's Magazine*, August 1894, 275–77; Scull, *Hoboken's Lackawanna Terminal*, 9, 12; Billington, *Innovators*, 113; Smith, *Romance of the Hoboken Ferry*, 21.

5. Cudahy, *Over and Back*, 39.

6. *Cassier's Magazine*, August 1894, 278–81, 287; *Scientific American*, 8 December 1888, 351–52, 5 May 1894, 279; *Scientific American Supplement*, 1 November 1890, 12,359–61, 30 January 1892, 13,400, and 23 November 1895, 16,587; Cudahy, *Over and Back*, 56–64, 116, 119; Norman Brouwer, "Harbor Master," www.southstseaport.org/magazine/articles/1997a-02.shtm.

7. *Map of the State of New Jersey*; Douglas, *All Aboard*, 242; Smith, *Romance of the Hoboken Ferry*, 138.

8. Stevenson, *Across the Plains*, 100–104.

9. Baxter and Adams, *Railroad Ferries of the Hudson*, 123; Cudahy, *Over and Back*, 132.

10. Cudahy, *Over and Back*, 92–94, 109, 342; *New York Times*, 22 February 1861, 1.

11. Smith, *Romance of the Hoboken Ferry*, 51, 87, 89, 95, 109–11.

12. *New Jersey Transport Heritage*, September 1995, unnumbered; Scull, *Hoboken's Lackawanna Terminal*, 6, 7, 12, 22, 26–33; Cudahy, *Over and Back*, 135–36.

13. *New Jersey Transport Heritage*, September 1995, unnumbered, October 2005, 1, and December 2005, 4; *Scientific American*, 18 October 1879, 240; Scull, *Hoboken's Lackawanna Terminal*, 66; Smith, *Romance of the Hoboken Ferry*, 119–20; Baxter and Adams, *Railroad Ferries of the Hudson*, 60.

14. Cudahy, *Rails under the Mighty Hudson*, 83–84.

15. Joe Greenstein, "New York City Studies Rail Freight Options," *Railway Age*, July 1999; *New York Times*, 2 March 2003, 14:1, 4 June 2003, B-4, B-8.

16. Scull, *Hoboken's Lackawanna Terminal*, 57–73; Smith, *Romance of the Hoboken Ferry*, 123–25; Baxter and Adams,

*Railroad Ferries of the Hudson,* 210–12; *Railway Age,* 21 December 1935; *New York Times,* 23 October 1935.

17. Steinman and Watson, *Bridges and Their Builders,* 186–87; *Breakthrough!* 2; *Scientific American,* 18 October 1879, 240, and 8 May 1880, 287–90; *Contributions from the Museum of History and Technology,* bulletin 240, 234; Hudson and Manhattan Railroad, www.hudsoncity.net/tubesenglish/1-constructionhistory.html.

18. *Contributions from the Museum of History and Technology,* bulletin 240, 234–35; *Scientific American,* 12 December 1874, 376, 3 April 1875, 210–11, 7 February 1880, 85; 8 May 1880, 290, and 7 August 1880, 85.

19. *Scientific American,* 18 September 1880, 177, 19 March 1881, 182, 26 March 1881, 196, 4 June 1881, 351, 356, 27 May 1882, 234, and 2 September 1882, 147; *Scientific American Supplement,* 4 November 1882, 5,690–92; Black, *Story of Tunnels,* 98; History of the Hudson and Manhattan Railroad, www.jerseycityhistory.net/hudsontubes.html.

20. *Breakthrough!* 2; *Scientific American,* 19 March 1881, 182, 15 July 1882, 39, 28 April 1883, 260, 21 May 1887, 324, and 7 September 1889, 145, 151; *Scientific American Supplement,* 22 February 1890, 11,786.

21. *Scientific American,* 3 January 1891, 3, 21 March 1891, 178, and 18 July 1891, 34; Finch, *Story of Engineering,* 485–86; *Frank Leslie's Popular Monthly,* February 1891, 251; Hudson and Manhattan Railroad, www.hudsoncity.net/tubesenglish/1-constructionhistory.html, 2.

22. *Breakthrough!* 2, 4; *Track Map of the Hudson and Manhattan Railroad;* Black, *Story of Tunnels,* 101, 105–6, *Newsletter of the Society for Industrial Archeology,* Fall 2000, 1; Scull, *Hoboken's Lackawanna Terminal,* 74; Burgess and Kennedy, *Centennial History,* 471; *Unionist-Gazette,* 22 July 1909, 1; Moore, *Destruction of Penn Station,* 63; *PATH Gazette,* 3; *New York Herald,* 26 February 1908; Cudahy, *Rails under the Mighty Hudson,* 13, 24, 41–45.

23. *Track Map of the Hudson and Manhattan Railroad;* Burgess and Kennedy, *Centennial History,* 469; Cunningham, *Newark,* 246.

24. Scull, *Hoboken's Lackawanna Terminal,* 75.

25. Klein, *Encyclopedia of North American Railroads,* 75.

26. Scull, *Hoboken's Lackawanna Terminal,* 75–77; Cranmer, *New Jersey in the Automobile Age,* 39–40, 122–23; Cudahy, *Rails under the Mighty Hudson,* 59–63.

27. Hudson and Manhattan Railroad, www.hudsoncity.net/tubesenglish/1-constructionhistory.html, 2.

28. Hudson and Manhattan Railroad. www.hudsoncity.net/tubesenglish/1-constructionhistory.html, 9.

29. Burgess and Kennedy, *Centennial History,* 465; Jacobs, *History of the Pennsylvania Railroad,* 83.

30. Burgess and Kennedy, *Centennial History,* 467–70.

31. Cudahy, *Rails under the Mighty Hudson,* 32, 33.

32. *Star-Ledger,* 28 July 2005, 16; *Trenton Times,* 30 September 2005, C8.

33. Ballon, *New York's Pennsylvania Stations,* 153–58, 186, 192; Wikipedia, s.v. "Pennsylvania Station (New York City)."

34. *Newsletter of the New Jersey Association of Railroad Passengers,* 26 October 2007, 3.

35. Wikipedia, s.v. "Pennsylvania Station (New York City)"; Diehl, *Late, Great Pennsylvania Station,* 14, 28; *Railway & Locomotive Historical Society Newsletter,* Spring 2007, 6–9; Ballon, *New York's Pennsylvania Stations,* 104.

## 8. The Railroad and the New Jersey Bedroom Communities (1840–2006)

1. Myers, *Story of New Jersey,* 298; Taber, "Commuter Railroad," preface; Douglas, *All Aboard,* 237; *New Yorker,* 16 April 2007, 62.

2. Lurie and Mappen, eds., *Encyclopedia of New Jersey,* 675–76.

3. Myers, *Story of New Jersey,* 298; Cranmer, *New Jersey in the Automobile Age,* 38, 39.

4. Douglas, *All Aboard,* 242.

5. Kobbé, *Kobbé's Jersey Central.*

6. *New York Times,* 6 February 1873, 2.

7. Baxter and Adams, *Railroad Ferries of the Hudson,* 114; Kobbé, *Kobbé's Jersey Central.*

8. Cunningham, *Newark,* 245–46, Cranmer, *New Jersey in the Automobile Age,* 39; *PATH Gazette,* 17; Moore, *Destruction of Penn Station,* 63.

9. *West Jersey Rails Quarterly,* June 1997, 2-37–2-40; *West Jersey Rails,* 1:47, 48; *New Jersey Transport Heritage,* September 1995, 3; Corporate Succession Philadelphia and Camden Ferry Company, http://broadway.pennsyrr.com/rail/prr/Corphist/p_cfy.html.

10. Kramer, *Pennsylvania-Reading Seashore Lines,* 60.

11. *West Jersey Rails,* 1:47.

12. Kramer, *Pennsylvania-Reading Seashore Lines,* 60; *National Railway Bulletin* 59, no. 4 (1994): 23; West Jersey History Project, www.westjerseyhistory.org/articles/camdenbrief/index.shtml.

13. *Haddon Gazette,* 22 January 1981; *West Jersey Rails,* 1:48.

14. Kramer, *Pennsylvania-Reading Seashore Lines,* 60.

## 9. The Jersey Central (1849–1976)

1. Osgood, "Historical Highlights of the Jersey Central Lines." 3–5; Botkin and Harlow, *A Treasury of Railroad Folklore,* 68; Cunningham, *Railroads,* 68–70.

2. Cunningham, *Railroads,* 70; *Flags, Diamonds, and Statues,* Fall 1975, 12; Mason, *Early Somerville,* 9.

3. *Flags, Diamonds, and Statues,* Fall 1975, 15; Mason, *Early Somerville,* 9; *Somerset Messenger Gazette,* 20 January 1972.

4. Anderson, *Central Railroad,* 1; Taber, *Delaware, Lackawanna & Western Railroad,* 37.

5. Cunningham, *Railroads,* 67–71, 143; Anderson, *Central Railroad,* 2, 31; Osgood, "Historical Highlights of the Jersey Central Lines," 8; Snell, *Hunterdon and Somerset Counties,* 110; *New Jersey Transport Heritage,* February 1996, 3.

6. Cunningham, *Railroads,* 72; Anderson, *Central Railroad,* 15, 22–23; *New Jersey Transport Heritage,* February 1996, 3.

7. Anderson, *Central Railroad,* 5, 9; Cunningham, *Railroads,* 143, 147.

8. Anderson, *Central Railroad,* introduction, 10; *New Jersey Transport Heritage,* February 1996, 3.

9. Reilly, *Central Railroad Company of New Jersey,* 5, 6; Snell, *Hunterdon and Somerset Counties,* 111; *New York Times,* 19 March 1872.

10. Reilly, *Central Railroad Company of New Jersey,* 5.

11. Cunningham, *Railroads,* 150–52, 154, 158–60.

12. Reilly, *Central Railroad Company of New Jersey,* 6.

13. Wikipedia, s.v. "Central Railroad of New Jersey"; Anderson, *Central Railroad,* 79; Kramer, *Pennsylvania-Reading Seashore Lines,* 10; Della Penna, *24 Great Rail-Trails of New Jersey,* 88.

14. Bianculli, *Trains and Technology,* 1:155–57.

15. Anderson, *Central Railroad,* 65–71, 78, 83; *Railway History Monograph,* July 1973, 9; *New Jersey Transport Heritage,* February 1996, 4.

16. Anderson, *Central Railroad,* 80, 83; Kramer, *Pennsylvania-Reading Seashore Lines,* 10.

17. Anderson, *Central Railroad,* 85.

18. Treese, *Railroads of New Jersey,* 52; Anderson, *Central Railroad,* 78, 124; Kobbé, *Kobbé's Jersey Central,* 92–94, 99; *New Jersey Transport Heritage,* August 2006, 6.

19. Anderson, *Central Railroad,* 89; Bianculli, *Trains and Technology,* 4:128, 141, 188; Condit, *Port of New York,* 146–47.

20. Anderson, *Central Railroad,* 164–66.

21. Wikipedia, s.v. "Central Railroad of New Jersey."

22. *Train Sheet,* Winter 1977–78, 1, 2; Kramer, *Pennsylvania-Reading Seashore Lines,* 42; Waltzer and Wilk, *Tales of South Jersey,* 112, Anderson, *Central Railroad,* 126.

23. Baer, Coxey, and Schopp, *Trail of the Blue Comet,* 268–69, 272, 275, 301; Waltzer and Wilk, *Tales of South Jersey,* 110–12; *Train Sheet,* Winter 1977–78, 3; *West Jersey Rails,* 1:34, 36; *West Jersey Rails Quarterly,* Autumn 2005, 6; *National Railway Bulletin* 62, no. 6 (1997): 17.

24. Baer, Coxey, and Schopp, *Trail of the Blue Comet,* 295, 301–2, 319; Kramer, *Pennsylvania-Reading Seashore Lines,* 42; Waltzer and Wilk, *Tales of South Jersey,* 113–14; Treese, *Railroads of New Jersey,* 67, 85; *West Jersey Rails,* 1:5, 36; Anderson, *Central Railroad,* 170.

25. *New York Times,* 16 September 1958, 15, and 17 September 1958, 1; Baer, Coxey, and Schopp, *Trail of the Blue Comet,* 412.

26. *Central Railroad of New Jersey Historical Journal 2002,* 11.

27. Anderson, *Central Railroad,* 125, 214.

## 10. The PJ&B, a Really Short Shortline (1865–Present)

1. MacAdam, *West Windsor, Then and Now,* 26, 28; White, *John Bull,* 93; *Princeton Packet,* 23 July 1996, 1A, and 7 October 2005, 3A; *Trains,* June 1987, 44, 46; *Star Ledger,* 27 September 2000.

2. *Princeton Packet,* 23 July 1996, 9A; *Star Ledger,* 27 September 2000; Lipp, "Princeton Branch," 5–7; JJC to J. M. Fox, 24 February 1939.

3. *Trains,* June 1987, 46; *Princeton Packet,* 23 July 1996, 9A; Lipp, "Princeton Branch," 7–10.

4. *Princeton Packet,* 23 July 1996, 1A, 9A; *Star Ledger,* 27 September 2000; Lipp, "Princeton Branch," 15.

5. Louisa Potter Strong, "An Anecdote of Class of 1877," 1907, Princeton Historical Society.

6. MacAdam, *West Windsor, Then and Now,* 23, 24; *Princeton Press,* 14 March 1874, 2, and 21 March 1874, 2.

7. *Princeton Packet,* 7 April 1976; *Star Ledger,* 27 September 2000; *New York Times,* 3 March 2002, sec. 14, 8.

8. John R. Wilmot, "The Princeton Branch," *Trains,* June 1987, 50.

9. F. L. Sheppard to F. H. Earle, 18 December 1902; Earle to Sheppard, 11 and 14 February 1903; Sheppard to W. W. Atterbury, general manager, Pennsylvania Railroad, 16 February 1903 and 1 June 1905; *Princeton Packet,* 23 July 1996, 9A; *Star Ledger,* 27 September 2000; *Trains,* June 1987, 50; Lipp, "Princeton Branch," 16–18; JJC to J. M. Fox, 24 February 1939, all stored by the Historical Society of Princeton.

10. *Trains,* June 1987, 51.

11. *Trains,* June 1987, 50; Genovese, *New Jersey Curiosities,* 137.

12. *Star Ledger,* 27 September 2000; *Trains,* June 1987, 48; Lipp, "Princeton Branch," 18–19.

13. Historical Society of Princeton, vertical file: "Railroads"; *New York Times,* March 31, 2002, 14:1, 8; *Star Ledger,* 27 September 2000.

14. Lipp, "Princeton Branch," 18; *Trenton Times,* 29 July 2006, A3, and 22 May 2007, A1.

## 11. The Rascals at Bay in "Fort Taylor" (1868)

1. B. White, *Book of Daniel Drew,* 218.

2. Jensen, *American Heritage History of Railroads in America,* 136–37; Folson, *Myth of the Robber Barons,* 4, 5; Klein, *Encyclopedia of North American Railroads,* 234–35.

3. Adams and Adams, *Chapters of Erie,* 5.

4. Klein, *Encyclopedia of North American Railroads,* 84–86; Jensen, *American Heritage History of Railroads in America,* 139.

5. Benét and Benét, *A Book of Americans,* 95–96.

6. *New York Times,* 16 March 1868, 4; White, *Book of Daniel Drew,* 43–54, 59, 215–32; Jensen, *American Heritage History of Railroads in America,* 136–37.

7. McPherson and Williams, eds., *Railroad Trains and Train People in American Culture,* 98; Gordon, *Scarlet Woman of Wall Street,* 168; Adams and Adams, *Chapters of Erie,* 18–23, 28–30; White, *Book of Daniel Drew,* 280.

8. Gordon, *Scarlet Woman of Wall Street,* 173–74.

9. White, *Book of Daniel Drew,* 280.

10. Gordon, *Scarlet Woman of Wall Street,* 173–75; Baxter and Adams, *Railroad Ferries of the Hudson,* Douglas, *All Aboard,* 156–57; Baer, Coxey, and Schopp, *Trail of the Blue Comet,* 68–69; Klein, *Encyclopedia of North American Railroads,* 85.

11. *Collier's Encyclopedia,* vol. 13, s.v. "Andrew Johnson"; White, *Book of Daniel Drew,* 257–58; Gordon, *Scarlet Woman of Wall Street,* 177–78.

12. Gordon, *Scarlet Woman of Wall Street,* 181; *New York Times,* 16 March 1868, 4.

13. Gordon, *Scarlet Woman of Wall Street,* 186; McPherson and Williams, eds., *Railroad Trains and Train People in American Culture,* 98; White, *Book of Daniel Drew,* 261–63, 277.

14. Gordon, *Scarlet Woman of Wall Street,* 192; Klein, *Encyclopedia of North American Railroads,* 86; Jensen, *American Heritage History of Railroads in America,* 136–37; Adams and Adams, *Chapters of Erie,* 48–49, 57–58, 61, 64, 70–76; White, *Book of Daniel Drew,* 325–26, 366–68, 404–5; Answers.com, s.v. "Daniel Drew."

15. White, *Book of Daniel Drew,* 282–83, 289–90, 404–5; Gordon, *Scarlet Woman of Wall Street,* 18, 378; Hoyt, *Pen and Pencil Pictures on the Delaware, Lackawanna and Western Railroad;* Wikipedia, s.v. "Drew University."

16. McPherson and Williams, eds., *Railroad Trains and Train People in American Culture,* 101; Treese, *Railroads of New Jersey,* 163; Baer, Coxey, and Schopp, *Trail of the Blue Comet,* 193–95.

17. Baer, Coxey, and Schopp, *Trail of the Blue Comet,* 68–72; Jensen, *American Heritage History of Railroads in America,* 142.

## 12. Henry Drinker and the Musconetcong Tunnel (1872–75)

1. Bianculli, *Trains and Technology,* 4:96, 102; Cunningham, *Railroads,* 156.

2. Lehigh University transcript, undated, supplied by P. Metzger, curator of the Special Collections Department.

3. Musconetcong Mountain Conservancy, www.nynjtc.org/clubpages/mmc.html.

4. Archer, *History of the Lehigh Valley Railroad,* 105, 108.

5. Drinker, *Tunneling,* 219–31; *Science Record,* 1876, 290.

6. Drinker, *Tunneling,* 230.

7. Cunningham, *Railroads,* 156.

8. Chris Marshall, alumni director, Lehigh University, to author, 7 October 2005.

9. Railfan.net Forums—Bellewood Park, http://forums.railfan.net.

10. Railfan.net Forums-LV-Musconetcong Tunnel, http://forums.railfan.net; Aerial Photos, www.railwaystation.com/airne.html; *Trenton Times*, 7 January 1998, A2.

## 13. The Railroad King of Blairstown (1876)

1. Heilich, *History of the Blairstown Railway*, 81; Snell, *Hunterdon and Somerset Counties*, 655; Cunningham, *Railroads*, 144; Schwieterman, *When the Railroad Leaves Town*, 178.

2. Cunningham, *Railroads*, 146, 148; Snell, *Hunterdon and Somerset Counties*, 656; Lane, *Indian Trail*, 386.

3. Snell, *Hunterdon and Somerset Counties*, 656; Honeyman, *Northwestern New Jersey*, 579–80; Lane, *Indian Trail*, 387.

4. Cunningham, *Capsules*, 47; Schwieterman, *When the Railroad Leaves Town*, 178.

5. Heilich, *Blairstown Railway*, 11, 14, 17; Bertholf, *Images of America: Blairstown*, 33; *Paulinskill Valley Trail*, 32.

6. Bertholf, *Images of America: Blairstown*, 34–35; Heilich, *Blairstown Railway*, 20, 33, 57; Schwieterman, *When the Railroad Leaves Town*, 179.

7. Heilich, *Blairstown Railway*, 7.

8. Edson, *Railroad Names*, 17; Heilich, *Blairstown Railway*, 20; Schwieterman, *When the Railroad Leaves Town*, 179; Mohowski, *New York, Susquehanna & Western Railroad*, 67, 69.

9. Della Penna, *24 Great Rail-Trails of New Jersey*, 126; *Paulinskill Valley Trail*, 3, 11; Heilich, *Blairstown Railway*, 45.

10. Cunningham, *Capsules*, 47; Snell, *Hunterdon and Somerset Counties*, 657.

11. Della Penna, *24 Great Rail-Trails of New Jersey*, 125–43; Schwieterman, *When the Railroad Leaves Town*, 180–81; *Paulinskill Valley Trail*, 3.

## 14. The Great Frog War at Hopewell (1876)

1. Henry, *This Fascinating Railroad Business*, 76.

2. Haussamen, *When the Railroads Came to Somerset County*, 19; Cunningham, *Railroads*, 39, 202; Snell, *Hunterdon and Somerset Counties*, 112–15.

3. Snell, *Hunterdon and Somerset Counties*, 112–13.

4. Haussamen, *When the Railroads Came to Somerset County*, 38–39; Snell, *Hunterdon and Somerset Counties*, 113–14; *Rutgers Alumni Monthly*, May 1925, 245–47.

5. Cunningham, *Railroads*, 202–3; Haussamen, *Iron Horse in Somerset County*, 46; Snell, *Hunterdon and Somerset Counties*, 114.

6. *Somerset Unionist*, 10 March 1870, 2; Wikipedia, s.v. "Mercer and Somerset Railway."

7. Lewis, *Hopewell Valley Heritage*, 19; Beck, *Roads of Home*, 122; *Frog War!*

8. Cunningham, *Railroads*, 201.

9. *Railroad History* 96:5354; Train Beginnings, www.pennridge.org/p/p-trainbeg.html; Delaware & Bound Brook Railroad, http://members.tripod.com/njrails/19th_Century/Delaware_Bound_Brook_Delaware_Bound_brook.htm; Snell, *Hunterdon and Somerset Counties*, 114; Hunter and Porter, *Hopewell*, 181.

10. Lee, *Down along the Old Bel-Del*, 11; *Frog War!*

11. Scharring-Hausen, ed., *Help Hopewell Honor Her Heroes*, 43.

12. Beck, *Roads of Home*, 123.

13. *Somerset Messenger*, 25 November 1875, 3.

14. Cunningham, *Railroading*, 39; Beck, *Roads of Home*, 123.

15. Hunter and Porter, *Hopewell*, 181.

16. Beck, *Roads of Home*, 123.

17. *New York Times*, 7 January 1876, 1 and 8 January 1876, 2; Beck, *Roads of Home*, 124; Lewis, *Hopewell Valley Heritage*, 19; Lee, *Down along the Old Bel-Del*, 11; Scharring-Hausen, ed. *Help Hopewell Honor Her Heroes*, 43; Cunningham, *New Jersey Sampler*, 160; Hunter and Porter, *Hopewell*, 181, 182; Cunningham, *Railroads*, 203; Cunningham, *Railroading*, 39, 40; *Frog War!*

18. Hunter and Porter, *Hopewell*, 182; Haussamen, *When the Railroads Came to Somerset County*, 40; Beck, *Roads of Home*, 119; Lee, *Down along the Old Bel-Del*, 11; Snell, *Hunterdon and Somerset Counties*, 116.

19. *Combination Atlas Map of Mercer County*, as printed on the end papers of Lewis's *Hopewell Valley Heritage*.

20. Beck, *Roads of Home*, 120.

21. *Frog War!*

22. Hunter and Porter, *Hopewell*,, 182–83.

23. Scharring-Hausen, R. L., ed. *Help Hopewell Honor Her Heroes*, 43, 45.

## 15. Frog Wars Redux (1879)

1. Wikipedia, s.v. "Frog War."

2. Cunningham, *Railroads*, 123; Kramer, *Pennsylvania-Reading Seashore Lines*, 4; *In Historic Cape May County, N.J.*

3. Wilson, *Jersey Shore* 477.

4. Cook and Coxey, *Atlantic City Railroad*, 66; Wilson, *Jersey Shore* 477–78; *In Historic Cape May County, N.J.*

5. Schwieterman, *When the Railroad Leaves Town*, 193–94.

6. *New York Times*, 31 July 1896, 1; Cunningham, *Railroads*, 298.

7. *New York Times*, 1 August 1896, 2; Cunningham, *Railroads*, 298.

8. Cook and Coxey, *Atlantic City Railroad*, 70; Wilson, *Jersey Shore* 478–79.

9. Cook and Coxey, *Atlantic City Railroad*, 69.

10. *Trenton Times*, 23 December 1906, 2.

11. *Tuckahoe Railroad History*, a flier published by the Historical Preservation Society of Upper Township; Burgess and Kennedy, *Centennial History*, 632.

12. Schwieterman, *When the Railroad Leaves Town*, 196–97.

13. Della-Penna, *24 Great Rail-Trails of New Jersey*, 110–13.

14. *Cape May Seashore Lines*, brochure, Tuckahoe, N.J.

## 16. Thomas Edison and Leo Daft

1. *Transactions of the Newcomen Society*, 1949–51, 153; Josephson, *Edison*, 22, 242; *Frank Leslie's Popular Monthly*, September 1889, 372, 379; Middleton, *Time of the Trolley*, 12, 13; *Railway Mechanical Engineering*, 137; Marshall, *Rail: Records*, 133; *Railroad History*, 130:6, 157:83.

2. Josephson, *Edison*, 12, 19–23, 26–40.

3. Middleton, *Time of the Trolley*, 14, 15; Josephson, *Edison*, 238–42; *Transactions of the Newcomen Society*, 1949–51, 154; *A Century of Progress*, 1880.

4. *Scientific American*, 5 June 1880, as reported in *Scientific American*, 3 February 1894, 72; Josephson, *Edison*, 240.

5. Middleton, *Time of the Trolley*, 16; Josephson, *Edison*, 240.

6. Josephson, *Edison*, 241–42.

7. Josephson, *Edison*, 400; *Railroaders*, 226–33.

8. Scull, *Hoboken's Lackawanna Terminal*, 49.

9. *Mystic's 2005 U.S. Stamp Catalog*, 2:23, 32, 96.

10. Menlo Park Museum, www.menloparkmuseum.com; World's Largest Light Bulb, www.roadsideamerica.com/sights/sightstory; Wikipedia, s.v. "Edison, New Jersey."

11. Middleton, *Time of the Trolley*, 16; Ransome-Wallis, *World Railway Locomotives*, 143, 161; *Scientific American*, 8 December 1883, 352; *Transactions of the Newcomen Society*, 1949–51, 154; Lighting a Revolution, http://americanhistory.si.edu/lighting/webnotes/webnote1.htm; Cable Car Home Page, www.cable-car-guy.com/html/ccmanb12.html; Leo Daft, 1883, www33.brinkster.com/iiii/inventions/3rdrail.asp; Marshall, *Rail: Records*, 133; Rowsome, *Trolley Car Treasury*, 72–76.

12. Jersey Shore Now, www.jerseyshorenow.com.

13. *Scientific American Supplement*, 24 December 1887, 9,982; Middleton, *Time of the Trolley*, 16; *Scientific American*, 8 December 1888, 361; *Transactions of the Newcomen Society*, 1949–51, 154; Jersey Shore Now, www.jerseyshorenow.com.

## 17. A Railroad Bicycle and a Bicycle Railroad (1880 and 1892)

1. W. Barnet Le Van, "High Railway Speeds," *J. Franklin Institute*, July 1880, 18.

2. Hubbard, *Encyclopedia of North American Railroading*, 29, 30; *J. Franklin Institute*, July 1880, 18; *Railroad History* 96:56; *Railroad Gazette*, 7 May 1880, 246; Bianculli, *Trains and Technology*, 1:152.

3. *Railroad History* 96:57; *J. Franklin Institute*, July 1880, 12; *Scientific American*, 1 November 1884, 281; *Engineering*, 24 March 1882, 270; *Star-Ledger*, 1 June 1947.

4. Beck, *Forgotten Towns of Southern New Jersey*, 105–8; Bolger, *Smithville*, 111–12; *Historic Smithville Park*, undated brochure of the Burlington County Board of Chosen Freeholders, Department of Resource Conservation; *Star-Ledger*, 1 June 1947; *Burlington County Times*, 11 May 1980; *A Brief History of Smithville*, a brochure published by the Burlington County (N.J.) Cultural and Heritage Commission, n.d.

5. Bolger, *Smithville*, 153.

6. Peterson, *Patriots, Pirates, and Pineys*, 93; Beck, *Forgotten Towns of Southern New Jersey*, 108; speech to Numismatic and Antiquarian Society by E. Newbold Cooper, 11 October 1954 (copy in Burlington County Historical Society); *Burlington County Times*, 15 January 1972; *Mount Holly Herald*, 13 May 1976; Bolger, *Smithville*, 53, 55, 207, 209.

7. Hubbard, *Encyclopedia of North American Railroading*, 29, 30; Bolger, *Smithville*, 130, 209–10; *Congressional Record*, June 21, 1954, A4523; *Philadelphia Record*, 16 March 1946; NJHM—The Iron Grave 1, www.njhm.com/bicyclerai11.htm, 5; *South Jersey Magazine*, Spring 1981, 8; *Burlington County Times*, 15 January 1972; *Mount Holly Herald*, 13 May 1976.

8. Hubbard, *Encyclopedia of North American Railroading*, 29; *Philadelphia Record*, 16 March 1946; *Burlington County Times*, 15 January 1972; *Mount Holly Herald*, 13 May 1976; Bolger, *Smithville*, 208, 211.

9. *Mount Holly News*, 26 December 1893; *Mount Holly Herald*, 13 May 1976.

10. Bolger, *Smithville*, 212, 215; *Philadelphia Record*, 16 March 1946; *Brief History of Smithville*; *Mount Holly Herald*, 25 July 1957, 10; newspaper clippings at Burlington County Library.

11. *Mount Holly News*, 13 April 1897; Bolger, *Smithville*, 213.

12. *South Jersey Magazine*, Spring 1981, 8; newspaper clippings at Burlington County Library; *Mount Holly Herald*; 13 May 1976; Bolger, *Smithville*, 214.

13. *Congressional Record*, June 21, 1954, A4523; NJHM—The Iron Grave 1, www.njhm.com/bicyclerai11.htm; Mt. Holly, New Jersey, www.mthollynj.com/chap12.html; blackpoo16; blackpoo17 (on-line); *Mount Holly Herald*, 13 May 1976.

14. Bolger, *Smithville*, 222.

15. *Historic Smithville Park*; *Brief History of Smithville*.

16. *Scientific American*, 7 September 1889, 150; 28 March 1891, 191; 17 February 1894, 97, 100; and 24 March 1894, 182; Abdill, *A Locomotive Engineer's Album*, 68; *Mount Holly Herald*, 13 May 1976.

## 18. Death of a President at Elberon (1881)

1. Wilson, *Jersey Shore*, 505; Ackerman, *Dark Horse*, 409; Bailey, *John Bull, a Replica of the Past*, 2; Cunningham, *New Jersey Sampler*, 137 and *Railroads*, 207.

2. *Collier's Encyclopedia*, vol. 10, s.v. "Garfield, James Abram."

3. McCabe, *Our Martyred President* 533, 536–38, 541.

4. *Philadelphia Times*, as reported by McCabe, *Our Martyred President* 533–34.

5. McCabe, *Our Martyred President* 541–42.

6. McCabe, *Our Martyred President* 595–97; *American Heritage of Invention and Technology*, Winter 2006, 5.

7. Mappen, *Jerseyana, the Underside of New Jersey History*, 93; McCabe, *Our Martyred President* 532, 601, 614, 635, 638.

8. Peskin, *Garfield*, 605; *New York Times*, 6 September 1881, 1; McCabe, *Our Martyred President* 642.

9. *New York Times*, 6 September 1881, 1.

10. Cunningham, *New Jersey Sampler*, 138.

11. Anderson, *Central Railroad*, 75.

12. *New York Times*, 6 September 1881, 1; McCabe, *Our Martyred President*, 642, 648, 653, 655, 657.

13. Ackerman, *Dark Horse*, 424–25; Geary, *Fatal Bullet*, n.p.; Peskin, *Garfield*, 605; McElroy, *James A. Garfield, His Life and Times*, 102; *New York Times*, 6 September 1881, 1; *Century*, 23:303; Cunningham, *Railroads*, 207; Cunningham, *New Jersey Sampler*, 138; McCabe, *Our Martyred President* 642, 648, 653, 655, 657.

14. Kingsbury, *Assassination of James A. Garfield*, 43, 45; Peskin, *Garfield*, 608–9; McCabe, *Our Martyred President*, opp. 49.

15. McCabe, *Our Martyred President* 712–16.

16. H. M. Plunkett, *Josiah Gilbert Holland* (New York: C. Scribner's, 1894), 152.

17. *Railroad History*, 158:105.

18. Wilson, *Jersey Shore*, 505; Stewart, *American Place Names*, 149; Wikipedia, s.v. "Long Branch"; Long Branch, NJ., www.virtualnjshore.com/lbranch.html; New Jersey Transit, www.njtransit.com.

19. Anderson, *Central Railroad*, 76; Salvini, *Boardwalk Memories*, 10, 11.

## 19. William F. Allen and the "Day of the Two Suns" (1883)

1. Botkin and Harlow, *A Treasury of Railroad Folklore*, 514.

2. *Scientific American*, 13 Oct. 1883, 227; Botkin and Harlow, *A Treasury of Railroad Folklore*, 515; Mencken, *Railroad Passenger Car*, 91; *Railroad History*, 159:19, 22, 26–28.

3. Cunningham, *Capsules*, 46; Botkin and Harlow, *A Treasury of Railroad Folklore*, 515; *Proceedings of the General Time Convention and Its Successor the American Railway Association*, 1893, 681, 684; *Technology and Culture*, January 1989, 27, 33; *Railroad History*, 148:13, 14.

4. Capo, *It Happened in New Jersey*, 66, 67; *Tales of New Jersey*, 40; *Frank Leslie's Popular Monthly*, April 1884, 386–87, 390.

5. *Proceedings of the General Time Convention and Its Successor the American Railway Association*, 1893, 684, 687, 702; *Technology and Culture*, January 1989, 43, 44.

6. *Proceedings of the General Time Convention and Its*

*Successor the American Railway Association,* 1893, 692, 698, 702; *Technology and Culture,* January 1989, 45–49; Capo, *It Happened in New Jersey,* 68, 69; *Scientific American,* 13 Oct. 1883, 227; Botkin and Harlow, *A Treasury of Railroad Folklore,* 516; *Scientific American Supplement,* 15 March 1884, 6,834; *Frank Leslie's Popular Monthly,* April 1884, 387–88; *Railroad History,* 148:20, 21.

7. Capo, *It Happened in New Jersey,* 69; Cunningham, *Capsules,* 46; *Scientific American,* 13 Oct. 1883, 227; Botkin and Harlow, *A Treasury of Railroad Folklore,* 516; *Scientific American Supplement,* 15 March 1884, 6,834, and 20 December 1884, 7,472–73; *Frank Leslie's Popular Monthly,* April 1884, 389.

8. *Railroad Gazette,* 16 November 1883.

9. Cunningham, *Capsules,* 46; *Railroad History,* 148: 21.

## 20. The "Hoodoo" Trolley Car and Other Streetcar Tales (1887–1940s)

1. Rowsome, *Trolley Car Treasury,* 74, 76.

2. Answers.com, s.v. "List of New Jersey street railroads"; Salvini, *Boardwalk Memories,* 21; Cranmer, *New Jersey in the Automobile Age,* 84, Murphy and Murphy, *Paterson and Passaic County,* 114; Rowsome, *Trolley Car Treasury,* 74; Middleton, *Time of the Trolley,* 60, 174.

3. Eid, *Trolleys to the Fountain,* 1–5.

4. *Unionist-Gazette,* 17 June 1909, 1, 4; Middleton, *Time of the Trolley,* 366.

5. *New Brunswick Daily Times,* 29 August 1905 and 1 September 1905; *New Brunswick Weekly Times,* 1 September 1905; *Trenton Daily State Gazette,* 2 September 1905.

6. *New Brunswick Daily Times,* 31 August 1905; *Trenton Daily State Gazette,* 1 September 1905.

7. Quinby, *Interurban Interlude,* 12–16; Rowsome, *Trolley Car Treasury,* 192; *New York Times,* 22 July 1911, 1.

8. *Daily True American,* 12 November 1903; *New Brunswick Daily Times,* 11 November 1903.

9. Murray, *Profiles in the Wind,* 84–85; Regina W. Murray to author, 22 October 2006.

10. Cranmer, *New Jersey in the Automobile Age,* 85; Middleton, *Time of the Trolley,* 88, 364.

11. Rowsome, *Trolley Car Treasury,* 145–49.

12. Cope, *Story of Cape May County Trains and Trolleys,* 49, 50.

13. *National Railway Bulletin* 63, no. 4 (1998): 16, 17.

14. Middleton, *Time of the Trolley,* 397, 424; *Trains,* January 2006, 56.

15. *New Jersey Transport Heritage,* April 2006, 1–3, 8.

16. Rowsome, *Trolley Car Treasury,* 7.

## 21. A Pair of Majestic Railroad Terminals (1889 and 1907)

1. *New York Times,* 28 October 2003, B1; Wikipedia, s.v. "Pennsylvania Station (New York City)"; Diehl, *Late, Great Pennsylvania Station,* 18–20.

2. Condit, *Port of New York,* 203–7.

3. *New Jersey History,* Fall/Winter 1990, 37–38.

4. Anderson, *Central Railroad,* 18, 21; Reilly, *Central Railroad Company of New Jersey,* 5; Condit, *Port of New York,* 65–66, 141–42; Osgood, "Historical Highlights of the Jersey Central Lines," 8; Treese, *Railroads of New Jersey,* 50; Kobbé, *Kobbé's Jersey Central,* 35; *CRRofNJ Newsletter,* January 1996, 3.

5. *Train Sheet,* Spring 1984, 7; Kobbé, *Kobbé's Jersey Central,* 29.

6. Department of Environmental Protection, www.state .nj.us/dep/parksandforests/parks/liberty_state_park/liberty_

crrnj.html; Berg, *Buildings and Structures of American Railroads,* 431, 436; *Central Railroad of New Jersey Historical Journal* 2002, 29; Condit, *Port of New York,* 142–43.

7. Cunningham, *Railroads,* 255; Condit, *Port of New York,* 203–7; Bianculli, *Trains and Technology,* 3:165; Anderson, *Central Railroad,* 100, 101.

8. Central Railroad of New Jersey Terminal, www.njcu.edu/ programs/jchistory/Pages/C_Pages/Central_Railroad_of_New_ Jersey.html; GET NJ—Liberty State Park, Jersey City, www .libertystatepark.org; *CRRofNJ Newsletter,* January 1996, 3, 4; Scull, *Hoboken's Lackawanna Terminal,* 83; *Midlander* 6, no. 4 (n.d.): 10.

9. *Central Railroad of New Jersey Historical Journal* 2002, 43–45.

10. Cunningham, *Railroads,* 259; Scull, *Hoboken's Lackawanna Terminal,* 22, 25.

11. *New Jersey History,* Fall/Winter 1990; Condit, *Port of New York,* 170; Cunningham, *Railroads,* 260; Smith, *Romance of the Hoboken Ferry,* 51, 87, 89, 95, 109–11; Scull, *Hoboken's Lackawanna Terminal,* 26, 35, 38.

12. *Railroad Gazette,* 9 August 1895; Cunningham, *Railroads,* 259–61; Scull, *Hoboken's Lackawanna Terminal,* 33; Condit, *Port of New York,* 172–73, 211–12.

13. Scull, *Hoboken's Lackawanna Terminal,* 7, 84–88; *Record,* 2 June 2006.

14. Douglas, *All Aboard,* 300.

## 22. A Cape May Speedster (1895)

1. *Scientific American,* 21 September 1895, 179; Comstock, *The Iron Horse,* 122.

2. *Scientific American,* 1 December 1894, 347; Bianculli, *Trains and Technology,* 1:189; *Railroad History* 98:62; Cook and Coxey, *Atlantic City Railroad,* 70.

3. Hubbard, *Encyclopedia of North American Railroading,* 202.

4. Cook and Coxey, *Atlantic City Railroad,* 70; Hubbard, *Encyclopedia of North American Railroading,* 202; *Railroad History* 98:62; Bianculli, *Trains and Technology,* 1:190.

5. Sinclair, *Development of the Locomotive Engine,* 489–91.

6. Carter, *Unusual Locomotives,* 55.

7. *Railroad History* 98:62.

8. Cook and Coxey, *Atlantic City Railroad,* 71.

9. *Journal of the Franklin Institute,* March 1835, 257–59.

## 23. The (Not So) Fast Line (1901–37)

Most of the newspaper references shown below were found in the pages of the *New Brunswick Daily Times.* Similar stories were printed in the *New Brunswick Weekly Times, New Brunswick Press* (daily and weekly), *New Brunswick Home News, Trenton State Gazette* (daily and weekly), *Cranbury Press, Trenton Sunday Advertiser, Daily True American,* and *Trenton Times* on, or near, the dates shown.

1. Cranmer, *New Jersey in the Automobile Age,* 85; *New Brunswick Daily Press,* 27 September 1903; *New Brunswick Daily Times,* 22 July 1903; *Trenton Daily State Gazette,* 2 July 1902.

2. *Princeton Press,* 14 December 1901; *Daily True American,* 11 December 1901, 19 June 1902, and 7 August 1902; *New Brunswick Daily Times,* 11 December 1901, 9 April 1902, 10 May 1902, 21 May 1902, and 8 September 1903; *Trenton Daily State Gazette,* 29 January 1902, 16 April 1902, and 27 November 1902.

3. *Trenton Daily State Gazette,* 26 August 1902.

4. *Daily True American,* 29 March 1902, 17 November

1902, 19 January 1903, and 30 October 1903; *Trenton Evening Times*, 3 November 1902; *New Brunswick Daily Times*, 3 September 1902, 20 October 1902, 3 November 1902, 26 April 1903; 31 August 1903, 19 March 1904, 29 November 1905, 8 December 1905, and 13 February 1906; *Trenton Daily State Gazette*, 11 December 1901, 26 February 1902, and 10 May 1902.

5. *Daily True American*, 17 April 1903 and 8 August 1903; *New Brunswick Daily Times*, 17 April 1903, 28 August 1903, 12 October 1903, 30 October 1903, 6 April 1904, 5 January 1905, 14 March 1905, and 4 August 1905; conversation with Robert Yuell, executive director of the Plainsboro Museum; *Trenton Daily State Gazette*, 28 July 1909.

6. *New Brunswick Daily Times*, 11 December 1903, 12 December 1903, 3 May 1904, 13 May 1904, 18 July 2004, 3 August 1904, 19 August 1904, 24 August 1904, and 5 August 1905; *Trenton Daily State Gazette*, 10 December 1903 and 14 May 1904; *New Brunswick Daily Press*, 17 March 1904; *Daily True American*, 14 May 1904.

7. *New Brunswick Daily Times*, 12 August 1905.

8. Conversation with Yuell; *New Brunswick Daily Times*, 24 February 1908, 3 May 1910, 4 May 1910, 6 May 1910, 17 April 1911, and 24 February 1912.

9. *New Brunswick Daily Times*, 1 March 1904, 22 January 1912, 13 February 1913, 2 October 1914, 20 November 1914, 28 August 1915, 7 February 1916, and 15 March 1916.

10. *New Brunswick Weekly Times*, 30 August 1904 and 12 July 1909; *New Brunswick Daily Times*, 7 May 1906 and 13 April 1910; *Trenton Daily State Gazette*, 7 May 1906, 8 May 1906, 12 May 1906, 23 May 1906, and 31 December 1906.

11. *New Brunswick Daily Times*, 22 July 1908, 22 August 1910, and 7 June 1915.

12. *New Brunswick Weekly Times*, 17 June 1904, 21 September 1906, and 23 April 1907.

13. *Cranbury Press*, 8 April 1913; *New Brunswick Daily Times*, 15 April 1913, 23 July 1913, and 7 March 1914.

14. Conversation with Yuell; *New Brunswick Daily Times*, 17 April 1906 and 20 April 1909; *Trenton Daily State Gazette*, 6 January 1906.

15. Conversation with Yuell; Answers.com, s.v. "Newark-Trenton Fast Line"; *Railroad History*, 171:23.

16. Railroads in Historic Burlington City, N.J., http://08016.com/railroads.html; Cranmer, *New Jersey in the Automobile Age*, 85.

## 24. Catastrophe at the Thoroughfare (1906)

1. *Trenton Times*, 31 October 1906, 5.

2. *Atlantic City*, an 1898 leaflet published by the Passenger Department of the Pennsylvania Railroad.

3. *Seaside Views—Atlantic City*, 15; *Trenton Times*, 29 October 1906, 1; Wilson, *Jersey Shore*, 848; Cunningham, *Railroads*, 127.

4. *Trenton Times*, 31 October 1906, 5.

5. Haine, *Railroad Wrecks*, 69.

6. Reed, *Train Wrecks*, 90; *New York Times*, 13 August 1880, 1, and 31 July 1896, 1.

7. *Trenton Times*, 29 October 1906, 1, 30 October 1906, 1, 31 October 1906, 5; 2004 *World Almanac*, 186–87; Wilson, *Jersey Shore*, 848.

8. *Trenton Times*, 30 October 1906, 1; *New York Times*, 30 October 1906, 1, 8; Haine, *Railroad Wrecks*, 69.

9. *New York Times*, 30 October 1906, 1, 2; Haine, *Railroad Wrecks*, 69.

10. *West Jersey Rails*, 2:14, 15.

11. Wilson, *Jersey Shore*, 848–49.

12. Reed, *Train Wrecks*, 90, 91; Haine, *Railroad Wrecks*, 134–37; *New York Times*, 16 September 1958, 1, 14, 15.

## 25. Making Tracks in New Jersey (1914–Present)

1. *National Railway Bulletin* 67, no. 3 (2002): 7; May, *Model Railroads*, 39.

2. *National Railway Bulletin* 67, no. 3 (2002): 9; Turner, *Along the Upper Road*, 372; Ponzol, *A Century of Lionel Timeless Toy Trains*, 18–20, 39; Grant, *International Directory of Company Histories*, 16:335–36; *Railroad History*, 181:31.

3. May, *Model Railroads*, 33, 36; Ponzol, *A Century of Lionel Timeless Toy Trains*, 19–25; Sutton, *Complete Book of Model Railroading*, 10, 14; *New Jersey Transport Heritage*, February 2006, 6; Grant, *International Directory of Company Histories*, 16:336.

4. Walthers, *Handbook for Model Railroaders*, 2; *Handbook for Model Builders*, 7.

5. *New Jersey Transport Heritage*, April 2006, 3; *Railroad History*, 181:28.

6. Wikipedia, s.v. "Lionel Corporation"; Ponzol, *A Century of Lionel Timeless Toy Trains*, 81, 101; Grant, *International Directory of Company Histories*, 16:33.

7. RailStop.com. www.railstop.com/History/Mantua/MantuaHistory.asp; Grant, *International Directory of Company Histories*, 16:336.

8. *Model Railroader*, October 1967, 2, 82; Sutton, *Complete Book of Model Railroading*, 12, 14; RailStop.com; Wikipedia, s.v. "Tyco Toys"; Grant, *International Directory of Company Histories*, 12:494–96.

9. *National Railway Bulletin* 67, no. 3 (2002): 15, 16; Wikipedia, s.v. "Lionel Corporation"; Ponzol, *A Century of Lionel Timeless Toy Trains*, 77, 87, 104, 120, 122, 140, 144; Grant, *International Directory of Company Histories*, 16:337–38; *American Heritage*, November/December 2006, 65.

10. Marshall, *Model Railroad Engineering*, ix.

11. Model Railroad Club flier; *Railroad History*, 181:47, 51.

12. *Northlandz*, a brochure distributed in Flemington, N.J.; Genovese, *New Jersey Curiosities*, 141–42.

13. Turner, *Along the Upper Road*, 373; Wikipedia, s.v. "Lionel Corporation."

## 26. The Outlaw Railroad Strike and the "Indignation Specials" (1920)

1. Bianculli, *Railroad History on American Postage Stamps*, 138–40, 144–46; Historical introduction to the Seattle General Strike, http://flag.blackened.net/revolt/hist_texts/seattle1919.html.

2. PRR Chronology, 1920, www.prrths.com (June 2004 ed.)

3. *Trenton Times*, 9 April 1920, 3, and 10 April 1920, 1, 3; PRR Chronology, 1920; *New York Times*, 10 April 1920, 1, 11 April 1920, 1, 12 April 1920, 1, 13 April 1920, 4, and 15 April 1920, 2.

4. *Trenton Times*, 10 April 1920, 1, 3, 12 April 1920, 1, 3, and 13 April 1920, 1; *New York Times*, 10 April 1920, 1–2, 11 April 1920, 1, 3, 12 April 1920, 1, and 13 April 1920, 1.

5. *Trenton Times*, 13 April 1920, 1; *Railway & Locomotive Historical Society Newsletter*, October 2005, 4; *New York Times*, 13 April 1920, 1, 3.

6. *Trenton Times*, 13 April 1920, 1; *New York Times*, 14 April 1920, 1–2.

7. *Trenton Times*, 13 April 1920, 1; *New York Times*, 13 April 1920, 1.

8. *Trenton Times*, 15 April 1920, 1, 5; PRR Chronology, 1920; *Princeton Packet*, 16 April 1920, 1.

9. *New York Times*, 14 April 1920, 1–2.

10. *Trenton Times*, 14 April 1920, 1, and 15 April 1920, 1.

11. *New York Times*, 14 April 1920, 1– 2, 15 April 1920, 3, and 16 April 1920, 3; *Railway & Locomotive Historical Society Newsletter*, October 2005, 4.

12. *Trenton Times*, 16 April 1920, 1, 17 April 1920, 1, 18 April 1920, 1; *New York Times*, 18 April 1920, 1, 19 April 1920, 1, 21 April 1920, 1–2; *Railway & Locomotive Historical Society Newsletter*, October 2005, 4.

13. Bianculli, *Railroad History on American Postage Stamps*, 145; *Trenton Times*, 15 April 1920, 6, and 16 April 1920, 1.

14. *Trenton Times*, 17 April 1920, 1; *New York Times*, 10 April 1920, 1, and 15 April 1920, 1.

15. CEC of the CPA: Down with the Betrayers of the Workers, www.marxisthistory.org; *New York Times*, 12 April 1920, 3, and 15 April 1920, 2; IWW/AI International Workers of the World, www.anarchy.no/iwwai.html; Answers.com, s.v. "International Workers of the World."

16. *Trenton Times*, 12 April 1920, 1, and *Trenton Times*, 14 April 1920, 1; *Railway & Locomotive Historical Society Newsletter*, October 2005, 4; *New York Times*, 11 April 1920, 2, 15 April 1920, 3 and 25 April 1920, 1.

17. *New York Times*, 18 April 1920, 1, and 22 April 1920, 2.

## 27. Modern Light Rail in the Garden State (1929–Present)

1. Newark City Subway, http://world.nycsubway.org/us/newark; Hyer and Zec, *Railroads of New Jersey*, 39; *Star-Ledger*, 31 March 2003; *Newark Light Rail map*; Middleton, *Time of the Trolley*, 401; *Railpace Newsmagazine*, September 2006, 5.

2. RAILROAD NET—Newark's Best Kept Secret: The City Subway. www.railroad.net/articles/railfanning/newarksubway/index.php; Newark City Subway, http://web.preby.edu/jtbell/transit/Newark/Subway; Carstens, *Traction Planbook*, 44, 45.

3. New Jersey Transit, www.njtransit.com.

4. Wikipedia, s.v. "Hudson-Bergen Light Rail"; *Hudson-Bergen Light Rail Map*.

5. *New York Times*, 11 December 2003, B5; Wikipedia, s.v. "Hudson-Bergen Light Rail."

6. *Railpace Newsmagazine*, May 2004, 20; New Jersey Transit, www.njtransit.com.

7. *Railpace Newsmagazine*, May 2004, 20; *Courier-Post*, 11 August 2006, www.southjerseynews.com/lightrail; Wikipedia, s.v. "River LINE"; Camden/Trenton, NJ: River LINE Light Rail, http://web.preby.edu/jtbell/transit/Camden-Trenton; *Trenton Times*, 12 March 2006, A7; Treese, *Railroads of New Jersey*, 5.

8. *Courier-Post*, 11 August 2006. www.southjerseynews.com/lightrail; Camden/Trenton, NJ: River LINE Light Rail, http://web.preby.edu/ jtbell/transit/Camden-Trenton.

9. *Trenton Times*, 29 January 2006, D4, and 12 March 2006, A7.

10. *River LINE Owner's Manual*.

## 28. The Dirigible Railroad at Lakehurst (1932–37)

1. *Collier's Encyclopedia*, vol. 13, s.v. "Invention," vol. 16, s.v. "Montgolfier," and vol. 19, s.v. " Pilâtre de Rozier, Jean François."

2. New Jersey Facts—History, www.njfacts.com/history.shtml; Era of the Dirigible, www.centennialofflight.gov/essay/Lighter_than_air/dirigibles/LTA9.htm; Capo, *It Happened in New Jersey*, 144; *New York Times*, 24 May 1908, 1, and 22 July 1919, 1.

3. *Collier's Encyclopedia*, vol. 13, s.v. "Invention," and vol. 14, s.v. "Lighter-than-Air Craft"; Abandoned and Little-Known

Airfields: Eastern New Jersey, www.airfields-freeman.com/NJ/Airfields_NJ_E.htm; Our Airship History, www.nlhs.com/ourltahist.htm.

4. *New York Times*, 16 October 1928, 2–4; *Short Line*, July 1994, 3,4; USS *Los Angeles* (ZR-3), Airship 1924–1939, www.history.navy.mil/photos/ac-usn22/z-types/zr3.htm.

5. *Short Line*, July 1994, 3–5; Rick Zitarosa to author, 24 September 2005.

6. *New York Times*, 15 October 1928, 2.

7. Zitarosa to author; Baer, Coxey, and Schopp, *Trail of the Blue Comet*, 296; *New York Times*, 15 October 1928, 1, 2, and 9 October 1936, 13; Bianculli, *Railroad History on American Postage Stamps*, 118; *CRR of NJ Historical Society Newsletter*, January 1996, 3.

8. *Collier's Encyclopedia*, vol. 14, "Lighter-than-Air Craft"; *Short Line*, July 1994, 3–5; Lakewood Lore—Navy Dirigible USS *Shenandoah*, www.lkwdpl.org/lore/lore152.htm; Capo, *It Happened in New Jersey*, 144–45; USS *Los Angeles* (ZR-3), Airship 1924–1939, www.history.navy.mil/photos/ac-usn22/z-types/zr3.htm; National Archives Postcard Dirigible Akron, http://americahurrah.com/Postcards/NA1akron.html.

9. Capo, *It Happened in New Jersey*, 151–52.

10. Time Travel Trail, www.oceancountygov.com/discover/oc_time.htm; Shore Region History, www.njbeach.info/s_historic.htm; *Short Line*, July 1994, 5.

## 29. Calamity at Woodbridge (1951)

1. Cunningham, *Railroads*, 41; Reed, *Train Wrecks*, 11; Douglas, *All Aboard*, 44; *Railroad History*, 158:105.

2. Haine, *Railroad Wrecks*, 127; Reed, *Train Wrecks*, 52.

3. *New York Times*, 7 February 1951, 1, 25; *Asbury Park Press*, 28 January 2001; *Home News Tribune*, 5 January 2001; Eastlake, *Great Train Disasters*, 41, 42; Track diagram from ICC investigation report, http://dotlibrary2.specialcollection.net.

4. *Asbury Park Press*, 28 January 2001.

5. *New York Times*, 7 February 1951, 1, 25; conversation with Frank LaPenta, eyewitness to Woodbridge accident, 29 November 2006.

6. Haine, *Railroad Wrecks*, 128.

7. *New York Times*, 8 February 1951, 1.

8. *New York Times*, 9 February 1951, 1, 19.

9. Haine, *Railroad Wrecks*, 128–29.

10. *Home News Tribune*, 5 January 2001.

## 30. Railroad Retreat and Renaissance in the Garden State (1950–Present)

1. Wikipedia, s.v. "Amtrak"; TGVweb-Acela Express, www.trainweb.org/tgvpages/acela.html.

2. Wikipedia, s.v. "Consolidated Rail Corporation" and "Penn Central Transportation."

3. *Trains*, May 1994, 28.

4. Cranmer, *New Jersey in the Automobile Age*, 37, 50–51, 120; Rosenbaum and Gallo, *NJ Transit Rail Operations*, 5.

5. NJ Transit History, www.geocities.com/transit383/njthist; Wikipedia, s.v. "Aldene Connection"; Cudahy, *Rails under the Mighty Hudson*, 53, 61, 91–92; *Trains*, May 1994, 28; Hyer and Zec, *Railroads of New Jersey*, 1–2.

6. Rosenbaum and Gallo, *NJ Transit Rail Operations*, 4; New Jersey Transit, www.njtransit.com; Wikipedia, s.v. "New Jersey Transit" and "Penn Central Transportation"; NJ Transit History, www.geocities.com/transit383/njthist; *Trains*, June 1987, 44.

7. Rosenbaum and Gallo, *NJ Transit Rail Operations*, 5; New Jersey Transit, www.njtransit.com.

8. Rosenbaum and Gallo, *NJ Transit Rail Operations*, 11.

9. NJ Transit timetable, Morristown Line, effective 5 April 1987.

10. Rosenbaum and Gallo, *NJ Transit Rail Operations*, 23; Pierson, *Narratives of Newark*, 266; Wikipedia, s.v. "Morris and Essex Railroad."

11. Rosenbaum and Gallo, *NJ Transit Rail Operations*, 31, 34, 38.

12. Bianculli, *Trains and Technology*, 3:150–51.

13. Pierson, *Narratives of Newark*, 266.

14. Rosenbaum and Gallo, *NJ Transit Rail Operations*, 51, 52, 85; Bianculli, *Trains and Technology*, 4:79.

15. Rosenbaum and Gallo, *NJ Transit Rail Operations*, 63–64; NJ Transit History, www.geocities.com/transit383/njthist; Kramer, *Pennsylvania-Reading Seashore Lines*, 4–6.

16. Rosenbaum and Gallo, *NJ Transit Rail Operations*, 5; *River LINE Owners Manual*; Wikipedia, s.v. "New Jersey Transit"; NJ Transit History, www.geocities.com/transit383/njthist; Cudahy, *Rails under the Mighty Hudson*, 92–93; *Star-Ledger*, 28 July 2005, 16; *Trenton Times*, 30 September 2005, C8, and 29 October 2005, A1; PATCO High Speed Line, http://world.nycsubway.org/us/phila/patco.html; DRPA, www.drpa.org/drpa/drpa_history.html; NJ Transit History, www.geocities.com/transit383/njthist; New Jersey Transit, "Economic Benefits of the Trans-Hudson Express Tunnel," www.accesstotheregionscore.com/images/ERA_Report_2006.pdf, 3, 6–9; *Lackawanna Coalition Railgram*, Winter 2006; *New York Times*, 21 June 2003, B8.

17. *Trenton Times*, 29 January 2006, D2, D4.

## 31. Preserving the Railroad

1. *Historic Preservation*, March/April 1989, 42.

2. *Historic Preservation*, March/April 1989, 42; *Hunterdon County Democrat*, 18 October 1873, as reported in Anderson, *Central Railroad*, 58.

3. *Historic Preservation*, March/April 1989, 44, 48; Millmore, *Railroad Stations of Northern New Jersey*, 193–94.

4. *Historic Preservation*, March/April 1989, 44, 45, 48, 49; *Historic Sites and Districts in Somerset County, New Jersey*, 15, 17; Millmore, *Railroad Stations of Northern New Jersey*, 113–14.

5. *Lambertville Station Restaurant*, brochure; Grow, *Waiting for the 5:05*, 101; Potter, *Great American Railroad Stations*, 150–51; Blumenson, *Identifying American Architecture*, 92.

6. Berg, *Buildings and Structures of American Railroads*, 298–99; *Somerset Messenger-Gazette*, 13 November 1969, 20 January 1972, and 29 September 1972; *Flags, Diamonds, and Statues*, Fall 1975, 15, 16.

7. *Trenton Times*, 12 December 1999, A3; Hunter and Porter, *Hopewell*, 183.

8. *Historic Preservation*, March/April 1989, 42–49.

9. Baxter and Adams, *Railroad Ferries of the Hudson*, 51; Cunningham, *Railroads*, 255; Central Railroad of New Jersey Terminal, www.njcu.edu/programs/jchistory/Pages/C_Pages/Central_Railroad_of_New_Jersey.html, 2; Liberty State Park, Jersey City, www.libertystatepark.org, 1.

10. *New Jersey Transport Heritage*, April 2006, 3; *Trains*, January 2006, 77.

## 32. Reliving the Past

1. Hyer and Zec, *Railroads of New Jersey*, 61–62; Black River and Western Railroad, www.brwrr.com; *Newark Sunday News*, 7 August 1966, 17–18; Black River and Western Railroad, flier, Ringoes, N.J.

2. *Tourist Trains*, 248; *Cape May Seashore Lines*, brochure, Tuckahoe, N.J.; *History of Tuckahoe Railroads*, brochure of the West Jersey Chapter of the National Railway History Society, 30 April 2005.

3. *Tourist Trains*, 253; *New Jersey Transport Heritage*, September 1996, 7; Railroad.Net, www.njmt.org/about_us.htm.

4. Rick Zitarosa to author, 24 September 2005; *Tourist Trains*, 249; *New Jersey Museum of Transportation*, brochures from Allaire, N.J., 1978, 1998; www.njmt.org/about_us.htm; *Newark Sunday News*, 7 August 1966, 17–18.

5. *New Jersey Transportation Heritage Center*, a brochure from Phillipsburg, N.J.; *United Railroad Historical Society*, brochure, Middletown, N.J.; *History of Tuckahoe Railroads*; Schwieterman, *When the Railroad Leaves Town*, 197; *New Jersey Transport Heritage*, December 2005, 4.

6. Treese, *Railroads of New Jersey*, 74–80; *Tourist Trains*, 251; *New Jersey Transport Heritage*, February 2006, 6.

## 33. And, in Closing . . .

1. Vance, *North American Railroad*, 34; www.vernonstories.com/01jvb.htm; biography for Ross Winans at www.whistler.arts.gla.ac.uk/biog/Wina_R.htm.

2. *True Democratic Banner*, 24 October 1872, as reported by Taber, "Commuter Railroads," 297A.

3. *New Jersey Transport Heritage*, August 2005, 4; *Morristown Jersey Man*, 30 August 1858, as reported by Taber, "Commuter Railroads," 199.

4. *Train Sheet*, Spring 1994, 5; *Newark Daily Mercury*, 11 November 1851, as reported by Taber, "Commuter Railroads," 142.

5. Sceurman and Moran, *Weird N.J.*, 222–23; Mott, *Ghost Stories of New Jersey*, 95–105.

6. Douglas, *All Aboard*, 244–45; Berg, *Buildings and Structures of American Railroads*, 318; *Railroad Gazette*, 29 April 1887.

# Bibliography

Abdill, George B. *A Locomotive Engineer's Album*. New York: Bonanza Books, 1965.

Ackerman, Kenneth D. *Dark Horse*. New York: Carol and Graf, 2003.

*Acts Incorporating the Delaware and Raritan Canal Company, the Camden and Amboy Railroad and Transportation Company, and the New Jersey Railroad and Transportation Company*. Trenton, N.J.: Phillips and Boswell, Printers, 1849.

Adams, Charles F., Jr., and Henry Adams. *Chapters of Erie*. Ithaca, N.Y.: Cornell University Press, 1966.

*American Practice in Block Signaling*. New York: Railroad Gazette, 1891.

Anderson, Elaine. *The Central Railroad of New Jersey's First 100 Years, 1849–1949*. Easton, Pa.: Center for Canal History and Technology, 1984.

Archer, Robert F. *The History of the Lehigh Valley Railroad*. Berkeley, Calif.: Howell-North Books, 1977.

Armytage, W. H. G. *A Social History of Engineering*. Cambridge: MIT Press, 1961.

*Atlantic City*. Millville, N.J.: South Jersey, 2000. A reprint of the 1898 leaflet published by the Passenger Department of the Pennsylvania Railroad.

Baer, Christopher T., William J. Coxey, and Paul W. Schopp. *The Trail of the Blue Comet*. Palmyra, N.J.: West Jersey Chapter, National Railway Historical Society, 1994.

Bailey, Ronald T. *John Bull, a Replica of the Past*. Strasburg, Pa., n.d.

Bailey, Shirley R., and Jim Parkhurst. *Early South Jersey Railroad Stations*. Millville, N.J.: South Jersey, 1981.

Ballon, Hilary. *New York's Pennsylvania Stations*. New York: W. W. Norton, 2002.

Baxter, Raymond J., and Arthur G. Adams. *The Railroad Ferries of the Hudson*. Woodcliff Lake, N.J.: Lind, 1987.

Beck, Henry Charlton. *Forgotten Towns of Southern New Jersey*. New Brunswick, N.J.: Rutgers University Press, 1964.

———. *The Roads of Home*. New Brunswick, N.J.: Rutgers University Press, 1956.

———. *Tales and Towns of Northern New Jersey*. New Brunswick, N.J.: Rutgers University Press, 1964.

Beers, F. W., ed. *Atlas of Hunterdon County, New Jersey*. New York: Beers, Comstock, and Cline, 1873.

Benét, Rosemary, and Steven Vincent Benét. *A Book of Americans*. New York: Farrar and Rinehart, 1933.

Berg, Walter G. *Buildings and Structures of American Railroads*. New York: John Wiley, 1893.

Bertholf, Kenneth, Jr. *Images of America: Blairstown*. Charleston, S.C.: Arcadia, 1998.

Bianculli, Anthony J. *Railroad History on American Postage Stamps*. Mendham, N.J.: Astragal Press, 2004.

———. *Trains and Technology*. 4 vols. Newark: University of Delaware Press, 2001–3.

Billington, David P. *The Innovators*. New York: John Wiley, 1996.

*Biographical Encyclopedia of New Jersey in the Nineteenth Century*. Philadelphia: Galaxy, 1877.

Black, Archibald. *The Story of Tunnels*. New York: McGraw-Hill, 1937.

Blumenson, John J.-G. *Identifying American Architecture*. Nashville: American Association for State and Local History, 1977.

Bolger, William C. *Smithville: The Result of Enterprise*. Burlington County (N.J.): Cultural and Heritage Commission, 1980.

Botkin, B. A., and Alvin F. Harlow, ed. *A Treasury of Railroad Folklore*. New York: Bonanza Books, 1953.

*Breakthrough!* Brochure. New York: Port Authority Trans-Hudson Corporation, 1978.

*A Brief History of Smithville*. A brochure published by the Burlington County (N.J.) Cultural and Heritage Commission, n.d.

Burgess, George H., and Miles C. Kennedy. *Centennial History of the Pennsylvania Railroad*. Philadelphia: Pennsylvania Railroad, 1949.

Capo, Fran. *It Happened in New Jersey*. Guilford, Conn.: Globe Pequot Press, 2004.

Carey, Henry Charles. *Beauties of the Monopoly System of New Jersey, by a Citizen of Burlington*. Philadelphia: C. Sherman, Printer, 1848.

Carstens, Harold H., ed. *Traction Planbook*. Ramsey, N.J.: Model Craftsman, 1968.

Carter, Ernest F. *Unusual Locomotives*. London: Frederick Muller, 1960.

Cawley, James, and Margaret Cawley. *Along the Delaware and Raritan Canal*. Cranbury, N.J.: A. S. Barnes, 1970.

*Central Railroad of New Jersey Historical Journal 2002*. Dunellen, N.J.: Central Railroad Company of New Jersey Historical Society, 2002.

*A Century of Progress: The General Electric Story*. Schenectady: Hall of History Foundation, 1981.

*Charters of Rail Road and Other Companies between New York and Philadelphia*. New York: T. Snowden, Printer, 1834.

Comstock, Henry B. *The Iron Horse*. New York, Galahad Books, 1971.

Condit, Carl W. *The Port of New York*. Chicago: University of Chicago Press, 1980.

Cook, W. George, and William J. Coxey. *Atlantic City Railroad*. Oaklyn, N.J.: West Jersey Chapter of the National Railway Historical Society, 1980.

Cope, Nathan. *The Story of Cape May County Trains and Trolleys*. N.p.: n.p., 1993.

Cranmer, H. Jerome. *New Jersey in the Automobile Age*. Princeton, N.J.: D. Van Nostrand, 1964.

Cudahy, Brian J. *Over and Back: The History of Ferryboats in New York Harbor.* New York: Fordham University Press, 1990.

———. *Rails under the Mighty Hudson.* New York: Fordham University Press, 2002.

Cunningham, John T. *Capsules of New Jersey History.* Trenton, N.J.: New Jersey Manufacturers Insurance, 1974.

———. *The New Jersey Sampler.* Upper Montclair: New Jersey Almanac, 1964.

———. *Newark.* Newark: New Jersey Historical Society, 1988.

———. *Railroading in New Jersey.* Newark: Associated Railroads of New Jersey, 1951.

———. *Railroads in New Jersey: The Formative Years.* Andover, N.J.: Afton, 1997.

Della Penna, Craig P. *24 Great Rail-Trails of New Jersey.* Amherst, Mass.: New England Cartographics, 1999.

Diehl, Lorraine B. *The Late, Great Pennsylvania Station.* Lexington, Mass.: Stephen Greene Press, 1985.

Douglas, George H. *All Aboard.* New York: Paragon House, 1992.

Dredge, James. *A Record of the Transportation Exhibits at the World's Columbian Exposition of 1893.* New York: John Wiley, 1894.

Drinker, Henry S. *Tunneling, Explosive Compounds, and Rock Drills.* New York: John Wiley, 1878.

Dunbar, Seymour. *A History of Travel in America.* New York: Tudor, 1937.

Eastlake, Keith. *Great Train Disasters.* Osceola, Wisc.: Motorbooks, 1997.

Edson, William D. *Railroad Names.* Potomac, Md.: privately published, 1984.

Eid, Joseph. *Trolleys to the Fountain.* Brick, N.J.: privately published, 1980.

Finch, James Kip. *The Story of Engineering.* Garden City, N.Y.: Doubleday, 1960.

*First Joint Report of the Associated Delaware & Raritan Canal Co., Camden & Amboy R.R. & Transportation Co., and New Jersey R.R. & Transportation Co. to the Stockholders, April 1867.* Philadelphia: H. G. Leisenring's Steam Printing House, 1867.

Folsom, Burton W. *The Myth of the Robber Barons.* Herndon, Va.: Young America's Foundation, 1991.

*Frog War! The Mercer and Somerset Story.* Videotape. Browns Mills, N.J.: Lakeside Productions, 1992.

Geary, Rick. *The Fatal Bullet.* New York: Nantier-Beall-Minoustchine, 1999.

Genovese, Peter. *New Jersey Curiosities.* Guilford, Conn.: Globe Pequot Press, 2003.

Gordon, John Steele. *The Scarlet Woman of Wall Street.* New York: Weidenfeld and Nicolson, 1988.

Grant, Tina, ed. *International Directory of Company Histories.* 82 vols. Detroit, Mich.: St. James Press, 1996.

Grow, Lawrence, *Waiting for the 5:05.* New York: Main Street/Universe Books, 1977.

Haine, Edgar A. *Railroad Wrecks.* New York: Cornwall Books, 1993.

Halsey, Edmund D. *History of Morris County.* New York: W. W. Munsell, 1882.

*Handbook for Model Builders.* New York: Lionel Corp., 1940.

Haussamen, Brock. *The Iron Horse in Somerset County.* North Branch, N.J.: Somerset County College, 1984.

———. *When the Railroads Came to Somerset County.* North Branch, N.J.: Raritan Press, 2000.

Heilich, Frederick W., III. *The History of the Blairstown Railway.* Livingston, N.J.: Railroadians of America, 1981.

Henry, Robert S. *This Fascinating Railroad Business.* Indianapolis: Bobbs-Merrill, 1942.

*Historic Sites and Districts in Somerset County, New Jersey.* Somerville, N.J.: Somerset County Cultural and Heritage Commission, 2004.

Holbrook, Stewart H. *The Story of American Railroads.* New York: Crown, 1947.

Honeyman, A. VanDoren. *Northwestern New Jersey.* New York: Lewis Historical, 1927.

Howell, J. Roscoe. *Ashbel Welch, Civil Engineer.* A reprint of article published in the *Proceedings of the New Jersey Historical Society,* October 1961 and January 1962. Lambertville, N.J.: Lambertville Historical Society, n.d.

Hoyt, J. K. *Pen and Pencil Pictures on the Delaware, Lackawanna and Western Railroad.* New York: W. H. Cadwell, 1874.

Hubbard, Freeman. *Encyclopedia of North American Railroading.* New York: McGraw-Hill, 1981.

*Hudson-Bergen Light Rail Map.* Newark: N.J. Transit, 2006.

Hunter, Richard W., and Richard L. Porter. *Hopewell: A Historical Geography.* Titusville, N.J.: Township of Hopewell, 1990.

Hyer, Richard, and John Zec. *Railroads of New Jersey.* Privately published, 1975.

*Illustrations of Incidents in Tunnel Construction.* New York: Hudson and Manhattan Railroad Co., 1909.

*In Historic Cape May County, N. J.* Cape May County Department of Public Affairs, n.d.

Jacobs, Timothy. *The History of the Pennsylvania Railroad.* New York: Bonanza Books, 1988.

Jensen, Oliver. *The American Heritage History of Railroads in America.* New York: Bonanza Books, 1981.

Jones, Wilson E. *The Pascack Valley Line.* Madison, N.J.: Railroadians of America, 1996.

Josephson, Matthew. *Edison.* New York: McGraw-Hill, 1959.

Kingsbury, Robert. *The Assassination of James A. Garfield.* New York: Rosen, 2002.

Kirby, Richard Shelton, and Philip Gustave Laurson. *The Early Years of Modern Civil Engineering.* New Haven: Yale University Press, 1932.

Klein, Aaron E. *Encyclopedia of North American Railroads.* New York: Exeter Books, 1985.

Kobbé, Gustav. *Kobbé's Jersey Central.* New York: Gustav Kobbé, 1890.

Kramer, Frederick A. *Pennsylvania-Reading Seashore Lines.* Ambler, Pa.: Crusader Press, 1980.

Lane, Wheaton J. *From Indian Trail to Iron Horse.* Princeton: Princeton University Press, 1939.

*Lease and Contract Dates June 30th, 1871, between the Delaware and Raritan Canal Company, the Camden and Amboy Railroad and Transportation Company, and the New Jersey Railroad and Transportation Company, Philadelphia and Trenton Railroad Company, Parties of the First Part, and the Pennsylvania Railroad Company, Party of the Second Part, 31 June 1871.*

Lee, Warren F. *Down along the Old Bel-Del.* Albuquerque: Bel-Del Enterprises, 1987.

Lee, Warren F., and Catherine T. Lee. *A Chronology of the Belvidere-Delaware Railroad Company (A Pennsylvania Railroad Company) and the Region Through Which It Operated.* Albuquerque: Bel-Del Enterprises, 1989.

Lewis, Alice Blackwell. *Hopewell Valley Heritage.* Hopewell, N.J.: Hopewell Museum, 1973.

Lipp, Delmar. "A Short History of the Princeton Branch of the Pennsylvania Railroad." Paper read at the meeting of the Historical Society of Princeton on 2 March 1939.

Lurie, Maxine N., and Marc Mappen, eds. *Encyclopedia of New Jersey.* New Brunswick, N.J.: Rutgers University Press, 2004.

MacAdam, Henry Innes. *West Windsor, Then and Now.* Princeton, N.J.: Princeton Corridor Rotary Club, 1997.

*Map of the NJ Transit Passenger Rail System.* Newark: NJ Transit.

*Map of the State of New Jersey.* Published by the State Highway Commissioners, 1925.

Mappen, Marc. *Jerseyana, the Underside of New Jersey History.* New Brunswick, N.J.: Rutgers University Press, 1992.

Marshall, David. *Model Railroad Engineering.* New York: Harper and Brothers, 1942.

Marshall, John. *Rail: The Records.* Enfield, Engl.: Guinness Superlatives, 1985.

Mason, Henry P. *Early Somerville.* A brochure printed for the Somerset Trust Company and reprinted in the *Somerset Messenger Gazette.*

May, Earl Chapin. *Model Railroads in the Home.* New York: Funk and Wagnalls, 1939.

McCabe, James D. *Our Martyred President.* Philadelphia: National, 1881.

McElroy, Richard L. *James A. Garfield, His Life and Times.* Canton, Ohio: Daring Books, 1986.

McPherson, James Alan, and Miller Williams, eds. *Railroad Trains and Train People in American Culture.* New York: Random House, 1976.

Mencken, August. *The Railroad Passenger Car.* Baltimore: Johns Hopkins University Press, 1957.

Menzies, Elizabeth G. C. *Passage between Rivers.* New Brunswick, N.J.: Rutgers University Press, 1976.

Middleton, William D. *The Time of the Trolley.* Milwaukee: Kalmbach, 1967.

Millmore, Robert W. *Railroad Stations of Northern New Jersey.* Morristown, N.J.: Red Gables, 2003.

Mohowski, Robert E. *The New York, Susquehanna & Western Railroad.* Baltimore: Johns Hopkins University Press, 2003.

Moore, Peter. *The Destruction of Penn Station.* New York: Distributed Art Publishers, 2000.

Mott, A. S. *Ghost Stories of New Jersey.* Edmonton: Lone Pine, 2006.

Mott, Edward H. *Between the Ocean and the Lakes: The Story of Erie.* New York: Ticker, 1908.

Murphy, J. Palmer, and Margaret Murphy. *Paterson and Passaic County: An Illustrated History.* Northridge, Calif.: Windsor, 1987.

Murray, Regina Waldron. *Profiles in the Wind.* Princeton, N.J.: privately published, 1998.

Myers, William Starr. *The Story of New Jersey.* New York: Lewis Historical, 1945.

*Mystic's 2005 U. S. Stamp Catalog.* Camden, N.Y.: Mystic Stamp, 2005.

*New Jersey Almanac, 1964–65.* Upper Montclair, N.J.: New Jersey Almanac, 1963.

Osgood, Joseph O., Jr. "Historical Highlights of the Jersey Central Lines." Manuscript, 1949.

Pangborn, J. G. *The World's Railway.* 1894; facs., New York: Bramhall House, 1974.

*PATH Gazette.* Diamond Jubilee souvenir edition published by the Port Authority Trans-Hudson Corporation, New York, 25 February 1983.

*The Paulinskill Valley Trail.* Hackettstown, N.J.: Paulinskill Valley Trail Committee, n.d.

Peskin, Allan. *Garfield.* Kent, Ohio: Kent State University Press, 1978.

Peterson, Robert A. *Patriots, Pirates, and Pineys.* Medford, N.J.: Plexus, 1998.

Phillips, Lance. *Yonder Comes the Train.* New York: A. S. Barnes, 1965.

Pierson, David Lawrence. *Narratives of Newark (in New Jersey).* Newark: Pierson, 1917.

Plunket, Harriette Merrick. *Josiah Gilbert Holland.* New York: C. Scribner's, 1894.

Ponzol, Dan. *A Century of Lionel Timeless Toy Trains.* New York: Friedman/Fairfax, 2000.

Potter, Janet Greenstein. *Great American Railroad Stations.* New York: John Wiley, 1996.

*Proceedings of the General Time Convention and Its Successor the American Railway Association.* New York: American Railway Association, 1893.

Quinby, E. J. *Interurban Interlude.* Ramsey, N.J.: Model Craftsman, 1968.

*The Railroaders.* New York: Time-Life Books, 1973.

*Railway Mechanical Engineering.* New York: American Society of Mechanical Engineers, 1979.

Ransome-Wallis, P., ed. *World Railway Locomotives.* New York: Hawthorne Books, 1959.

Raum, John O. *History of New Jersey.* Philadelphia: John E. Potter, 1877.

———. *History of the City of Trenton.* Trenton, N.J.: W. T. Nicholson, 1871.

Reed, Robert C. *Train Wrecks.* New York: Bonanza Books, 1968.

Reilly, Frank T. *Central Railroad Company of New Jersey: Its History and Employees.* Williamsport, P.R.: Reed Hann Lithographic Co., 2004.

———. Locomotive listing, 1 February 1982. Manuscript.

*River LINE Owner's Manual.* Newark: New Jersey Transit.

*Rogers Locomotive Catalog, 1876.* Ed. John H. White Jr. Newark: New Jersey Historical Society, 1983.

Rosenbaum, Joel, and Tom Gallo. *NJ Transit Rail Operations.* Piscataway, N.J.: Railpace, 1996.

Rowsome, Frank, Jr. *Trolley Car Treasury.* New York: Bonanza Books, 1956.

Salvini, Emil R. *Boardwalk Memories.* Guilford, Conn.: Insider's Guide, 2006.

Sceurman, Mark, and Mark Moran. *Weird N.J.: Your Travel Guide to New Jersey's Local Legends and Best Kept Secrets.* New York: Barnes and Noble Books, 2004.

Scharring-Hausen, R. L., ed. *Help Hopewell Honor Her Heroes.* Glen Moore, N.J., 1921 A program for a fund-raiser to erect a library and museum. A copy resides at the Hopewell Museum, Hopewell, N.J.

Schwieterman, Joseph P. *When the Railroad Leaves Town.* Kirksville, Mo.: Truman State University Press, 2001.

Scull, Theodore W. *Hoboken's Lackawanna Terminal.* New York: Quadrant Press, 1987.

*Seaside Views—Atlantic City.* Philadelphia: Allen, Lane and Scott, ca. 1870s. Reprinted by *South Jersey* Magazine, Millville, N.J., 2001.

Sinclair, Angus. *The Development of the Locomotive Engine: A History of the Growth of the Locomotive from Its Most Elementary Form, Showing the Gradual Steps Made toward the Developed Engine, with Biographical Sketches of the Eminent Engineers and Inventors Who Nursed It on Its Way to the Perfected Form Today.* A reprint of the 1907 ed. annotated by John H. White Jr.; Cambridge: MIT Press, 1970.

Smith, Harry J., Jr. *Romance of the Hoboken Ferry.* New York: Prentice-Hall, 1931.

Snell, J. B. *Early Railways.* London: Octopus Books, 1972.

Snell, James P. *History of Hunterdon and Somerset Counties, New Jersey.* Philadelphia: Everts and Peck, 1881.

———. *History of Warren County.* Philadelphia: Everts and Peck, 1881.

Steinman, David B., and Sara Ruth Watson. *Bridges and Their Builders.* New York: G. P. Putnam's Sons, 1941.

Stevenson, David. *Sketch of the Civil Engineering of North America.* London: John Weale, 1859.

Stevenson, Robert Louis. *Across the Plains.* New York: Charles Scribner's Sons, 1925.

Stewart, George R. *American Place Names.* New York: Oxford University Press, 1970.

Stockton, R. F. *Defence of the System of Internal Improvements of the State of New Jersey.* Philadelphia: King and Baird, Printers, 1864.

*Stories of New Jersey.* New York: M. Barrows, 1938.

Stover, John F. *American Railroads.* 2d ed. Chicago: University of Chicago Press, 1997.

Sutton, David. *The Complete Book of Model Railroading.* Englewood Cliffs, N.J.: Prentice-Hall, 1964.

Taber, Thomas T. "Commuter Railroad." Manuscript, 1945–47.

Taber, Thomas T., III. *The Delaware, Lackawanna & Western Railroad in the Nineteenth Century, 1828–1899.* Muncy, Pa.: privately published, 1977.

*Tales of New Jersey.* Newark: New Jersey Bell Telephone, 1963.

*Tourist Trains.* 38th ed. Waukesha, Wisc.: Kalmbach, 2003.

*Track Map of Hudson and Manhattan Railroad.* New York: Electric Railroaders Association, 1960.

Treese, Lorett. *Railroads of New Jersey.* Mechanicsburg, Pa.: Stackpole Books, 2006.

Trumbull, L. R. *A History of Industrial Paterson.* Paterson: Carleton M. Herrick, 1882.

Turnbull, Archibald D. *John Stevens, an American Record.* New York: Century, 1928.

Turner, Jean-Rae. *Along the Upper Road.* Hillside, N.J.: Rotary Club of Hillside, 1977.

Vance, James E., Jr. *The North American Railroad.* Baltimore: Johns Hopkins University Press, 1995.

Walthers, W. K. *Handbook for Model Railroaders.* Wauwatosa, Wisc.: Modelmaker, 1939.

Waltzer, Jim, and Tom Wilk. *Tales of South Jersey.* New Brunswick, N.J.: Rutgers University Press, 2001.

Watkins, J. Elfreth. *The Camden and Amboy Railroad: Origins and Early History.* Washington: Gedney and Roberts, 1892.

Welch, Ashbel. *Report on Safety Signals.* Address to the Railroad Convention held at the St. Nicholas Hotel, New York, 17 October 1866. Lambertville, N.J.: Hazen and Roberts, Printers, 1870.

*West Jersey Rails: A Series of Stories about Southern New Jersey Railroad History.* 2 vols. Oaklyn, N.J.: National Railway Historical Society, 1983, 1985; reprint of vol. 1, 1999.

White, Bouck. *The Book of Daniel Drew.* Larchmont, N.Y.: American Research Council, 1965. (White contended that the writings were Daniel Drew's own words as found in a log that was unearthed. It is more likely that this was a device used by White to tell his story, which is based on fact, because Drew was said to be illiterate and incapable of keeping such a log or diary.)

White, John H. *The American Railroad Passenger Car.* Baltimore: Johns Hopkins University Press, 1978.

———. *The John Bull.* Washington: Smithsonian Institution Press, 1981.

———. *A Short History of American Locomotive Builders in the Steam Era.* Washington: Bass, 1982.

Wilson, Harold F. *The Jersey Shore: A Social and Economic History of the Counties of Atlantic, Cape May, Monmouth, and Ocean.* Vol. 1. New York: Lewis Historical, 1953.

*World Almanac.* New York: World Almanac Books, 2004.

# Index

ANTHONY J. BIANCULLI is a retired mechanical engineer and the author of *Railroad History on American Postage Stamps* as well as a series of four books on *Trains and Technology*, a treatise on the American railroad in the nineteenth century.